Warfare and the Wounded Earth

Environmental Dimensions of Conflict

Edited by

Dr Kanika Sharma

Published in association with

The Indian Society of International Law
New Delhi

Vij Books
New Delhi (India)

First Published in India in 2026

Published by

Vij Books
(An imprint of Vij Books India Pvt Ltd)
(Publishers, Distributors & Importers)
4836/24, Ansari Road
Delhi – 110 002
Phones: 91-11-43596460, Mob: 98110 94883
e-mail: contact@vijpublishing.com
web : www.vijbooks.in

ISBN: 978-93-47436-00-0 (HB)

ISBN: 978-93-47436-32-1 (PB)

ISBN: 978-93-47436-69-7 (EBook)

Contents

Foreword

The environment has been a voiceless victim of armed conflict. In reality, environmental damage begins much before the conflict starts. Today, every country in the world maintains a military force, which is an essential component of its government. The military forces consume vast quantities of resources, including rare earth elements, critical minerals, hydrocarbons, common metals, and water. The militaries also need large areas of land and sea for their bases and testing of equipment. In many cases, such areas could be of greater ecological importance. Military training creates emissions and destroys landscape and marine habitats. Militaries are also huge energy users whose greenhouse gas emissions (GHG) make a significant contribution to the climate crisis. The carbon dioxide emissions of the large militaries would be greater than those of many of the world's countries combined. It is estimated that the militaries are responsible for about 5.5 per cent of all GHG emissions globally.

The ongoing armed conflicts in several parts of the world have severely damaged the environment. In the last 26 months, the armed conflict has caused unprecedented levels of environmental damage in the Gaza Strip. Military operations have caused significant damage to agriculture and ecosystems—including contamination of soil, plants and the food chain. Remote sensing data indicate that, as of now, more than 97 per cent of the tree crops in Gaza, 84 per cent of annual crops, 95 per cent of shrub land, and 89 per cent of grass/fallow land have been damaged. The conflict has significantly degraded water infrastructure, leading to severely limited, low-quality water supply to the population. Soils have been significantly contaminated with chemicals and heavy metals from munitions. Heavy destruction of piped systems, and increasing use of cesspits for sanitation have increased contamination of the aquifer, marine and coastal areas. With the conflict continuing, air, water, and soil pollution persists, and the few remaining vegetated areas are at risk of destruction.

Russia-Ukraine armed conflict has worsened climate and environmental challenges in Ukraine. Approximately 1.7 million hectares of Ukrainian forests are affected by war. This war has also hampered the country's ability to monitor and respond to changes in the environment. Chemicals from munitions and other pollutants, and damage to inland waterways and marine infrastructure, are likely to have long-term consequences for human health and the biodiversity of ecosystems, particularly in the Black Sea and the Sea of Azov. If Ukraine were to rebuild using conventional materials and technologies, the reconstruction itself would generate 97 million tonnes of CO_2. Nearly as much as the first two years of war. Reportedly, Ukraine intends to ask Russia for $43 billion in climate compensation. When Ukraine submits its claim, it will be the beginning of a debate on the role of the environment in conflicts and the climate responsibilities of states.

In the last 15 years of conflict, Syria is left with pressing challenges. A report on Syrian armed conflict states that it has resulted in nearly 618,000 deaths and 113,000 disappearances in the last 15 years; however, it is silent on the environmental impact of the conflict. Visible damage from military actions includes huge amounts of conflict-rubble in destroyed cities and towns, damaged water infrastructure and industrial facilities, and widespread toxic remnants of war such as mines and unexploded ordnance. This has caused deforestation, biodiversity loss, aggravated water scarcity and soil degradation, having serious impacts on agriculture and weakening the country's capacity for climate adaptation.

Every weapon, whether a bullet or a bomb, has a direct and indirect impact on the natural environment. The use of explosive weapons can cause massive damage to civilians and industrial infrastructure, resulting in heavy toll on the environment. More recently, in June 2025, the United States used GBU-57 MOP (Massive Ordnance Penetrator) to destroy nuclear facilities in Iran. These bombs are among the heaviest and most powerful non-nuclear bombs in the US arsenal, weighing in at 30,000 pounds and 20 feet long. It is difficult to estimate at this stage whether this attack on nuclear enrichment facilities has caused any radioactive contamination.

Nuclear weapons are dangerous and destructive. Taken together, the nuclear-weapon states have more than 12,000 nuclear weapons in their arsenal. If nuclear weapons are used, virtually every country would be impacted regardless of involvement in the conflict. The direct and indirect consequences of the use of nuclear weapons in war would be devastating for humankind and the biosphere. After the explosion, smoke and dust from the firestorms would block sunlight from reaching the Earth's surface, causing an abrupt drop in global temperatures and rainfall, leading to shorter growing seasons and a decrease in overall agricultural production and fish stocks worldwide. According to an estimate, only about 2 percent of current nuclear-weapons, exploded on cities, would abruptly cause ice age temperatures, putting over two billion people at risk of starvation in just the following two-years. In fact, we are not even aware of the consequences of nuclear war, including its environmental and social effects. The UN General Assembly has recently voted to establish a 21-member independent scientific panel to undertake a new comprehensive study on the effects of nuclear war, with its final report due in 2027.

In the context of the development of international law, the protection of the environment during armed conflicts is relatively recent. We find it mentioned in only two international humanitarian law treaties: the 1976 Convention on the Prohibition of Military or Any Other Hostile Use of Environmental Modification Techniques, and Articles 35(3) and 55 of the 1977 Additional Protocol I to the Geneva Conventions. Unfortunately, a good number of states are not party to these treaties, and the safeguards do not bind them or non-state actors. Further, these treaties are not applicable in a non-international armed conflict.

Keeping the above in view, the Indian Society of International Law held a one-day seminar on November 6, 2025, the International Day for Preventing the Exploitation of the Environment in War and Armed Conflict. This book, "*Warfare and the Wounded Earth: Environmental Dimensions of Conflict*," edited by Dr Kanika Sharma, Assistant Professor (Sr), is an outcome of the discussions held during the seminar, and I congratulate all scholars who have contributed for the book. I am sure that these contributions will stimulate further research and discussions to strengthen the protection of the environment during conflicts, and that militaries will adopt preventive measures to safeguard the natural environment.

Prof (Dr) Manoj Kumar Sinha
President
The Indian Society of International Law,
New Delhi

December 10, 2025

Preface

Conflicts alter. Armed conflicts have always reshaped the political, social, and economic foundations of nations. Yet one of their most profound and enduring consequences—environmental degradation—remains insufficiently understood, inconsistently documented, and inadequately addressed within international legal and policy frameworks. The ongoing wars of the twenty-first century, from Ukraine to Gaza and beyond, provide stark evidence that environmental harm is not a peripheral by-product of warfare but a central concern with long-term, transboundary, and intergenerational implications. The degradation of ecosystems, contamination of soil and water, destruction of biodiversity, and collapse of environmental governance mechanisms trigger consequences that persist long after the guns fall silent.[1] These impacts transcend national borders, affecting regional stability, food security, public health, and the broader climate system on which all life depends.

> *"Protecting the environment before, during, and after armed conflict must rise to the same level of political importance as protecting human rights, because a healthy environment is a foundation upon which peace and many human rights are realised."*[2]

In recognition of the gravity of this issue, the United Nations General Assembly declared 6 November as the *International Day for Preventing the Exploitation of the Environment in War and Armed Conflict.* Marking this day in 2025, the Centre for Advanced Studies in International Humanitarian

1 The US military is one of the worst polluters on the planet. It is responsible for contaminating foreign countries with dioxin, depleted uranium, UXO, and various explosive remnants, whether directly or indirectly. Jon Mitchell, 2020, *Poisoning the Pacific: The US Military's Secret Dumping of Plutonium, Chemical Weapons, and Agent Orange*, London: Rowman & Littlefield, p. 5.

2 David Jensen, UN Environment's Head of Environmental Cooperation for Peacebuilding. Available at: https://www.unep.org/news-and-stories/story/why-legal-principles-war-and-environment-matter.

Law and Military Law at the Indian Society of International Law (ISIL) organised a one-day seminar on "Protection of Environment During War and Armed Conflict." This seminar served as a pivotal platform for scholars, practitioners, and policymakers to examine the complex interactions between armed conflict and environmental protection, and to explore how existing international humanitarian law (IHL) and environmental law can be strengthened to better safeguard the natural world in times of war. The present volume brings together selected papers from that seminar, offering a timely and multidisciplinary contribution to an issue of growing urgency.

Wartime environmental damage manifests in multiple forms.[3] First, there is the deliberate targeting of the environment as a method of warfare. Historical precedents—from the destruction of dams in Korea to the extensive use of Agent Orange in Vietnam and the burning of Kuwaiti oil wells in 1991—demonstrate that ecosystems have often been weaponised to achieve strategic objectives. Such acts inflict catastrophic and often irreversible harm on forests, agricultural lands, water bodies, and the atmosphere, disrupting human survival systems for decades.[4]

Second, environmental destruction occurs indirectly as foreseeable collateral damage arising from attacks on military, industrial, or energy infrastructure. Oil spills, chemical leaks, and toxic emissions are among the most common environmental consequences of modern warfare. The Iran–Iraq War, with its attacks on offshore platforms and refineries, produced severe marine and atmospheric pollution, illustrating how military operations can trigger environmental crises that extend far beyond the battlefield.

Third, although relatively rare, the manipulation of natural processes—such as cloud seeding or attempts to generate tidal waves—demonstrates the potential for environmental modification techniques to be used as weapons. These practices underscore the need for robust international norms and verification mechanisms, such as those embodied in the ENMOD Convention, to prevent the abuse of environmental systems for hostile purposes.

3 Britta Sjostedt, 2020, *The Role of Multilateral Environmental Agreements: A Reconciliatory Approach to Environmental Protection in Armed Conflict*, London: HART, pp. 10-20.

4 UN Environment Programme (UNEP) and UN Centre for Human Settlements (UNCHS), The Kosovo Conflict: Consequences for the Environment and Human Settlements, Nairobi, 1999 (Kosovo Report); UNEP, Lebanon Post-Conflict Environmental Assessment, Nairobi, 2007.

Fourth, and arguably most pervasive, is the indirect environmental damage that follows institutional collapse during armed conflict. With governance systems disrupted, illegal logging, mining, wildlife trafficking, uncontrolled waste disposal, and unsustainable exploitation of natural resources have become widespread. Refugee flows place additional pressure on fragile ecosystems, while the breakdown of environmental regulation accelerates land degradation and biodiversity loss. These cumulative impacts may, in many cases, exceed the direct environmental harm caused by kinetic military operations.

The contemporary conflicts in Ukraine and Gaza exemplify the scale and complexity of wartime environmental damage. Prolonged bombardment, attacks on energy infrastructure, and disruptions in water and waste management have created cascading environmental and humanitarian crises.[5] Research suggests that countries may require up to half a century to restore pre-conflict levels of environmental performance. In an era defined by climate change, rapid biodiversity loss, and pervasive pollution, the intersection between armed conflict and environmental stress amplifies the vulnerabilities of ecosystems and societies alike.[6]

The case of Sierra Leone serves as a cautionary illustration of how climate change, environmental degradation, and conflict can interact to produce long-term insecurity.[7] As climate-related disasters intensify and socio-political institutions struggle to cope,[8] the environmental dimensions of conflict become increasingly central to peacebuilding efforts. As Krampe (2024) notes, addressing both the direct ecological impacts of conflict and the institutional weaknesses that follow is essential for achieving sustainable peace.[9]

---

5 Secretariat of the Convention on Biological Diversity, Global Biodiversity Outlook 5, Montreal, 2020.

6 Military CO_2 emissions tend to remain high several years after large-scale armed conflicts as the state needs to retain a robust military presence to deal with breakaway or newly emerging rebel groups, or due to fears that international tensions will rise again. This effect is also present in states neighbouring armed conflict that increase military expenditure.

7 Sierra Leone: Technical Assistance Report-Climate Policy Diagnostic, International Monetary Fund, Fiscal Affairs Dept., December 11, 2024, eISBN: 9798400294846.

8 Britta Sjostedt and Karen Hulme, Re-evaluating International humanitarian law in a triple planetary crisis: New challenges, new tools, *International Review of the Red Cross* (2023), Vol. 105, No. 924, pp. 1238–1266.

9 Krampe F, et.al., Armed conflict causes long-lasting environmental harms, *Environment and Security*, 2025, pp. 1-15, DOI: 10.1177/27538796251323739.

This book seeks to advance scholarly and policy debates on these vital issues. The chapters collectively explore the legal, ethical, ecological, and security dimensions of environmental protection during armed conflict. They highlight gaps in existing international frameworks, analyse state and non-state practices, and propose pathways to strengthen global norms and accountability mechanisms. By drawing on historical case studies, contemporary conflicts, and evolving legal standards, the contributors offer a comprehensive analysis that underscores the urgency of integrating environmental protection more fully into IHL, environmental law, and peacebuilding strategies.

The editor is deeply grateful to Prof. (Dr.) Manoj Kumar Sinha, President of the Indian Society of International Law (ISIL), New Delhi, for his insightful Foreword, and to Prof. V. G. Hegde, Executive President of ISIL, for his continuous encouragement. The editor also extends sincere thanks to M/s Vij Books, New Delhi, for their commitment and professionalism in bringing this edition to publication.

This volume is offered in the hope that it will stimulate further research, foster informed debate, and contribute to the global endeavour to protect the environment—our shared heritage—even in the darkest hours of war, because there is no Earth B.

Dr Kanika Sharma

10 December, 2025 Assistant Professor (Sr)

Contributors

Gp Capt Kishore Kumar Khera VM retired from the Indian Air Force after 33 years as a fighter pilot. He had a diplomatic tenure. He commanded a fighter squadron and led the first-ever fighter deployment from India to the USA for an international exercise. He served in the Plans and Ops Branch at Air HQ. He was a pioneer member of the COBRA Group and headed the Operational Planning and Assessment Group. He conceptualised, planned and orchestrated the largest-ever IAF operational exercise, Gagan Shakti. He was a Research Fellow at the Institute of Defence Studies and Analyses from 2017 to 2019. Currently, he is an independent analyst and has authored nine books and about fifty articles on security and strategic affairs. The President of India awarded him the Vayu Sena Meda.

Charu Grover has served as a visiting faculty at Bharati Vidyapeeth Institute of Management and Research and as an Assistant Professor at Gitarattan International Business School (affiliated to Guru Gobind Singh Indraprastha University). She has authored and co-authored articles in the domains of Competition Law, Corporate Law, and International Law, to name a few. She is currently pursuing her doctoral degree at the Department of Laws, Panjab University. She has qualified for the UGC NET examination. She was awarded a scholarship to attend the summer course offered by the Xiamen Academy of International Law, China. She is constantly working towards enhancing her knowledge and skills in the realm of academia and research.

Dr Gurpal Singh, Assistant Professor, Panjab University Regional Centre, Muktsar, has 20 years of teaching experience. He completed his PhD from Panjab University, Chandigarh and Post Graduate Diploma in Human Rights PGDHR from the Indian Institute of Human Rights, New Delhi. He has authored and published over 20 research papers in reputed journals and specialises in legal education and academic research.

Gaurav Kumar, PhD scholar at National Law University Delhi. He is also a team member of the UNESCO Chair for legal dimensions of clean sport at NLU Delhi. He has done LLB from Campus Law Centre, Delhi University and LLM in criminal law from the Indian Law Institute. His areas of interest in law are international environmental law, international humanitarian law, sports law, and criminal law.

Bismita Saikia is a Research Scholar in the Department of Law at Tezpur University, Assam. She holds a postgraduate degree in Law from the Department of Law, Tezpur University, and an undergraduate degree in Law from the Centre for Juridical Studies, Dibrugarh University. She is UGC-NET and SLET (North East Region) qualified. Her areas of interest include international law, human rights law, and environmental law.

Dr Gitanjali Ghosh is an Associate Professor of Law and Head at the Department of Law, Tezpur University. Previously, she has served as an Assistant Professor of Law at the National Law University and Judicial Academy, Assam, and as a Researcher at the Centre for Women and the Law, National Law School of India University, Bengaluru. She holds a doctoral and postgraduate degree in law from the National Law School of India University, Bengaluru and an undergraduate degree in law with a gold medal from the North-Eastern Hill University, Shillong. She is also a recipient of a UGC Junior Research Fellowship. She is actively involved in teaching and research in the areas of international law, human rights law, family law, child law, gender and law, and customary law.

Dr Parineet Kaur is an Assistant Professor at the Indian Law Institute, New Delhi. She has been the Head, Centre of Advanced Studies in Intellectual Property and Technology Law, at the Indian Society of International Law. She is a graduate in Economics from Sri Guru Gobind Singh College of Commerce, University of Delhi, and has completed her LL B from Campus Law Centre, Faculty of Law, University of Delhi, and also LL M. She has a Ph D in the area of Copyright and Competition Law in Entertainment Industry from Dr. Ram Manohar Lohiya National Law University Lucknow, India. She is UGC NET qualified. She also represented India at the prestigious "BRICS Forum of International Rule of Law" in Beijing and has presented papers at various national and international conferences, and has many publications to her credit. Her areas of specialisation include Intellectual Property Law, Entertainment Law, Competition Law, International Law, and Human Rights Law. She has co-edited two books: *International Refugee Law* and *Modern Warfare and International Humanitarian Law: Evolving Challenges and Normative Developments*, and has edited another book: *Intellectual Property Laws and Space Laws: Emerging Frontiers of Innovation* *and Regulation*, published by the Indian Society of International Law, New Delhi.

Dr Kanika Sharma is Senior Assistant Professor and Head, Centre for International Humanitarian Law and Military Law at the ISIL She has received a PhD and LL M with a Gold Medal from the University of Jammu, Jammu and Kashmir. She has qualified UGC NET-JRF. Having 9 years of experience, she has delivered lectures in the field of humanitarian and refugee law at national and international universities. She has published various papers in Journals of repute and also presented papers in National and International Conferences. She has co-edited two Books *viz. Modern Warfare and International Humanitarian Law* and *International Refugee Law*. She is a course coordinator of PG Diploma Course in Human Rights, International Humanitarian and Refugee Law conducted by the Indian Academy of International Law and Diplomacy, the teaching wing of the Indian Society of International Law.

Dr Vasudha Bali is an Assistant Professor of Law at Vivekananda Institute of Professional Studies, New Delhi. She holds a PhD in Sports Law from the Indian Law Institute, New Delhi, with her doctoral research titled *"Sports Law in India: Towards Gender Equality."* She is a recipient of the ICSSR Doctoral Fellowship (2022–24) and has qualified for the UGC-NET. Dr Bali also holds a Postgraduate Diploma in International Human Rights, Humanitarian Law, and Refugee Law from the Indian Society of International Law, New Delhi and various Certificate Courses in Sports Law. Her research areas include sports law, gender justice, and human rights. She has published in reputed journals such as the *Global Sports Policy Review* and *ILI Law Review*, and contributed chapters on sports governance, human rights, and environmental law. Dr Bali frequently presents her work at national and international conferences and is dedicated to promoting gender equality, Human Rights and ethical governance in sports law.

Wg Cdr (Dr) U C Jha is Secretary General at the Indian Society of International Law, New Delhi. His areas of research include International Humanitarian Law, Military Law, and Human Rights Law. He took premature retirement from the Indian Air Force in 2001. He has completed Ph D in 'Law and Governance' from Jawaharlal Nehru University, New Delhi. He was invited by the Parliamentary Standing Committee on Defence on a few occasions to present views on the Armed Forces Tribunal Bill; Common Code for the Armed Forces; and the Stress Management in the Armed Forces. Dr Jha was invited by the Diplomatic Academy of MFA of Russia to attend seminar on "Civilian Capacity: Enhancing the

Deployment of Rule of Law Expertise" held in Moscow." He was invited by the UN High Commissioner for Human Rights at Geneva to make a presentation on the independence, impartiality and competence of the judiciary, including military courts. He has delivered a series of lectures on international humanitarian law during the South Asian Teaching Sessions conducted by the International Committee of the Red Cross at Dhaka, Colombo, Islamabad, Kathmandu, and Tehran and various universities in India. He has authored 35 books and contributed more than 165 articles on subjects relating to military legal system, international humanitarian law and human rights in various international and Indian journals and newspapers.

Bharathi M, LL M (International Law), practiced as an advocate from the year of 2022 in both civil and criminal at the Principal District Court, Srivilliputtur, Virudhunagar, Tamil Nadu and actively participated in international academic discussions, including attending an international conference at TNDALU in collaboration with the Indian Society of International Law. She is passionate about exploring new ideas and engaging in international law conferences to gain valuable insights and contribute to scholarly discourse.

Ms Yash Sinha has completed her LLM degree from South Asian University, New Delhi. Her primary research interests are focused on the intersecting domains of International Humanitarian Law, International Environmental Law and International Human Rights Law. Her academic experience includes working as a Research Associate under Dr. Stellina Jolly at South Asian University, New Delhi. In this capacity, she provided extensive research assistance, notably contributing in the preparation of the Toolkit and Training Manual for *'Monitoring Human Rights in Climate Change by National Human Rights Institutions in South Asia'*. She has also undertaken Research Internships at prestigious national and international organisations, including the Indian Society of International Law (ISIL), Asian African Legal Consultative Organisation (AALCO), National Green Tribunal (NGT), New Delhi etc. In addition, she has authored the book chapter titled *'Loitering Munition and Its Implication Under IHL'* in the edited volume of Modern Warfare and International Humanitarian Law – Evolving Challenges and Normative Development.

Dr Niharika is an Assistant Professor (Senior Scale) in Faculty of Law, University of Lucknow and has a teaching experience of more than 9 years. Her area of research pertains to LGBTQ+ studies, Environmental law and International Law. She has completed her B.A.LL.B. (Hons.) and

LL.M. (Bronze Medallist) from Dr. Ram Manohar Lohiya National Law University, Lucknow. She has completed her Ph.D. from Faculty of Law, University of Lucknow on the critical issue of Transgender Rights. She has published one book, 15 articles in National and International Journals, contributed nine book chapters, delivered a number of talks on national radio, IIT Roorkee, NLU, IGNOU and other institutions. She has worked as co-director on ICSSR major project on "Role of Public Policies in better Environmental Management of Municipalities in the State of Uttar Pradesh with special reference to Smart Cities of the State".

Shobhit Pratap Singh is a Ph D Scholar (NET-JRF) at Faculty of Law, University of Lucknow. His research area includes Public International Law, Jurisprudence, and Legal Theory, with a particular focus on sovereignty, reparations, state responsibility, refugee law, global south, and theoretical implications such as subjects and sources of law, and interpreting the connotations of various schools of legal thought. He is pursuing his doctoral thesis on the topic – 'A Study on the Evolving Characteristics of Sovereignty in International Law in the light of Emerging Theoretical Narrative of Meta-modernism', under the supervision of Dr. Niharika, Faculty of Law, University of Lucknow. Shobhit holds a degree in BA LL B and LL M from Dr Ram Manohar Lohiya National Law University, Lucknow and Gujarat National Law University. Currently, he is working on to refine his thematic research areas to expand the contextual understanding by publishing, presenting papers, and attending seminars.

Prof (Dr) D Bhuvaneswari is the Director, College Development Council and Head, Department of International Law and Organisation at the Tamil Nadu Dr Ambedkar Law University, with over twenty-three years of academic and administrative service. She holds a BL (First Rank, Bharathiar University), an ML (First Class with Gold Medal, University of Madras), and a PhD in International Law with a specialisation in extradition. A distinguished scholar, she has presented over 50 papers and presentations at the national and international arena, published 30 journal articles and chapters, and organised major academic programmes, including international conferences on present-day trends like AI, women's rights etc, colloquia, national workshops, symposia, round tables, and faculty development programmes on research methodology. The author has supervised the work of four PhD scholars.

Abarajitha R B is an advocate and product of the esteemed School of Excellence, The Tamil Nadu Dr. Ambedkar Law University with a BA.LLB(HONS). He is presently pursuing LLM from the aforesaid academia, specialising in International Law and Organisation. Having keen interest in research and oration, the co-author has merited over 20 international, national conferences and symposiums through paper presentations and research paper publications since her UG. The author further intends to master in space law by exploring the multidisciplinary convergence of human rights, investment law, diplomacy, international relations, etc in the space race by delving into the global stands further insisting on the stands of India in the present realm. She further finds her interest in the convergence of the international legal order amidst the era of global curriculum.

Vinay Juneja is currently working as Assistant Professor (Law) in Vivekananda Institute of Professional Studies - Technical Campus (VIPS-TC). His areas of interest and research work are Insolvency Bankruptcy Code (IBC), Competition Law, Mergers and Acquisition, Public International Law, International Economic Law, geo-economics, International Human Rights and International Humanitarian Law.

Prof (Dr) T V Subba Rao, is presently working as Professor-Emeritus, VIPS, Delhi, and started his career as a teacher of Law in 1978. He held many academic, administrative and supervisory in the University system. Amongst the many, a few are: Acted as a Visiting Professor, Director, Research and Development Council; Chairperson, Postgraduate Council, National Law School University, Bangalore; Formerly Chairperson, Undergraduate Council, NLSIU.

Tushar Pal is an Assistant Professor (Law) at UPES, Dehradun and is also currently pursuing his PHD with his research interests in energy transition. With a foundation in law and a focus on Energy and Environmental Laws, Mr Pal's work has begun to make significant contributions to the Renewable Energy Sector. In the past year, his research and practice have centred around Human Rights Law and SDGs. This includes addressing critical issues interlinking Environmental and Human Rights Laws.

Dr Meenakshi Harith is the Librarian at the Indian Society of International Law (ISIL), New Delhi, with over 25 years of experience in library and information science. She holds a Ph D in Library Science, Master's degree in Library Science and Sociology, LL B, and a Postgraduate Diploma in International Law and Diplomacy. Dr Harith has contributed extensively to legal bibliography, having compiled numerous subject-specific bibliographies for the Indian Journal of International Law and the ISIL Yearbook of International Humanitarian and Refugee Law since 2001. Her expertise includes bibliometrics, information retrieval, digital resource management, and legal information systems. She has actively participated in national and international conferences, professional training programs, and webinars. Dr Harith continues to lead efforts to digitise and expand access to international legal literature, aiming to develop ISIL's e-library into a specialized national resource on international law.

Part I

Military Preparations and Environment

War Preparations and Environment

Kishore Kumar Khera

Abstract

Peace pays. But it extracts a heavy price. A strong, well-equipped and well-trained military force is an essential tool for sustained peace. How does a military keep itself war-ready? It is by continuously analysing the likely battle space and re-equipping, re-organising and retraining for evolving scenarios.

Wars are often finite in their geography, scale, scope, frequency and duration, but war preparations are omnipresent across the globe and around the clock. While wars have a devastating, visible, immediate impact on the environment, it is war preparation in peacetime that causes long-term degradation. War preparation or military training is a diffuse activity and accordingly seems to have a limited impact on the environment. This impact spread across the length and breadth of the country and its maritime zones, slowly but systematically eroding our environment. Overall degradation of the environment of war preparation far exceeds that of wars. Use of explosives, air, soil and water contamination with heavy metals and chemicals, fossil fuels, water and electricity consumption, deforestation and displacement for training, noise and physical disturbance of maritime life are some of the seemingly small factors. But the sustenance of such activities over decades leaves an indelible mark on our environment that is more devastating than localised wars of limited duration.

While warfare's immediate environmental devastation is widely acknowledged, the persistent and widespread ecological impacts of military preparedness during peacetime often go unnoticed. This article examines how continuous military training and readiness activities—essential for national security—contribute significantly to long-term environmental degradation.

Introduction

Wars destroy. Wars, by their very nature, generate immediate and visible environmental destruction. Scorched landscapes, oil spills, destroyed infrastructure, and toxic residues in the aftermath of conflict remain etched in public consciousness.[1] However, the less visible and often overlooked aspect is the ecological footprint of preparing for war in peacetime. Unlike wars—finite in space and time—preparations are continuous, diffuse, and systemic. They occur on land, at sea, and in the skies, permeating every aspect of military operations. Their environmental impacts accumulate silently, leaving behind a trail of long-term degradation. The less visible costs of military training, exercises, and readiness in peacetime far outweigh those of actual conflict in terms of scale and persistence. Every sortie, naval deployment, and ground exercise consumes fossil fuels, disturbs ecosystems, and produces emissions.[2] Cumulatively, these activities degrade natural environments on a scale rarely examined outside environmental and security scholarship. The paradox, however, is striking: while militaries exist to preserve peace and stability, their constant preparations for war produce enduring and widespread ecological consequences.[3]

The pursuit of peace has historically depended upon the maintenance of credible military capabilities. States, in their quest to deter aggression and secure sovereignty, invest heavily in raising, equipping, and training their armed forces. Among the three principal branches of the armed forces—army, navy, and air force—the environmental impacts of preparations differ in scale, type, and geography. The army, with its extensive land requirements, disrupts terrestrial ecosystems. The navy, through exercises and operations at sea, disturbs delicate marine life and pollutes maritime zones. The air force, heavily dependent on fossil fuels and high-emission aircraft, contributes substantially to atmospheric pollution and climate change. This tripartite impact represents a persistent, often overlooked ecological footprint of militaries worldwide. Add to these the impact of new domains of Space and Cyberspace in warfare, and the environment suffers. The militarisation of outer space has shifted from speculative debate to operational reality. Nations maintain constellations of satellites

1 United Nations Environment Programme (UNEP), From Conflict to Peacebuilding: The Role of Natural Resources and the Environment (Nairobi. UNEP, 2009), p34.

2 Neta C. Crawford, "Pentagon Fuel Use, Climate Change, and the Costs of War," *Costs of War Project*, Watson Institute, Brown University, 2019.

3 John Keeley, *The Environmental Consequences of War* (Cambridge: Cambridge University Press, 1999), p15.

for communication, navigation, reconnaissance, and missile warning. Preparation for space warfare involves not only the deployment of satellites but also the testing of anti-satellite (ASAT) weapons, missile defence systems, and electronic warfare tools. While space is imagined as a void immune to terrestrial concerns, its militarisation carries distinct and enduring environmental consequences.

This essay examines in detail the environmental impacts of war preparations by various wings of the armed forces. It argues that while military readiness is indispensable, its ecological costs demand recognition, mitigation, and reform. By highlighting the scale and depth of environmental disruption, the discussion seeks to contribute to a more balanced understanding of security—one that includes not only territorial integrity but also environmental sustainability. This article, drawing on historical evidence, contemporary practices, and scientific findings, explores the environmental consequences of military preparations. It situates the discussion within the larger context of security and sustainability, and asks whether it is possible to reconcile the imperatives of defence with ecological responsibility.

The Imperative of Military Preparedness

No state can afford complacency in matters of defence. The strategic environment is inherently uncertain, with threats evolving in form and intensity. Modern militaries are thus compelled to maintain a constant state of readiness through training, exercises, research and development, procurement, and infrastructure expansion.

The Security–Sustainability Contradiction

The fundamental inconsistency is evident: states require strong militaries to preserve sovereignty and peace, yet sustaining these forces erodes the very environment upon which human security ultimately depends. The challenge lies in reconciling two imperatives—security from external threats and security from ecological collapse. The debate is complicated by:

- **National Security Exemptions:** Defence sectors often operate outside environmental accountability frameworks.
- **Technological Secrecy:** Military R&D and procurement lack transparency, making independent assessment difficult.
- **Public Perception:** Citizens accept environmental costs as necessary sacrifices for national security, limiting political pressure.

Preparation for war entails:

- **Training and Exercises:** Field manoeuvres, live-fire drills, naval deployments, and air operations designed to replicate battlefield conditions along with inherent electromagnetic emissions.
- **Testing and Development:** Research laboratories and testing ranges producing and trialling advanced weapons systems.
- **Infrastructure:** Bases, logistics hubs, airfields, naval dockyards, and communication networks.
- **Energy and Resource Consumption:** High dependence on fossil fuels, electricity, and water to sustain operations.

While these activities ensure deterrence and operational efficacy, they demand massive natural resources, generate waste, and disrupt ecological balances. Unlike civilian industries—often subject to environmental regulations—militaries worldwide enjoy exemptions in the name of national security, amplifying their environmental footprint.

Shaking Statistics

- Approximately 5.5% of global greenhouse gas emissions are attributed to military activities—including training, operations, manufacturing, and supply chains. If militaries globally were treated as a single country, they'd rank as the fourth-largest emitter in the world, exceeding even Russia's total emissions.[4]
- In absolute terms, the global military carbon footprint is estimated at around 2,750 million tonnes of CO_2-equivalent (Mt CO_2e).[5]
- The US military alone—the largest branch in terms of energy use—has emitted nearly 4,000 Mt CO_2e between 1979 and 2023, comparable to India's annual emissions. [6]

4 Stuart Parkinson and Linsey Cottrell, Estimating the Military's Global Greenhouse Gas Emissions, Scientists for Global Responsibility (SGR) and the Conflict and Environment Observatory (CEOBS), November 2022.

5 Stuart Parkinson, How big are global military carbon emissions?, Responsible Science Journal No 5, *July 8, 2023.*

6 Neta C. Crawford, The Pentagon, Climate Change, and War: Charting the Rise and Fall of US Military Emissions, Oxford University, 2022.

- For NATO, military activities in 2023 are estimated to have produced 233 million tonnes of CO_2e, surpassing emissions of countries like Colombia or Qatar.[7]

Climate Blind Spot

Military emissions have historically been excluded from international climate agreements—like the Kyoto Protocol and Paris Agreement—due to exemptions on the grounds of national security. As a result, these emissions are largely unreported and unaccounted for in national carbon inventories. Geopolitical tensions and increased rearmament (e.g., following the war in Gaza and Ukraine) are likely to push military emissions even higher. Experts argue for more transparent reporting, rigorous accounting, and integration of military emissions into national and global climate strategies. A classical case is in the maritime domain, wherein the navies justify their environmental exemptions by citing national security imperatives. Yet, the ecological costs are mounting. Unlike terrestrial damage, which may be remediated through afforestation or soil treatment, marine degradation is harder to reverse. The invisibility of underwater impacts—noise, sonar, UXO—renders them politically neglected. Mitigation strategies exist: quieter propulsion systems, renewable energy integration at bases, stricter spill controls, and compliance with international conventions. However, the secrecy and autonomy of navies often limit transparency and external accountability.

The global military contributes roughly 2.75 billion tonnes of CO_2-equivalent annually. This figure surpasses the emissions from both civil aviation (2%) and shipping combined (3%). Therefore, military emissions exceed both civil aviation and shipping combined. However, due to consistent underreporting, inconsistent data, and treaty exemptions, these emissions remain a major "blind spot" in climate action and policy.

Comparative Impact: War versus Preparations

It may appear counterintuitive, but the aggregate environmental cost of peacetime preparations often surpasses that of actual wars. Wars, though devastating, are episodic. Preparations, in contrast, are ceaseless, spanning decades and enveloping entire nations.

7 Susan Chako, NATO's 2023 military spending produces emissions rivalling entire countries, Down to Earth, July 7, 2024.

Consider the Vietnam War - the extensive use of Agent Orange left large tracts barren, but the cumulative emissions and resource consumption of the US military during the Cold War far exceeded the localised devastation of the Vietnam conflict. Similarly, while the Gulf War oil spills were disastrous, the routine emissions from maintaining fleets, aircraft, and bases in West Asia for decades represent a heavier long-term burden. Thus, while warfare dramatises environmental destruction, preparations normalise it. This normalisation renders the ecological toll invisible to public debate, yet no less consequential.

Paradoxically, military lands sometimes serve as biodiversity havens. Restricted access prevents urbanisation, industrialisation, and intensive agriculture. The Salisbury Plain in the UK and certain Indian ranges harbour endangered species precisely because of their seclusion.[8] Yet, this inadvertent conservation benefit must not obscure the degradation caused by active training. The challenge lies in balancing military necessity with ecological stewardship.

The Hidden Environmental Burden of Military Preparations

Use and Habitat Transformation

Armies are inherently land-centric institutions. Their training, manoeuvres, and logistics demand vast tracts of land. Tank manoeuvres churn topsoil, artillery firing leaves craters, and deforestation creates open ranges. In India alone, approximately two million hectares are under defence control,[9] much of it reserved for training, ranges, and cantonments. Comparable patterns exist globally: the US Army manages more than 12 million acres across hundreds of bases.[10] These lands, often ecologically sensitive, are transformed to suit military needs. Forests are cleared for firing ranges, wetlands are drained for armoured manoeuvres, and grasslands are converted into cantonments. Soil compaction from repeated tank manoeuvres reduces infiltration and alters hydrological cycles, creating long-term ecological shifts.

8 English Nature, *Biodiversity of Salisbury Plain Training Area* (London: English Nature, 2002).

9 Comptroller and Auditor General of India, *Report on Defence Land Management* (New Delhi: Government of India, 2011).

10 U.S. Department of Defence, *Base Structure Report FY 2018* (Washington, D.C.: DoD, 2018).

Naval readiness requires extensive coastal infrastructure: dockyards, air stations, ammunition depots, and logistics hubs. Construction of such facilities transforms coastal habitats, often encroaching upon mangroves, estuaries, and coral reefs. In India, the expansion of naval bases in the Andaman and Nicobar Islands has raised concerns over coral reef degradation and turtle nesting sites.[11] Similarly, the US Naval Base at Guam has altered local ecosystems through dredging, land reclamation, and deforestation.[12] These transformations carry long-term consequences for coastal biodiversity and natural defences against storms and erosion.

Air forces require large bases with long runways, hangars, fuel depots, and housing. The construction and expansion of such facilities transform landscapes. Wetlands, grasslands, and agricultural lands are often acquired for runways.[13] In India, the expansion of air bases in the Northeast has raised concerns over deforestation and the displacement of tribal communities.[14] Jet fuel storage and handling also pose risks of leakage and fire. Spills at bases have contaminated soils with benzene, toluene, and other hydrocarbons, requiring costly remediation.[15]

Space militarisation requires vast terrestrial infrastructure: launch pads, radar tracking stations, command centres, and testing ranges. The construction and maintenance of these facilities often disrupt local ecosystems. In the United States, the expansion of missile defence testing ranges in Alaska and California displaced indigenous communities and altered migratory bird populations.[16]

Soil Degradation and Contamination

Training with heavy armoured vehicles and artillery profoundly alters soil structures. Topsoil is eroded, vegetation cover is lost, and large craters from

11 Ritwick Dutta, "Military Expansion and the Environment in the Andaman Islands," *Economic and Political Weekly* 39, no. 3 (2004): pp303–307.

12 U.S. Environmental Protection Agency, *Impact of Guam Naval Base Expansion* (Washington, D.C.: EPA, 2010).

13 Peter Hough, *Environmental Security: An Introduction* (London: Routledge, 2014), 132.

14 Sanjoy Hazarika, Strangers of the Mist: Tales of War and Peace from India's Northeast (New Delhi: Penguin, 1994), 217.

15 U.S. Environmental Protection Agency, *Petroleum Contamination at Military Bases* (Washington, D.C.: EPA, 2016).

16 U.S. Missile Defence Agency, *Environmental Impact Statement for Ground-Based Midcourse Defence* (Washington, D.C., 2004).Bottom of Form

artillery shells alter the landscape. Over the decades, these changes render training areas ecologically fragile. A US Army Corps of Engineers study found that tracked vehicle manoeuvres compact soil to depths of over 30 centimetres, reducing fertility and recovery potential.[17]

Chemical contamination is equally severe. Residues from explosives, propellants, and heavy metals from ammunition accumulate in soils. Lead from small arms firing ranges, for example, leaches into the surrounding land and groundwater. Studies in Germany and the United States show elevated lead concentrations near long-used ranges, exceeding safety limits for human and ecological health.[18]

Naval gunnery, missile testing, and torpedo drills leave behind unexploded ordnance (UXO) and debris on the seabed.[19] Over time, corrosion releases toxic residues, contaminating sediments and harming benthic organisms. In some cases, old dumping grounds for munitions—such as those in the Baltic Sea—pose continuing hazards to marine ecosystems.[20]

Air-to-ground weapons testing—bombs, rockets, and missiles—requires extensive ranges. These activities scar landscapes with craters, release chemical residues, and produce UXO hazards. The Nevada Test and Training Range, used for decades by the US Air Force, remains heavily contaminated with ordnance, metals, and propellant residues.[21] In India, the IAF's use of the Pokhran range for live bombing has raised concerns over desert ecology, groundwater contamination, and the displacement of local communities.[22]

Aircraft operations release not only CO_2 but also nitrogen oxides, sulphur oxides, and particulate matter at high altitudes. These emissions have

17 U.S. Army Corps of Engineers, *Soil Impacts from Military Vehicles* (Washington, D.C., 2003).

18 H. J. Pichtel, "Distribution of Lead in Soils at an Outdoor Firing Range," *Bulletin of Environmental Contamination and Toxicology* 72, no. 2 (2004): pp.335–343.

19 R. P. Whitney et al., "Environmental Effects of Naval Gunnery Practice," *Marine Pollution Bulletin* 58, no. 3 (2009): pp.394–401.

20 International Union for Conservation of Nature (IUCN), *Munitions Dumped at Sea: A Threat to the Environment* (Gland: IUCN, 2010).

21 National Research Council, *Environmental Remediation at the Nevada Test Site* (Washington, D.C.: National Academies Press, 2002).

22 Tripathi and Shukla, "Groundwater Contamination from Defence Activities in Rajasthan," *Indian Journal of Environmental Protection* 20, no. 5 (2000): pp.377–384.

stronger radiative forcing effects than ground-level pollutants.[23] Contrails and induced cirrus clouds alter atmospheric dynamics, contributing to warming. Military aviation, less regulated than civilian aviation, remains a significant yet underreported contributor to climate change.

Maintenance of aircraft involves extensive use of solvents, degreasers, and hydraulic fluids, many of which are hazardous. Improper disposal contaminates soils and groundwater around bases. At Kadena Air Base in Okinawa, PFAS contamination has been documented in local water supplies due to firefighting foams.[24]

War preparations in space also involve extensive testing of launch vehicles, many of which use toxic propellants such as hydrazine. Hydrazine is carcinogenic, and spills during fuelling or accidents contaminate soils and groundwater near launch sites.[25] The Baikonur Cosmodrome in Kazakhstan has repeatedly suffered ecological damage from unspent fuel in failed launches, harming local ecosystems and human health.[26]

Water Resource Strain and Pollution

Army bases, often located in arid or semi-arid regions for strategic depth, consume vast quantities of water. Cantonments require potable water for thousands of personnel, vehicle maintenance, and training. Water extraction on such scales depletes aquifers.[27] Moreover, training activities frequently pollute surface and groundwater. Leached residues of perchlorates, nitrates, and heavy metals contaminate aquifers. In India's Pokhran range, repeated testing of artillery and missiles has raised concerns over groundwater quality, though systematic studies remain

23 Intergovernmental Panel on Climate Change (IPCC), *Aviation and the Global Atmosphere* (Geneva: IPCC, 1999).
Intergovernmental Panel on Climate Change (IPCC), *Aviation and the Global Atmosphere* (Geneva: IPCC, 1999).

24 Jon Mitchell, *Poisoning the Pacific* (Lanham: Rowman & Littlefield, 2020), pp.165–169

25 National Research Council, *Toxicity of Propellants Used in Spacecraft* (Washington, D.C.: National Academies Press, 1998).

26 Philip C. Saunders, *China's Space Program: A Net Assessment* (Washington, D.C.: CSIS Press, 2015), pp.72–75.

27 Ashok Swain, "Environmental Cooperation in South Asia," in *Environmental Peace-making*, eds. Ken Conca and Geoffrey D. Dabelko (Washington, D.C.: Woodrow Wilson Centre Press, 2002), 61–85.

sparse due to security restrictions.[28] Globally, the problem is evident: US bases in Okinawa and Germany have reported contamination from per- and polyfluoroalkyl substances (PFAS) due to firefighting foams.[29]

Forest Loss and Deforestation

The army's frequent demand for training ranges necessitates deforestation. Deforestation for training ranges also displaces wildlife, fragments habitats, and reduces carbon sequestration capacity. The immediate effect is habitat fragmentation. Wildlife corridors are disrupted, leading to biodiversity loss. Species sensitive to human disturbance, such as big cats, elephants, or ground-nesting birds, are particularly affected.[30] Unlike commercial deforestation—often offset through compensatory afforestation—military clearances are seldom subjected to equivalent scrutiny. In Northeast India, expansion of training facilities in the 1980s and 1990s led to significant deforestation, exacerbating soil erosion in already fragile ecosystems.[31] Similarly, the British Army's Salisbury Plain Training Area, though paradoxically a biodiversity hotspot due to restricted civilian access, has suffered deforestation and soil compaction.[32]

While some military lands act as inadvertent wildlife sanctuaries due to limited civilian intrusion, the ecological costs of active training—fires, deforestation, and noise—remain substantial.

Noise Pollution and Wildlife Disturbance

Military hardware is inherently noisy—jet engines, artillery barrages, mechanised columns, and sonar pings create extreme acoustic disturbances. Beyond human habitation, such noise disrupts avian breeding patterns, terrestrial animal migration, and marine mammal communication. The consequences cascade across food chains and ecological webs. Prolonged

28 B. D. Tripathi and R. K. Shukla, "Groundwater Contamination from Defence Activities in Rajasthan," *Indian Journal of Environmental Protection* 20, no. 5 (2000): pp.377–384.

29 Jon Mitchell, Poisoning the Pacific: The US Military's Secret Dumping of Plutonium, Chemical Weapons, and Agent Orange (Lanham: Rowman & Littlefield, 2020), 118–122.

30 Ruchi Badola and Syed Ainul Hussain, "Conflict in Paradise: Human–Wildlife Conflict in Protected Areas," *Conservation and Society* 4, no. 3 (2006): pp.340–348.

31 Ministry of Environment and Forests, *Report on Forest Diversion for Defence Projects* (New Delhi: Government of India, 1999).

32 English Nature, *Biodiversity of Salisbury Plain Training Area* (London: English Nature, 2002).

exposure affects not only human populations in nearby settlements but also wild and marine life. Studies in the Netherlands demonstrated that bird populations near artillery ranges displayed altered breeding and nesting behaviours, leading to reduced reproductive success.[33] Similar patterns are reported near tank firing ranges in Eastern Europe.

Military aircraft generate extreme noise, with take-off levels exceeding 140 decibels.[34] Communities near air bases, such as those around the Indian Air Force's Jodhpur station or the US Air Force's Ramstein base in Germany, have long protested against noise pollution. Beyond human discomfort, such noise disrupts avian populations, particularly migratory species that rely on acoustic cues.[35] Supersonic flights, still part of training regimens, create sonic booms that can damage property and unsettle wildlife. Although restricted in populated areas, such flights continue over deserts, seas, and sparsely populated regions, with ecological consequences often overlooked.

The psychological stress induced in wildlife by such disturbances remains poorly studied but is likely significant. Nocturnal species, in particular, suffer from altered activity cycles when training occurs at night.

Energy Consumption and Carbon Emissions

Militaries are among the largest institutional consumers of energy worldwide. According to the Stockholm International Peace Research Institute (SIPRI), the US military is the world's single largest institutional consumer of petroleum. Similar patterns, albeit on smaller scales, exist globally. Mechanised columns, logistics convoys, and cantonments consume large volumes of fossil fuels and electricity. The US Army, for instance, consumed more than 270,000 barrels of oil daily during the Iraq War buildup, much of it for training and logistics.[36] Even in peacetime, large-scale exercises involve thousands of vehicles, each burning diesel or petrol.

33 H. Van der Zande, W. J. Ter Keurs, and W. J. van der Weijden, "The Impact of Outdoor Shooting Activities on the Density of Birds in the Western Netherlands," *Biological Conservation* 41, no. 4 (1987): pp.285–297.

34 Federal Aviation Administration (FAA), *Aircraft Noise Levels and Their Impact* (Washington, D.C.: FAA, 2012).

35 Richard Fuller et al., "Daytime Noise Predicts Nocturnal Singing in Urban Robins," *Biology Letters* 3, no. 4 (2007): pp.368–370.

36 Michael Klare, Blood and Oil: The Dangers and Consequences of America's Growing Petroleum Dependency (New York: Metropolitan Books, 2004), 201.

Warships, especially aircraft carriers and destroyers, consume enormous amounts of fossil fuels. A naval destroyer burns approximately 1,000 barrels of fuel per day at cruising speed.[37] Multiply this by the number of vessels engaged in routine operations and exercises, and the carbon footprint becomes staggering. Nuclear-powered carriers avoid direct fuel combustion, but their life-cycle environmental costs—from uranium mining to radioactive waste—are significant.[38] Exhaust emissions from naval vessels include carbon dioxide, sulphur oxides, nitrogen oxides, and particulate matter, all of which contribute to climate change and regional air pollution. In port cities such as Mumbai or San Diego, naval berthing significantly adds to local air quality deterioration.[39]

Air forces epitomise speed, reach, and technological sophistication. Yet, they are also the most energy-intensive of all military branches. Modern fighter aircraft consume several thousand litres of aviation turbine fuel (ATF) in a single sortie[40]. For example, the F-15 fighter jet burns nearly 25,000 litres over three hours of flight.[41] Large-scale exercises such as Red Flag in Nevada involve hundreds of aircraft, producing emissions comparable to those of small cities.

Routine training sorties, transport missions, and patrols across nations cumulatively release millions of tonnes of greenhouse gases annually. According to the *Costs of War Project*, the US Department of Defence emitted 59 million metric tonnes of CO_2 equivalent in 2017, much of it from air operations.[42]

37 U.S. Congressional Research Service, *Navy Ship Propulsion Technologies* (Washington, D.C.: CRS, 2006), p.12.

38 Allison Macfarlane and Rodney C. Ewing, eds., *Uncertainty Underground: Yucca Mountain and the Nation's High-Level Nuclear Waste* (Cambridge, MA: MIT Press, 2006), p.177.

39 California Air Resources Board, *Emissions from Port Operations* (Sacramento: CARB, 2015).

40 U.S. Department of Defence, *Energy for the War fighter: Operational Energy Strategy* (Washington, D.C.: DoD, 2011), p.8.

41 John A. Warden, *The Air Campaign* (Washington, D.C.: National Defence University Press, 1989), p.54.

42 Neta C. Crawford, "Pentagon Fuel Use, Climate Change, and the Costs of War," *Costs of War Project*, Watson Institute, Brown University, 2019.

Displacement and Human Costs

Preparation for war frequently entails the acquisition of land, leading to the displacement of civilian populations. In India, the creation of field firing ranges in Rajasthan and Jammu & Kashmir displaced entire villages.[43] Such displacements also have secondary environmental costs: resettled populations exert pressure and further degrade new ecosystems.

Fires and Accidental Hazards

Live-fire exercises occasionally trigger forest fires, particularly in dry seasons. The Indian Army has reported multiple fire incidents in Uttarakhand during summer training.[44] Such fires destroy biodiversity, alter soil chemistry, and release significant carbon emissions. Similarly, unexploded ordnance (UXO) left in training areas poses long-term risks, restricting civilian use of land and endangering both humans and wildlife.

Maritime Exercises and Ecological Disruption

Navies are indispensable for the protection of maritime interests, sea lines of communication, and territorial waters. Yet their preparations for war—ranging from fleet exercises to live-fire drills—carry substantial ecological costs. Unlike armies, whose impacts are largely terrestrial, naval activities affect delicate marine ecosystems.[45] Large-scale exercises such as the RIMPAC (Rim of the Pacific Exercise) or India's Malabar exercises involve dozens of warships, submarines, and aircraft operating in concert.[46] These events, repeated annually, consume vast quantities of fuel, generate underwater noise, and release pollutants. Their scale, often comparable to wartime operations, transforms regional seas into zones of disturbance for extended durations.

Underwater Noise and Marine Mammals

The most direct and widely studied impact of naval activities is underwater noise pollution. Active sonar, essential for anti-submarine warfare,

43 R. S. Mann, "Displacement due to Defence Projects in India," *Economic and Political Weekly* 38, no. 2 (2003): pp.137–142

44 Ministry of Defence (India), *Annual Report 2015–16* (New Delhi: Government of India, 2016).

45 Michael Renner, *The Security Implications of Climate Change* (Washington, D.C.: World watch Institute, 2007), p.41.

46 U.S. Navy, *RIMPAC 2020 Exercise Overview* (Washington, D.C.: Department of the Navy, 2020).

generates high-intensity sound waves that travel hundreds of kilometres underwater. Research has established links between sonar use and mass strandings of cetaceans such as whales and dolphins.[47] In 2000, a NATO exercise in the Bahamas was followed by the stranding of 17 whales, an incident later attributed to mid-frequency active sonar.[48] Chronic noise from ship engines, propellers, and drills also interferes with marine mammal communication, which depends on sound for navigation, feeding, and reproduction.[49] Fish and invertebrates are similarly affected, displaying altered behaviour and stress responses. Over time, such disturbances can deplete populations and disrupt food chains.

Oil Spills and Chemical Discharges

Even in peacetime, naval operations pose risks of oil spills and chemical leaks. Routine refuelling at sea (underway replenishment) occasionally results in accidental discharges. The International Tanker Owners Pollution Federation records multiple instances of naval vessels responsible for localised spills.[50] Moreover, cleaning agents, firefighting foams, and paint residues containing heavy metals leach into seawater from naval bases and dry docks.[51] Ship-breaking activities, often tied to naval decommissioning, add to marine pollution, especially in South Asian yards where environmental regulations are weak.[52]

Ballast Water and Invasive Species

Naval vessels, like their commercial counterparts, use ballast water for stability. Discharge of ballast water introduces invasive species into non-native environments, disrupting local ecosystems.[53] Although the

47 Christopher Clark et al., "Acoustic Masking in Marine Ecosystems: Intuitions, Analysis, and Implications," *Marine Ecology Progress Series* 395 (2009): pp.201–222.

48 U.S. National Oceanic and Atmospheric Administration (NOAA), *Report on the Bahamas Marine Mammal Stranding Event of 2000* (Washington, D.C.: NOAA, 2001).

49 Hal Whitehead, *Sperm Whales: Social Evolution in the Ocean* (Chicago: University of Chicago Press, 2003), pp.89–91.

50 International Tanker Owners Pollution Federation, *Oil Tanker Spill Statistics 2018* (London: ITOPF, 2019).

51 Andrew DeWit, "The Environmental Footprint of Naval Operations," *Naval War College Review* 67, no. 1 (2014): pp.113–127.

52 Greenpeace International, *End of Life Ships: The Human Cost of Breaking Ships* (Amsterdam: Greenpeace, 2005).

53 IMO, Ballast Water Management Convention (London: IMO, 2004).

International Maritime Organisation (IMO) mandates ballast water management, compliance by naval fleets remains inconsistent due to operational security exemptions.[54]

Nuclear Risks

Nuclear-powered submarines and carriers pose unique risks. Accidents, though rare, can have catastrophic consequences. The 1989 sinking of the Soviet submarine Komsomolsk in the Norwegian Sea released radioactive materials, while several decommissioned submarines remain scuttled with reactors intact.[55] Such legacies underscore the long-term risks of nuclear naval propulsion.

Military planners have long considered the deployment of nuclear-powered or nuclear-armed systems in orbit. While the Outer Space Treaty (1967) prohibits nuclear weapons in space, nuclear-powered satellites have been launched, some of which have crashed back to Earth. The 1978 crash of the Soviet Cosmos 954 satellite spread radioactive debris across Canadian territory.[56] Future military competition in orbit risks reviving such hazards.

Space Debris Proliferation

The most visible ecological consequence of military space preparations is the generation of orbital debris. China's 2007 ASAT test, which destroyed the Fengyun-1C satellite, created more than 3,000 trackable fragments and hundreds of thousands of smaller pieces.[57] These fragments orbit Earth for decades, posing collision risks to civilian satellites and the International Space Station. The cascading effect—known as the Kessler Syndrome—could render some orbital bands unusable.[58] Military doctrines that emphasise "space dominance" encourage redundancy and rapid replenishment of constellations, adding to orbital congestion. Launches themselves release

54 Elizabeth DeSombre, "Flagging Standards: Globalization and Environmental, Safety, and Labor Regulations at Sea" (Cambridge, MA: MIT Press, 2006), p.201.

55 David Fairhall, "Nuclear Submarine Accidents: Komsomolsk Case Study," *The Guardian*, April 10, 1989.

56 David Wright, Laura Grego, and Lisbeth Gronlund, *The Physics of Space Security* (Cambridge, MA: American Academy of Arts and Sciences, 2005), pp.56–57.

57 Brian Weeden, "2007 Chinese Anti-Satellite Test Fact Sheet," Secure World Foundation, 2010.

58 Donald J. Kessler and Burton G. Cour-Palais, "Collision Frequency of Artificial Satellites: The Creation of a Debris Belt," *Journal of Geophysical Research* 83, no. A6 (1978): pp. 2637–2646.

carbon soot into the stratosphere, where it persists, altering atmospheric chemistry and contributing to climate forcing.[59]

Cyber as a Warfighting Domain

At first glance, cyberspace may appear immaterial, a domain of code and algorithms divorced from ecological consequences. Yet, the infrastructure underpinning cyber operations—data centres, server farms, undersea cables, and satellite communications—carries substantial environmental costs. Preparations for cyber warfare amplify these costs in ways that are rarely acknowledged.

Data centres, which host military cloud networks, simulations, and cyber training environments, are energy-intensive. Globally, data centres consume nearly 1% of all electricity, and military networks add significant demand.[60] Cyber war-gaming and AI-driven simulations require immense computational power, further straining energy grids. If powered by fossil fuels, this translates into higher greenhouse gas emissions. Military cyber units often operate in isolated, secure networks that duplicate civilian infrastructure, effectively doubling resource consumption. Unlike commercial firms that increasingly adopt renewable energy solutions, military secrecy and reliability requirements make adoption slower.

The hardware used in cyber defence and offence—servers, encryption devices, specialised processors—becomes obsolete quickly due to rapid technological change. This accelerates the generation of e-waste.[61] Military-grade electronics, often classified, cannot easily enter civilian recycling streams. Disposal is usually centralised and shrouded in secrecy, leading to storage or incineration rather than environmentally sound recycling. Toxic substances such as lead, mercury, and brominated flame retardants in e-waste pose long-term risks to soil and water systems. In some cases, surplus military electronics are offloaded to secondary markets in developing countries, where unsafe dismantling exposes workers and communities to hazards.[62]

59 Martin Ross and Darin Toohey, "Particle Emissions from Commercial Spaceflight: A Climate Concern," *Eos* 90, no. 43 (2009): pp.409–410.

60 International Energy Agency (IEA), *Data Centres and Energy: Fact Sheet* (Paris: IEA, 2020).

61 Ruediger Kuehr and Eric Williams, *Computers and the Environment: Understanding and Managing Their Impacts* (Dordrecht: Kluwer Academic, 2003).

62 Jim Puckett et al., *Exporting Harm: The High-Tech Trashing of Asia* (Seattle: Basel Action Network, 2002).

Global cyber connectivity relies heavily on undersea fibre-optic cables. Military cyber strategies include both defending and attacking these cables. The physical preparation of cable-laying operations, coastal landing stations, and repair activities disturb seabed ecosystems. During wartime preparations, navies may map cables for sabotage or lay redundant cables for secure networks, adding to ecological disruption.[63]

Cyber and electronic warfare overlap in the use of jamming, spoofing, and electromagnetic interference. Prolonged use of electromagnetic tools during exercises increases the electromagnetic footprint, potentially affecting avian navigation and pollinators such as bees, which rely on geomagnetic cues.[64] While research remains inconclusive, precautionary principles suggest that the intensification of electromagnetic emissions is not environmentally neutral.

Mitigation and the Way Forward

Till humanity realises the futility of war, military preparedness is essential for national security. This has profound ecological costs. Armies transform landscapes, degrade soils, and consume water. Navies disturb marine ecosystems, pollute seas, and risk nuclear accidents. Air forces emit vast greenhouse gases, create noise and chemical pollution, and transform land for airbases. These impacts, though diffuse and often invisible, exceed the environmental toll of actual wars.

The paradox is stark: militaries exist to secure peace and sovereignty, but in doing so they undermine the ecological foundations of security itself. Recognition of this dilemma is the first step. The second is reform: adopting greener technologies, integrating environmental safeguards into training, and increasing transparency. Ultimately, true security cannot be defined solely in territorial terms. It must encompass ecological sustainability, for without stable environments, there can be no lasting peace. The challenge before states is to reconcile military necessity with ecological responsibility—ensuring that preparations for war do not render peace uninhabitable.

Recognising the environmental burden of military preparedness does not imply weakening defence. Rather, it necessitates innovation and

63 Nicole Starosielski, *The Undersea Network* (Durham, NC: Duke University Press, 2015).

64 Alfonso Balmori, "Electromagnetic Pollution from Phone Masts: Effects on Wildlife," *Pathophysiology* 16, no. 2–3 (2009): pp.191–199.

accountability. Technological innovation offers partial solutions, yet adoption remains limited, constrained by operational conservatism, costs, and the primacy of combat readiness over sustainability. Several pathways exist:

Green Military Technologies

- Development of biofuels and synthetic fuels for aircraft and vehicles.
- Adoption of hybrid-electric propulsion for naval vessels.
- Investments in renewable energy infrastructure at bases.

Sustainable Training Practices

- Increased reliance on simulators to reduce live-fire exercises.
- Recycling of expended materials and safe disposal of hazardous waste.
- Rotation of training areas to allow ecological recovery.

Regulatory Oversight

International environmental treaties must gradually incorporate military activities. Exemptions that shield armed forces from scrutiny need recalibration to balance secrecy with sustainability.

Civil-Military Collaboration

Defence lands can serve dual purposes: as biodiversity reserves when not used for training. Examples from the UK and India show that restricted military zones often harbour rich ecosystems due to limited civilian encroachment. Managed wisely, militaries can become stewards of conservation rather than agents of degradation.

Transparency and Research

Encouraging military–academic partnerships to study environmental footprints can yield evidence-based solutions. Public awareness can catalyse reforms without undermining operational readiness.

Conclusion

Peace is often celebrated as the ultimate aspiration of nations. Yet, paradoxically, sustaining peace demands a significant investment in military preparedness. The adage "if you want peace, prepare for war" encapsulates a dilemma for states: while armed forces deter aggression and secure borders, their perpetual readiness carries unseen costs. Prominent among these is environmental degradation, a consequence that rarely figures in public debate yet has profound implications. Environmental consequences of war are widely acknowledged: scorched earth policies, toxic contamination, and infrastructural devastation leave visible scars.

The environment is the ultimate foundation of security. While armies, navies, and air forces secure borders, it is fertile soil, clean air, and potable water that sustain societies. Ignoring the ecological costs of war preparations is therefore shortsighted. The challenge is not to dismantle militaries but to ensure that their pursuit of preparedness does not compromise the ecological stability upon which peace itself rests.

The preparation for war in new domains underscores a broader lesson: environmental impacts are not confined to physical battlefields. Space debris endangers satellites essential for climate monitoring and disaster relief. Cyber infrastructures accelerate fossil fuel use even as militaries profess commitments to green energy. Thus, environmental security must expand its scope. A comprehensive view of sustainability in defence requires integrating ecological accountability into military space launches, cyber infrastructure design, and international arms control negotiations. Only by acknowledging these hidden costs can nations balance security imperatives with planetary stewardship.

As global environmental crises intensify, the nexus between defence and ecology demands urgent attention. Militaries must evolve into institutions that defend not only sovereignty but also sustainability. Peace indeed pays, but unless managed wisely, its price may be the irreversible degradation of our planet. There is no Earth B.

Environmental Destruction by Military Forces

Charu Grover & Gurpal Singh

Introduction

International Humanitarian Law (IHL) regulates the conduct of armed conflicts. Unless there is an armed conflict, IHL cannot be applied. This thought leads us to address the pertinent question of what exactly qualifies as an "armed conflict." Therefore, before moving on to related issues regarding the extent of hostilities, it is important to examine the legal definition of armed conflict.

To begin contemplating it, the ethical distinctiveness of armed warfare is a fair place to start. A lot of people have opined that it is not a big deal for combatants to deliberately harm and kill other people. To be straightforward, this differs greatly from the moral code that governs interpersonal relationships between humans. Speaking pragmatically, in every human community's standard moral code, causing harm or death to another person deliberately with the intention is considered one of the worst acts that can be done by any human. Thus, this popular perspective on war proposes a drastic departure from the accepted moral framework[1].

The concept of war is unique. Establishing peace becomes the primary and foremost objective. An absolute war may be a way to end the war, but it is not the most suitable or conducive means of ensuring a peaceful resolution. Instead, it would annihilate one of the parties, which would result in the end of the battle. In such a scenario, it would appear that there is a need for a substitute for total war. In such a scenario, armed conflicts should be

1 The Impact of War on the Environment, available at:https://www.researchgate.net/publication/ 387591902_ The_Impact_of_War_on_the_ Environment accessed on 28th September 2025.

conducted in a way that underscores the possibility of durable peace. This may be the most important principle of humanitarianism.

The subject of humanitarianism has responded to the unique circumstances that emerge during violent wars. Although suffering is a common consequence of battle, there are universal principles that bring people together. This also puts forth an argument that even war has its boundaries. Obviously, people don't want to live in a constant state of war; they ultimately want it to end and to heal the wounds caused by war. Therefore, when hostilities have ended, a dedication to human ideals that can serve as the foundation for a community must be upheld. It is important to note that the branch of IHL seeks to guarantee compliance with the most fundamental human ideals, including freedom from suffering, community, and dignity. In the face of ultimate battle, it stands as the human community's last option.

The first paragraph of this article describes IHL as the corpus of international law that is responsible for how an armed conflict is conducted. Therefore, the occurrence of an armed conflict is a basic condition for the application of international humanitarian law. Furthermore, it is important to remember that IHL regulates the conduct of armed conflict, not its emergence. It lays down the acceptable behaviours once a war is in progress. It doesn't focus on how the conflict began or who was responsible[2].

The Latin phrase "jus in bello", which means "law in war," is often used to refer to the corpus of international law responsible for governing the conduct of armed conflicts. The majority of people consider this to be equivalent to what is presently known as IHL. Another Latin phrase, jus ad bellum, or "law to war," is the legal skeleton that governs the origin of armed hostilities. It is also imperative that the primary goal of preventing the occurrence of armed conflicts is given importance, which is also occasionally referred to as the jus contra bellum, or "law against war." The differentiation between jus in bello and the jus ad bellum is the crux of international humanitarian law.

It has been exhibited in the past that IHL only comes into play when there is an armed conflict in existence. Thus, a primary part of this body of legislation is the legal definition of armed conflict. This leads to several significant questions. Firstly, how can one distinguish between a riot or other civil unrest and an armed conflict? Although identifying these

2 Ibid.

boundaries can be arduous, international courts and tribunals have assisted in this regard.

As per Common Article 2 of the 1949 Geneva Conventions, "all cases of declared war or of any other armed conflict which may arise between two or more of the High Contracting Parties, even if the state of war is not recognised by one of them," is underlined and explained by the Conventions. Thus, it can be understood to a large extent that the existence of an armed conflict does not require a declaration of war. If hostilities surpass a particular level, international humanitarian law will underlie the relevant provisions. Since transgressions of the laws and customs can only be understood when they take place, the idea of armed conflict is also pertinent to international criminal law.

The Common Article 2 underlines that even if, in certain situations, when there is a lack of objection to the occupation, the provisions of the Geneva Conventions shall apply. This shall happen when a state party's territory is absolutely or partially occupied. This further exemplifies the scope of the Conventions to take note of the circumstances in which an occupation occurs in the absence of a declaration of war or armed conflict. The severe consequences include those affected by such an occupation. Such people may still be eligible for the protections provided under the Geneva Convention IV.

As regards the determination of the scope of an armed conflict, two different types are recognised by the definition underlined by the Appeals Chamber in the case of Tadić. "A resort to armed force between States" is something the first test is being referred to as. Although it is not of complete necessity or requirement, it is usually illustrated as one or both states formally declaring war. "Prolonged armed violence between governmental authorities and organised armed groups or between such groups within a State" is something the second test refers to. This concept realises that disputes involving non-state actors may potentially be covered by the branch of IHL. Both conflicts in which no states are involved as a consequence of direct intervention and conflicts that concern a combination of states and non-state parties are covered by the test[3].

As we have deliberated in the paper till now, IHL is a branch of law that becomes operational when there is an armed conflict. The issue of whether

3 International Humanitarian Law, available at: https://www.icrc.org/sites/default/files/document/file_list/en_-_handbook_humanitarian_law_-_web.pdf accessed on 28th September 2025.

specific acts are within the geographic scope of the conflict, however, could arise. The ICTY Appeals Chamber has underlined in its jurisdictional ruling in the Tadić case that "the temporal and geographical scope [of the conflict] extends beyond the exact time and place of hostilities." Involving the length of the conflict, at least some of the provisions of IHL are applicable throughout the "entire territory" of the parties. As a result, "a breach of the laws or customs of war may take place at a place and time where no fight is taking place in reality.

International and non-international armed conflicts are the two major bifurcations of armed conflict by IHL. In a broader sense, it is believed that civil conflicts fell outside the purview of international law before the 1949 Geneva Conventions. In this regard, the states should perform the obligation for handling them internally. However, the brutal character of wars like the Spanish Civil War (1936–1939) resulted in a growing global awareness of the need for rules in this domain. Since that time, the significance of limiting internal armed conflicts has only skyrocketed. A vast majority of armed wars after World War II lack an international nature.

An example of the adverse impact on nature was war operations conducted in the Gulf region. This was the first time environmental effects took place on such a large scale. These consequences resulted from both conventional military operations and deliberate and conscious activity against nature. Such a phenomenon can be termed ecoterrorism. The situation of war in such areas significant amounts of waste getting into the water reservoirs and soil. The observations regarding the impact of war on the environment have been successful in showing that destroying oil wells can be severely damaging to the environment. As per a source, it is estimated that about 60 million barrels of oil have spilt and leaked from the burning and leaking shafts. This resulted in creating nearly 300 backwaters with a total area of 49 km. Persistently, as a result of evaporation, several pollutants are leaked into the atmosphere. The majority of them end up in soil and groundwater. The products of the burning oil, such as fumes and gases, caused the precipitation of "acid rain". The pollution, which was another result of the war, caused a different phenological response in desert plants. In the performance of the military operations, missiles containing substandard uranium were used[4].

In 1945, the disastrous consequences of the utilisation of nuclear weapons were discovered. This happened when the US Army dropped a uranium

4 Ibid.

bomb, called the "Little Boy," on Hiroshima and a bomb called the "Fat Boy" on Nagasaki.

In the 1960s, significant amounts of plutonium, which is considered one of the most fatal radioactive elements, were released into the environment. The tiny particles, which became a part of the stratosphere, systematically covered the surface of the planet. This resulted in the so-called global radioactive fallout.

The Interrelationship between Armed Conflicts and Environmental Damage

The concepts of "armed conflict" and "environment" can be easily comprehended by each individual. Emanating from the French term "environ," which literally means "to surround," the word "environment" stands for the natural world in which humans and other organisms exist. However, the definition of "armed conflict" in its most comprehensive sense has changed over legal debates and is still changing today. Over the period of time, the concept of "armed conflict" has expanded and now includes both international and non-international military confrontations[5].

There has been an unprecedented utilisation of combat manoeuvres. This stems from the ecosystem, or flora and fauna. The aforesaid serves as a pertinent issue in the twenty-first century. The bitter truth is that the world community has been undermining the environment's contribution and suffering for years, although it has been a passive victim of wars and conflicts. Until a decade after World War II, the issue of environmental damage was ignored to a large extent. The same can be concluded due to the lack of discussions concerning the same post-war.

In the case of Prosecutor v. Tadic, three kinds of armed conflicts were laid down. These were: International Armed Conflicts, Non-International Armed Conflicts and Occupation Operations. The International Armed Conflicts involve two or more State Parties in an act of war. Non-International Armed Conflicts concern the involvement of either party that is not a State Party. Such a party is rather a non-state actor involved in a complex and prolonged conflict. As regards the Occupation Operations, this armed conflict takes place on the territories of other States.

5 Armed conflict causes long-lasting environmental harms available at: https://www.researchgate.net/publication/389753708_" Armed_conflict_causes_long-lasting_environmental_harms" accessed on 28th September 2025.

The armed conflicts have the capacity to adversely impact the environmental systems of countries. This involves a two-tier effect, direct and indirect consequences. As regards the direct consequences, it has been observed that heavy metals are released during the war into the soil. These heavy metals also penetrate the water. Due to the aforesaid, there has been an increase in severe health consequences. These consequences include cancer and an increase in antimicrobial resistance. In 1999, there was a depletion of uranium from modern weapon systems during NATO's engagement in the Kosovo War. This impacted the local population to a large extent as per the United Nations Environment Programme [UNEP]. Furthermore, to quote another relevant example, the Russian strikes on Ukrainian infrastructure in the realm of energy highlighted the serious issues and effects of conflict on the environment[6].

As regards the indirect consequences, the armed conflicts have been instrumental in triggering behavioural changes. During wartime, the governments could not effectively control and there was a lack of livelihood security. Apart from the battle zone, Environmental effects may arise from internal displacement and irregular capacity of the government. Lastly, active combat and the basic upkeep and training of armed forces are two ways that armed conflicts contribute to carbon emissions.

There have been some pertinent advancements in our knowledge of how armed conflict impacts the environment, but uncertainties associated with the same are still the same. The majority of the existing knowledge has its roots in case studies, which are either centred around a particular country or environmental problems, leaving a lot of room for exploration and discovery. To shut the gap involves significant policy ramifications. Abridging this gap would serve to be of academic interest for many, especially when it comes to creating interventions that lessen long-term environmental deterioration in post-conflict contexts[7].

The military operations that affect the environment adversely can immediately affect the civilian population. A good example of the same is that through the destruction of objects that are an important part for their survival, causing property damage, to name a few. The damage to dams may cause significant environmental and civilian harm.

6 Ibid.

7 The interplay of environment and armed conflicts, available at: https://www.hpnlu.ac.in/PDF/fbabce1a-2e7c-43ae-ae51-693232aa9713.pdf accessed on 28th September 2025.

Indirectly, and over a period of time, causing harm to the environment has affected the ability to live on the land. Particularly, the ability of citizens to obtain water for drinking or agricultural purposes may be impacted by particular environmental-harming actions made by conflicting parties, such as pollution or altering river routes. It is pretty much known that there is a connection between environmental damage and civilian displacement, which is detrimental in and of itself. When the natural environment has been seriously harmed, civilians will frequently leave the region either right away or quickly. Therefore, environmental damage caused by military actions may be a factor in relocation. Long-term environmental degradation can pose serious obstacles to efforts at reconciliation, extending conflict and the negative effects that come with it. damage to the environment that fuels climate change, including the rise in greenhouse gas emissions[8]. It is pertinent to register that such an injury compromises the safety of the global population. Thus, it is becoming more widely acknowledged as a security issue, frequently intensifying conflict and eroding stability. Populations affected by conflicts are particularly susceptible to the effects of climate change. Therefore, reducing environmental damage and other climate change-causing causes is a long-term way to safeguard civilians, partly by averting or lessening future conflicts and the risks and damages that come with them. Additionally, when State or non-state actors aim to successfully restrict the potential harm, they must give thought to different groups of the civilian population who confront distinct vulnerabilities in the face of environmental disaster.

Effects of Armed Conflicts on the Environment

Although it is part of the common knowledge that conflict inevitably harms the environment, this isn't the only conceivable effect. The warfare may be obligated to lessen the disturbing and destructive human activity. Another way of looking at things is that there won't be much of an environmental impact from war. The comprehensive impact of war on the is an empirical question because each of these scenarios has some value attached to it[9].

The theoretical argument that conflict damages the surroundings of the participating nations has not received much attention. To be victorious in the conflict, military forces indulge in harming their own environment or

8 Ibid.

9 The effect of warfare on the environment, available at:https://www.researchgate.net/publication/227574694_The_effect_of_warfare_on_the_environment accessed on 28th September 2025.

the opposing side's environment. Arable ground may be flooded to limit army movement; oil wells, fresh water, crops, land, and animals may be damaged to restrict their use by an enemy; and woods may be burned to deprive timber or hiding spots. To exemplify the war effort, both parties may also increase the exploitation of their own resources or the resources that have been taken from the opposing side. By limiting the extent of persistent environmental damage, the prevailing war can also improve a participating nation's ecology. This kind of effect may be direct or indirect. It may differ depending on the environmental characteristics and economic sectors. To quote an example, the destruction of motor vehicles and industrial buildings may result in lowering the transportation and output.

Concerning the indirect environmental benefits, a smaller number of fishing vessels may be sent out to sea as a aftermath of fishermen joining the army or trying to avoid areas of conflict, which would increase fish stocks[10]. Because the military frequently declares certain areas "off limits" to civilians, biodiversity may also rise indirectly. The overall effects of warfare on the ecosystem might not be of high volume. In this regard, one of the major reasons can be that some wars may not be intense enough or of a certain type to have a major impact on the environment (e.g., surgical strikes may not affect vast areas). Second, there may be little to no overall influence from war because the conflicting negative and positive effects on a particular area of the ecosystem may balance each other out.

Armed conflicts have crucial effects on ecosystems. The ecosystem services of prominence, such as carbon sequestration, soil stabilisation, and water management, are degraded as a result of military operations that involve the employment of heavy weapons, landmines, and other damaging technologies. In addition to the aforesaid, since displaced groups may overuse natural resources, such as gathering firewood, accessing water, and acquiring food to suit their immediate survival needs, the widespread displacement of populations as a result of war frequently puts unsustainable strains on ecosystems.

Natural resources may also be destroyed or contaminated as a result of armed conflict. Deforestation and groundwater pollution can result from bombing and infrastructure targeting. For instance, in Syria, the Islamic State utilised incendiary bombs to burn farms and crops. The environmental risks posed by armed conflict can also have a major impact on civilians' physical safety. The reason for this may be increased competition for

10 Ibid.

natural resources. Such increased competition can lead to violence and displacement[11].

Widespread environmental deterioration and destruction can result from armed conflicts' profound and protracted effects on ecosystems. Armed conflicts can impact ecosystems in the following ways:

i. **Habitat Destruction**: Because of military actions, bombardment, and infrastructure development, armed conflicts may destroy natural habitats. Important ecological processes like pollination and nutrient cycling may be disrupted, and biodiversity, including plant and animal species, may be lost as a result.

ii. **Soil Degradation**: During armed conflicts, the use of chemicals, heavy artillery, and explosives can contaminate the soil, lowering soil fertility and having long-term health consequences on local residents and animals.

iii. **Water Pollution**: Chemical weapons and other military operations contribute to polluting water, impacting groundwater and surface water supplies. In addition to potentially leading to the loss of aquatic ecosystems and biodiversity, this could have serious negative effects on human health.

iv. **Disturbance in Wildlife**: Armed conflicts may contribute to the eviction of wildlife and the hunting of it for food. Important species may become extinct as a result, and ecological systems like seed distribution and predator-prey dynamics may be disturbed.

v. **Climate Change**: By using explosives and burning fossil fuels, armed conflicts can release significant volumes of greenhouse gases into the atmosphere, which can contribute to climate change. The adversely affected natural ecosystems can also result in higher carbon emissions and less carbon sequestration.

Challenges associated

International law has been responsible for the protection of the environment during wartime. Although their sufficiency has been questioned in recent decades, several aspects of international law protect the environment during armed conflicts. The numerous branches of

11 War and the Environment: The Ecological Consequences of Armed Conflict, available at:https://theacademic.in/wp-content/uploads/2024/10/67.pdf accessed on 28th September 2025.

law, such as International criminal law, international humanitarian law, international human rights law, and international environmental law, have been instrumental in laying down measures for protection at the time of war. These sets of rudimentary principles of international law work to stop, lessen, and repair environmental damage at various stages. Nevertheless, every military action has any way resulted in physical and psychological injuries, fatal injuries, and destruction of property and the environment[12].

The peacebuilding operations may become considerably more difficult if the environmental issues facing war-torn countries are not addressed and dealt with. The United Nations Environment Programme (UNEP) has been responsible for conducting a preliminary review of the environmental harm done to Ukraine and the probable effects on the environment and public health. The persistent hostilities in Ukraine have recently brought the connections between the environment and conflict to the forefront. The law of international liability provides a strong foundation for the accountability of states in case of environmental harm resulting from armed conflict. The instruments, such as Hague Convention IV of 1907 and Additional Protocol I to the Geneva Conventions (AP I), specifically put forth the responsibility of States for violations of jus in bello. The Draft Principles on Protection of the Environment in Relation to Armed Conflicts (ILC Draft Principles) have been recently updated. In consonance with the update, the International Law Commission (ILC) affirms states' international responsibility for the environmental effects of armed conflict. However, regardless of whether jus in bello has been adversely affected, a State that has violated jus ad bellum—the law governing the utilisation of force—would be liable for all damages, including environmental harm. Meanwhile, the weakness in the framework of the law of armed conflict is to be filled as jus in bello continues to develop to improve environmental protection[13].

In terms of the bifurcations, the challenges associated with mitigating the environmental damage caused by armed conflict can be divided into four parts: technical, political, and financial.

The technical challenges include the infrastructural collapse. The infrastructural collapse includes the deterioration of the basic amenities

12 Remedying the environmental impacts of war: Challenges and perspectives for full reparation, available at:https://international-review.icrc.org/sites/default/files/reviews-pdf/2023-12/remedying-the-environmental-impacts-of-war-924.pdf accessed on 28th September 2025.

13 Ibid.

such as water treatment, sanitation, and waste management systems. In case of destruction of waste management systems, the consequences can be such as rubbish burning and open dumping. These behaviours present health risks. They can increase the pollution level. Due to rapid urbanisation and population growth, the waste management systems have been suffering. If a nation like India is taken into consideration, several issues emanate concerning the lack of effective waste management systems. These issues can be reliance on unhygienic landfills for disposal, incomplete processing capacity, inefficient collection and transportation methods, and a lack of waste segregation at the source. The national government has launched a number of initiatives to address these issues, such as encouraging the use of recycling and composting methods and waste segregation at the source. The implementation on a larger scale is still a bothersome issue. The recent times have been great in terms of waste management as a practice; certain fundamental reforms are still needed in the Indian waste management industry. These reforms comprise formalising the unorganised sector, strengthening waste segregation, and improving the quality of trash processing facilities. Another technical challenge can be a lack of access of data in a conflict area.

If one looks into the political challenges, the principle of state sovereignty is fully capable of hindering international intervention, which was in operation to mitigate environmental damage within a nation's borders. Even when environmental degradation affects on transboundary, the efforts of the diplomats are complicated by the principle of non-interference associated with another state's internal affairs. Also, the state institutions and governance structures, especially those in charge of environmental management, are frequently seriously weakened by conflict. This prevents long-term environmental recovery by making post-conflict nations susceptible to corruption and uncontrolled resource extraction.

As regards the financial challenges, the illicit exploitation and trade of natural resources, such as timber, minerals, and oil, is a common source of funding for conflicts. If any attempts are made to create sustainable, lawful economies to finance rehabilitation, such efforts are undermined by this.

Long-term economic and environmental losses result from war's destruction of the institutions, monitoring capabilities, and financing systems required to uphold environmental laws and manage natural resources responsibly. As a consequence of the high perceived political and economic risk, conflict-affected areas find it tough to draw in green private sector investment or issue cutting-edge financial instruments (such as Green Bonds) for cleanup.

A Way Ahead

On analysis of the various conventions on International Humanitarian Law, there are a few analyses that are discussed in the upcoming paragraph.

- Although novel technologies, like the use of depleted uranium, are not yet being discussed, barring the general principles of the law of war. But it is of significance to understand the restrictions on the means of warfare. These involve military tactics, and they lead to indirect environmental protection. The environment is indirectly protected by the legislations that protect the civilian property[14].
- The majority of the present laws are not always applicable because most of the armed conflicts nowadays can be categorised as non-international conflicts. One of the biggest impediments to preventing the frequently severe environmental destruction caused by internal conflicts is the lack of availability of national laws.
- The international population is unable to vigil over legal infractions. They also lack tools to assess responsibility and perpetuate the methodical compensation procedures and processes for environmental harm, which have been a grave consequence of global armed conflicts. The presence of such a mechanism and its application could serve as an absolute deterrent to prevent environmental harm and reduce the impact of violations committed during the war.
- Since there are no globally accepted benchmarks for determining the threshold of these principles, it is easier to defend nearly any environmental damage if the intervention of the military is deemed to be high enough. This would aid in restricting the process of determining how well these ideas may be utilised in practice to stop environmental harm. Due to a lack of scientific clarity regarding the probable effects of a specific weapon, the ICRC puts a lot of

14 Toward an Environmental and Climate-Sensitive Approach to Protection in UN Peacekeeping Operations, available at:https://www.ipinst.org/wp-content/uploads/2022/10/Environmental-and-Climate-Sensitive-Approach-to-UN-Peacekeeping-Operations.pdf accessed on 28th September 2025.

weight on the significance of adopting a cautious approach[15].

- The reduction of the level of natural resources and environmental destruction may be a major component of other crimes included under the Rome Statute. It can be said with certainty that both the national criminal courts of ICC Parties and the International Criminal Court (ICC) may prosecute and hold it criminally liable. This holds merit both in the case of international disputes between State Parties and domestic armed conflicts taking place inside State Parties. There has been a persistent practice of misusing and extracting natural resources during conflicts. This practice may be prosecuted under the war crime of plunder. The same will be in particular interest to the parties.

- Unless otherwise laid down, the terms of multilateral environmental accords (MEAs) should be construed as continuing to apply during both international and non-international armed conflicts. The scholars and researchers of law, including the International Law Commission, are ignorant of the point of view that IHL supersedes International Environmental Law (IEL), which is of merit at the time of armed conflict[16].

Recommendations

In relation to the aforesaid key findings, there are certain solutions which are as follows-

- The content of international law has been utilised to prosecute environmental violations taking place during an armed conflict, which should be taught to international judges and legal professionals to enhance the material of case law that is now available. By outlining a real caution of prosecution with regard to infractions, the case law that followed would be of help in clarifying current regulations and exemplifying deterrence. The requisite education and training should encompass things like options for directly involving international law provisions in national laws.

- The facets of international law that safeguard the environment at the time of conflict should be implemented meticulously at the

15 Ibid.

16 The Impact of War on the Environment, available at:https://www.researchgate.net/publication/387591902_The_Impact_of_War_on_the_Environment accessed on 28th September 2025.

national level to ensure that environmental infractions committed during battle are penalised and dealt with. This will lead to the building of targeted capacity-building programs for legal practitioners that address the court.

- The member states of the United Nations might consider a permanent body akin to the U.N. Compensation Commission (UNCC). Such an organisation was established by the Security Council to handle claims concerning compensation related to the Gulf War, which took place during 1990–1991. The same could be established, either under the supervision of the General Assembly or the Security Council.
- The U.N. ought to consider defining "conflict resources". This would facilitate outlining the magnitude to which the improper use of some natural resources is to be considered as a "threat to peace and security." Such an inadequate utilisation can be used to fund war. It is important to define the term "conflict resources". They refer to natural resources whose continuous exploitation and trade during a conflict result in grave human rights abuses. It would be in utmost good faith that the identification of conflict resources is made. The imposition of international sanctions is something that can be given attention to.
- Natural resource concessions provided during hostilities frequently lack legal backing and might not relate to best practices for benefit-sharing and analysis of environmental impacts.
- Every year, in consonance with the occasion of the International Day for Preventing the Exploitation of the Environment in War and Armed Conflict, the U.N. General Assembly shall receive a brief and clear report on the environmental effects of armed conflicts: The Assembly must take into consideration interrogating the Secretary-General to present an annual report on the consequences of armed conflicts on the environment. The report should highlight the direct and indirect effects that current international and non-international armed conflicts have on the environment. The report should outline suggestions for addressing the various risks to human life posed by harm to each nation's natural resources[17].

17 Ibid.

Conclusion

Till now, we have discussed the concept of armed conflict, how it damages the environment, challenges associated with reducing the environmental damage occurring because of armed conflict. In this section of the research article, we shall discuss the ways to prevent the environmental damage that can take place because of armed conflicts.

In the modern world, the industrialised nations are obligated to curb greenhouse gas emissions associated with conflicts. A plausible way to achieve this is by shifting towards less militarised technologies. Such technologies must be substituted by eco-friendly security technologies. The instances of the same consider the idea of reducing dependency on fossil fuels and implementing energy-efficient techniques. In addition to the same, developed countries can apply resources in the direction of research and advancement of sustainable low-tech solutions. The factors, such as the utilisation of electric vehicles while complying with the requirement of duty of care, could serve as a viable solution. It is important to note that ensuring the reliable availability of long-lasting electricity infrastructure for military endeavours is important.

The phenomenon of climate justice underlines the socioeconomic and environmental gaps between various industrialised nations. This has resulted in the emergence of certain terminologies, such as countries of the North, countries of the South, and developing nations. These differences put forth the issues about the right of developing countries to aim for industrialisation and urbanisation. While addressing such issues, it is important to underline the historical and persistent responsibility for greenhouse gas emissions. The carriers of such responsibilities are generally the most industrialised nations. The issue of climate justice remains central to international climate negotiations. Due to such importance being bestowed on climate justice, there is a need for a balance between industrial development and preservation imperatives[18].

Another suggestion concerning the mitigation of environmental damage is avoiding situating troops in such ecosystems that are not strong enough. The underlying thought here is the prevention of potential damage to these ecosystems. These ecosystems are often rich in biodiversity. In addition to all of this, they perform important ecological functions. By avoiding such

18 Armed conflict causes long-lasting environmental harms, available at:https://www.researchgate.net/publication/389753708_" Armed_conflict_causes_long-lasting_environmental_harms accessed on 28th September 2025.

placements, the principal objective is to minimise negative impacts on the environment and align with the aim of sustainable development.

Furthermore, another suggestion is to "map areas of ecological importance and fragility". To put it in simpler terms, it means to identify and state locations that are of importance when it comes to their ecological value. Such areas can be degraded easily. There is a process of mapping that helps in judging the areas on a number of factors. Such factors are the presence of biodiversity, habitat types, ecosystem services, and susceptibility to human activities or natural disasters. On mapping these areas, the people in power and decision-makers can better understand the needs of the environment. They can understand the importance of conservation of resources. These people also develop a sound understanding of activities such as development or resource extraction and their management. This activity on the part of the decision makers and people in power serves as a valuable tool for environmental planning. They can also serve as blueprints for conservation.

Another suggestion is designating demilitarised zones (DMZs). Such a designation can lead to the prohibition of military activities. Such military activities include weapon testing and training exercises, to name a few. The ultimate advantage of this will be the reduction of the direct physical impact of military operations on the environment. The instances of such operations include the destruction of the habitat, pollution, and disturbance of wildlife. This further permits the preservation of rare or endangered species. DMZs can serve as symbols of peace and cooperation. They bear the responsibility for collaboration on environmental issues that transcend political boundaries.

Also, it is extremely important to try to prevent environmental damage from the adverse effects of armed conflicts. Four aspects of preventive protection should be taken into account:

1) The environment and other armed conflict victims are entitled to legal rights that cannot be waived or agreed upon, thanks to the protection that international humanitarian law (IHL) provides. This is determined by Article 7 common to the four 1949 Geneva Conventions.

2) The states parties to the conflict may agree, at any point during the armed conflict and even before the start of hostilities, to provide additional environmental protection beyond that established by

IHL, as determined by Article 6 common to the four 1949 Geneva Conventions; and;

3) The sources of legal protection of the environment in IHL comprise the four Geneva Conventions of 1949, the Additional Protocols of 1977, and the Hague Conventions of 1899 and 1907;

4) Finally, the legal protection is not being specifically and explicitly addressed, but is more related to the legal protection of victims of armed conflict in general, which can be adapted to provide special protection for the environment at various stages of outbreaks of hostilities, considering the environment as one of the victims of armed conflict.

The phrases "protection of the environment" and "the prevention of environmental harm" are used in comparable contexts. Between the two terms, there are differences and subtleties. Protection is the degree to which constructive measures are made to protect the environment from harmful influences. Prohibition and prevention can be assigned to the term such as limitations. Here, the limitations imply the ability to carry out actions that will harm the environment. Thus, in general environmental discourse, the concept of environmental protection is related to the broad spectrum of ecologically beneficial obligations.

To quote an example, military manuals present one avenue for developing a unified set of norms that armed forces could follow in all types of armed conflict. Along with the Military Manual on the Protection of Cultural Property, which was published by UNESCO in 2016, the ICRC has contributed to some model recommendations to assist states in identifying military manuals that prioritise international law. The U.N. Secretary-General made it clear in 1999 that U.N. peacekeeping forces must adhere to IHL-related standards. The order of the U.N. Secretary-General states that U.N. forces are expressly forbidden from applying military tactics that could result in needless suffering or injury, or which are likely to cause extensive and serious harm to the environment[19].

To sum it up, in this research article, it was aimed to explain the body of law concerning armed conflicts, which is called the International Humanitarian Law. IHL, as the body of international law, is responsible for how an armed conflict is conducted. IHL regulates the conduct of armed conflicts, not their emergence. It underlines the acceptable behaviours once a war is in

19 Ibid.

progress. It doesn't focus on how a conflict began or who was responsible. We also discussed the definition of armed conflicts and how they can be determined and defined. We discussed the interrelationship between an armed conflict and environmental damage. But that's not enough. It was essential to address the challenges associated with mitigating the environmental damage. Lastly, we highlighted certain recommendations to mitigate environmental damage resulting from the armed conflict.

Part II

Environmental Harm During Armed Conflict

Scorched Earth Tactics and Environment

Gourav Kumar

Introduction

In the last century, more than two hundred armed conflicts have inflicted not only human and economic losses but also severe ecological damage. The military's contribution to environmental degradation and climate change is substantial, though frequently excluded from mainstream discourse. Radioactive waste, chemical residues, and other byproducts of military operations are often left untreated, persisting for decades in affected regions. National security priorities consistently override environmental concerns, reinforcing the perception that ecological costs are acceptable collateral. The environmental impact of conflicts themselves varies greatly. Some international armed conflicts may be brief but highly destructive. Some civil wars may last for decades but be fought at low intensity. Many contemporary conflicts have blurred the lines, lasting years but featuring sustained periods of high-intensity warfare. Who is fighting, where they're fighting and how they're fighting all strongly influence the environmental impact of a conflict.[1] The environmental impacts of the war in Gaza are unprecedented, as per the preliminary assessment published by the UN Environment Programme (UNEP), the community is facing rapidly growing soil, water and air pollution and risks of irreversible damage to its natural ecosystems. UNEP reiterates its call for an immediate ceasefire to protect lives and, eventually, help mitigate the conflict's environmental impacts. Not only are the people of Gaza dealing with untold suffering from the ongoing war, but the significant and growing environmental damage in Gaza risks locking its people into a painful, long recovery. Although

1 Conflict and Environment Observatory, *How does war damage the environment?* (4 June 2020) *available at:* https://ceobs.org/how-does-war-damage-the-environment/ (last visited on August 22nd 2025)

many questions regarding the exact type and quantity of contaminants affecting the environment in Gaza still remain, people are already living with the consequences of conflict-related damage to environmental management systems and pollution today. Water and sanitation have collapsed. Important infrastructure still continues to be shattered. Coastal areas, soil and ecosystems have been severely impacted. The conflict has unbridled recent limited progress on Gaza's environmental management structure, including the development of water desalination and wastewater treatment facilities, rapid growth in solar power, and investments in the restoration of the Wadi Gaza coastal wetland. The fighting has produced an estimated 39 million tonnes of debris, or 107 kg per square metre across the Gaza Strip. This is more than five times the amount of debris produced during the fighting in Mosul, Iraq, in 2017. Dust and contamination from unexploded ordnance, asbestos, industrial and medical waste and other dangerous materials are among the threats that debris brings to both human health and the environment. Human remains buried beneath the rubble need to be handled carefully and delicately. In order to facilitate other forms of recovery and restoration, the enormous and intricate process of clearing the debris must begin as soon as possible. The systems for hygiene, sanitation, and water are virtually non-existent. Due to the closure of Gaza's five wastewater treatment facilities, a variety of pathogens, fertilisers, microplastics, and dangerous chemicals have contaminated freshwater, land, beaches, and coastal waters. This poses immediate and long-term threats to the health of Gazans, marine life, and arable lands. The solid waste management system is severely damaged since five out of six solid waste management facilities in Gaza were damaged. By November 2023, 1,200 tonnes of rubbish were accumulating daily around camps and shelters. A shortage of cooking gas has forced families to burn wood, plastic and waste instead, endangering women and children in particular. This, coupled with fires and burning fuels, is likely to have sharply lowered Gaza's air quality, though no open-source air quality data is available for Gaza. Munitions containing heavy metals and explosive chemicals have been deployed in Gaza's densely populated areas, contaminating soil and water sources, and posing a risk to human health, which will persist long after the cessation of hostilities. Children are particularly at risk from unexploded ordnance. Lead and other heavy metals are predicted to leach when solar panels are destroyed, thereby posing a new threat to Gaza's water and soil. Israel's attempts to demolish Hamas's network of tunnels could worsen environmental harm.[2] Depending on the construction standards of the tunnels and the extent to which water is being pumped into them, the preliminary assessment warns of long-term risks to human health from groundwater contamination and to buildings constructed on potentially unstable land surfaces.[3]

Due to the fertility of its western mountains, where rain-fed agriculture flourished, Yemen was known to geographers in antiquity by the Latin term "Arabia Felix," or "Fertile Arabia." A significant environmental crisis has been brought on during the past century by a multitude of human-caused elements, both local and direct, as well as international and indirect. This problem has been made much worse by political unrest in recent decades and, more recently, full-scale warfare. The primary symptom of these issues is water scarcity. Although the shortage is more noticeable in rural areas, where 70% of the population resides, it is better reported in metropolitan areas. Although Yemen's most urgent environmental concern is water scarcity, other environmental problems are closely related. Thousands of unique endemic species in the UNESCO-listed Socotra archipelago were uprooted, and the foundations of hundreds of historic buildings in the city of Sana'a and elsewhere collapsed or were undermined.[4]

Large amounts of fuel are needed and consumed in high-intensity conflicts, which result in significant CO2 emissions and contribute to climate change. The first three years of Russia's invasion of Ukraine produced 230 MtCO2e, which is equal to the combined yearly emissions of Slovakia, Austria, Hungary, and the Czech Republic. For the first time, an attempt has been undertaken to determine the emissions resulting from a dispute. Both the extensive use of explosive ordnance and large-scale vehicle movements have the potential to cause extensive physical harm to delicate landscapes and geodiversity.

---

2 Al-Maghalseh, Maher. "The Environmental Impact and Societal Conditions of PV Power Plants: A Case Study of Jericho Gate-Palestine Stat Of." *Wadi Alshatti University Journal of Pure and Applied Sciences* (2025): 16-31.

3 United Nations Environment Programme, *Damage to Gaza causing new risks to human health and long-term recovery – new UNEP assessment* (18 June 2024) *available at* https://www.unep.org/news-and-stories/press-release/damage-gaza-causing-new-risks-human-health-and-long-term-recovery(last visited on July 23,2025).

4 "Socotra, the Galapagos of the Indian Ocean, Becomes a Disaster Zone," BBC, May 24, 2018, https://www.bbc.com/news/world-middle-east-44235159. (last visited on August 13th 2025).

This paper examines the enduring and evolving phenomenon of scorched-*earth tactics* and their environmental consequences in contemporary armed conflicts. It revisits the historical foundations of scorched earth strategies while critically examining how modern warfare—characterised by precision weapons, hybrid conflicts, cyber operations, and resource-driven battles continues to devastate ecosystems, biodiversity, and human livelihoods. The study situates these practices within the framework of international humanitarian law and emerging environmental norms, analysing gaps in accountability, enforcement, and reparations. Finally, this paper argues for a paradigm shift in the treatment of the environment during armed conflicts, moving beyond anthropocentric notions of collateral damage toward an eco-centric model of protection, restoration, and accountability.

Historical Background

For almost as long as armies have conducted combat operations, scorched-earth tactics have been employed. Although the method is less widespread now, it has been used recently, most notably during Russia's invasion of Ukraine in 2022.[5] The term is thought to be a translation of the Chinese phrase jiāotüge (zhèngcè), which means "scorched earth (policy)" and was first used in English in a 1937 report on the Second Sino-Japanese War (1937–45). To prevent advancing Japanese soldiers from receiving any kind of assistance, retreating Chinese burned crops and destroyed cities during the Japanese invasion of China.[6] Here's its history and some of its most notable uses, including during World War II and in Vietnam. Before one can discuss the use of scorched earth policies, it must be understood what such tactics entail. In general, a scorched earth policy is a strategy that aims to destroy anything that may be of use to the enemy, whether that be natural resources, military equipment, or even local citizens. While the latter was banned under the 1977 Geneva Convention, the destruction of resources remains a key strategy for some warring nations. The Scythians were the first to use the scorched earth tactic. Nomadic herders from what is now Kazakhstan, Russia and Ukraine, they did battle against the Persians and Darius the Great. To gain the upper hand, they moved in secret, destroying the Persians' food and poisoning their wells. Before their opponents could figure out what happened, they would retreat into the forest.

5 https://www.warhistoryonline.com/war-articles/scorched-earth-tactics.html

6 https://www.britannica.com/topic/scorched-earth-policy

The Armenians, the Greeks against Alexander the Great, and the Gauls, who employed scorched earth tactics against the Romans, were among the other ancient societies that adopted the strategy due to its effectiveness. According to legend, the countryside of what is now France and the Benelux was devastated by the Gauls under Vercingetorix before the war. Even though the Romans were severely harmed by this devastation, they managed to defeat and subjugate the Gauls.[7]

The use of explosive weapons in urban areas creates a number of environmental risks, including vast quantities of debris and rubble, which can cause air and soil pollution. Pollution can also be caused by damage to light industry and environmentally sensitive infrastructure, such as water treatment plants. The loss of energy supplies can have reverberating effects that are detrimental to the environment, shutting down treatment plants or pumping systems, or can lead to the use of more polluting fuels or domestic generators. This raises a critical inquiry: what are the environmental consequences of the military's exceptional status, and how does warfare accelerate ecological decline? The Battle of Verdun (1916) offers an illustrative case study of the intersection between modern warfare and environmental destruction. On 21 February 1916, German forces initiated an unprecedented artillery assault on the French lines, firing an estimated 200,000–300,000 shells within a single day from approximately 1,300 positions. This marked a significant transformation, like armed conflict, epitomising the industrialisation of warfare. The objective was attritional—aimed not at territorial gain but at exhausting the enemy through sustained violence. The natural environment proved defenceless against such mechanised destruction. The Battle of Verdun soon became emblematic of industrial warfare's ecological consequences. The French command's uncompromising order "Ils ne passeront pas" ("They shall not pass") ensured that the conflict devolved into a prolonged struggle over every meter of land. After ten months of continuous battle, the region's cultural and ecological landscapes had been obliterated. By the end of the battle, nothing remained of this once culturally and historically rich region of northern France. The core battlefield zone, the Zone Rouge, is still considered a death trap today. For decades, only scrub oaks could grow in the poisoned soil, which remains littered with unexploded ordnance and hazardous munitions. For ten relentless months, the lives of humans, animals, and plants were consumed, showing just another expendable

7 https://www.warhistoryonline.com/war-articles/scorched-earth-tactics.html

resource of war. The fighting was so ceaseless that soldiers were rotated in shifts, battling not just the enemy but also the devastation of the land itself.

Scorched Earth policy

Scorched earth policy as a method of warfare is principally limited by the relevant rules established in order to prevent the use of weapons or methods of warfare that are not consistent with the basic rules of international humanitarian law, determining how hostilities have to be conducted (Warfare, Methods and Means). According to Art. 35 (1) Additional Protocol I ('AP I') 'in any armed conflict, the right of the Parties to the conflict to choose methods and means of warfare is not unlimited.' In its Advisory Opinion on Legality of the Threat or Use of Nuclear Weapons ([1996] ICJ Rep 226), the International Court of Justice (ICJ) upheld this customary rule by declaring that "methods and means of warfare, which would preclude any distinction between civilian and military targets, ... are prohibited. Art. 51 (4) (b)–(c) AP I further prohibits attacks that 'employ a method or means of combat which cannot be directed at a specific military objective; or attacks which employ a method or means of combat the effects of which cannot be limited as required by the Protocol and which consequently are of a nature to strike military objectives and civilians or civilian objects without distinction'. As a result, it is forbidden to use scorched earth tactics on enemy territory that aim indiscriminately at civilian targets and cause excessive collateral damage. The last provision is especially crucial for scorched earth policies, limiting their lawfulness to military attacks, which are able to distinguish between the different statuses of objects under humanitarian law.[8]

It is to be observed that the scorched-earth policy as a method of warfare may have disastrous effects on the environment. The strategic breach of the Yellow River dyke exemplifies that the environment can be used as a weapon of war by modification of its status in order to prevent the advance of belligerent armed forces (environmental warfare). Whereas the destruction of the environment during armed conflict is often a side-effect of military battles (environmental collateral damage), the environmental destructions as part of scorched earth tactics are used intentionally. Methods of warfare that cause excessive damage to the environment are explicitly taken into consideration by Articles 35 (3) and 55 (1) AP I, stating that methods

8 Alexander Schwarz and Maria Grigat, 'Scorched Earth Policy' in Rüdiger Wolfrum (ed), Max Planck Encyclopedia of Public International Law (Oxford University Press, online edn) https://opil.ouplaw.com/display/ 10.1093/law:epil/9780199231690/law-9780199231690-e2172 (last visited on 30th August 2025).

or means of warfare that are intended, or may be expected, to cause widespread, long-term, and severe damage to the natural environment are prohibited. Although the exact scope of Arts 35 and 55 is controversial, a breach of the rules demands that the damage to the natural environment must be either intentional or expected; mere collateral damages to the environment are not covered by the prohibitions. However, in practice, the relevance of both rules is rather limited: the requested conditions of 'widespread, long-term and severe damage' suggest that the threshold is very high and only exceptional examples are taken into account (Oeter 127, 216). Furthermore, the scope of both rules is limited as the prescribed effects must be met cumulatively. Therefore, the threshold would not have been crossed by the Iraqi forces setting fire to the oil wells during the 1991 Gulf War (US Department of Defence 636). Nevertheless, the principle of proportionality, applicable to the natural environment (Henckaerts and Doswald-Beck [2005] 143), protects the environment as an illicit target as long as damages to the environment are disproportionate to the military advantage (Oeter 213). Additionally, the environment is indirectly protected from scorched earth policies by Art. 56 AP I, which prohibits the military attack of works or installations containing dangerous forces, 'namely dams, dykes and nuclear electrical generating stations, if such attack may cause the release of dangerous forces and consequent severe losses among the civilian population' (Environment, Protection in Armed Conflict).[9]

The artillery fire at Verdun was unrelenting, transforming the battlefield into a site of unprecedented destruction. Never before had so many soldiers perished within such a confined geographical space. Among the survivors, psychological trauma, then termed shell shock, was widespread, marking a turning point not only in military history but also in the relationship between war and the natural environment.

Environmental Harm in Modern Conflicts

The ecological devastation was absolute. Contemporary accounts describe the land as stripped bare, with no fertile soil or humus remaining. Continuous bombardment had displaced the topsoil repeatedly, scattering it beyond recognition. Agricultural recovery in such conditions was inconceivable; ploughing or cultivation became permanently impossible. The forests and fields were obliterated, and not a single square meter of land was left undisturbed. What remained was a pockmarked terrain of

9 ibid

shell craters, offering only meagre protection in the form of hastily dug trenches. This transformation also altered the conduct of warfare itself. Soldiers were increasingly detached from direct contact with the enemy; face-to-face combat became rare. Instead, the outcome of battles was determined by the range and destructive capacity of artillery shells. The defining characteristic of the First World War was thus the invisibility of the enemy; death often arrived from five to ten kilometres away. Trenches offered limited protection, as even the act of lifting one's helmet above the parapet could be fatal under the constant threat of long-range fire. One of the most infamous examples of this devastation was the hill known as Le Mort-Homme ("the Dead Man"). Subjected to relentless bombardment, the hill itself physically diminished, losing an estimated ten meters of elevation by the conclusion of the battle. This striking alteration of the landscape illustrates the extent to which industrialised warfare reshaped not only human society but also the very topography of the natural world.

Verdun may be regarded as an experimental site for the emerging technologies of modern warfare, including weapons of mass destruction.[10] It marked one of the earliest instances in which poison gas was deployed via artillery shells, enabling chemical agents to be delivered with greater precision to enemy positions and indiscriminately killing all life within their trajectory. The unprecedented scale of munitions production and deployment further altered the character of the conflict. Supplies of artillery shells appeared inexhaustible, fundamentally changing military strategy. Whereas earlier battles were constrained by the limited availability of men and ammunition, Verdun was characterised by continuous resupply, permitting commanders to adopt a strategy of relentless bombardment.

In total, both sides launched an estimated sixty million shells over the course of the battle. The engagement may thus be understood as one of the most resource-intensive undertakings in human history, consuming vast quantities of raw materials, industrial output, and human lives. What distinguished the First World War from earlier conflicts was not only the unprecedented scale of destruction but also the systemic reorganisation of national economies into "war economies."[11] This shift enabled industrial production to compensate for massive levels of consumption that would have been unimaginable in the nineteenth century. The industrialisation of

10 Burgess, George K. "Applications of Science to Warfare in France." *The Scientific Monthly* 5, no. 4 (1917): 289-297.

11 Halperin, Sandra. "Dynamics of conflict and system change: The Great Transformation revisited." *European Journal of International Relations* 10, no. 2 (2004): 263-306.

warfare, evident at Verdun, foreshadowed the even greater mobilisation of resources and ecological devastation that would occur during the Second World War.

By the height of the First World War, the pace of industrial arms production had accelerated to such an extent that munitions manufactured in a single month equalled the total stock available at the outbreak of the conflict. The capacity to wage war was no longer determined merely by manpower or immediate resources at the front but increasingly by the industrial and technological power of the home front. This marked a profound shift in military logistics: sustaining warfare now required continuous innovation and large-scale industrial reorganisation. Arms production became not only a matter of ensuring long-term supply but also of maintaining technological superiority through constant advancement.

Within decades, this trajectory culminated in an unprecedented global arms build-up. By the Second World War, bomber fleets possessed the capability to incinerate entire urban centres within minutes. The practice of carpet bombing devastated vast territories, discharging extraordinary volumes of ordnance and fundamentally altering both landscapes and civilian life. Following the cessation of hostilities, millions of tons of unused munitions suddenly became redundant, resulting in the largest episode of weapons overproduction in history.

Analysing Case Studies related to the Scorched Earth

The disposal of these materials created additional environmental challenges. Off the coast of Nova Scotia, one of the primary transatlantic routes between Europe and North America, wartime military activity had been particularly intense.[12] In the postwar period, this area became a repository for surplus ordnance, with long-term ecological risks that remain insufficiently studied. Thus, the industrialisation of warfare not only intensified the destructiveness of conflict but also left behind enduring legacies of contamination and waste.

Recent developments in regions of Vietnam most affected by Agent Orange give some reason for optimism. Even so, it will take decades before a complex ecosystem can re-establish itself there. For years to come, people everywhere on the planet will be contending with the ecological

12 Carton, Geoffrey, and Andrzej Jagusiewicz. "Historic disposal of munitions in US and European coastal waters, how historic information can be used in characterizing and managing risk." *Marine technology society Journal* 43, no. 4 (2009): 16-32.

consequences of past military conflicts. But the burdens of history are not the only weight on the world's environment; the environmental impacts of war extend far beyond the period of violent conflict itself.

That is why the study of warfare ecology begins not with battle, but with preparations for war. Just military preparations alone consume about 15 million square kilometres of land and account for nearly 6% of global raw material use. This militarised consumption of resources is a critical component of humanity's overall exploitation of nature. American military forces alone consume as much oil in a single year as the entire nation of Sweden, making them the world's single largest institutional consumer. During the Iraq War in 2003, the United States and its allies used 30% more oil per month than was consumed during the whole of World War I. Modern machinery of war has an insatiable thirst: a jet fighter burns as much fuel in one hour as 500 compact cars would in the same time; an aircraft carrier consumes the energy equivalent of a small town in a single day. Altogether, the military sector is responsible for roughly 10% of global CO_2 emissions.

Meanwhile, a national security mindset and the primacy of military strength have long shielded armed forces from the environmental standards that apply to the civilian sector. There are, however, glimpses of change. In Western Germany, a military training area recently permitted 100 hectares to be converted into a nature sanctuary. Is this a sign of a budding environmental awareness within the military? Perhaps. But one exception will always remain. In battle, the imperative is survival. The one who shoots faster and more effectively wins. Concerns about forests in 20 years, the impact on agriculture, or the deformities suffered by future generations remain secondary. As long as armed conflict remains a viable instrument of power, the environmental costs of war will be immense, and nature will be left footing the bill.

International Legal Framework

Scorched-earth tactics, characterised by the deliberate destruction of environmental resources, civilian infrastructure, and property to deny strategic advantage to an adversary, pose complex challenges under international law. While historically employed to impede enemy forces, such practices often inflict severe and long-lasting consequences on civilians and the natural environment. Over the past decades, international law has increasingly recognised environmental protection as a critical component of humanitarian protection during armed conflicts. This recognition is reflected in treaty law, customary international humanitarian law (IHL), and international criminal law. Key instruments include the Additional Protocol I (AP I) to the Geneva Conventions (1977)[13] The Rome Statute of the International Criminal Court (1998) established customary IHL principles.

Additional Protocol I to the Geneva Conventions (1977)

Additional Protocol I (AP I) is the primary treaty explicitly addressing environmental protection in the context of armed conflict. Its provisions seek to balance military necessity with the imperative to preserve the natural environment and civilian life. Article 35(3) states that parties to a conflict must not employ methods or means of warfare intended, or expected, to cause *"widespread, long-term and severe damage to the natural environment."* This provision establishes a preventive framework: it prohibits environmental harm even in the absence of direct civilian casualties. The terms *widespread*, *long-term*, and *severe* define a high threshold, emphasising that the law targets significant ecological and humanitarian consequences rather than minor or incidental damage. Article 55(1–2)[14] Further codifies environmental protection as an obligation of belligerents. Paragraph 1 mandates that *"care shall be taken in warfare to protect the natural environment against widespread, long-term and severe damage,"* highlighting the interdependence of environmental integrity and civilian survival. Paragraph 2 explicitly prohibits attacks on the environment by way of reprisal. The scope encompasses forests, agricultural lands, water systems, urban infrastructure, and other environmental features critical to civilian life. Collectively, these provisions affirm that environmental protection is not merely incidental but an integral element of IHL.

Despite its normative importance, AP I's enforcement is constrained by its high threshold. Damage must meet the criteria of being *widespread, long-term, and severe* to trigger legal liability, leaving smaller-scale or cumulative destruction potentially unregulated. Moreover, AP I applies only to conflicts involving parties that have ratified the Protocol, limiting universality.

13 Protocol Additional to the Geneva Conventions of 12 August 1949, and relating to the Protection of Victims of International Armed Conflicts (Protocol I), 8 June 1977,

14 Protocol Additional to the Geneva Conventions of 12 August 1949, and relating to the Protection of Victims of International Armed Conflicts (Protocol I), 8 June 1977

Rome Statute of the International Criminal Court (1998)

The Rome Statute codifies environmental destruction as a potential war crime in international armed conflicts.

Article 8(2)(b)(iv) criminalises the act of *"intentionally launching an attack in the knowledge that such attack will cause incidental loss of life or injury to civilians or damage to civilian objects or widespread, long-term and severe damage to the natural environment which would be clearly excessive in relation to the concrete and direct overall military advantage anticipated."*[15]

This provision introduces three critical elements for establishing criminal liability:

1. Intentionality and Knowledge: The perpetrator must have intended the attack or been aware that their actions were likely to result in environmental and civilian harm.
2. Threshold of Damage: The environmental destruction must be *widespread, long-term, and severe*, consistent with AP I standards.
3. Proportionality: Liability arises only when the harm caused is *clearly excessive* relative to the anticipated military advantage.

The Rome Statute thus imposes individual criminal responsibility, enabling prosecution at the ICC for severe scorched-earth operations. However, the requirement of proportionality and the high threshold of environmental damage limit the scope of prosecutions, particularly in cases involving incremental or diffuse ecological harm. While Rome Statute Article 8(2)(b)(iv) strengthens accountability mechanisms, it applies exclusively to international armed conflicts, leaving non-international conflicts less explicitly regulated in terms of environmental harm.

Customary International Humanitarian Law

Customary IHL extends environmental protection to all armed conflicts, irrespective of treaty ratification. The ICRC's Study on Customary IHL identifies several relevant norms: For example, Rule 45[16] Provides that the natural environment is protected as a civilian object. Attacks against it are

15 Rome Statute of the International Criminal Court, 17 July 1998, art 8(2)(b)(iv).

16 ICRC, *Customary International Humanitarian Law*, Volume I: Rules (Cambridge University Press 2005) Rule 45.

unlawful unless required by military necessity. Rule 46[17] Provides that the Parties must avoid causing widespread, long-term, severe damage to the environment, whereas Rule 70[18] Provides that the Belligerents are prohibited from using methods of warfare that cause superfluous injury or unnecessary suffering, which encompasses tactics producing severe environmental harm. Customary law thereby establishes that environmental destruction is inherently limited by principles of necessity and proportionality. Unlike treaty law, customary norms also extend to non-international armed conflicts, filling a critical gap in the legal framework.

Additional instruments, while not directly binding in armed conflict, reinforce the normative framework against environmental harm:

- ENMOD Convention (1976): Prohibits hostile environmental modification techniques with widespread, long-lasting, or severe effects.
- Rio Declaration (1992) & Stockholm Declaration (1972): Recognise environmental protection as a core principle of human welfare, indirectly informing the interpretation of IHL obligations.

These instruments reflect the broader trend of integrating environmental protection into the principles of international law, emphasising that environmental integrity is inseparable from human rights and civilian protection.

Human rights and environmental justice

The term 'environmental justice', which can be defined using a range of theoretical approaches, encompasses a wide range of justice considerations.[19] One formulation of environmental justice can be drawn from the emerging fields of eco-crime and green criminology, which provide an understanding of environmental justice based on conventional criminological discourses as they apply to environmental harm (see Walters 2010; White 2008). Another account of environmental justice is based on the theory of distributive justice whereby just outcomes are assessed

17 ICRC, *Customary International Humanitarian Law*, Volume I: Rules (Cambridge University Press 2005) Rule 46.

18 ICRC, *Customary International Humanitarian Law*, Volume I: Rules (Cambridge University Press 2005) Rule 70.

19 Schlosberg, David. *Defining environmental justice: Theories, movements, and nature.* OUP Oxford, 2007.

according to the equality and fairness with which environmental benefits and burdens are distributed between individuals, communities and States.

Environmental justice can therefore be interpreted as operating on two planes: intra- and intergenerational justice. These two layers of justice do not operate independently. As Brown Weiss pointed out: 'in the present generation, one cannot expect people to fulfil obligations to future generations if they are not able to satisfy their basic needs' (2008: 216). She argued that a failure to address the needs of communities today would exacerbate the inequalities facing future generations.[20] One of the main ways that human rights principles can be used to combat environmental injustice is by promoting the protection and fulfilment of human rights for everyone, but especially for developing nations. This will enable these communities to focus on the environmental legacy they will leave for future generations and more effectively engage with sustainable development practices.

In 2008, Edith Brown Weiss penned what could be regarded as a rather prescient paper on equity and climate change. She maintained that climate change was a problem for environmental justice in terms of how it affects some communities, nations, or generations. She used John Rawls' theory of justice (1971) to pinpoint the issue of attaining distributive justice regarding the consequences among members of the same generation of the changing climate.[21]

Environmental justice is also inseparable from the question of energy justice. Fence-line communities disproportionately bear the brunt of pollution from petrochemical and fossil-fuel facilities, while simultaneously facing higher household energy burdens. The transition to renewable energy must therefore be equitable and human rights-centred, ensuring that communities most affected by pollution are not excluded from the benefits of clean energy. Historical experience warns of transitions that perpetuate exploitation, as in the shift from slavery to sharecropping in the American South. A just energy transition requires democratised decision-making, equitable access to clean energy, and opportunities for workforce development in line with human dignity.

20 Lewis, Bridget. "Human rights and environmental wrongs: Achieving environmental justice through human rights law." *International Journal for Crime, Justice and Social Democracy* 1, no. 1 (2012): 65-73.

21 Weston, Burns H. "Climate change and intergenerational justice: Foundational reflections." *Vt. J. Envtl. L.* 9 (2007): 375.

Sustainable Development Goals as a Moral Framework

The Sustainable Development Goals (SDGs) provide what can be described as a global moral compass at a time of deep political division and global uncertainty. With their core promise to "leave no one behind", the SDGs aim to irreversibly eradicate poverty sustainably and equitably. Yet, soberingly, only about 15% of the SDG targets are currently on track, largely due to ongoing conflicts, crises, and systemic inertia.

The greatest missing ingredient, as emphasised by several speakers, is human willpower. While the technical knowledge, financial capacity, and institutional frameworks exist, the failure lies in mustering the collective determination to act. Still, the abundance of humanitarians and social leaders worldwide offers hope, underscoring that humanity can still rise to meet the challenge.

Framing Climate and Environmental Justice

The concept of climate justice extends beyond environmental protection; it integrates human rights and the principle of a just transition. This means ensuring that the shift to sustainable economies and low-carbon futures does not marginalise vulnerable communities.

Globalisation, though often criticised, need not be inherently harmful — but exclusion from participation in economic systems has historically bred inequality and resistance. Climate change exacerbates these inequities, disproportionately impacting minorities, indigenous groups, and marginalised populations. COVID-19 further revealed these vulnerabilities, making evident the urgent need for a new, inclusive, and fair global economy aligned with the SDGs. Mary Robinson's seven principles of climate justice remain a touchstone, emphasising equity, dignity, accountability, and participation of affected communities.

Accountability and the Role of Law

Many legal scholars stressed that legal accountability is indispensable. Without enforceable laws and mechanisms of redress, efforts to mitigate climate change and environmental harm remain insufficient. The emergence of discussions around ecocide, which reflects the massive destruction of ecosystems, reflects growing recognition that environmental crimes should be elevated to the level of international crimes, akin to genocide, war crimes, crimes against humanity, and aggression.[22]

Corporate actors, in particular, often define their responsibility too narrowly, limiting accountability to Scope 1 and 2 emissions (direct operations), while ignoring Scope 3 impacts (supply chains). Yet, most environmental and human rights abuses occur precisely in the value chain. Thus, the need for system-level reforms is urgent, supported by enforceable international law.

Ecocide as the Fifth International Crime

Currently, the International Criminal Court (ICC) recognises four crimes: Genocide, Crimes against humanity, War crimes, and the Crime of aggression.

A proposal now gaining traction is to recognise ecocide as the fifth crime under the Rome Statute. Ecocide would hold individuals criminally liable for knowingly causing widespread, long-term, or severe damage to the environment.

The rationale is moral as much as legal: just as genocide is a crime against all humanity, so too is the destruction of our shared environment a crime against all people. In recent years, Belgium has already incorporated ecocide into its criminal code, the EU has adopted a directive requiring member states to legislate against severe environmental crimes, and similar proposals have emerged in Brazil, Spain, Scotland, Mexico, Italy, the Netherlands, and the UK.[23] Such developments highlight a growing consensus thereby environmental destruction must be treated as a crime of universal concern, beyond the discretion of individual states.

Analysing IHL environmental provisions

Failure to respond to the environmental challenges of war-torn societies can greatly complicate the task of peacebuilding.[24] The United Nations Environment Programme (UNEP) is conducting an initial assessment

22 Killean, R. (2025). Ecocide's evolving relationship with war. *Environment and Security*, *0*(0).

23 Bosio, Eleonora. "The environmental protection under the International Criminal Law: the new crime of ecocide." (2023).

24 Ken Conca and Jennifer Wallace, "Environment and Peacebuilding in War-Torn Societies: Lessons from the UN Environment Programme's Experience with Post-conflict Assessment", Global Governance, Vol. 15, No. 4, 009, p. 486.

of the harm done to Ukraine's environment and the possible effects on the environment and public health in order to inform and get ready for a thorough post-conflict assessment. The ongoing hostilities in Ukraine have recently brought the relationship between the environment and conflict to the fore. The law of international responsibility provides a solid foundation for states' accountability for environmental harm resulting from armed conflict. On the one hand, the Hague Convention IV of 1907 and Additional Protocol I to the Geneva Conventions hold States accountable for jus in bello violations.[25] Under Article 3 of Hague Convention IV, "a belligerent party which violates the provisions of the said Regulations shall, if the case demands, be liable to pay compensation". Article 91 of AP I contains the same liability rule by providing that "[a] Party to the conflict which violates the provisions of the Conventions or of this Protocol shall, if the case demands, be liable to pay compensation". The international responsibility of States for environmental consequences of armed conflict is affirmed by the International Law Commission (ILC) in the recently adopted Draft Principles on Protection of the Environment in Relation to Armed Conflicts (ILC Draft Principles)[26]. However, regardless of whether jus in bello has been broken, a State that has violated jus ad bellum—the law governing the use of force—would be liable for all damages, including environmental harm. Meanwhile, international environmental law and human rights law are to fill in the gaps in the framework of the law of armed conflict, as jus in bello is constantly changing to improve environmental protection.[27] Thus, it follows that any belligerent State that has breached the obligations under the law of armed conflict or any other applicable rules of international law shall be held accountable for all damage it has caused, including environmental damage.

The legal principle with respect to military attach is that the responsible State is obliged to "wipe out all the consequences of the illegal act and re-establish the situation which would, in all probability, have existed if that act had not been committed". Article 31 of the 2001 ILC Draft Articles on the Responsibility of States for Internationally Wrongful Acts (ARSIWA) enshrines this idea as a duty to "make full reparation" for any harm

25 Protocol Additional (I) to the Geneva Conventions of 12 August 1949

26 ILC, Draft Principles on Protection of the Environment in Relation to Armed Conflicts, with Commentaries, UN Doc. A/77/10,

27 Michael Bothe, Carl Bruch, Jordan Diamond and David Jensen, "International Law Protecting the Environment during Armed Conflict: Gaps and Opportunities", International Review of the Red Cross, Vol. 92, No. 79, 2010.

material or moral caused by a State's internationally wrongful act.[28] The responsible State must provide complete reparations for the harm it has caused in accordance with Article 34 of the ARSIWA. These reparations may be made in the form of restitution, compensation, or satisfaction. In this way, the duty to offer "full reparation" calls for reestablishing the circumstances that would have existed in the absence of the wrongdoing in order to mitigate the effects of the act as much as possible.

While the law of State responsibility contains the principle of full reparation, the question is how to define the specific types of state general obligation. What are the specific requirements for the re-establishment? Does it call for restoring every component of the damaged environment to its pre-existing physical condition? How can we ascertain whether the serious adverse effects have been reduced and the situation has been restored to the state that would have existed had the wrongdoing not been committed? In sum, what kind of reparation, and how much reparation, amounts to "full reparation" and, further, how should full reparation be realised? This issue is further complicated by the state of impossibility of active restoration in many situations as particularly in the context of a changing environment suffering from the triple crisis of climate change, pollution and loss of ecology.

By establishing a far lower yardstick of damage than that required by AP I, the ENMOD Convention, which forbids the usage of the environment as a "weapon" or more precisely as a "method" of warfare, offers the environment much broader protection. The variety of methods contained under the ENMOD Convention, however, seems limited, and it ignores the environment's status as a target, which is the range of targets that are shielded from destruction, damage, or injury. The environment is not defined in any of the widely ratified bello treaties, and their provisions generally use anthropocentric language or simply refer to the "natural environment". However, an analysis of the law of armed conflict does not show the exact meaning and scope of this term, i.e. what exactly is immensely protected as the "natural environment".

Apart from the restricted safeguards provided by international humanitarian law, the regulations of international environmental law exhibit significant promise in preventing environmental harm during times of conflict. More generally, some environmental treaties are still in effect during times of

28 ILC, Draft Articles on Responsibility of States for Internationally Wrongful Acts, with Commentaries, UN Doc. A/56/10, in Yearbook of the International Law Commission, Vol. 2, Part 2, 2001 (ARSIWA), Art. 31

armed conflict; in such cases, multilateral agreements or environmental treaties can reinforce and supplement environmental protection. A careful examination of the environmental treaties' provisions shows that environmental protection can extend to the inherent value of natural ecosystems, even though different environmental treaties have different definitions of "environment" that vary depending on their respective topics. For example, under the United Nations (UN) Convention on the Law of the Non-Navigational Uses of International Watercourses, the term "environment" is broader and is more than the living resources of international watercourses, the flora and fauna dependent upon those watercourses.

The ILC describes the broader aspect of the environment. Particularly, the 2006 Draft Principles on the Allocation of Loss in the Case of Transboundary Harm Arising out of Hazardous Activities[29] defines environment as "includes natural resources, both abiotic and biotic, such as air, water, soil, fauna and flora and the interaction between the same factors, and the characteristic aspects of the landscape". As per the ILC, "environment could be defined in different ways for different purposes, and it is appropriate to bear in mind that there is no universally accepted definition". Additionally, the Commission has adopted the inclusion of "environmental values" and "non-service values" such as the enjoyment of natural ecosystems and other associated facilities.

The recent usage of this term by international courts and tribunals is also encouraging in broadening the scope of the environment and giving environmental justice in the case of pure environmental damage, namely, damage caused to the environment, in and of itself. In its Advisory Opinion in the Nuclear Weapons case, the International Court of Justice (ICJ)[30] Eloquently noted that "the environment is not an abstraction but represents the living space, the quality of life and the very health of human beings, including generations unborn". Later, in the proceedings of the United Nations Compensation Commission (UNCC), despite not attempting to define the term "direct environmental damage" in UN Security Council Resolution 687. The Panel explicitly stated that "there is no justification for the contention that general international law precludes compensation

29 International Law Commission, *Draft Principles on the Allocation of Loss in the Case of Transboundary Harm Arising out of Hazardous Activities*, with commentaries, Yearbook of the International Law Commission, 2006, vol II, Part Two.

30 Legality of the Threat or Use of Nuclear Weapons (Advisory Opinion) [1996] ICJ Rep 226

for pure environmental damage". In the Iron Rhine case decided by the Permanent Court of Arbitration, "environment" was broadly referred to as "including air, water, land, flora and fauna, natural ecosystems and sites, human health and safety, and climate".

A dynamic approach to environmental protection

The International Law Commission (ILC) adopts a dynamic approach to environmental considerations in armed conflict, emphasising that such considerations "cannot remain static over time but should develop as understanding of the environment develops." This evolving conception of the environment shapes the notion of environmental protection in conflict situations and supports the pursuit of full reparation for environmental damage in the aftermath of hostilities.

Contemporary perspectives view the environment not as a mere collection of objects to be safeguarded, but as a dynamic, interactive system. This systemic understanding is crucial in assessing wartime environmental damage. The International Committee of the Red Cross (ICRC), in its comments on the ILC Draft Principles, stressed that assessments must rely on "current knowledge, including on the connectedness and interrelationships of different parts of the natural environment as well as on the effects of the harm caused." In this light, the ILC highlighted that present-day scientific knowledge of ecological systems must inform the application of the "widespread, long-term and severe" damage criteria. More specifically, the risk of damage must be assessed not only in terms of harm to individual objects but also in terms of the potential impact on fragile, interdependent systems comprising both living and non-living components.

The Panel of Commissioners considered that in assessing what measures are reasonably necessary to clean or restore a damaged environment, "primary emphasis must be placed on restoring the environment to preinvasion conditions, in terms of its overall ecological functioning rather than on the removal of specific contaminants or restoration of the environment to a particular physical condition".

The practice of the ICJ and the UNCC has demonstrated a nuanced but critical distinction between the objectives of "returning the environment to its original state" and "maintaining the overall ecological functioning of the environment".[31] Recalling that the proper objective of reparation for wartime environmental damage should take into account the contemporary understanding of the environment, the interactivity within the environment, and the coupling of human and natural systems, the principle of full reparation can be achieved through the objective of restoring the overall ecological functioning of the damaged environment.

In her Preliminary Report on the Protection of the Environment in Relation to Armed Conflicts, Special Rapporteur Marie G. Jacobsson observed that the effect on the environment of an armed conflict may remain long after the conflict and has the potential to prevent an effective rebuilding of the society, to destroy pristine areas or to disrupt important ecosystems.[32] The ICRC also drew attention to the fact that damage to the environment due to armed conflicts may have long-term consequences that continue after the end of hostilities. As an illustration, in Kuwait and Saudi Arabia, the adverse effects of the oil well fires during the 1990–91 Gulf War were revealed more than ten years later in the form of desert covered with inches of oily residue that eventually hardened into a pavement-like substance, and lakes of oil that trapped livestock, birds and other wildlife.

An effective way to identify and assess long-term risks to the environment in relation to armed conflict, so as to inform necessary future actions, is to monitor the consequences during conflict and in its aftermath. In this regard, the ICRC suggests establishing possible mechanisms and procedures for addressing the immediate and long-term consequences of environmental damage. One of the unique features of the work of the UNCC is the implementation of comprehensive monitoring and assessment projects to ascertain the level of damage. As expressed by the Panel of Commissioners, even if the results generated show that no damage has been caused or that damage has occurred, but remediation or restoration efforts are not possible or advisable in the circumstances, a monitoring and assessment activity could be of benefit. Also, such an activity could help to alleviate concerns regarding potential risks or damage and avoid unnecessary and wasteful measures to deal with non-existent or negligible risks.

31 Kong, Lingjie, and Yuqing Zhao. "Remedying the environmental impacts of war: Challenges and perspectives for full reparation." *International Review of the Red Cross* 105, no. 924 (2023): 1441-1462.

32 Lehto, Marja-Liisa, Special Rapporteur. "First Report on Protection of the Environment in Relation to Armed Conflicts." UN International Law Commission, A/CN.4/720, 30 April 2018.

Establishment of the causal nexus

Establishment of the causal nexus is another challenge facing the assessment of wartime environmental claims.[33] The law of State responsibility requires establishing a link of causality between a culpable act and the damage suffered. The causal link must be "sufficiently direct and certain", and the damage must be neither too remote nor too speculative.

Given that the causation between environmental damage and wrongful acts during the conflict is not always clear and straightforward, a strict interpretation of the rules on evidence places a heavy burden on the claimant, particularly with respect to damages resulting from concurrent causes. In this regard, the solution for attaining full reparation is to develop specific causality standards applicable to wartime environmental damage. As set out by the UNCC, in the case of Iraq's invasion and occupation of Kuwait, regard must be paid to the contribution of any pre-existing or subsequent causes where such causes can be identified, "not in determining the restoration objective to be achieved by remediation, but in determining the proportion of the costs of remediation that can reasonably be attributed to the invasion".[34] The Panel of Commissioners made it plain that Iraq is not exonerated from liability for loss or damage simply because other factors might have contributed to the loss or damage. Evidence present in relation to each head of loss or damage is the basis for ascertaining the existence of a direct causal nexus.

In specifying the legal test for causation, the ICJ highlighted that "the causal nexus required may vary depending on the primary rule violated and the nature and extent of the injury".

This is consistent with the position taken by the UNCC, which held that due account of the contribution from other factors should be taken in order to determine what proportion of the damage is attributable to the responsible actor.

33 Schmitt, Michael N. "Green war: an assessment of the environmental law of international armed conflict." *Yale J. Int'l L.* 22 (1997): 1.

34 Schneider, Michael E., 'The Role of Iraq in the Uncc Process with Special Emphasis on the Environmental Claims', in Timothy J. Feighery, Christopher S. Gibson, and Trevor M. Rajah (eds), *War Reparations and the UN Compensation Commission: Designing Compensation After Conflict* (New York, 2015; online edn, Oxford Academic, 23 Apr. 2015),

Compensation and valuation of wartime environmental damage

In environmental adjudication, compensation is a common remedy, as it seeks to replace the loss sustained. However, a calculation of monetary compensation for pure environmental harm makes the standard of full reparation extremely difficult, if not impossible, to realise.

Valuing environmental losses is a challenging exercise because, on the one hand, restitution is often impossible to achieve, and on the other, the valuation of environmental damage requires special techniques. In the Gabčíkovo-Nagymaros[35] Project case, the ICJ noted "the often-irreversible character of damage to the environment" and "the limitations inherent in the very mechanism of reparation of this type of damage". This is particularly evident in the context of armed conflict. It is often the case that armed conflict causes massive and widespread environmental harm, and restitution is often costly and sometimes impossible in the case of irreversible harm. In addition, despite having a non-economic value requiring restoration to the state prior to the damage occurring, pure environmental damage may be incapable of being calculated in market terms. As a result, compensation raises the problem of assessing the quantum of environmental damage – i.e., whether it should be based on the costs of reinstatement measures, on an abstract quantification computed using a theoretical model, or on some other basis. The legal precedents for international environmental compensation are generally limited, indicating that the rules of international law relating to the valuation of environmental damage remain underdeveloped.

Conclusion

The history and new practice of scorched earth warfare reveal a troubling continuity: the deliberate destruction of land, resources, and ecosystems remains a recurrent military strategy, despite clear prohibitions under international humanitarian law. As conflicts in Gaza, Yemen, and Ukraine demonstrate, the environmental consequences of modern warfare are not incidental but systemic acts, thereby polluting soil and water, destroying biodiversity, accelerating climate change, and dismantling fragile environmental governance systems. The ecological toll is enduring, persisting long after hostilities cease, often locking affected populations into cycles of poverty, ill health, and environmental degradation. While the Geneva Conventions and Additional Protocol I recognise limits on methods

35 [1997] ICJ Rep 88

and means of warfare, the enforcement gap remains stark. Scorched earth tactics continue to expose the inadequacy of anthropocentric legal frameworks that prioritise military necessity over ecological survival. If the environment is to be meaningfully protected in times of conflict, a paradigm shift is required, for example, one that treats nature not as collateral but as a subject of protection in its own right. This demands stronger accountability mechanisms, the recognition of ecocide as an international crime, and a commitment to restoration and reparations as central pillars of post-conflict recovery. Ultimately, the environmental costs of war underscore that true security cannot be achieved through military dominance alone. Without embedding ecological considerations at the core of humanitarian law and peacebuilding, humanity risks repeating a scorched legacy, one where the survival of ecosystems and future generations remains the greatest casualty of armed conflict.

Environmental Impact of the Russia-Ukraine Conflict

Bismita Saikia & Gitanjali Ghosh

Abstract

The Russia-Ukraine conflict that began in 2014 with the annexation of Crimea escalated with Russia's invasion of Ukraine in February 2022. The conflict has not only led to colossal human suffering and geopolitical instability, but it has also substantially affected the environment. Its environmental toll has been alarming, resulting from various military activities like shelling and airstrikes that have caused deforestation, water and air pollution, soil contamination, etc. There have been attacks on numerous industrial infrastructures and risks to nuclear facilities, which have amplified environmental risks and threatened environmental security both regionally and globally. This paper seeks to analyse the impact of the conflict on the environment, evaluate the legal framework related to environmental protection during armed conflicts, and its applicability during the Russia-Ukraine conflict. It also aims to highlight the urgent need to address the issue of environmental protection in times of conflict and the need for stronger protection for the environment.

Introduction

Wars or armed conflicts, be they international or non-international, usually bring widespread destruction, whose impact extends beyond just the battlefield and affects every aspect of human life, including the surrounding environment.[1] When the aspect of the consequences of armed conflict is discussed, the immediate attention or focus goes to the

---

1 United Nations, *How Conflict Impacts Our Environment* (UN, 2025) https://www.un.org/en/peace-and-security/how-conflict-impacts-our-environment accessed 10 September 2025.

destruction of life and infrastructure, the number of human casualties, or the number of people who are displaced and forced to leave their residences. However, another victim of armed conflict is the environment, which is often forgotten as it doesn't immediately make it to the headlines, which is why it is called the "silent victim".[2] Its impact frequently goes unreported or underreported, and usually remains unmeasured, although its impact can be long-lasting.

The Russia-Ukraine armed conflict, which started in 2014 with the annexation of Crimea, escalated into a full-fledged conflict in February 2022.[3] This conflict shows the grievous impact of conflict situations on the environment. It has changed the environmental landscape of both States, especially Ukraine, as civilian properties were damaged, factories, farmlands, forests, power plants, as well as water systems were targeted and affected.[4]

From a legal point of view, environmental protection in times of armed conflict is considered an important responsibility. Various branches of law work in this regard. The provisions of International Humanitarian Law (IHL) set a limit to what can and cannot be done during warfare, and its provisions prevent belligerent States from causing unnecessary damage to the environment.[5] The Additional Protocol I to the Geneva Convention prevents the States involved in a conflict from causing widespread, long-term, and severe damage to the environment.[6] The Rome Statute of the International Criminal Court (Rome Statute) also contains provisions that

2 D. Carutasu, *Effects of Military Conflicts* (International Conference Knowledge-Based Organisation, Romania, 2024).

3 Council on Foreign Relations, *War in Ukraine* (CFR Global Conflict Tracker, 15 September 2025) https://www.cfr.org/global-conflict-tracker/conflict/conflict-ukraine accessed 17 September 2025.

4 D. Hryhorczuk et al, "The Environmental Health Impacts of Russia's War on Ukraine" *Journal of Occupational Medicine and Toxicology* (2024) pp. 1-14 at p. 1.

5 International Committee of the Red Cross, *Answers to Your Questions – International Humanitarian Law* (ICRC, December 2014).

6 G. Carter, 'Do Articles 35 and 55 of Additional Protocol I to the 1949 Geneva Convention effectively protect the environment during an armed conflict?' (UWE Blogs, 27 November 2023) https://blogs.uwe.ac.uk/bristol-law-school/do-articles-35-and-55-of-additional-protocol-i-to-the-1949-geneva-convention-effectively-protect-the-environment-during-an-armed-conflict/ accessed 10 August 2025.

allow for the prosecution of such acts of environmental destruction under certain circumstances.[7]

International Environmental Law (IEL) creates an additional layer of protection for the environment. The Convention on the Prohibition of Military or Any Other Hostile Use of Environmental Modification Techniques (ENMOD Convention) goes on to prevent the use of environmental modification techniques that can be put to hostile use.[8] The idea of having environmental crime as a separate core international crime has also gained momentum in the present time.[9] Recently, the ILC has drafted the Principles on Protection of the Environment in Relation to Armed Conflicts (PERAC), in which they have attempted to build a connection between environmental protection and humanitarian concerns before, during, and after conflict, which justifies the need to protect the environment during a humanitarian crisis.[10]

Nonetheless, in terms of its enforcement in real life, it faces some serious obstacles and issues, which means that the enforcement of these laws remains weak and often goes unpunished, and this is highlighted through the Russia-Ukraine conflict. Thus, it becomes essential to study this conflict and the environmental impacts of this conflict through a legal lens, as it will help to understand the capability and effectiveness of the existing international rules, identify the gaps, and contribute towards having stronger laws in this regard.

Environmental Consequences of the Russia-Ukraine Armed Conflict

The Russia-Ukraine conflict that escalated in February 2022 gradually turned into one of the longest and most destructive conflicts so far,[11] with far-reaching repercussions for human beings and the environment.[12]

7 *Environmental Damage in the Context of International Criminal Law* (FTB Chambers, 12 June 2023) https://www.ftbchambers.co.uk/news/blog-view/environmental-damage-in-the-context-of-international-criminal-law accessed 10 August 2025.

8 ICRC, supra note 5

9 S. Meheta and P. Merz, "Ecocide - A New Crime against Peace" *Environmental Law Review,* vol. 17 (2015), pp. 3-7 at p. 3.

10 International Law Commission, *Draft Principles on the Protection of the Environment in Relation to Armed Conflicts* (adopted 2022).

11 B. Frederick et al, *Consequences of the Russia-Ukraine War and the Changing Face of Conflict* (RAND Corporation, Research Brief RB-A3141-1, May 2025).

12 Joint Research Centre, 'War worsens climate and environmental challenges in Ukraine' (European Commission, 11 April 2025) https://joint-research-centre.ec.europa.

Although human suffering is widely publicised, environmental damage is also equally alarming.[13] To gain a deeper understanding of the conflict's impact, it is important to first examine how the conflict began and how the actions of the belligerent states have caused severe environmental damage that will continue to affect the region for years to come.

The Beginning of the Armed Conflict

The conflict between the two major European States, Russia and Ukraine, is not a recent issue. These two States have always had a tense relationship, especially ever since Russia claimed and ultimately took control over Crimea in 2014.[14] So, this is not the first time that Russia has challenged Ukraine's sovereignty and territorial integrity since Ukraine gained independence in 1991. But this time it is much more brutal, terrible, intense, cut-throat, and inordinate.

The usurping of Ukraine by Russia, which unfolded on 24 February 2022, is still going on, and the conflict and its impacts have escalated to such an extent that it is considered the *"most extensive belligerent action between States since the end of World War II."*[15] This act of Russia of using and operating force and pressure on Ukraine by giving the justification of self-defence is a violation of the provisions of the Charter of the United Nations, to begin with.[16] The extremity of the conflict is evident in the massive displacement and forced migration of millions of people from Ukraine.[17]

Russia has long opposed the increasing influence and alliance of the West with its neighbouring countries.[18] When Russia invaded Ukraine, the

---

eu/jrc-news-and-updates/war-worsens-climate-and-environmental-challenges-ukraine-2025-04-11_en#:~:text=Since%202022%2C%20the%20war%20led,mass%20movements%20in%20their%20territories. accessed 12 August 2025.

13 Ibid.

14 J. Masters, "Ukraine: Conflict at the Crossroads of Europe and Russia" (Council on Foreign Relations, 14 February 2023) https://www.cfr.org/backgrounder/ukraine-conflict-crossroads-europe-and-russia accessed 10 August 2025.

15 P. S. Baruch and O. Beeri, "The Russian Invasion of Ukraine: Legal Aspects" (INSS Insight, 10 March 2022) https://www.inss.org.il/publication/russia-invasion-law/ accessed 7 August 2025.

16 Charter of the United Nations, adopted 26 June 1945, entered into force 24 October 1945, 1 UNTS XVI, art 2.

17 Council on Foreign Relations, supra note 3.

18 E. Gotz and P. Ekman, "Russia's War Against Ukraine: Context, Causes, and Consequences" *Problems of Post-Communism*, vol. 71(3) (2024), pp. 193-205 at p.193.

Russian leader claimed the purpose was "demilitarising and de-Nazifying Ukraine."[19] The leader of Russia stated that he wants to end the agony and suffering of the people, which, according to them, began after the annexation of Crimea in 2014. Russia affirmed that there were cases of genocide to wipe out the pro-Russian population in Ukraine.[20] Thus, it has consistently rejected labelling its actions as an invasion or a war.[21]

Since Ukraine's independence in 1991, Ukraine has placed a strong emphasis on its sovereignty. However, Russia has always maintained the view on Ukraine that "Ukraine never had stable traditions of genuine statehood."[22] The events of 2014 can also be traced back to Russia pressuring Ukraine's then-President to abandon plans of joining the European Union, which triggered unrest and set the stage for further conflict.[23]

When Ukraine expressed its willingness to join NATO, Russia felt the threat from the West. According to Russia's leader, NATO's ultimate goal is "to split society in Russia and ultimately destroy it."[24] After Ukraine expressed its desire to join NATO, Russia began moving troops near Ukraine's border, calling it military training. At that point, NATO had already warned Ukraine of the strong possibility of war.

Environmental Impact of the Russia-Ukraine Armed Conflict

The full-scale invasion of Ukraine by Russia has led to immeasurable destruction and impact that extends far beyond just human suffering. It has resulted in severe and widespread destruction of the environment, specifically in Ukraine. There has been direct destruction of infrastructure, habitats, and species, as well as indirect harm in the form of pollution and destruction of important environmental resources.

As of June 2023, there has been an estimated $56.4 billion in environmental damage to Ukraine, as per Ukrainian and international analysis.[25] It has

19 P. Kirby, "Why Has Russia Invaded Ukraine and What Does Putin Want?" (BBC News, 24 February 2023) https://www.bbc.com/news/world-europe-56720589 accessed 7 August 2025.

20 E. Fortuin, " 'Ukraine Commits Genocide on Russians': The Term 'Genocide' in Russian Propaganda" *Russian Linguistics*, vol. 46(3) (2022), pp. 313–347 at p. 314.

21 Ibid.

22 P. Kirby, supra note 19.

23 J. Masters, supra note 14.

24 Kirby, supra note 19.

25 Hryhorczuk et al, supra note 4, 8.

been found that 30% of protected areas in Ukraine have been affected in indirect ways, and around 30% of the territory of Ukraine is affected by direct impacts of the conflict, by the use of landmines or UXO, etc.[26]

Air Pollution

The conflict has led to extreme changes in air quality in Ukraine. A large number of bombings and fires at industrial locations, added by movements of a large number of tanks and military trucks, had released dangerous amounts of pollutants in the air.[27] A leading example in this regard was the situation of Kyiv in March 2022, which recorded 28 times higher concentration of fine dust particles (PM2.5) than the safe guideline as provided by the World Health Organisation.[28]

The destruction of civilian buildings and infrastructures also adds to the air pollution as they release huge amounts of dust, asbestos, and other toxic substances.[29] Numerous fuel storage facilities were also attacked, leading to the burning of huge amounts of fuel that released thick black smoke across various cities.[30] In 2022, the country experienced 25 times more forest fires than in 2021, which affected not just local areas but also wider regions, depending on wind patterns.[31]

Water Pollution and Destruction of Water Systems

There have been massive contaminations of water systems in Ukraine resulting from the conflict. As a direct consequence, people faced a shortage of water, and the polluted water increased the risk of waterborne diseases, because of the release of munitions residues, explosives, fuels, and other

26 Ibid, 1.

27 Hryhorczuk et al, supra note 4, 3.

28 Ibid.

29 Ibid.

30 *Ukraine Conflict Environmental Briefing: Fossil Fuel Infrastructure* (Conflict and Environment Observatory and Zoï Environment Network, November 2022) https://ceobs.org/ukraine-conflict-environmental-briefing-fossil-fuel-infrastructure/#:~:text=or%20political%20manipulation.-,Case%20study:%20Attack%20on%20the%20KLO%20oil%20storage%20depot%2C%20Kalynivka,the%20damaged%20infrastructure%20across%20Ukraine. accessed 15 August 2025.

31 O. Brown et al, *The Impact of Russia's War Against Ukraine on Climate Security and Climate Action* (OSCE, 2023).

chemicals into freshwater resources, including the collapse of wastewater management.[32]

The Nova Kakhovka Dam was destroyed on 6 June 2023, causing one of the most serious cases of water pollution and ecological damage in Europe, and the worst disaster of its kind since Chernobyl.[33] Because of the destruction of this dam, forest and agricultural areas, and dozens of villages and towns were quickly flooded.[34] Thousands of people living on both sides of the river had to evacuate their homes.[35] It was reported that the floodwater had also dislodged the landmines, becoming a huge concern for the nearby residents.[36]

In the Dnipro River, around 150 tons of machine oil were spilt, accompanied by a huge quantity of debris, sewage, and other organic wastes.[37] It affected the marine environment to a great extent, resulting in the perishing of thousands of fish, and it also affected thousands of domestic animals as they drowned or were poisoned after consuming the water.[38] So, the marine and coastal environments along the Dnipro-Black Sea corridor have sustained severe damage leading to lower water salinity in coastal zones, triggering harmful algal blooms (cyanobacteria), killing large populations of mussels, fish eggs, and changing underwater habitat structure: notably, macrophyte beds (seaweeds, submerged plants) were washed away, then replaced by more freshwater-tolerant species in formerly saline or brackish zones.[39]

Thus, the long-term impact of the conflict on the water resources of Ukraine can be extremely deadly. It is because, with the destruction of the

32 O. Shumilova et al, "Impact of the Russia–Ukraine Armed Conflict on Water Resources and Water Infrastructure" *Nature Sustainability*, vol. 6 (2023), pp. 579–586 at p. 579.

33 K. Hook, Statement, US Helsinki Commission Briefing, "Russia's Ecocide in Ukraine: Environmental Destruction and the Need for Accountability."

34 "Ukraine dam: What we know about Nova Kakhovka incident" (BBC News, 8 June 2023) https://www.bbc.com/news/world-europe-65818705 accessed 17 August 2025.

35 Ibid.

36 Ibid.

37 K. Sergatskova, "Aftermath of the Kakhovka Dam Collapse" (Wilson Center, 20 June 2023) https://www.wilsoncenter.org/blog-post/aftermath-kakhovka-dam-collapse accessed 17 August 2025.

38 Ibid.

39 Y. Kvach et al, "Biodiversity effects of the Russia–Ukraine War and the Kakhovka Dam Destruction: Ecological Consequences and Predictions for Marine, Estuarine, and Freshwater Communities in the Northern Black Sea" *Ecological Processes*, vol. 14 (2025), pp. 1–25 at p. 1.

dam and its reservoir, more than 1 million hectares of farmland in three regions have been left with no source of reliable water for the next three to five years.[40] The lack of irrigation will increase the risk of soil damage, desertification, and land degradation. Sea mines, drifting ordnance, and underwater explosions pose direct risks to marine fauna, especially species sensitive to acoustic disturbance, like dolphins, and those with limited mobility. Furthermore, habitat disruptions such as damage to coastal wetlands, estuaries, and marine plant beds, along with disrupted conservation activity and weakened monitoring, have undermined the ability of ecosystems to recover.[41]

Soil Contamination

Various reports suggest that the frontline areas of Ukraine are heavily polluted with shells and landmines.[42] Many weapons didn't explode at the time they were fired, and as per estimates, almost one-third of the land in Ukraine is contaminated with unexploded artillery shells and cluster munitions.[43] Cleaning the affected areas could be extremely expensive for Ukraine, costing billions, as it will require qualified individuals, technology, and machinery.

The famous chernozem (black soils) of Ukraine, considered one of the most fertile across the globe and very crucial for global food supply, has also suffered significantly.[44] The explosions, their remains, and the unexploded shells and mines have resulted in reduced crop yields and pose a danger to overall food contamination.[45] According to national assessments, the

40 Sergatskova, supra note 5.

41 *Ukraine Conflict Environmental Briefing: The Coastal and Marine Environment* (Conflict and Environment Observatory, February 2023) https://ceobs.org/ukraine-conflict-environmental-briefing-the-coastal-and-marine-environment/#4 accessed 17 August 2025.

42 "'It is an elephant': Ukraine's unexploded mine problem" (UN, 5 June 2025) https://news.un.org/en/story/2025/06/1164121#:~:text=Massive%20contamination%2C%20'real%20and%20perceived,potentially%20contaminated%20land%20is%20safe.&text=An%20Explosive%20Ordnance%20Disposal%20Specialist,of%20contamination%20from%20the%20war. accessed 17 August 2025.

43 Hryhorczuk et al, supra note 4, 6.

44 M. Cavallito, "How war is contributing to environmental degradation in Ukraine" (Resoil Foundation, 18 April 2025) https://resoilfoundation.org/en/environment/ukraine-war-contaminated-soil/ accessed 20 August 2025.

45 "Ukraine: Impact" (The Monitor) https://the-monitor.org/country-profile/ukraine/impact?year=2023# accessed 20 August 2025.

indirect loss to agriculture is much greater compared to the direct physical damage to cropland.[46]

Apart from this, battlefields change the original landscape of a geographical region. Large vehicles, their tracks, trenches, fortifications, etc., affect the natural structure of the soil.[47]

Risk to Biodiversity and Protected Areas

Ukraine is often called the "Green Heart" of Europe, owing to its rich biodiversity; however, the conflict has caused serious damage to the biodiversity and unique system of the country, like its grasslands, wetlands, forests, etc., which is home to about 70,000 species of flora and fauna.[48] Around 30 percent of the protected areas in Ukraine, including 23 national parks and reserves, have been affected by the use of heavy machinery, wildfires, shelling, deforestation, landmines, scattered debris, etc.[49]

Many of the species in Ukraine are at a greater risk of extinction now because of the severe impact of the conflict on the environment. Various animals and birds, like the Eurasian brown bears, the Eurasian lynx, the European Bison, etc., are at risk as their conservation efforts were affected soon after the beginning of the conflict.[50] Black Sea dolphins are also at risk.[51] The conflict has forced a large number of animals to leave their habitats, and the disruption of these habitats is likely to take a toll on their populations.

46 M. Nehrey and R. Finger, "Assessing the Initial Impact of the Russian Invasion on Ukrainian Agriculture: Challenges, Policy Responses, and Future Prospects" *Heliyon*, vol. 10 (2024), pp. 1–20 at p. 7.

47 Hryhorczuk et al, supra note 4, 6.

48 B. Vykhor and A. Beckmann, *Assessing the Environmental Impacts of the War in Ukraine* (WWF CEE, 13 June 2022) https://wwfcee.org/our-offices/ukraine/assessing-the-environmental-impacts-of-the-war-in-ukraine accessed 20 August 2025.

49 "New Coordination Center to Assess Environmental Impacts of the War on Ukraine" (UNDP, 10 March 2023) https://www.undp.org/ukraine/press-releases/new-coordination-center-assess-environmental-impacts-war-ukraine accessed 20 August 2025.

50 C. Howell, "War Threatens Ukraine's Wildlife" (Conservation Frontlines, April 2022) https://conservationfrontlines.org/2022/04/war-threatens-ukraines-wildlife/ accessed 20 August 2025.

51 E. Hauser, "In the Black Sea Porpoises and Dolphins Struggle to Survive Year of Russian Invasion" (Deep Sea Reporter, 7 August 2025) https://www.deepseareporter.com/in-the-black-sea-porpoises-and-dolphins-struggle-to-survive-year-of-russian-invasion/ accessed 20 August 2025.

Additionally, international conservation sites are also affected, as reports indicate that the ecological character of 16 occupied Ramsar Sites has undergone change, and around 15 others have potentially undergone change.[52]

Radiation Risks

Nuclear and radiological risks have always been one of the most serious environmental threats during any conflict. The Zaporizhzhia Nuclear Power Plant (ZNPP) became the first civilian nuclear facility to be directly affected during the Russia-Ukraine conflict.[53] The plant had quite frequently been enduring shelling, power outages, and disruptions in its cooling-water supply.[54] Although safety measures were taken to lower the chances of any disaster, they cannot eliminate the possibility of danger associated with it. Reports suggesting the shutdown of all six reactors within the plant, and the destruction of the Kakhovka Dam, further intensified the risks by reducing the amount of water needed for the reactors' cooling, thereby leaving the ZNPP solely dependent on the limited resources available to it.[55]

It is said that this scenario represents a low-probability but high-consequence risk, whereby even with reactors being shut down, the ongoing shelling could trigger accidents.[56] In case of any accidents in these nuclear plants

52 O. Vasyliuk and E. Simonov, "Ramsar wetlands under fire in Ukraine" (Ukraine War Environmental Consequences Work Group, 2 September 2025) https://uwecworkgroup.info/ramsar-wetlands-under-fire-in-ukraine/#:~:text=On%20March%2010%2C%202023%2C%20Ukraine,six%20wetlands%20of%20international%20importance. accessed 20 August 2025.

53 A. Zurita, "The Zaporizhzhia Nuclear Power Plant Taken as Military Target: Legal and Technical Global Challenges" (CIDOB, April 2024) https://www.cidob.org/en/publications/zaporizhzhia-nuclear-power-plant-taken-military-target-legal-and-technical-global accessed 22 August 2025.

54 A. J. Nelson and C. Norteman, "What to do about the Zaporizhzhia Nuclear Power Plant" (Brookings, 23 March 2023) https://www.brookings.edu/articles/what-to-do-about-the-zaporizhzhia-nuclear-power-plant/#:~:text=The%20power%20to%20the%20plant,restart%2C%20which%20comes%20with%20risk. accessed 22 August 2025.

55 "Update 162 – IAEA Director General Statement on Situation in Ukraine" (IAEA, 7 June 2023) https://www.iaea.org/newscenter/pressreleases/update-162-iaea-director-general-statement-on-situation-in-ukraine#:~:text=Director%20General%20Grossi%20will%20travel,shutdown%20state%20of%20the%20reactors. accessed 22 August 2025.

56 E. Lyman, "An Attack on the Zaporizhzhia Nuclear Plant Could Still Be Catastrophic" (Union of Concerned Scientists, 7 July 2023) https://blog.ucsusa.org/edwin-lyman/

could lead to a major radiological release that can spread through wind and weather, contaminating farmland, water bodies, and water systems, etc., affecting people across Ukraine and potentially reaching up to several neighbouring countries.[57]

Apart from the nuclear sites, other industrial sites in Ukraine are also at risk of getting targeted during the conflict, and any damage to these sites could release dangerous pollutants that spread beyond Ukraine's borders. As long as the occupation of Russia remains over ZNPP, these threats remain quite serious, making this not just a safety issue for Ukraine, but a cross-border environmental and public health concern with long-term effects.

Impact on the Climate

The conflict has led to major impacts on the climate. In the first year of conflict, around 39.6 million tons of CO_2 were released, where 21.9 million tons came directly from the fighting, and 17.7 million tons came from fires.[58] The occupation of Russia and continuous attacks between the two countries have severely damaged the clean energy sector of Ukraine. As per the Ministry of Energy in Ukraine, many wind and solar plants have been disabled or occupied.[59] The conflict has actually reversed Ukraine's progress towards renewable energy and forced the country to use resources diverted from its climate goals, highlighting its backwardness in achieving the global shift to clean energy.

Health Concerns

As civilians and emergency workers are exposed to many environmental dangers during the conflict, it has created serious health problems. The bombings, missile strikes, wildfires, etc., release harmful gases and smoke, and the destruction of infrastructures like homes, factories, schools, and

---

an-attack-on-the-zaporizhzhia-nuclear-plant-could-still-be-catastrophic/ accessed 22 August 2025.

57 Hryhorczuk et al, supra note 4, 7.

58 M. Shrestha, "The War in Ukraine is Fuelling the Climate Crisis" (Development and Cooperation, 1 August 2023) https://www.dandc.eu/en/article/russias-war-aggression-causing-significant-greenhouse-gas-emissions-and-revealing#:~:text=Direct%20fighting%20and%20military%20transport,14.6%20million%20tonnes%20of%20CO2. accessed 22 August 2025.

59 L. Limb, "Ukraine's Green Fightback: Wind Farms, Solar Schools and Counting the Cost of 'Destroying Nature'" (Euro News, 23 February 2024) https://www.euronews.com/green/2024/02/24/ukraines-green-fightback-wind-farms-solar-schools-and-counting-the-cost-of-destroying-nature. accessed 22 August 2025.

other buildings leaves behind debris polluted with asbestos, heavy metals, and cement dust. As a result of this, soil and water are also contaminated, mostly affecting people in rural areas where they often depend on groundwater.[60] These hazards, followed by the problem of displacement, loss of livelihood, lack of necessities, like medicines and treatments, etc., lead to both physical and mental health problems.[61]

Many studies highlight the likelihood that the rates of diseases like cancer.[62] And mental health struggles will increase extensively.[63] It is said that similar to the Camp Lejeune case in the U.S, where, because of water contamination, people had to suffer for decades of illness, and required huge medical and financial support, the communities in most affected areas in Ukraine may also need long-term care from specialists in environmental health and toxicology, making public health recovery one of the most difficult and costly challenges of the war.[64]

Legal Framework Protecting the Environment during Armed Conflict

International Humanitarian Law

IHL is the branch of law that governs the conduct of parties during armed conflicts, ensuring the protection of civilians and civilian objects. Moreover, if there is a conflict between IHL rules and those of other branches of international law during war, the rules of IHL take precedence.[65]

60 Hryhorczuk et al, supra note 4.

61 "Three Years of War: Rising Demand for Mental Health Support, Trauma Care and Rehabilitation" (WHO, 24 February 2025) https://www.who.int/europe/news/item/24-02-2025-three-years-of-war-rising-demand-for-mental-health-support-trauma-care-and-rehabilitation#:~:text=Shifting%20health%20needs,both%20physical%20and%20psychological%20recovery. accessed 22 August 2025.

62 C. Caglevic et al, "The Armed Conflict and the Impact on Patients with Cancer in Ukraine: Urgent Considerations" *American Society of Clinical Oncology*, vol. 8 (2022), pp. 1–7 at p. 2.

63 A. Kurapov et al, "The Mental Health Impact of the Ongoing Russian-Ukrainian War 6 Months After the Russian Invasion of Ukraine" *Frontiers in Psychiatry*, (2023), pp. 1–9 at p. 2.

64 E. Z. Stakhiv, *Ecocide in Ukraine – The Toxic Legacy of Russia's War* (Testimony before the Commission on Security and Cooperation, Helsinki Commission, U.S. Congress, 16 July 2024).

65 M. O. Medvedeva, M. M. Hnatovskiy and T. R. Korotkiy, *International Humanitarian Law: Handbook on International Legal Protection of the Environment during Armed Conflict* (Feniks, Odesa 2016).

Article 35(3) of Additional Protocol I to the Geneva Conventions provides that "*It is prohibited to employ methods or means of warfare which are intended, or may be expected, to cause widespread, long-term and severe damage to the natural environment.*"[66] This provision talks about both the aspects, i.e., weapons that are used in conflicts as a means, as well as the tactics or strategies that are used as methods in a conflict. This provision doesn't apply only in those circumstances where the end goal is to cause environmental damage, but it is equally applicable when such damage is foreseeable as a consequence of military action.

The threshold for prohibited environmental damage set by this provision is high, as the terms "widespread, long-term, and severe" are used.[67] Furthermore, it strikes a balance between military necessity and environmental protection. Although IHL permits attacks on legitimate military targets, it prohibits using methods that may cause unnecessary or disproportionate harm to the natural environment. This requires a proportionality assessment, weighing the anticipated military advantage against the potential environmental damage.

Recognising the value of the natural environment, Article 55 provides that all feasible care should be taken by the parties involved in an armed conflict to avoid causing widespread, long-term, and severe damage to the natural environment.[68] The scope of this provision extends beyond incidental environmental protection, thereby explicitly prohibiting attacks on the environment for the purpose of causing harm. It also addresses the principle of proportionality and precaution by providing that even at times of targeting legitimate military objectives, parties to a conflict must plan and conduct operations in a way that minimises environmental harm. Article 55 also says that the environment cannot be attacked as a form of revenge. Moreover, the presence of civilians in an area doesn't mean that it can't be targeted in war; nonetheless, soldiers must take all possible steps to protect the environment. This helps reduce damage to nature and prevents harm to people who depend on it for survival.

66 Protocol Additional to the Geneva Conventions of 12 August 1949, and Relating to the Protection of Victims of International Armed Conflicts (Protocol I), Adopted 8 June 1977, UNTS 1125, UN Doc. A/CONF.183/2, art 35(3).

67 M. Bothe et al, "International Law Protecting the Environment During Armed Conflict: Gaps and Opportunities" *International Review of the Red Cross*, vol. 92(879) (2010), pp. 569–592 at p. 575.

68 Additional Protocol I, art 55.

Article 54 emphasises protecting the necessities of life, like food, water, crops, etc., which are extremely significant and essential for the survival of civilians; thus, the parties involved in conflict cannot deliberately destroy or remove them to starve people or weaken the enemy.[69]

Structures like dams, nuclear power plants, etc., are protected under Article 56, as attacking them could be extremely dangerous, as it may cause flooding, radiation exposure, or massive explosions. Even if these installations are being used for military purposes, attacks on them are prohibited as they would create catastrophic and indiscriminate effects that would extend far beyond the battlefield.[70]

Various customary IHL rules also highlight the aspect of environmental protection. Rule 43 talks about the general protection of the environment, wherein it establishes that protecting the environment from widespread, long-term, and severe damage is part of customary international law, meaning it applies to all states and all types of conflicts.[71] Rule 44 prohibits any kind of attack on forests, agricultural areas, water installations, and similar important resources, when the main aim is to damage the environment itself.[72] Additionally, Rule 45 restricts the poisoning of the environment by way of contamination of rivers, lakes, or through any other medium, as its impact would be both indiscriminate and disproportionate.[73]

International Criminal Law

The Rome Statute also recognises intentional environmental harm as a war crime under some specific circumstances under Article 8(2)(b)(iv).[74] It specifically covers international armed conflicts and criminalises any attack that would knowingly cause widespread, long-term, and severe damage to the natural environment, exceeding the military advantage gained, thereby highlighting the principle of proportionality under the IHL.

69 Additional Protocol I, art 55.

70 Additional Protocol I, art 56.

71 J.M. Henckaerts and L. Doswald-Beck, *Customary International Humanitarian Law: Volume I – Rules* (Cambridge University Press, 2005) Rule 43.

72 Ibid, Rule 44.

73 Ibid, Rule 45.

74 *Rome Statute of the International Criminal Court*, adopted 17 July 1998, entered into force 1 July 2002, 2187 UNTS 90, art 8(2)(b)(iv).

Article 8(2)(e)(iv) talks about non-international armed conflicts and doesn't explicitly mention the environment; nevertheless, it focuses on the protection of civilians and civilian objects.[75] This provision restricts any intentional attacks against any building which is dedicated to "*religion, education, art, science, or charitable purposes, historic monuments, hospitals, and places where the sick and wounded are collected*", so long as they are not military objectives.[76]

International Environmental Law

The ENMOD Convention was adopted in 1976 and entered into force in 1978. Article I(1) sets out to prohibit States from deliberately manipulating the environment as a method of warfare or hostility.[77] It provides that it is the obligation of every State that has signed and agreed to the Convention not to use the environment as a weapon in war or conflicts in any way that can cause widespread, long-term, or severe damage to the environment of any other State Party.[78]

The provisions of the said convention strictly ban using any environmental modification technique to manipulate any natural processes, when the intention behind such action is to cause destruction, damage, or injury to another State. No State can use any Environmental Modification Techniques to trigger earthquakes, tsunamis, volcanic eruptions, or alter weather patterns to cause prolonged rainfall or drought, manipulate the climate, or interfere with the ozone layer or outer space environment.

Applicability of the Legal Farmwork during the Armed Conflict

The importance of the IHL during the Russia-Ukraine conflict is quite clear since both countries have signed the Geneva Convention as well as the Additional Protocol I, making these rules directly relevant to how they carry out their military operations.[79] The aim of the IHL extends

75 Ibid, art 8(2)(e)(iv).

76 Ibid.

77 *Convention on the Prohibition of Military or Any Other Hostile Use of Environmental Modification Techniques*, adopted 10 December 1976, entered into force 5 October 1978, 1108 UNTS 151, art I.

78 Ibid.

79 Human Rights Watch, "Russia-Ukraine: International Law, Occupation, Armed Conflict, and Human Rights" (HRW, 23 February 2022) https://www.hrw.org/news/2022/02/23/russia-ukraine-international-law-occupation-armed-conflict-and-human-rights accessed 24 August 2025.

beyond regulating attacks and providing protection to civilians and other noncombatants from the hazards of the conflict.[80] It also addresses the aspect of environmental damage during conflicts.[81] The Nova Kakhovka Dam destruction is one such incident that can be discussed. Considering the provisions of IHL, the dam is treated as a work containing dangerous force, and its destruction caused massive flooding, large-scale displacement of people, with the destruction of various forest and agricultural areas, resulting in one of the most serious cases of water pollution and ecological damage in Europe.[82] This incident highlights the importance of having environmental protection provisions under IHL and raises serious questions about the lawfulness of the damage caused under the principles of distinction, proportionality, and precautions.

The ENMOD Convention is also important in this regard, as Russia and Ukraine are parties to this Convention, whose main objective is to ban the use of any environmental modification techniques for triggering natural disasters for military purposes and the use of the environment as a weapon in conflicts.[83] Nonetheless, its application in terms of this particular conflict is quite debatable, as it is to be specified whether destroying infrastructure like dams and causing massive flooding as a result of it, could be seen as a kind of deliberate environmental manipulation.[84] Although the scope of ENMOD is narrower than that of IHL, it still provides an additional legal framework.

The Rome Statute becomes fully applicable in the Russia-Ukraine conflict, with Ukraine becoming a party to it at the beginning of 2025, allowing the Court to investigate and prosecute alleged war crimes and environmental destruction, although Russia is not a State Party.[85] Earlier, although Ukraine

80 Ibid.

81 "The Environment and Warfare" (ICRC) https://www.icrc.org/en/law-and-policy/environment-and-warfare accessed 24 August 2025.

82 M. Tignino, T. Kebebew and C. Pellaton, "International Law and Accountability for the Nova Kakhovka Dam Disaster" (Lieber Institute, 13 July 2023) https://lieber.westpoint.edu/international-law-accountability-nova-kakhovka-dam-disaster/ accessed 24 August 2025.

83 J. Jarose, "A Sleeping Giant? The ENMOD Convention as a Limit on Intentional Environmental Harm in Armed Conflict and Beyond" *American Journal of International Law*, vol. 118 (2024), pp. 468–509 at p. 469.

84 Ibid, 506.

85 "Ukraine Becomes the 125th State Party to the ICC Rome Statute" (Coalition for the International Criminal Court, 22 January 2025) https://www.coalitionfortheicc.org/

had not ratified the Rome Statute, it had accepted ICC's jurisdiction over crimes committed on its territory twice, i.e., in 2014 and 2015.[86] The applicability of the Rome Statute is evident through various incidents that have caused both civilian and environmental harm. The ICC could investigate the Nova Kakhovka Dam destruction, as it had foreseeable consequences impacting human lives as well as the natural surroundings, and took place in Ukrainian soil. There have also been attacks near nuclear facilities, like the drone strike near the South Ukraine Nuclear Power Plant.[87] And the attack on the Chernobyl Radiation Shelter structure in 2025.[88] Although these attacks didn't result in the immediate release of radiation, nonetheless, it does highlight a serious risk associated with the safety of both humans and the environment, further highlighting the importance of the ICC to exercise jurisdiction over such acts that threaten critical infrastructure with large-scale environmental consequences. Reports by Amnesty International and other organisations have documented large-scale destruction of energy facilities, water supply systems, and industrial plants, showing the Statute's relevance for holding individuals accountable for actions that harm civilians and the environment.[89]

As per the Ukrainian authorities and other international observers, the Russian military actions have caused serious harm to the environment,

---

ukraine-becomes-125th-ICC-state-party#:~:text=Ukraine%20signed%20the%20Rome%20Statute,to%20join%20the%20ICC%20Statute. accessed 24 August 2025.

86 C. Kmiotek, "Ukraine Ratifies Rome Statute but Must Address Concerns Over ICC Jurisdiction" (Atlantic Council, 21 August 2024) https://www.atlanticcouncil.org/blogs/ukrainealert/ukraine-ratifies-rome-statute-but-must-address-concerns-over-icc-jurisdiction/ accessed 24 August 2025.

87 Reuters, "IAEA Says Drone Detonated Near Ukraine's South Ukraine Nuclear Plant" (Reuters, 25 September 2025) https://www.reuters.com/world/europe/iaea-says-drone-detonated-near-ukraines-south-ukraine-nuclear-plant-2025-09-25/ accessed 25 September 2025.

88 "Watch: Russian Drone Strikes Chernobyl Radiation Shelter; Zelenskyy Calls Out 'Terrorist Threat'" (Times of India, 15 February 2025) https://timesofindia.indiatimes.com/world/europe/watch-russian-drone-strikes-chernobyl-radiation-shelter-zelenskyy-calls-out-terrorist-threat/articleshow/118244799.cms accessed 25 September 2025.

89 "Russia/Ukraine: Latest Massive Missile Strike on Critical Infrastructure is a War Crime" (Amnesty International, 28 November 2024) https://www.amnesty.org/en/latest/news/2024/11/russia-ukraine-latest-massive-missile-strike-on-critical-infrastructure-is-a-war-crime/ accessed 25 September 2025.

with 8,000 registered cases of environmental destruction.[90] These large-scale effects, along with attacks on civilian buildings, show that the Rome Statute can be used to hold people responsible for harming both people and the environment.

ILC Draft Principles on Protection of the Environment in Relation to Armed Conflicts

The principles in the draft emphasis the importance of protecting the environment before, during, and after wars and in situations of one country's occupation over the other.[91] When the environment is affected, it takes a toll on the health of people, affects jobs, and cultural heritage, which highlights that the protection of nature is directly related to human safety. The principles provide that it is the responsibility of the States to come up with appropriate laws and take proper actions to prevent any environmental damage.[92]

Before a conflict begins, States are encouraged to set up special protected areas that are places of rich environmental, ecological, or cultural value, and which will be ensured extra protection during conflict situations.[93] Importance is also given to the lands of indigenous people under the draft principles.[94] Environmental considerations should be integrated into military planning, peacekeeping operations, and the relocation of populations during conflicts.[95]

The principles provide that during conflicts, the existing rules of IHL should be expanded.[96] They prohibit the use of any such methods of warfare that are likely to cause widespread, long-term or serious environmental damage and restrict any kind of attack that damages the environment, except when it

90 S. Vakulina, "Russian Environmental Attacks in Ukraine caused €85 Billion in Damage, Kyiv Estimates" (Euronews, 4 June 2025) https://www.euronews.com/2025/06/04/russian-environmental-attacks-in-ukraine-caused-85-billion-in-damage-kyiv-estimates accessed 25 September 2025.

91 International Law Commission, *Draft Principles on the Protection of the Environment in Relation to Armed Conflicts* (adopted 2022) Principle 1.

92 Ibid, Principle 3.

93 Ibid, Principle 4.

94 Ibid, Principle 5.

95 Ibid, Principles 6, 7, 8.

96 Ibid, Principle 13.

is a legitimate military target.[97] The principles also strengthen the principles under the IHL, namely, the principle of distinction, proportionality, and precautions.[98] It also bans reprisals against the environment and the looting of natural resources.[99] The use of environmental modification techniques, for deliberate attempts to change the weather pr ecosystem for hostile uses, is also prohibited under the principles.[100] The occupying powers must ensure to protect the environment of the occupied territories in accordance with applicable international law and follow the local environmental laws, make proper use of the natural resources sustainably, and avoid any activity that can cause cross-border environmental harm.[101]

After the conflicts, the draft principles highlight the importance of restoration and cooperation.[102] The peace agreements should include environmental recovery measures. The States and organisations are encouraged to actively share information necessary for ensuring the post-conflict assessment and timely rebuilding process.[103] The belligerent parties are expected to remove any remnants of conflict, like explosives and other toxic materials, and ensure compensation and relief for the environmental damage that has been done in the course of the conflict.[104]

Thus, the Draft Principles combine binding rules of existing law with aspirational elements like corporate due diligence, pre-designation of protected areas, and post-conflict remediation frameworks, creating a hybrid system that links IHL and IEL, with the main goal to ensure environmental protection at all stages of armed conflicts and provide guidance to the development of international law.

Gaps and Challenges pertaining Legal Framework Protecting the Environment during Armed Conflict

IHL aims to minimise the effects of armed conflicts, including the harm caused to the environment during such conflicts. The key provisions

97 Ibid.

98 Ibid, Principle 14.

99 Ibid, Principles 15, 16.

100 Ibid, Principle 17.

101 Ibid, Principles 19, 20, 21.

102 Ibid, Principles 22, 24.

103 Ibid, Principle 23.

104 Ibid, Principles 26, 25.

under AP I to the Geneva Conventions are Articles 35 and 55, which set a very high standard or threshold for holding someone accountable for causing environmental harm, thereby making its enforcement difficult.[105] Various provisions under the IHL only ensure indirect protection to the environment, focusing more on civilian safety and property. Furthermore, the lack of precedents and effective monitoring systems further weakens enforcement, while customary principles like distinction, necessity, and proportionality offer limited environmental safeguards during the chaos of war.[106]

Article 8 of the Rome Statute acknowledges certain environmental damages as a war crime under certain circumstances; however, its application is quite limited owing to the requirement of proof that damage needs to be "widespread, long-term, and severe," which leaves many cases out of environmental harm.[107] There are also limits to the Court's jurisdiction, as it can only act if the case involves a State Party to the Statute, the nationality of the accused is of a State Party, or if the UN Security Council makes a referral, which can constrain accountability.[108] Additionally, collecting reliable evidence in active conflict zones exacerbates the issue of accountability. Moreover, the larger part of Article 8 mainly focuses on attacks against civilians and civilian property, treating environmental damage as a secondary issue. The lack of past cases prosecuting environmental war crimes further reduces the Statute's effectiveness as a deterrent.[109]

105 R. Argren, "The Obligation to Prevent Environmental Harm in Relation to Armed Conflict" *International Review of the Red Cross*, vol. 105(924) (2023), pp. 1208–1226 at p. 1214.

106 L. Kong and Y. Zhao, "Remedying the Environmental Impacts of War: Challenges and Perspectives for Full Reparation" *International Review of the Red Cross*, vol. 105(924) (2023), pp. 1441–1462 at p. 1457.

107 B. Leebaw, "Scorched Earth: Environmental War Crimes and International Justice" *Perspectives on Politics*, vol. 12(4) (2014), pp. 770–788 at p. 788.

108 M. Vinicius, "The Role of the International Criminal Court in Preventing Crimes Against Humanity and Rebuilding Societies Emerging from Conflict" (Policy Center for the New South, April 2025) https://www.policycenter.ma/publications/role-international-criminal-court-preventing-crimes-against-humanity-and-rebuilding#:~:text=Unlike%20its%20ad%2Dhoc%20predecessors,of%20societies%20emerging%20from%20conflict accessed 25 September 2025.

109 A. Al-Dlabeeh et al, "The Role of International Criminal Law in Violations of the Environment During Armed Conflict" *Journal of Environmental Management and Tourism*, vol. 13(3) (2022), pp. 643–648 at p. 647.

Regarding the ENMOD Convention, although its focus is on intentional environmental manipulation, which is undoubtedly very important, nonetheless, the scope of it is narrow.[110] The threshold for accountability is also high, with no permanent system for enforcement or monitoring.[111] On top of this, confirming that such techniques were used deliberately is both technically complex and politically sensitive, which makes it even harder to hold violators accountable.

Conclusion and Suggestions

The Russia-Ukraine conflict clearly highlights how the environment becomes a silent casualty in times of conflict. The environment suffers extensive damage during times of conflict; however, it is not treated with the same urgency as the protection of human life and infrastructure. The widespread ecological harm is visible through the contamination of water resources, soil degradation, wild forest fires, and industrial and air pollution. Various incidents of the destruction of crucial infrastructures, including attacks near nuclear power plants, demonstrate how these attacks can trigger catastrophic environmental consequences, which may worsen humanitarian crises and result in long-term damage to ecosystems.

Although IHL, ENMOD Convention, and the Rome Statute recognise the need to safeguard the environment during armed conflict, some significant gaps and challenges affect the applicability and enforcement of the relevant provisions. It is mostly the high threshold for accountability and the absence of a strong enforcement mechanism that limit the effectiveness. Moreover, the lack of precedents in relation to accountability under the relevant provisions also highlights that environmental crimes often remain under-prioritised in the pursuit of justice, overshadowed by direct human rights violations.

Thus, it is the need of the hour to rethink how international law addresses environmental protection in times of conflict, as without stronger norms, monitoring systems, and accountability mechanisms, the environment will remain a neglected victim of conflict.

Apropos suggestions, the legal framework needs to be strengthened by lowering the threshold set for environmental damage under IHL, ENMOD, and the Rome Statute. Also, the definition of war crime should be extended to explicitly include severe environmental destruction arising

110 Jarose, supra note 83.

111 Ibid.

from both intentional and reckless acts, or active efforts can be made towards recognising ecocide as the fifth core international crime. Apart from that, an independent body should be established with the obligation to monitor, record, and investigate environmental damage caused by conflict. Additionally, the ICC's jurisdiction may be strengthened to prioritise the prosecution of environmental crimes committed in armed conflicts. Further, all States should integrate environmental safeguards into military training. Lastly, there is a need for stronger cooperation with NGOs and other international organisations to ensure rapid responses to environmental crises during armed conflicts.

Environmental Damage in Non-International Armed Conflict

Parineet Kaur

Introduction

Environment has been a mute victim of every armed conflict, be it an international or non-international. The actions taken by the military or non-state actors during the course of armed conflict have, through the ages, led to significant environmental destruction. The natural environment, during the course of conflict, could be intentionally targeted or manipulated to serve as a weapon. Environmental degradation and exploitation can thus be both a cause and a consequence of armed conflict. In this chapter, the environmental damage during non-international armed conflict (NIAC) has been analysed.

After the Second World War, the NIAC has been much more common than international armed conflict. According to the Peace Research Institute Oslo, there were 74 non-state armed conflicts in 2024.[1] The majority of NIACs do not in fact remain confined within the borders of a single country, but eventually affect neighbouring countries in some way.[2] During

1 *Conflict Trends: A Global Overview, 1946–2024*, Peace Research Institute Oslo (PRIO), 2025, p. 24, available at: <https://static.poder360.com.br/2025/06/relatorio-prio-conflict-trends-divulgado-em-junho-de_2025.pdf> accessed on 26 October 2025.

2 *Stockholm International Peace Research Institute (SIPRI) Yearbook 2012 (Oxford University Press, Oxford, 2012).* The early 1990s saw the outbreak of fighting in Rwanda, which by April 1994 had expanded into Democratic republic of Congo (DRC) and resulted in a stream of refugees pouring into gorilla habitat. Indeed, approximately 50 percent of Rwanda's civilian populations were displaced during this conflict, of which 860,000 refugees were concentrated in the vicinity of Virunga National Park. Shortly after the influx of Rwandan refugees in 1994/1995 into DRC, came the 1996 war between the armed forces of DRC and the rebel movement of Kabila, backed by Angola, Rwanda and Uganda. Subsequently fighting again broke out in 1998 between

and following armed conflict, an armed and lawless society can have both direct and indirect impacts on the environment. These impacts occur for subsistence, strategic, or commercial reasons, and often have political, social, and economic root causes. The NIAC have also contributed to severe famine and to rendering land unusable through the wholesale distribution of antipersonnel landmines and ERWs. During NIAC, in a territory, where the nation state has been weak, non-state actors remain major culprits in the destruction of the natural environment and exhaustion of natural resources.[3] Armed conflict between competing entities within a state has significant impacts on both the human societies involved and environment. Unfortunately, armed conflict is particularly prevalent in areas important for biodiversity. For instance, Colombia is one of the countries with the greatest biodiversity of the world and harbours ecosystems of critical importance. Columbia has faced severe ecological challenges, mainly due to unsustainable exploitation of natural resources and the devastating effects of protracted armed conflicts. The conflict has resulted in increased deforestation, habitat destruction, and loss of biodiversity, directly linking violence to ecological degradation.[4]

Over 80 percent of the major armed conflicts in the second half of the 20th century happened in the biodiversity hotspots, areas that contain the entire populations of more than half of all species of plants and more than 42 percent of all vertebrates. Two-thirds of the world's 34 hotspots have experienced armed conflict warfare during that time.[5] Hotspots are also characterised as being under particular threat because poverty in the poor countries where hotspots are mostly found puts great pressure on the resources found in the natural environment. Armed conflict in the hotspots makes conservation even more challenging, as refugees from the

---

Rwandan and Ugandan troops and the DRC army. The streams of refugees that were displaced during these conflicts led to uncontrolled firewood harvesting, and increased poaching in the Virungas National Park and the death of few silverback mountain gorillas, and disruption of natural animal migration patterns. UNEP World Conservation Monitoring Centre, October 2003, pp. 5-6.

3 Alyson J.K. Bailes, *Global Security Governance: A World of Change and Challenge, Stockholm International Peace Research Institute (SIPRI) Yearbook 2005* (Oxford University Press, Oxford, 2005), pp. 1–27.

4 Carlos A. Sierra *et al.*, "Monitoring Ecological Change During Rapid Socio-Economic and Political Transitions: Colombian Ecosystems in the Post-Conflict Era", *Environmental Science & Policy*, vol. 76 (2017), pp. 40–41.

5 T. Hanson, T.M. Brooks, G.A.B. da Fonseca, M. Hoffmann, J.F. Lamoreux, G. Machlis, C.G. Mittermeier, R.A. Mittermeier and J.D. Pilgrim, "Warfare in Biodiversity Hotspots", *Conservation Biology*, vol. 23 (2009), pp. 578–587.

fighting often turn to the forests for food and building materials, putting additional pressure on biodiversity.[6]

Environmental Damage in Non-International Armed Conflict

Since the last three decades or so, armed conflicts in important habitats for wildlife have affected numerous countries. A partial list includes Afghanistan, Angola, Bosnia, Colombia, the Democratic Republic of Congo, Cambodia, Central African Republic, Colombia, Guatemala, India, Indonesia, Liberia, Mexico, Myanmar, Nepal, Pakistan, Peru, the Philippines, Sierra Leone, Senegal, Sri Lanka, the Solomon Islands, Sudan and South-Sudan. Armed conflict in some of these countries has often taken the form of low-level conflicts that continued for years, with the same territory changing hands several times. In addition to the tragic toll on civilian populations, such conflicts have had considerable environmental impacts: Opposing armies engage in deforestation and defoliation, hunt wildlife for food, lay thousands of antipersonnel land mines, and clash over valuable natural resources (such as timber and diamonds) to finance their arms purchases. The biggest tragedy is that during NIAC, ecological assaults in combat zones are often kept secret or widely ignored, resulting in more devastating humanitarian and environmental harm.

There is hardly any scientific literature on the effects of NIAC on the environment. It is generally limited to the sub-Saharan African continent[7] and there to the effects of conflict on large mammals such as primates, elephants and rhinoceroses, and on the effects on national parks. Due to these limitations, study under this chapter is confined to three regions, covering 13 situations in the world.[8]

6 Jeffery A. McNeely and Susan A. Mainka, *Conservation for a New Era: Conservation and Armed Conflict* (International Union for Conservation of Nature (IUCN), Switzerland, 2009), available at: <http://data.iucn.org/dbtw-wpd/html/2009-026/section11.html> accessed on 11 October 2025.

7 Africa is the oldest continent on Earth. The array of ecosystems and organisms contained within its forests, rivers, deserts, wetlands, mountains, and savannas, is unequalled in the world. The human species evolved at the margins of the equatorial forests of Africa, and people have substantially influenced African ecosystems for hundreds of thousands of years. The civil wars and internal strife's have been responsible for more African forest destruction in the past 60 years than in the preceding 10,000.

8 The destruction of the natural environment of Afghanistan has been extensive during the international and the non-international armed conflict. It started after the Soviet occupation of Afghanistan in 1979 and continues even now.

Angola

The long civil war in Angola from 1975 to 2002 and the continuous hostilities among rival groups that have persisted since then, have brought with them severe consequences on forests and wildlife. Deforestation is considered one of the major environmental results of this state of violence and devastation. Angola remains one of the most heavily landmine-contaminated countries in the world. The continued presence of landmines is a significant impediment to Angola achieving its potential to host one of the continent's most diverse wildlife populations. The Angolan Government has committed to clearing its landmines by 2025, however, it could not achieve this goal. Angola has some of the world's most important wilderness and the country has the potential to host one of the most diverse wildlife populations on the continent. However, the presence of landmines and other remnants of the civil war render large areas of the country unsafe both for wildlife and for the local people.[9] During the London 2018 Illegal Wildlife Trade Conference, Angola's Minister of the Environment stated that the threat of landmines prevents Angola from developing a wildlife-focused tourism trade that could be helpful in promoting conservation in remote regions of the country.[10] The landmines have robbed Angola of its rich biodiversity, as thousands of animals, including antelopes and elephants, have fallen prey to them. In addition, many subsistence farmers have lost cattle to landmine incidents and are, as a result, forced to kill wildlife in order to avoid starvation. Landmines also restricted the movement of people, as refugees are often unable to return to their homes and farm their land. Many people have lost their lives in attempts to rebuild their farming activities around the landmines. In the past 30 years, about 80,000 Angolans have been killed or maimed by landmines.[11]

9 Christopher Vandome, *Mine Action in Angola: Clearing the Legacies of Conflict to Harness the Potential of Peace* (The Royal Institute of International Affairs, Chatham House, London, 2019), p. 13.

10 Paula Coelho, Statement at the *Illegal Wildlife Trade Conference: London 2018*, during the launch of the Chatham House Africa Programme paper by Christopher Vandome and Alex Vines, *Tackling Illegal Wildlife Trade in Africa* (Chatham House, London, 2018).

11 Srisakdi Charmonman, "A Survey of Landmines in Top Ten Countries with Most Landmines", *International Journal of the Computer, the Internet and Management*, vol. 23, no. 2 (May–August 2015), pp. 49–53.

Central African Republic

The Central African Republic (CAR) is located in the heart of Africa and its rich biodiversity reflects influences from both the east and west of the continent.[12] The topography of the country is largely defined by low-lying and undulating hills, and for this reason, most of the habitat differentiation in the CAR is caused by climate, mainly variations in rainfall. The CAR has four main climate zones, extending from north to south.[13] The CAR's vegetation zones correspond to these climate zones and include Sahelian savanna, consisting of open savannas; Sudanian savanna, consisting of vast grasslands with small groups of trees; Congolian forest-savanna mosaic, which includes wooded savanna and dry, deciduous forest; and Congolian dense forest, ranging from deciduous forest to semi-evergreen and evergreen forest.[14]

During most of the four decades since independence, the CAR remained calm in a region rife with civil unrest and armed conflict. In 1996, members of the CAR army mutinied thrice, demanding payment of back wages and improved benefits and working conditions. The army took to the streets, firing their weapons in the air and looting Bangui's main

12 The CAR's biodiversity is one of the least studied in Africa. It has approximately 700 species of birds and the region of Dzanga-Sangha is one of the most biologically diverse areas in the country. Harris, D. 1994. Interim check-list to the vascular plants of the Dzanga-Sangha Project Area Central African Republic. Unpublished report. *University of Oxford*, p. 31; J.M. Fay, C.A. Spinage, B. Chardonnet and A.A. Green, "Central African Republic", in R. East (ed.), *Antelopes: Global Survey and Action Plans* (International Union for Conservation of Nature (IUCN), Gland, 1990), pp. 99–109.

13 The Sahelien Zone is characterized by a longer dry season than rainy season, with annual rainfall totaling less than 1,200 mm. This zone is situated in the extreme north of the CAR, and covers about 10 percent of the country. The Sudano-Guinean Zone, which comprises the largest part of the country, is characterized by three to six months of dry season with annual rainfall of around 1,400 mm. The Sudano-Oubangian Zone, which covers most of the southern third of the country, is characterized by a three-month dry season, high humidity throughout the year, and annual rainfall greater than 1,500 mm. The Guinean-Congolese Zone, which is located in the extreme south (around Bangassou and south of Bayanga) is characterized by the absence of a true dry season, with annual rainfall exceeding 1,500 mm. Allard Blom and Jean Yamindou. 2001. *A Brief History of Armed Conflict and its Impact on Biodiversity in the Central African Republic (Biodiversity Support Program, Washington, n.d.), p. 9.*

14 A. Blom and J. Yamindou, "Status of the Protected Areas and Gazetted Forests of the Central African Republic", in A. Blom, *Ecological and Economic Impacts of Gorilla-Based Tourism in Dzanga-Sangha, Central African Republic* (Doctoral Thesis, Department of Environmental Sciences, Tropical Nature Conservation and Vertebrate Ecology Group, Wageningen University, The Netherlands, 2001).

commercial district.[15] The third mutiny had the most serious consequences on the economy, civil society, and the environment. People were forced to evacuate their homes and relocate to areas under the control of their own ethnic affiliation. The precious forest resource of the country remained under threat from years of conflict and widespread criminality. Illegal logging, firewood trafficking for charcoal, and timber trafficking contribute to a deforestation rate of about 1% of total rainforest coverage every year. The most sought-after wood species is *Sapele* – a reddish-brown hardwood widely used for making furniture, decorative veneers and musical instruments.

At the base of the criminal chain are traffickers from the Democratic Republic of the Congo, Congo-Brazzaville, Cameroon, Chad, Sudan and South Sudan While the CAR is the source for illegal logging, wood and products are trafficked through neighbouring countries via several road and waterway transit corridors. The illicit trade is exacerbated by weak law enforcement, porous borders and increasing transnational demand for the country's timber products. Timber trafficking has also been enabled by the CAR's protracted political instability, and has played a major role in funding the conflict that has decimated the country. Illegal timber exports have attracted militias and armed groups seeking funds to buy weapons in a power struggle that has collapsed the state and claimed the lives of thousands of citizens. Illicit timber exports have attracted multiple militias and armed groups seeking funds to buy weapons.[16]

Columbia

The Amazon rainforest in Colombia plays a significant role in regulating global climate by acting as a carbon sink, absorbing large quantities of CO_2, and releasing oxygen. In the recent times, Columbia has faced severe ecological devastation due to protracted armed conflicts. [17] The

15 Allard Blom and Jean Yamindou, *A Brief History of Armed Conflict and its Impact on Biodiversity in the Central African Republic* (Biodiversity Support Programme, Washington, 2001), pp. 11–12.

16 Oluwole Ojewale, "Conflict and Organised Crime are Razing CAR's Rainforests", *Institute for Security Studies*, available at: <https://issafrica.org/iss-today/conflict-and-organised-crime-are-razing-cars-rainforests> accessed on 26 October 2025.

17 Colombians have endured nearly 50 years of conflict as a result of civil war and the evolving organized criminal activity surrounding the drug market. Murders, forced displacement, torture, rape, "disappearances," kidnapping and extortion are part of the social fabric. The drug economy helped drive the expansion of all of the armed groups, which work as security services for the drug trafficking operations or are directly

unregulated exploitation of natural resources has further fuelled illegal activities and deepened socio-economic inequalities in the country.[18] Military operations in the country have led to the devastation of natural habitats, resulting in species displacement and ecosystem disruption, depriving animals of essential resources for survival. Armed conflicts have created conditions that facilitated illegal hunting and wildlife trafficking.[19] The breakdown of governmental structures and law enforcement during conflict allowed poachers to exploit wildlife and supply black markets with ivory, bushmeat, and other animal products. Such illicit trade accelerates the loss of biodiversity. In addition, the proliferation of weapons to non-state actors has exacerbated wildlife hunting, leading to a drastic reduction in the diversity of species.[20] The combined effects of these consequences undermine the overall health of ecosystems, human livelihoods, and the planet's ability to sustain life. According to Jodyvash (2025), the exploitation of natural resources, fuelled by armed conflict, has led to habitat destruction, deforestation, and a significant loss of species, exacerbating ecological imbalances and undermining the resilience of ecosystems.[21]

---

involved in the business. Over the past two decades, hundreds of thousands of people abandoned their homes and possessions because of the violence and were forced from the countryside into urban slums. Of Colombia's 44 million people, more than 3 million are internally displaced persons. Cecilie Rystad, *The Armed Internal Conflict in Colombia and the Peace Process with FARC-EP and the Colombian Government: A Case Study on the Work of the Security Council Towards Implementing the Colombian Peace Process* (2022–2023).

18 Rebecca M. Bratspies, "Territory is Everything: Afro-Colombian Communities, Human Rights and Illegal Land Grabs", *Colombia Human Rights Law Review*, vol. 4 (2020).

19 Colombia contains 7 percent of the world's mammals (358 species), 6 percent of the world's reptiles, and 10 percent of the world's amphibians. Colombia is also home to about 20 percent of the world's birds (1,721 species), more than any other country in the world. It is estimated that Colombia also has 1,900 species of fish, 970 species of crustaceans, 2,200 types of mollusks, 150 types of coral, and 290 types of starfish (echinoderms). Also see: Luz E. Nagle, "Placing Blame Where Blame is Due: The Culpability of Illegal Armed Groups and Narco-Traffickers in Colombia's Environmental and Human Rights Catastrophes", *William & Mary Environmental Law and Policy Review*, vol. 29 (2004), p. 61.

20 Colby Loucks *et al.*, "Wildlife Decline in Cambodia, 1953–2005: Exploring the Legacy of Armed Conflict", *Conservation Letters*, vol. 2 (2009), p. 82

21 Deforestation destroys the natural habitat of several indigenous species. It is estimated that 52 species of birds and mammals and over 700 species of plants and birds are endangered in Colombia, primarily due to deforestation, including the only big cat in Latin America, the jaguar. Elise Botero, *Coca Production and Climate Change in Colombia* (Earth Centre, Columbia University, New York, 2010); Mohammadreza

Democratic Republic of Congo

The Democratic Republic of Congo (DRC), is the second-largest country in Africa and the 11th-largest in the world. With a population of around 112 million, the DR Congo is the second most populous in Africa. The DRC holds the world's largest deposits of cobalt and tantalum, as well as significant reserves of copper, gold, diamonds, and other minerals (zinc, iron, uranium, etc). DRC possesses more species of birds and mammals than any other African country and is one of the most flora-rich countries on the continent.[22] The DRC harbours large ecosystem diversity and rich biodiversity, consisting of the largest fauna and the second largest flora (after South Africa) on the African continent, and the second largest tropical forest in the world after the Amazon. The forests of DR Congo are known as the "world's second lung." In addition to logging, they provide many livelihood opportunities, including ecotourism, conservation, agriculture and non-timber forest products such as foodstuffs, medicine or cosmetics.

Instability caused by the influx of refugees from Rwanda Civil War led to the First Congo War from 1996-1997. The second Civil war from 1998 to 2003, resulted in the deaths of 5.4 million people and the assassination of the President. Since the early 2000s, there have been more than 100 active armed groups in Congo. However, a peace agreement, brokered by the US, was signed by Rwanda and the DRC on 27 June 2025. The DRC has experienced a trade-off between natural resources of known commercial value and biodiversity of undetermined value during its two civil wars in 1996-1997 and 1998-2003. Despite its abundance in natural resources, it is one of the poorest countries in the world. Local communities in eastern DRC continue to face the double burden of the climate crisis and ongoing violent conflict and insecurity. Armed conflict also exacerbates environmental degradation and vulnerability to climate change, increasing poverty and limiting people's adaptive capacity.[23]

The impact of the mainly Rwandan refugees on the environment in the east DRC has been devastating. If they were accompanied by armed men, roaming refugees forced villagers to feed them or raid their fields. If they

---

Jodyvash, "Armed Conflicts and Their Impact on Biodiversity Preservation in Colombia: A Legal and Ethical Analysis", *Mexican Law Review*, New Series, vol. XVIII, no. 1 (July–December 2025), pp. 25–68.

22 J.A. Sayer, C. Harcourt and N.M. Collins, *The Conservation Atlas of Tropical Forests: Africa* (Macmillan Publishers Ltd, U.K., 1992), p. 288.

23 Katongo Seyuba, *Climate, Peace and Security in Eastern Democratic Republic of the Congo, SIPRI Insights on Peace and Security*, no. 2025/02 (March 2025), p. 20.

were unarmed, local people tried to help them. In all circumstances, refugees substantially increased the pressure of the human population on the available resources. In some instances, this resulted in the local population itself being forced to start moving, mainly towards small towns, or to increase its reliance on fish and wildlife.[24]

DRC's armed conflict led to widespread lawlessness. The environmental damages caused on Kahuzi-Biega National Parks in Congo and Rwanda due to armed conflict and coltan mining are as follows: (i) Forest clearance and use of timber to build camps to accommodate workers. (ii) Forest clearance to expose substrate for mining. (iii) Pollution of streams by silt from the washing process. (iv) Erosion of unprotected earth during rains leading to land-slips. (v) Cutting of firewood for warmth and cooking in camps. (vi) Hunting for animals for bushmeat to feed miners and camp followers. (vii) Animals maimed or dying after escaping from snares. (viii) Debarking of trees to make panning trays for washing coltan. (ix) Cutting of lianas to make a carrying basket for coltan. (x) Disturbance of animals due to large numbers of people residing in and moving through forests. (xi) Silting up of streams likely to kill invertebrates and reduce photosynthesis in aquatic plants. (xii) Reduced productivity of fish stocks in lakes and rivers affected by silt pollution. (xiii) Ecological changes due to loss of keystone species such as elephants and apes. (xiv) Loss of biodiversity: only a small population of elephants, gorillas, okapis, and other endangered species remain. Long-term changes in the watershed due to rapid run-off in deforested areas.[25]

In the DRC all elephant populations suffered during the war of 1995 - 2006. Populations of elephants were severely reduced by armed militias who competed to secure control and monetary off-take of easily extractable natural resources, such as gold, diamonds, and mineral ores, that could be extracted by low input artisanal methods. Saw-wood, charcoal and fisheries were also targets of control and conflict. Key resources included ivory and bushmeat, and African elephants were the most important of these targeted species.

24 A. Biswas and C. Tortajada-Quiroz, "Environmental Impacts of the Rwandan Refugees on Zaire", *Ambio*, vol. 26 (1996), pp. 403–408.

25 Ian Redmond, *Coltan Boom, Gorilla Bust: The Impact of Coltan Mining on Gorillas and Other Wildlife in Eastern Congo* (Dian Fossey Gorilla Fund Europe and the Born Free Foundation, 2001), pp. 9–10.

Ethiopia

Ethiopia has long been recognised for its wealth of natural resources, endemic species, and high biodiversity. Known as one of the longest-running civil wars in African history, the Ethiopia-Eritrea conflict lasted 30 years, primarily because both countries were struggling with a range of internal problems and civil discord. In the mid-1980s Ethiopia experienced a series of devastating droughts and insect plagues that led to widespread crop failures and livestock losses. However, the Government forced uprooting of hundreds of people from the north and their resettlement to the south, the mandatory relocation of homesteads into structured villages, and the strict regulation of peoples' movements and transport. The restriction on peoples' movements and transport, however, left people in many areas desperate for food and other commodities.

In Ethiopia, deforestation on lands adjacent to, and within, certain protected areas resulted in the loss of critical habitat, species isolations, and local species extinctions. Farming on steep slopes increased as well, as land became increasingly scarce and important. Attempts to farm on steep slopes, however, increased the rate of soil erosion and gullying and decreased crop yields, and eventually forced many to seek new farming opportunities on steep slopes at times, thereby exacerbating the deforestation protected-area issue.[26]

The diversion of finances and development energy toward conflict meant that Ethiopia's conservation organisation, and all protected areas, received insufficient funding and lacked in infrastructure and equipment. This contributed to ineffective enforcement of many conservation bylaws and the Government's exclusionary protected-area policy. These dilemmas were dealt with by periodically calling in the military to assist in the removal of those deemed encroachers. Use of the military to remove people angered and alienated the once-legitimate residents to an even greater extent, particularly when they felt their very survival was at stake.

The restriction on people's movement exacerbated deforestation and soil-erosion issues and led to the overgrazing of rangelands throughout Ethiopia. Many significant and widespread environmental changes took

26 Excessive soil erosion resulting from deforestation interfered with the operation of several of Ethiopia's hydro-power schemes and was the reason for repeated nationwide power outages during the rainy season. The decline in water quality throughout Ethiopia has been attributed to unregulated deforestation and soil erosion, as has been the decline in rainfall production and stream flow. These impacts had an effect on Ethiopia's wetlands, fisheries, and overall natural biodiversity.

place due to overgrazing, including shrub-land expansion, an increase in undesirable woody species, soil erosion and a decline in forage quality and quantity. These changes, in turn, exacerbated the exclusionary protected-area policy's settlement-encroachment issue, and were responsible for many similar habitat alterations within Ethiopia's protected areas. In Awash National Park, encroachment and settlement led to the illegal harvest of fuel wood and shelter wood, increased competition between wildlife and livestock, and forced many species to forage elsewhere. There was an increase in illegal hunting and disease transmission as well, which contributed to the decline of wildlife.

Many types of modern weaponry (primarily machine guns) were readily available through Ethiopia's black market during the period of conflict. Unfortunately, easy access to machine guns increased the frequency and intensity of conflict between ethnic groups. Death and injuries increased as a consequence, as did the displacement of entire ethnic groups from disputed lands. The displaced, in turn, sometimes tried to occupy nearby protected areas. Nechisar National Park was occupied for such reasons on several occasions. Because of the easy access to machine guns, hunting increased throughout Ethiopia, in addition to that which took place in most of the country's protected areas.[27] Food, leather, and medicinal products were the primary reasons cited by those caught in the act, in addition to income generation from the sale of ivory.

Iraq-Marsh Arabs

In Iraq, the Mesopotamian marshlands constitute the largest wetland ecosystem in the West Asia. They are a crucial part of intercontinental flyways for migratory birds, support endangered species, and sustain freshwater fisheries, as well as those of the Persian Gulf. In addition to their ecological importance and outstanding natural resources, these marshlands are unique from the global perspective of human heritage. They have been home to indigenous communities for millennia and are regarded as the site of the legendary 'Garden of Eden'. In the early 1970s,

27 Species most vulnerable to hunting during the period of conflict included the Lesser and Greater Kudu (*Tragelaphus strepsiceros*), Common Eland (*Tragelaphus oryx*), Buffalo (*Synercus caffer*), Beisa Oryx (*Oryx gazella*), Soemmerring's Gazelle, Swayne's Hartebeest, Grevy's Zebra, Mountain Nyala, Elephant, Giraffe (*Giraffa camelopardalis*), Hippopotamus (*Hippopotamus amphibius*), Cheetah (*Acinonyx jubatus*), Lion (*Panthera leo*), Spotted Hyena (*Crocuta crocuta*), and jackals (Canis sp.).

the marshlands, consisting of interconnected lakes, mudflats and wetlands, extended over 20,000 sq km of Iraq and Iran.[28]

In 1991, after the First Gulf War, the Marsh Arabs of southern Iraq[29] rose up against the Saddam Hussein government with the US encouragement. However, the rebellion was unsuccessful. Driven to punish their opponents who had sought refuge in the Mesopotamian marshlands, the Iraqi Government launched a massive engineering campaign to drain the second largest wetland system in the Arab world. Huge canals and earthworks were constructed to divert the waters of the Tigris and Euphrates around the marshes and into the Gulf to destroy the lifestyle and culture of the Marsh Arabs.[30] The destruction of the Mesopotamian marshlands has been documented by the UNEP.[31] The drainage of the wetlands was a deliberate and calculated act of genocide and ecocide.[32] The loss of the marshlands

28 *Environment in Iraq: UNEP Progress Report, 2003* (United Nations Environment Programme, Geneva, 2003), pp. 22–24.

29 Before the first Gulf War Southern Mesopotamia held South-western Asia's most extensive wetlands, at the confluence of the Tigris and the Euphrates. For thousands of years these wetlands had been occupied by the ancestors of the people known today as the Marsh Arabs. The culture of the Marsh Arabs, existing in harmony with the marsh environment, was completely dependent on marsh resources: the plants, animals and water of the marshes. The duration of the culture testifies to the sustainability of its uses of those resources. The reeds that grew in the marshes were the primary building material for houses and boats; the fish and waterfowl of the marshes were a primary source of food. The marshes themselves were known to outsiders for their spectacular displays of spring wildflowers.

30 Massive drainage works in southern Iraq in the late 1980s and early 1990s, together with the effects of major upstream damming devastated the wetlands (overall loss of 90%), such that only minor and fragmented parcels remain today. Massive loss and degradation had taken place by 2000, with the greatest change occurring between 1991 and 1995. The central and Al Hammar marshlands had been almost completely destroyed, with 97% and 94% of their respective cover transformed into bare land and salt crusts. The water-filtering role of the marshland had ceased and the remaining drainage canals carried polluted irrigation wastewater directly toward the Gulf, with potentially harmful impacts on local fish resources. *"The Marsh Arabs of Iraq: Do They Want to Go Back in Time?", The Economist (London), 5 June 2002.*

31 While the exact number of deaths and of persons displaced as a result will probably never be known, most sources give numbers of displaced persons between 200,000 and 400,000. *"The Marsh Arabs of Iraq: Do They Want to Go Back in Time?", The Economist (London), 5 June 2002.*

32 Aaron Schwabach, "Ecocide and Genocide in Iraq: International Law, the Marsh Arabs and Environmental Damage in Non-International Conflicts", *The Berkeley Electronic Press*, Paper 35 (2003).

has had a catastrophic impact on biodiversity and wildlife.[33] Today the Mesopotamian wetlands are parched earth crusted with salt.

Nepal

For almost a decade, Nepal suffered the worst kind of armed conflict. The armed uprising by the Maoist extremists began in February 1996. It grew over the years and gradually expanded to most parts of the country. The conflict came to an end when the Maoist joined the political mainstream in 2006. The Maoist conflict had several direct and indirect impacts on the environment in Nepal.[34] First, it resulted in the destruction of forests and other natural resources due to war like situation; second, the conflicting groups exploited natural resources to raise funds; third, the conflict situation was exploited by vested groups for smuggling and illicit trade in wildlife and natural resources; and the fourth, the displacement and resettlement of people may also result in adverse impact on stressed natural resources. During armed conflict, Maoist insurgents ultimately controlled many of Nepal's natural resources and conservation territories. As Maoists worked to replace the central Government on the ground and remake the state, they imposed a "war tax" on the trade of forest products and collected park fees from tourists.[35]

During the period of conflict, encroachment of forests land, poaching, destruction of forests cover, logging of wood, smuggling of wildlife species

33 Prominent losses include possible extinction of the endemic smooth-coated otter *Lutra perspicillata maxwellii*, bandicoot rat *Nesokia bunnii*, long-fingered bat *Myotis capaccinii* and an endemic species of barbel fish *Barbus sharpeyi*. Several water-birds are critically threatened, including African darter *Anhinga rufa* and sacred ibis *Threskiornis aethiopica*, which may now be extinct in the West Asia.

34 Nepal has been an agrarian economy with over 80 percent of the people dependent on agriculture for their livelihood. The land distribution has been inequitable and poor people live on lands that measure less than one hectare which can hardly support a family's needs. There is intense and widespread competition for available natural resources, leading to conflict for space, ownership and control. At the same time fast depletion of resources, the rapidly increasing population, the faulty land distribution system, insecure tenancy rights, etc have caused problems particularly for the tenant farmers and agricultural laborers. It has resulted in increasing pressure on natural resources leading to the environmental conflict. The degree of human reliance on the environment differs from place to place.

35 Yogesh Dongol and Roderick P. Neumann, "State Making through Conservation: The Case of Post-Conflict Nepal", *Political Geography*, vol. 85 (March 2021).

and other forest produce as well as loss of biodiversity were reported.[36] A large number of endangered animals such as one horned rhinos, musk deer, snow leopard and Royal Bengal tiger were poached during the peak of insurgency in Royal Bardia National Park and Royal Chitwan National Park and other places.[37] The Maoists conflict also caused loss of biodiversity in the wildlife sanctuaries and other protracted forest areas, primarily due to the withdrawal of security forces and officials due to the fear of the Maoists. A large number of Asian one horned Rhinos were poached between 2001-2004 in Royal Bardia National Park and Royal Chitwan National Park. Nepal's Royal Bengal Tiger population is being hunted for its skin and bones. Wildlife smuggling increased tremendously from 1998 to 2005.[38]

Nigeria

Armed conflicts in the North-East of Nigeria and the Niger Delta have left a lot of devastation on the environment and the livelihood of civilians. The armed conflict in Nigeria can be linked to Boko Haram[39] armed opposition groups in Cameroon, Chad, Niger, Nigeria and Islamic State West Africa;[40] and have been characterised by violence and brutality.[41] The root causes of the conflict have centered around climate and environmental issues, poverty, Islam, community allegiance, poor governance, and corruption. The bombing and destruction of the environment and infrastructure in the North-east of Nigeria is overwhelming. Armed conflict

36 B.C. Upreti, "Conflict in Nepal: Impact on Nepal and Its Cross-Border Consequences", in V.R. Raghavan (ed.), *Internal Conflict in Nepal: Transnational Consequences* (Vij Books India Pvt. Ltd., New Delhi, 2011), pp. 100–118.

37 "The Impact of Nepal's Armed Conflict on Conservation Efforts", available at: <http://nepal.usembassy.gov/env_page5.html> accessed on 3 March 2025.

38 Ek Raj Sigdel, "Poaching – How to Fight It", *The Kathmandu Post* (Kathmandu), 6 March 2003; K.C. Shandip, "Nepal Still a Hotspot for Illegal Wildlife Traders", *The Kathmandu Post* (Kathmandu), 7 April 2002.

39 The name Boko Haram was given to the group by residents of Maiduguri, Borno State where the group originated from. 'Boko' means 'fake' used primarily to signify Western education while 'Haram' means 'forbidden', consequently, Boko Haram is translated colloquially as 'Western education is sin'.

40 United Nations High Commissioner for Human Rights (UNHCHR), "Violations and Abuses Committed by Boko Haram and the Impact on Human Rights in the Countries Affected", *United Nations General Assembly* (New York), available at: <https://digitallibrary.un.org/record/819031?In=en> accessed on 23 October 2025.

41 Aondowase Targba, "The Impact of Armed Conflicts on Forced Migration Crises in Nigeria and Mali", *Journal of Migration and Human Security*, vol. 10, issue 4 (2022).

has caused severe environmental damage, including the destruction of infrastructure, pollution from oil spills and military activities, deforestation, land degradation, and displacement of communities. These effects disrupt ecosystems, contaminate water and soil, and contribute to long-term environmental insecurity, with particularly devastating consequences in regions like the North-East and Niger Delta. Civilians and their objects have been attacked, the environment which sustains them has not been left out and the resultant effect is massive movement of the population, resulting in internal displacements trapped in refugee crises.[42]

Rwanda

Rwanda is one of the smallest countries in Africa.[43] The 1990-1994 civil war in Rwanda killed hundreds of thousands of people and generated two million refugees within Rwanda and another two million who fled south to Burundi, Tanzania and Zaire.[44] Most refugees settled in and around protected areas of great conservation value. Two years later, the conflict sparked a civil war in Zaire itself. The despotic ruler was deposed in 1997, and the country renamed as the Democratic Republic of the Congo. Its new leader was assassinated and its neighbours Uganda, Burundi, Namibia, South Africa, and Zimbabwe all got enmeshed in conflict. Rwanda has two national parks, Volcanoes National Park in the west and the Akagera National Park in the east, and several forest reserves. The forest reserves in Rwanda include the Nyungwe Forest Reserve, and the Gishwati and Mukura Forest Reserves. These national parks and forest reserves suffered severely due to a prolonged armed conflict.

42 Theresa U. Akpoghome, Godwin U. Akpoghome and Oritsemisan P. Igbogbo, "Examining the Effects of Internal Armed Conflict on the Nigerian Environment and the Response of Government", *Journal of Environmental Law & Policy*, vol. 2, no. 1 (2022), pp. 22–54.

43 Rwanda is a small country---26, 338 sq km, having a relatively large population of an estimated 10.2 million (2008) and high rate of population growth. A central plateau at elevation between 1,400 and 2,200 meters dominates the country. It rises to the west, towards Congo, to heights of over 3,500 meters, and falls in elevation towards Tanzania in the east. The northwestern part, between the towns of Gisenyi and Ruhengeri, is the most famous for its five volcanoes. Jürgen Brauer, *War and Nature: The Environmental Consequences of War in a Globalized World* (AltaMira Press, London, 2011), pp. 122–123.

44 J.A. Berry and C.P. Berry, *Genocide in Rwanda: A Collective Memory* (Harvard University Press, Washington, D.C., 1999).

Sierra Leone

Sierra Leone, a former British protectorate and colony, became an independent nation in 1961. Since independence, the population has experienced five coups, decades of single-party rule and a ten-year civil war that lasted until 2002. The environmental causes and consequences of armed conflict have been prominent for the past 30 years. During the armed conflict, the Revolutionary United Front (RUF) fighters repeatedly targeted water holding tanks, wells and other water-related infrastructure in their thorough sacking of local villages across the country. This led to further deterioration in already poor water access situations. The acute water shortages, particularly later in the dry season, inhibited other activities during the recovery process. A lack of waste management capacity caused problems for sanitation, surface water degradation and damage to coastal areas. While most of Sierra Leone's infrastructure was damaged and neglected during the conflict, the lack of water system recovery has been particularly harmful.

Subsistence agriculture has long played the most prominent livelihood role in Sierra Leone. During the armed conflict, the damage to agriculture in rural areas has been very serious most notably in the loss of cash crop plantations and livestock. The direct damage to agricultural output was a combination of damage caused by rebel fighters as they sacked towns and villages, and the fact that most displaced owners abandoned their plots for several seasons or years. As a result of the damage to the commercial agricultural sector, recovery of the rural farm economy has been slow and capital-intensive.

During the conflict, forests were damaged by the activities of the RUF, the Sierra Leone Army and government-affiliated militias and mercenaries. Impacts on forest were particularly damaging because of the nature of the rebel activities that included the destruction of crops and vegetation in a senseless manner.[45] Problems such as desertification, deforestation, soil erosion, and water scarcity reduce food-growing potential, worsen health

45 In Sierra Leone, forests were also a refuge. During the armed conflict, entire communities escaped to the forests, sometimes living there for years. Today, many of these same communities have become dependent on forest resources to survive, including protected forests where people plant, poach, dig rock quarries and cut down timber. As population pressures mount, the lure of protected areas will only grow, putting a range of ecosystem services in jeopardy. *Sierra Leone: Environment, Conflict and Peace-building Assessment*, Technical Report, 2010, United Nations Environment Programme, Nairobi, p.62.

effects, decrease biodiversity, and diminish life-support capacity.[46] Any or all of these factors can lead to civil conflict and ignite a new cycle of armed conflict.[47]

During the conflict, the RUF and other related combatants increased the intensity of illicit artisanal diamond mining to support their operations. An estimated annual amount of between US$ 25 million and US$ 125 million in diamonds left the country each year throughout the war as part of the RUF's diamond trade.[48] The mining sites that were expanded were not rehabilitated in any way, leaving effluent, degraded sites and lost arable land. The mining also caused a great deal of persistent damage to the sector, in terms of reduced flows of natural capital and a heavily degraded environment.

Sri Lanka

The two decades of armed conflict in Sri Lanka had detrimental impacts on the environment.[49] The destruction of wildlife, flora and fauna all over the conflict-prone territories in Sri Lanka has been reported. As early

46 The loss of biodiversity in Sierra Leone has been a major concern since the early 1960s. The threat is manifested by various negative impacts: (i) Loss of unique habitats for wildlife within ecosystems. The loss of biodiversity in a country runs parallel with the loss of such "specialized" habitats, which are destroyed as the vegetation is removed; (ii) Loss of genetic resources and wild types for improving biotechnology; tissue culture, crossbreeding, genetic engineering, and pest control; and (iii) Loss of plant resources with medicinal potential to combat diseases and improve human livelihoods. Chris B. Squire, *Sierra Leone's Biodiversity and the Civil War: A Case Study Prepared for the Biodiversity Support Program* (Biodiversity Support Program, Washington, D.C., 2001), p. 9.

47 Jeffery A. McNeely, "War and Biodiversity: An Assessment of Impacts", in Jay E. Austin and Carl E. Bruch (eds.), *The Environmental Consequences of War: Legal, Economic and Scientific Perspectives* (Cambridge University Press, Cambridge, 2000), p. 355.

48 C. Fithen, *Diamonds and War in Sierra Leone: Cultural Strategies for Commercial Adaptation* (Ph.D. Dissertation, Department of Anthropology, University College London, 1999).

49 In the wake of discriminatory State policies and anti-Tamil violence in the 1950s, the Tamil struggle for rights, which began as non-violent protests, increasingly gave rise to Tamil militancy and armed revolt, with a central demand for a separate State. A number of Tamil politico-militant groups, including LTTE, emerged in the 1970s, as the discourse shifted from accommodation to separatism. Violent repression of Tamils by Sinhala nationalists increased in intensity, alongside increasing attacks by Tamil armed groups against the security forces. Elements in the Governments encouraged anti-Tamil violence which culminated in an extensive 1983 anti-Tamil attacks. It resulted in thousands of deaths, large-scale displacement, and destruction of Tamil property and migration abroad. The 1983 is commonly regarded as the start of armed

as in 1986, Wilpattu National Park was attacked by Tamil rebels, killing twenty-one staff and destroying facilities. This caused a withdrawal of conservation staff, and an increase in military activity in the area.[50] The incessant violence has brutally destroyed the biodiversity, natural resource base and wealth of the nation. The ecosystem and biodiversity profile have been harmfully affected due to the bombings, planting of landmines and aerial attacks. The ERW problem in Sri Lanka is not just about unexploded ordnance (UXO)[51]; there is also large contamination from abandoned ordnance as frontlines have shifted and army camps have been deserted. These unexploded munitions can be found in rural and urban areas. Elephants and their terrain, which are one of the most fiercely guarded wildlife reserves of Sri Lanka, have been adversely affected due to the ERW. It is estimated that approximately 482 sq km is contaminated by mines and UXO in the North.[52]

ERW prevents people using their land, although not to the same extent as landmines do. Once discovered, people are reluctant to use their land for agriculture and are afraid to let their children play freely. Nevertheless, sometimes economic needs outweigh the risk of contact. Although most explosives are not harmful to the environment, detonated explosives are toxic. White phosphorus is extremely toxic when released and can cause toxicity, which contaminates soil and water through secondary exposure.

---

conflict between the Government and LTTE. *Report of the Secretary-General's Panel of Experts on Accountability in Sri Lanka* (31 March 2011), p. 8.

50 Jeffery A. McNeely, "War and Biodiversity: An Assessment of Impacts", in Jay E. Austin and Carl E. Bruch (eds.), *The Environmental Consequences of War: Legal, Economic and Scientific Perspectives* (Cambridge University Press, Cambridge, 2000), p. 364.

51 Unexploded ordnance (UXO) refers to a wide range of explosive weapons in many different conditions: artillery shells, grenades, mortars, rockets and airdropped bombs as well as explosive submunitions (or bomblets) that form the contents of cluster munitions, either air-dropped or delivered from land-based systems. According to International Mine Action Standards (IMAS), UXO is 'explosive ordnance that has been primed, fuzed, armed or otherwise prepared for use or used. It may have been fired, dropped, launched or projected yet remains unexploded either through malfunction or design or for any other reason'.

52 Landmine and Cluster Munition Monitor (LCMM), a programme providing research and monitoring for the International Campaign to Ban Landmines (ICBL) and the Cluster Munition Coalition (CMC), has reported a total of 21,993 landmine-related casualties in Sri Lanka since the 1980s, including 1,419 civilian returnees. From 1999 to the end of 2009 the casualty figure was 1,310, including 123 killed, and 453 injured. Vidya Abhayagunawardena, "Vicious Killer", *Frontline*, vol. 28, issue 18 (27 August–9 September 2011).

There is also a significant accumulation of heavy metal contamination in areas that have been subjected to prolonged exchange of fire.[53]

In the early years of the militancy, a number of camps were established by militants in the forested area of Vanni for training and absconding. There were also a few encroachments for establishing settlements in the forests of Vanni. They came to the forests without the familiarity, understanding and knowledge of the natural environment. A consequence of their presence in the forests was the incursion of domesticated species of plants, particularly food plants. In many cases, they held an urban utilitarian view of the forest. Few militant groups were also engaged in illegal logging and marketing of the timber as a source of revenue.[54] The free availability of guns during the war and the use of wire snares appear to have had a serious impact on wildlife.[55] Wildlife population in Sri Lanka is believed to have declined significantly as the result of long-term armed conflict.[56]

Sudan

Sudan has faced continuous political violence and conflicts since gaining independence.[57] The war in Sudan between the Sudanese Armed Forces

53 Rosy Cave, *Explosive Remnants of War in Sri Lanka* (Landmine Action, London, 2003).

54 T. Saverimuttu, N. Sriskandarajah and V.I.S. Jayapalan, "Ecological Consequences of the War in the Tamil Homeland in Sri Lanka", *Proceedings of the International Conference on Tamil Nationhood and Search for Peace in Sri Lanka* (Ottawa, Canada, 1999).

55 Spotted deer (*Axis axis*) used to be the most common and numerically abundant large herbivore in the Wilpattu National Park. But today, its numbers have declined significantly. Deer meat or venison was sold outside the park. Other protected areas (like Yala East (Kumana) National Park, Flood Plains National Park) were also in danger of becoming 'empty forests' as illegal timber extraction and poaching continued. Uncontrolled hunting of wildlife not only reduces the population of the target species, but it causes serious changes in flora and fauna. The elephants in northern Sri Lanka have been subjected to disruption and illicit killing by military and guerilla forces since 1984 as the result of armed conflict. Dudley Joseph P., et. al., Effects of War and Civil Strife on Wildlife and Wildlife Habitats, Vol. 16, No. 2, *Conservation Biology*, April 2002, pp. 319-329.

56 Dudley Joseph P., et. al., Effects of War and Civil Strife on Wildlife and Wildlife Habitats, Vol. 16, No. 2, *Conservation Biology*, April 2002, p. 319-329.

57 The gold trade connects Sudan's civil war to the wider region and highlights the roles that commodities play in perpetuating violent conflict. Even before the start of the civil war in 2023, Sudan's main warring parties – the Sudanese Armed Forces (SAF) and the Rapid Support Forces (RSF) – were in competition for the country's natural resources. In fact, the fight to control gold assets was one of the drivers of the conflict. Artisanal and small-scale gold mining (ASGM) makes up the majority

(SAF) and the Rapid Support Forces (RSF) started on 15 April, 2023. The conflict has caused significant direct and indirect environmental damage, affecting both urban and rural populations. The conflict has heavily affected central and south-western states. While eastern states, such as Red Sea State, have seen little fighting, the influx of internally displaced persons (IDPs) has placed significant pressure on the environment. These pressures have also affected neighbouring countries that are hosting substantial refugee populations.

Impacts of armed conflict include increased deforestation, agricultural decline, pollution from damaged industrial and energy infrastructure, de-energisation events and the deterioration of health and sanitation systems. The conflict has impacted many hazardous facilities like oil refineries, industrial and chemical plants, and power stations. It has caused physical damage posing significant environmental risks. The widespread use of explosive weapons in urban areas[58] has contributed to significant damage to the urban fabric of Khartoum's conurbation. Landmines are a major problem in Sudan. UXOs and explosive ordnance are mixed in with the debris, complicating its management and posing risks to people returning home. Sudan's protected areas already faced growing threats from environmental degradation, infrastructure expansion, climate change, agricultural encroachment, pollution and invasive species. [59]

---

of the gold that Sudan produces, most of which ends up in the UAE, either directly or indirectly via neighbouring countries including Chad, Egypt, Eritrea and South Sudan. The UAE and Egypt have significant influence and support opposing parties to the civil war. Ahmed Soliman, Gold and the war in Sudan, Chatham House, March 26, 2025.

58 The use of explosive weapons in populated areas plays a prominent role in damaging and destroying the environment in situations of armed conflict. Destruction of commercial and industrial units, utility infrastructure, filling stations, workshops, fuel storage and garages, can result in the contamination and release of a host of toxic and hazardous chemicals from damaged buildings and infrastructure which can create airborne contaminants and can contaminate water resources and/or underlying soils, negatively impacting local population. Linsey Cottrell, Eoghan Darbyshire and Kristin Holme Obrestad, "Explosive Weapons Use and the Environmental Consequences: Mapping Environmental Incidents in Ukraine", *Journal of Conventional Weapons Destruction*, Vol. 26, No. 1, 2022, pp. 46–47.

59 "The Environmental Costs of the War in Sudan", 21 May 2025, available at: https://ceobs.org/the-environmental-costs-of-the-war-in-sudan/ accessed on 21 May 2025.

Syria

In Syria, initial protests against President Assad's regime in 2011 escalated into a full-scale war between the Syrian Government (backed by Russia and Iran) and anti-government rebel groups (backed by the US and a rotating number of US allies, including France, the UK, Italy, Saudi Arabia, Turkey, Jordan, and the UAE). Three campaigns drove the conflict: coalition efforts to defeat the self-proclaimed Islamic State, violence between the Syrian Government and opposition forces, and military operations against Syrian Kurds by Turkish forces.[60] The use of explosive weapons is Syria has caused widespread harm resulting from damage to or destruction of essential civilian infrastructure, such as hospitals, water and electricity. The use of explosive weapons in populated areas is also a major driver of population displacement, both within and across international borders, as people flee due to fear of, or as a result of, attacks that damage or destroy their homes or livelihoods. The destruction of buildings[61] has also generated enormous volumes of debris which may contain ERW or other hazardous materials that pose further dangers to civilians and can hinder clearance operations and make debris difficult to recycle. The volume of debris generated in Syria from the destruction in Aleppo and Homs is estimated at more than 20 million tonnes combined. It is estimated that its removal will require more than 1 million truckloads, generate emissions and pollution and take years to complete. A 7.8 magnitude earthquake and 7.5 magnitude aftershock on 6 February, 2023, struck northwest Syria, resulting in nearly 9,000 deaths and $5.1 billion in damages.[62] The collapse of local governance and damaged infrastructure has also affected waste management system, resulting in uncontrolled dumping, open burning of waste and co-disposal with conflict debris. This has caused further contamination and negatively impacts the environment.[63] In Syria, after 14 years civil war, many of the

60 Terry S. Gill, Classifying the Conflict in Syria, *International Law Studies*, Vol. 92, 2016, pp. 353-380.

61 Buildings destroyed by explosive weapons can release hazardous materials into the air and on the ground, such as toxic smoke and heavy metals, which can have both chemical and physical impacts on health, including in the long term. *The Broken Land: The Environmental Consequences of Explosive Weapons Use* (Action on Armed Violence (AOAV), London, 2020), p. 6.

62 "Conflict in Syria", *Centre for Preventive Action*, 2 October 2025, available at: <https://www.cfr.org/global-conflict-tracker/conflict/conflict-syria> accessed on 2 October 2025.

63 *Explosive Weapons with Wide Area Effects: A Deadly Choice in Populated Areas* (International Committee of the Red Cross (ICRC), Geneva, 2022), p. 54; "We Must Not Ignore Explosive Weapons' Environmental Impact", *CEOBS Blog*, 12 May

rivers are choked with pollutants, the forests are devastated, farms are in danger and enforced environmental regulations are non-existent. The civil war has destroyed one-third of country's forests due to clear-cutting for firewood, ferocious wildfires, and artillery and bombing.[64]

Legal Protection

Despite the obvious threat posed by situations of NIAC, none of the rules of IHL applicable to such situations specifically cater for protection of the environment. In many cases there is a link between the Martens Clause and environmental protection. However, the Martens Clause does not explicitly mention environmental damage during NIAC. There is no provision under IHL specifically dealing with environmental protection during the NIAC. Common Article 3 of the Geneva Conventions of 1949 and AP II of 1977 which deals with non-international armed conflict do not even mention the subject. A proposal submitted to the Diplomatic Conference to introduce into AP II, a proposal analogous to Article 35, paragraph 3, and Article 55 of AP I was explicitly rejected.[65] AP II prohibits attack upon installations containing dangerous forces, the prohibition of starvation of civilians, and other provisions aimed at protecting the civilian population could be indirectly relevant.[66] NIAC therefore, pose disturbing dilemmas for the protection of the natural environment. They constitute vast majority of armed conflict, but there is a lack of legal norms applicable to them.[67]

2021, available at: <https://ceobs.org/we-must-not-ignore-explosive-weapons-environmental-impact/ > accessed on 12 May 2021.

64 Zinab Shuker, "Syria's Environmental Crisis Is Its Achilles Heel", *The Century Foundation*, 16 June 2025, available at: <https://tcf.org/content/commentary/syrias-environmental-crisis-is-its-achilles-heel/>accessed on 16 June 2025.

65 Antoine Bouvier, "Protection of the Natural Environment in Times of Armed Conflict", *International Review of the Red Cross*, no. 285 (December 1991), p. 576.

66 According to Bouvier (1991), the concept of environmental protection is not totally absent from Additional Protocol II. Article 14 (Protection of objects indispensable to the survival of the civilian population), which prohibits attacks against "foodstuffs, agricultural areas for the production of foodstuffs, crops, livestock, drinking water installations and supplies and irrigation works", and Article 15, which prohibits any attack against "installations containing dangerous forces….if such attack may cause the release of [such] forces", contribute to protecting the environment in time of non-international armed conflict. Antoine Bouvier, "Protection of the Natural Environment in Time of Armed Conflict", *International Review of the Red Cross*, no. 285 (December 1991), pp. 556–578.

67 For instance, the action of the Iraqi government in Mesopotamia violated Article 14 of AP II, which provides: "Starvation of civilians as a method of combat is prohibited.

Conclusion

The relationship between NIAC and their impacts on the environment depends to a large extent on the intensity and duration of the conflict. According to Smith (2013), environmental damage in NIAC has been caused by both states and non-state actors. This damage can be as a result of targeting, methods and means of warfare, or illegal resource exploitation.[68] This study reveals that the main impacts of NIAC on the environment occurs through habitat destruction and loss of wildlife, over-exploitation and degradation of natural resources, and pollution. Habitats are sometimes directly affected during NIAC. For example, vegetation may be cut, burned, or defoliated to improve mobility or visibility for troops. In addition, the presence of landmines, ERW and hazardous wastes pose a threat to the local population.

When large numbers of displaced people are temporarily resettled, they often clear away vegetation, to farm and to obtain firewood—practices that swiftly lead to deforestation and erosion. Since internally displaced people are often located in ecologically marginal and vulnerable areas, the ability of the environment to subsequently recover may be limited. With habitat destruction, certain plant and animal species may become locally threatened, or even extinct. In Rwanda, two-thirds of the original area of Akagera National Park was removed from protected status, and numerous refugees and their livestock were resettled there. The result was the virtual

---

It is therefore prohibited to attack, destroy, remove or render useless, for that purpose, objects indispensable to the survival of the civilian population, such as foodstuffs, agricultural areas for the production of foodstuffs, crops, livestock, drinking water installations and supplies and irrigation works." In addition, under Article 17 of AP II, there is a prohibition on the forced movement of civilians. It provides: (1) The displacement of the civilian population shall not be ordered for reasons related to the conflict unless the security of the civilians involved or imperative military reasons so demand. Should such displacements have to be carried out, all possible measures shall be taken in order that the civilian population may be received under satisfactory conditions of shelter, hygiene, health, safety and nutrition. (2) Civilians shall not be compelled to leave their own territory for reasons connected with the conflict. Though, the Iraq was not a party to AP II, its action was violative of principles of distinction, proportionality and humanity. Discrimination requires that attackers distinguish military targets from civilian ones. Proportionality requires that the force used be proportional to the desired objective. Humanity requires that military forces avoid inflicting suffering, injury, or destruction beyond that actually necessary for the accomplishment of legitimate military objectives.

68 Tara Smith, *The Prohibition of Environmental Damage during the Conduct of Hostilities in Non-International Armed Conflict* (Ph.D. Thesis, Irish Centre for Human Rights, National University of Ireland, Galway, 2013).

local extinction of some species of plants and animals. Individual animals may also be killed or injured by landmines, as happened to elephants in Mozambique. In areas where fighting is occurring, troops often hunt large mammals in great numbers to obtain food. This practice can have a devastating impact on wildlife populations, especially if military action continues in an area for an extended period. During armed conflict, those in power are often in need of immediate revenue. To fund their military activities, they may turn to commercial-scale extraction of natural resources such as timber, ivory, and diamonds.

In the present century, the means and methods of warfare have become more destructive, and the environment continues to be a target. The Government as well as non-state actors have been deliberately and indiscriminately targeting the environment in order to destroy opposing troops of cover, food and water. The use of landmines, drones, violation of protected natural areas through troop movement, poaching for food, plundering of natural resources and scorched earth practice are some of the methods and means being adopted by combatants. To drive civilian population from an area and to demoralise opposing forces, armed forces are also attacking natural areas inhabited by indigenous people. Refugees and IDPs, who require shelter, food, water and cooking fuel, frequently impact the environment. Corrupt government officials also exploit situations to plunder natural resources as the blame apparently goes to refugees and displaced persons.

In 2020, the International Committee of the Red Cross has issued Guidelines on the Protection of the Natural Environment in Armed Conflict.[69] The International Law Commission (ILC), in 2022, has also drafted Principles for the Protection of the Environment in Relations to Armed Conflicts. These guidelines and principles are applicable to both international and non-international armed conflicts; however, they are soft laws, and their implementation during NIAC remains doubtful.[70] In terms of International

69 *Guidelines on the Protection of the Natural Environment in Armed Conflict* (International Committee of the Red Cross (ICRC), Geneva, 2020), Parts I–IV. Part I of the 2020 Guidelines covers IHL rules that provide specific protection to the natural environment as such. Part II contains general IHL rules that protect the natural environment. Part III comprises the rules on specific weapons that afford protection to the natural environment. Part IV includes IHL rules on respect for, implementation and dissemination of the rules protecting the natural environment.

70 Pouria Askary and Katayoun Hosseinnejad, "A Possible Legal Framework for the Exploitation of Natural Resources by Non-State Armed Groups", *International Review of the Red Cross*, vol. 105, no. 924 (2023), pp. 1522–1542.

Criminal Law, the Rome Statute Article 8 (2) (b) (4) mainly focuses on IAC, the provision criminalises the intentional attacks which are likely to cause widespread, long-term and severe damage to the natural environment. But the provision strictly applies only to IAC. Therefore, NIAC's accountability for environmental destruction often relies on domestic mechanisms.

Part III

Post-Conflict Legacy and Liability

Environmental Impact of Explosive Remnants of War

Kanika Sharma

In armed conflict, various types of high-explosive munitions are fired, dropped, or otherwise delivered during the fighting. A vast majority of these munitions' bursts at the time of delivery and thus pose no further danger; however, a small proportion do not. In addition, a large quantity of munitions and military equipment may be abandoned by the warring parties on the battlefield. Explosive remnants of war often found in war-affected areas may include artillery shells, hand grenades, mortar shells, cluster-bomb submunitions, air-dropped bombs, missiles and other similar weapons. In addition, there could be anti-personnel land mines, sea mines and booby traps that were emplaced, but not subsequently triggered or removed during the war. For instance, during the Second Indochina War of 1961-1975, the US dropped approximately 20 million bombs of various sizes and fired some 230 million artillery (including naval) shells; in addition to countless millions of rockets, mortar shells and over 100 million 40mm grenades. The overall failure rate of all high-explosive munitions expended by the US during this war was estimated to be of the order of 10 per cent. This war resulted in uncounted millions of dangerous duds, including a variety of delayed-action anti-personnel weapons.[1]

Long after armed conflicts are over, explosive remnants of war (ERW) may continue to cause death, injury and suffering to unsuspecting civilians besides harming the natural environment. For instance, in 2022, a 1,000 lb bomb was found in Frankfurt, Germany. This was a small fraction of the thousands of World War II unexploded ordnance found in the country each year. Anti-personnel mines (APMs) buried under the ground also

1 Arthur H. Westing, Explosive Remnants of War: Mitigating the Environmental Effects, Stockholm International Peace Research Institute, Sweden, 1985.

pose a direct threat to human lives, even years after a conflict has ended. Beyond the human toll, ERWs and APMs have a catastrophic impact on the environment, on land and underwater. They deny civilian populations access to their homes, agricultural land, water, roads, schools, health care facilities and other resources. The components of explosive weapons and their remnants (metals and explosive substances containing toxic elements) contaminate soils, subsoils, and water sources. They spread beyond populated areas, poisoning flora and fauna, having a significant impact on entire ecosystems. ERW can set in motion a chain of events leading to environmental harm, such as soil degradation or deforestation, potentially affecting entire species by degrading habitats and altering food chains.[2]

There is an increasing concern about the potential, immediate and long-term impacts on the natural environment of toxic substances and other pollutants that may be released by the use of heavy explosive weapons in populated areas. This has serious ramifications for the health and well-being of the local population. According to the UN, it will take 1100 years to clear ERWs all the active landmines in the world if no new are deployed. [3] This chapter covers the impact of ERWs and landmines on the natural environment.

Defining Explosive Remnants of War and Landmines

In 2003, when a Protocol to CCW [4] became effective, an estimated 60 million unexploded ordnances and landmines were scattered across 70 countries around the world. At the time, 24,000 people were either injured or killed by these conflict remnants every year. This number is undoubtedly out of date, as contemporary international and non-international armed conflicts have drastically increased the concentration and geographic spread of unexploded ordnance and landmines in and at the periphery of combat zones.

The term 'Explosive Remnants of War' (ERW), until 20023, was used as a broad term for explosive ordnance (such as mortar bombs, grenades,

2 The Geneva International Centre for Humanitarian Demining (GICHD), available at: www.gichd.org.

3 UN News, The deadly Legacy of Landmines, April 2, 2023, available at: https://news.un.org/en/story/2023/04/1135252.

4 The 1980 Convention on Prohibitions or Restrictions on the Use of Certain Conventional Weapons which may be Deemed to be Excessively Injurious or to have Indiscriminate Effects ('CCW').

cluster submunitions and air-dropped bombs) which have not exploded and are left as a hazard in the post-conflict environment. This resulted from ordnance being fired but failing to explode (unexploded ordnance - UXO) or from ordnance stores being abandoned during the fighting (abandoned explosive ordnance - AXO). The 2003 CCW Protocol V on Explosive Remnants of War defines ERW as 'unexploded ordnance and abandoned explosive ordnance." The term 'unexploded ordnance (UXO)' means explosive ordnance that has been primed, fused, armed, or otherwise prepared for use and used in an armed conflict. It may have been fired, dropped, launched or projected and should have exploded but has failed to do so. The term 'abandoned explosive ordnance' means explosive ordnance that has not been used during an armed conflict, that has been left behind or dumped by a party to an armed conflict, and which is no longer under the control of the party that left it behind or dumped it. Abandoned explosive ordnance may or may not have been primed, fused, armed or otherwise prepared for use.

ERW can be generated in many ways and present a variety of hazards due to the diverse types of ammunition used. In the post-conflict situation, the battlefields are often littered with explosive debris. The explosive threat from the debris can be divided into four categories (i) mine and unexploded military ordnance (UXO), (ii) abandoned armoured vehicles (AFV), (iii) small arms and light weapons (SALW), and (iv) abandoned, damaged/disrupted stockpiles of ammunition and explosives.

As regards landmines, the first treaty negotiations on landmines took place in the context of the CCW, which was adopted in 1980 with its attached protocols, including the Protocol on Prohibitions or Restrictions on the Use of Mines, Booby-Traps and Other Devices (CCW Protocol Il). It was the first international humanitarian law (IHL) treaty regulating conventional weapons since the early 20th century. The adoption of the CCW in 1980 was an achievement in two ways: first, the convention and its protocols only applied to international armed conflicts; and second, the substantive prohibitions and limitations contained in CCW Protocol II were not significantly different than what could be derived from the general rules of IHL. In view of the large number of civilian casualties and related socio-economic damages documented by humanitarian organisations, the states Parties to the CCW strengthened the rules on landmines, booby-traps, and other devices by adopting an amended version of CCW Protocol II in 1996 (Amended CCW Protocol II).[5]

The failure of the Review Conference of CCW to agree on a total prohibition of APM prompted States favouring a total ban to start negotiations outside of the consensus-based setting of the CCW. This led to the launch of the 'Ottawa Process' and the negotiation and conclusion of the 1997 APM Ban Treaty.[6] As of 1 October 2025, the APM Ban Treaty had been ratified by 166 States. In addition, a few non-party states have announced that they would destroy most of APM stockpiles held by them and would refrain from producing, acquiring, or using the APM in armed conflicts. However, a number of States such as China, India, Pakistan, Russia and the US have not become parties to the convention.

Article 2 of the Mine Ban Treaty defines APMs as a munition designed to be placed under, on, or near the ground and to be 'exploded by the presence, proximity or contact of a person.' The APM Ban Treaty is unique as it banned a weapon that was in widespread use at the time and was in the arsenals of many armed forces. It also contains elements that are not normally found in IHL treaties but are more often found in disarmament treaties, such as prohibitions on production and transfer, and requirements to destroy stockpiles. The Mine Ban Treaty prohibits APMs only. It does not prohibit anti-tank or anti-vehicle mines, which are regulated by the CCW and the general rules of international humanitarian law (IHL).

5 A number of improvements were adopted at the 1996 CCW Review Conference. among others, the scope of application was extended to cover non-international armed conflicts (Art. 1 (2) Amended CCW Protocol II); general restrictions on the use of APMs were strengthened (Art. 3); non-detectable APMs were banned (Art. 4) as well as mines with anti-sensing devices (i.e., mechanisms or devices specifically designed to detonate the munition through the presence of commonly available mine detectors as a result of their magnetic or other non-contact influence during normal use in detection operations; Art. 3 (5)). Slightly stronger restrictions on the use of remotely-delivered APMs (including a ban on the remote-delivery of long-lived APMs, ie those mines which are not in compliance with the provisions on self-destruction and self-deactivation) were also added (Art. 6 Amended CCW Protocol II). Finally, the Amended CCW Protocol II also contained, for the first time, a number of transfer prohibitions (Art. 8). The compliance obligations for CCW Protocol II were improved to some extent (Art. 14 Amended CCW Protocol II). Knut Dorman, Land Mines, MPEPIL, July 2015, available at: https://opil.ouplaw.com/display/10.1093/law:epil/9780199231690/law-9780199231690-e321.

6 The Convention on the Prohibition of the Use, Stockpiling, Production and Transfer of Anti-Personnel Mines and on their Destruction of 1997, known informally as the Ottawa Treaty, the Anti-Personnel Mine Ban Convention, or often simply the Mine Ban Treaty, aims at eliminating anti-personnel landmines around the world.

Characteristics: ERWs and APMs

UXOs are often extremely unstable and can detonate at the slightest touch. Injuries can often occur when people are farming or undertaking construction work in a contaminated area and touch, move or tamper with them. Some UXOs may contain motion-sensitive fuses or magnetic sensors; other UXO may have a timed self-destruct feature that may not have functioned properly. Because the state or condition of UXOs cannot easily be determined, they must all be considered extremely dangerous and should never be touched or disturbed by anyone except explosive ordnance disposal professionals. UXO accidents are often more lethal than landmines due to their higher explosive and fragmentation content. Characteristics of some of the UXO is as follows.

Rockets and Missiles: A rocket or a missile is an explosive device containing its own means of propulsion (the rocket motor) as well as explosives or other fillers (the warhead). Missiles are similar to rockets, although they are guided in their trajectory. Rockets and missiles can be fired from vehicles, ground-based launchers, aircrafts, ships and submarines, and from the shoulder. Rockets and missiles are used to deliver high explosives or other payloads like submunitions, leaflets, chemical or biological materials at greater distances and with greater accuracy than just about any other type of weapon. A rocket/missile is referred to according to its diameter. For example, a 122 mm BM-21 rocket has a diameter of 122 mm, but has, depending on the type, a length of 2.87 m or longer.

Unexploded rockets and missiles can be extremely dangerous, as disturbance may initiate any unspent rocket fuel and propel the rocket in an unguided fashion. If the warhead is still intact, the explosive potential is equal to when the rocket or missile is initially launched, and even greater if the rocket or missile does not launch, but explodes with a full load of fuel. Rocket fuel is also extremely corrosive, volatile and will burn exposed skin and can kill a person if the fumes are inhaled. Rocket fuel is also liable to explode if ignited. Some types of fuel will self-ignite on contact with air. For all these reasons, rockets and missiles should not be approached. The remains of exploded rockets and missiles can contain gas-bottles with compressed gases, which are needed for guidance or cooling the IR-seeker; in addition, hazardous pyrotechnic devices for guidance and arming can be found.

Bomb is an explosive device, usually dropped from aircraft, but conversions to warheads of artillery rockets are known. Bombs come in many different shapes and sizes. Bombs are usually made of metal and have a smooth, curved, normally aerodynamic shape. Air-delivered bombs can range in size from 25 kg to 5,000 kg and can be as long as three-and-a-half metres (around 12 feet). They are typically grey, green or brown in colour. Mostly the bombs contain HE, but other payloads like sets with flashlights, chemical agents or white phosphorous will be possible. Like other UXOs, bombs wear with age and exposure to the elements. They may be rusted, discoloured, and partially hidden by dirt or debris. Typical signs of bombing activity include large craters in the ground. Unexploded bombs may be found above or below the ground. They can penetrate up to 35m deep into the ground without exploding. About 100,000 unexploded bombs have been uncovered in Germany since the end of the Second World War. Often, the bombs are up to 250 kg. Some bombs are much larger. Bombs with a mass of 10 tons were used to destroy bridges and barriers. Thousands of bombs have penetrated the ground so deeply as to remain undiscovered for years.

Abandoned Ordnance (AO) is ordnance that has not been used, but is no longer in the control of any particular force. AO includes every kind of ammunition such as mortar rounds, grenades, bombs, rockets, artillery rounds and others. Caches of AO and poorly secured or maintained stockpiled munitions, sometimes located in or near communities, in military buildings, public buildings, schools, houses and so on, can produce catastrophic explosions. Poorly stored or maintained munitions may become more sensitive and suddenly explode. Absence of lightning rods or safety regulations, high temperatures and humidity can all increase the risk of explosions. Intense heat from fires can also cause abandoned ordnance to detonate. Small caches of abandoned ordnance may continue to be discovered years after a conflict has ended. In Cambodia for example, small caches of ordnance that have been abandoned, forgotten or lost continue to be discovered for more than 30 years. Abandoned military vehicles, weapons (such as artillery guns and tanks), and buildings may also contain abandoned ordnance, extremely volatile rocket fuels and ingredients such as chemicals and depleted uranium. In addition to the hazard posed by the ammunition, the securing of weapon and ammunition caches with booby traps is common.

Menace of ERW and APM

Nearly every armed conflict in modern times has left behind large amounts of explosive remnants. ERW found in conflict affected areas may vary in size from hand grenades the size of an apple to large aircraft bombs weighing more than 1000kg. Although they have failed to function as intended, ERW can sometimes require only the slightest disturbance to detonate. They remain unpredictable in behaviour, and their age and appearance can be deceptive. For instance, lethal explosives from the First World War found in France and Belgium are often found to be in perfect working order. Two apparently identical items of ordnance might behave very differently when handled, depending on what has happened to them before they are discovered.

ERW and APMs are a persistent problem and a deadly threat that kill and injure large numbers of men, women and children who disturb or tamper with them. As these weapons often take years and even decades to clear, their presence can hinder reconstruction, the delivery of humanitarian aid, farming and the return of people displaced by the fighting. It is estimated that at least 80 countries are affected by ERW and APMs.

ERW and APMs present hazardous contamination in almost all post-conflict environments. A survey found that more than 80 countries or disputed territories worldwide contain some level of ERW contamination. There are a number of countries, for example Belgium, Germany, Greece, Latvia, Lithuania, the Netherlands, Slovakia, Slovenia and the UK, that have a residual ERW problem, as a result of World Wars I and II. Today, at least 24 countries and territories in sub-Saharan Africa appear to suffer negative socio-economic effects from the presence of explosive remnants of war. ERW are posing significant problems in several countries in the Central and South Americas, including Nicaragua. Due to prolonged armed conflict in Asia and the Pacific, nineteen countries, including Afghanistan, Iraq, Nepal, Pakistan, Sri Lanka and Vietnam, have been affected by ERW. It has also caused socio-economic effects in 13 countries and territories in Europe, and at least seven in Central Asia. Seventeen countries and territories in the West Asia and North Africa (WANA) experience socio-economic impacts from ERW or mines.[7]

7 The West Asia and North Africa region is affected by mines/ERW because of the many wars and conflicts this region witnessed since the 1940s through today. There are 15 affected countries and territories in MENA contaminated with millions of mines and ERW. Regional projections vary greatly, totaling 52–66 million mines and ERW. The estimated contaminations of each country are as follows: Algeria: 2,783,555, Egypt: 21,600,000 (only 20–25 percent are mines), Iran: 12–16 million, Iraq: 8–12 million before the 2003 Coalition invasion, which surely increased those numbers, Israel: 260,000, emplaned by Israel for security reasons, Jordan: 203,000, Kuwait: small number after clearance of 5–7 million, Lebanon: 406,000 mines and 4 million ERW, the majority of which are cluster submunitions left after the last Israeli conflict with Hezbollah/Lebanon in July and August 2006, Libya: 1.5–3 million, Syria: 500,000

A few countries have been affected by ERWs for more than 150 years, as some unexploded weapons remain volatile for extended periods of time. For instance, at the end of the Second World War, Poland's territory was saturated with unexploded mines, missiles and other explosives of warfare. These ERW prevented the economic utilisation of nearly 20,000 sq km for more than five years. In areas that have experienced bombing or protracted battles, large quantities of ERWs may contaminate the land and harm vulnerable communities. Accidents involving them are often more lethal than landmines due to their higher explosive contents. The degradation of ERWs over time poses significant risks to human health through the contaminants that they release into the natural environment. A few serious situations of ERW and APM contamination are discussed in greater detail.

Iraq: Iraq is one of the most contaminated countries in the world. Northern Iraq (Iraqi Kurdistan) is very seriously affected both by ERW and mines, some of them dating back to WW II, while others are the legacy of the Iran-Iraq War, the Kurdish conflict and the 1991 Gulf War. In addition, Iraqi forces abandoned some stockpiles of munitions in northern towns and cities in 1991. The US and the UK military operations launched from Northern Iraq in 2003 have created more ERW. A survey in Northern Iraq has identified 4,000 distinct areas contaminated by ERW. Another survey by the University of Durham indicated that the presence of mines in rural areas poses a direct or indirect threat to most of Northern Iraq's rural population. In addition, reports by Handicap International and Iraqi Ministry of Defence assess the magnitude of the contamination as follows:

- Around 1,730 million square metres of contaminated land
- Some 20 million mines (as reported by the Ministry of Defence)
- The possibility of more than 50 million cluster bomblets
- Numerous unexploded ordnance sites
- A large number of abandoned munitions sites
- A total of over 1.6 million Iraqis affected
- Casualties (both injury and death) from failed cluster bomblets: 5,500 to 8,000

Tunisia: 3,240 mines and an unknown number of ERW, and Yemen: 150,000 to 2 million. Ayman Soyour, Landmine/ERWs and War on Terrorism in Mena, available at: https://commons.lib.jmu.edu/cgi/viewcontent.cgi?article=1667&context=cisr-journal.

Kuwait: Nearly 35 years after the invasion of Kuwait in 1990-1991 by 100,000 Iraqi soldiers under Iraqi President Saddam Hussein, landmines and ERWs still kill and injure civilians, some of whom were born after the end of the Gulf War. According to the latest statistics, there have been over 1700 casualties from landmines and other ERW since the Gulf War. Of these, over 648 have been fatal. It is estimated that Iraqi soldiers laid about two million landmines in Kuwait's deserts, coastlines and cities, and abandoned large quantities of unexploded ordnance. Bubiyan Island, off the northeast coast of Kuwait was used for military exercises, is also contaminated with ERW. Serious efforts of mine clearance have been made after the end of the war, and an estimated 1.65 million mines have been removed.[8] Yet, the United Nations Mine Action Service (UNMAS) estimates that the country's desert areas remain contaminated with landmines and unexploded ordnance and that the remaining 350,000 landmines are yet to be located in some desert areas in Kuwait.[9]

Vietnam: Vietnam is massively contaminated by cluster munition remnants (CMR) but no accurate estimate exists, even to the nearest hundred square kilometres. An ERW impact survey, started in 2004 and completed in 2014, was only published in 2018. It said that 61,308 square km or 19% of Vietnam's land surface area was affected by ERW: bombs, mines, and explosive ordnance. Unexploded ordnance left over from the Vietnam War has killed more than 42,000, while some 62,000 people have been injured in the country since the conflict ended in 1975.[10] Mine action in Vietnam contends with a number of environmental challenges in its diverse

8 As of 2023, the government has declared the clearance over 90% of the land that was contaminated with landmines following the Gulf War. However, there is still a significant amount of work to be done, due to many uncontrolled challenges such as (environmental terrain-geological and human conditions) yet the government remains committed to clearing all landmines and other ERW from Kuwaiti territory. The Kuwait Army EOD Units has played a major role in clearing landmines and other ERW from Kuwaiti territory since the liberation of Kuwait until today. The army has used a variety of methods to clear these hazards, including: Minesweeping, Explosive ordnance disposal (EOD), Hand-clearing and Seismic Survey. Available at: https://www.apminebanconvention.org/fileadmin/_APMBC-DOCUMENTS/Meetings/2023/IM23-4-Art5-Kuwait.pdf.

9 Sebastian Castelier and Aladdin Elbarbary, Killer mines in Kuwait keep Gulf War alive and deadly, November 28, 2023, available at: https://www.aljazeera.com/gallery/2023/11/28/killer-mines-in-kuwait-keep-gulf-war-alive-and-deadly.

10 US forces used 15 million tons of bombs and ammunition during the war and an estimated 800,000 tons of unexploded ordnance still contaminates 20% of the country's area. It may take more than 100 years to clear the contaminated area. Vietnam War ammo has killed 42,000 since, *Times of India*, 30 June 2009. Available at: http://

habitats ranging from tropical forest to coastal wetlands, all of which are aggravated by climate change. Heavy rainfall and flooding, particularly during monsoon seasons, displace items of explosive ordnance, making their detection and removal more challenging. Additionally, erosion and sediment transport caused by intense rainfall can bury or expose explosive ordnance, necessitating frequent re-surveying and clearance of affected areas. Vietnam will likely need at least 25 years more to clear its ERWs.

Syria: Since the outbreak of armed conflict in Syria a decade ago, explosive munitions have been deployed extensively by all parties. A portion of these munitions fail to detonate or remain abandoned due to several factors. The presence of UXO is a critical impediment to Syria's recovery and development, affecting the ability to farm, use roads, repair housing, or re-enter buildings such as schools or hospitals. ERWs have a resounding impact on civilian life, economic activity, and environmental health, making them a crucial issue demanding attention from the international community. ERW is likely to affect multiple generations of Syrians impacting: (i) Loss of life or limb through encounters with live munitions years after conflict subsides, particularly among children. (ii) Disruptions to economic development, especially related to rebuilding in urban areas and agriculture in rural areas.; and (iii) Environmental degradation as munitions break down and seep chemicals and rust into the ground and groundwater across the country.[11]

Croatia: In Croatia, it has been estimated that there are 13,000 square kilometres of potentially contaminated territory by explosive ordnance, representing almost 23% of Croatia's land area. The aerial bombing campaign carried out by the North Atlantic Treaty Organisation (NATO) in 1999 against the Federal Republic of Yugoslavia also left an abundant unexploded ordnance, as well as the 2001 conflict in North Macedonia with local Albanians. The consultation also revealed that, apart from conflicts and wars, military training exercises and incidents involving explosive

---

timesofindia.indiatimes.com/World/Rest-of-World/Vietnam-War-ammo-has-killed-42k-since/articleshow/4718385.cms.

11 Gaafar, R. (2021) 'The Environmental Impact of Syria's Conflict: A Preliminary Survey of Issues', Arab Reform Initiative [Preprint]. Available at: https://www.arab-reform.net/publication/the-environmental-impact-of-syrias-conflict-a-preliminary-survey-of-issues/.

ordnance carried by ships, planes or vehicles have also led to create "legacy sites" that still contain unexploded ordnance.[12]

Sri Lanka: The Sri Lankan Civil War (July 1983–May 2009), between the government and the Tamil Tigers, was a conflict marked by the extensive use of explosive weapons. It mainly impacted the majority-Tamil areas in the north and east (Tamil Eelam), and the violence left deep scars upon the communities in these areas. The land is still heavily marked by the legacy of landmines, air-dropped bombs, and other ERWs. A large number of civilians and ex-combatants still suffer from the effects of explosive contamination. Though serious efforts have been made, clearance of land remains slow. The contaminated areas are littered with landmines (including improvised mines), unexploded missiles, grenades, and other UXO. Shrapnel and casings from exploded ordnance caused considerable contamination, increasing the difficulty for those clearing the land. The socio-economic impact of ERW in Sri Lanka is long-lasting and does not end even when the land is declared mine-free.[13]

Sudan: The recent war in Sudan between the Sudanese Armed Forces (SAF) and the Rapid Support Forces (RSF) began on 15 April 2023. The widespread use of explosive weapons in urban areas has contributed to significant damage. The conflict has caused significant direct and indirect environmental damage, affecting both urban and rural populations. Impacts include increased deforestation, agricultural decline, pollution from damaged industrial and energy infrastructure, de-energisation events and the deterioration of health and sanitation systems. The war has impacted many hazardous facilities, like oil refineries, industrial and chemical plants, and power stations, posing significant environmental risks. Pulverised building materials such as asbestos can create inhalational exposure risks for residents and workers, while disposing of large debris volumes can cause environmental impacts unless managed properly. UXOs and explosive ordnance are mixed in with the debris, complicating its management and posing risks to people returning home. The conflict has heavily affected central and south-western states. While eastern states, such as Red Sea State, have seen little fighting, the influx of internally displaced persons (IDPs) has placed significant pressure on the environment. These pressures have also affected neighbouring countries that are hosting substantial refugee

12 Domagoj Hajdukovic, Post-conflict time: defusing ticking time bombs for a safe return of displaced populations, Parliamentary Assembly, Council of Europe, June 06, 2024.

13 Jennifer Dathan, The Effects of ERW contamination in Sri Lanka, *The Journal of Conventional Weapons Destruction*, Issue 22, No. 3, 2018.

populations. The conflict is also placing pressure on natural resources outside of protected areas, and it is crucial that protecting and restoring the fragile ecosystems that underpin livelihoods is part of any post-conflict recovery plan. Sudan's proximity to the Sahel, the Horn of Africa, and the Red Sea means the conflict poses a serious risk of regional destabilisation, placing additional pressure on climate-sensitive ecosystems and fragile environments in neighbouring countries.[14]

Gaza and Ukraine: As regards Gaza and Ukraine, the sheer scale of bombardment is unprecedented.[15] When a permanent ceasefire is reached and the rebuilding begins in both conflict-ridden territories, identifying, removing, and destroying thousands of ERW will be extremely dangerous. The long-term impacts and resulting effects on human health from pollution and damage to the natural ecosystems, can only be fully assessed once the war has ended. Since the start of Russia-Ukraine War in 2022, Ukraine has become the most ERW/landmine-contaminated country in the world. By an estimate, roughly 25,000 sq km of agricultural land is contaminated with ERWs and landmines. Unexploded bombs may be buried underground or under piles of rubble and may inadvertently detonate during clearing or reconstruction.[16] In early May 2024, the United Nations Mine Action Service (UNMAS) estimated that it would take at least 14 years to clear Gaza of ERW. Identifying and clearing UXO is expensive and it is estimated that it may take 30 contractors one month to find and defuse a single bomb in Gaza, at a cost of $40,000.[17] The war has increased Ukraine's vulnerability to climate change and complicated its efforts to reduce greenhouse gas

14 Leon Moreland, Tasneem Sied Ahmed, Abubakr Mohammad, Klara Funke, Eoghan Darbyshire and Doug Weir, The environmental costs of the war in Sudan, May 21, 2025, available at: https://ceobs.org/the-environmental-costs-of-the-war-in-sudan/.

15 M. Sio, Israel dropped 100,000 tons of explosives over Gaza, May 08, 2025, available at: https://www.aa.com.tr/en/middle-east/israel-dropped-100-000-tons-of-explosives-over-gaza-wiped-out-2-200-families-media-office/3561614.

16 The Russian-Ukrainian war is having a dramatic impact on the environment. The effects are still unknown. However, it is expected that the effects will be substantial. Since the conflict is ongoing, it is challenging to have ground-accurate data that could show an idea of the extension of the impact. Solokha, M. et. al., (2023) 'Russian-Ukrainian war impacts on the environment. Evidence from the field on soil properties and remote sensing', Science of The Total Environment, 902, p. 166122. Available at: https://doi.org/10.1016/j.scitotenv.2023.166122.

17 Yara M. Asi, Explosive Remnants of War in Gaza: A Long-Term Threat to Palestinian Life, July 17, 2024, available at: https://arabcenterdc.org/resource/explosive-remnants-of-war-in-gaza-a-long-term-threat-to-palestinian-life/.

emissions. During the first 12 months of the war, an estimated 21.9 million tons of carbon dioxide (CO_2) were released due to war-related activities and an additional 17.7 million tons of CO_2 were released from war-related fires.[18]

Some of the contaminants include elements such as lead, antimony, uranium, dinitrotoluene, trinitrotoluene, and other dangerous chemicals which are generally resistant to biological treatment. They remain in the biosphere for a prolonged period of time. These contaminants often leak into groundwater, contaminate foodstuff, damage organs via direct contact, and are often more resistant and expensive to clean up than the undegraded munitions themselves. In addition to the human toll, contamination from remnants of conflict is a significant obstacle to development. It leads to human displacement, delays the return and resettlement of displaced persons and blocks access to vital resources and social services. By denying access to land, water sources, other natural resource, the presence or suspected presence of remnants of war increases pressure on the resource, resulting in unsustainable natural resource management practices by communities affected by conflict.

Global Impact

Wars are no longer confined to designated battle zones. It has shifted to populated areas in cities and has become one of the most pressing threats to civilian lives in modern times across the globe. Weapons that are designed for open battlefields are now being used in densely populated environments impacting civilians. Combatants have a wide range of ammunition and explosives available to them. These may include small arms ammunition, pyrotechnics, grenades, mortar ammunition, projectiles, landmines, guided missiles, free flight rockets, aircraft bombs, and unmanned aerial vehicles and "cruise" missiles. Even when properly targeted, however, many explosive weapons fail to function as designed.[19] The consequences

18 de Klerk L, Shlapak M, Shmurak A, et. al., Climate damage caused by Russia's war in Ukraine. 2023.

19 The reasons for explosive ordnance failure could include (i) production defects (ii) improper storage (adverse climatic conditions can affect the explosive composition, meaning higher failure rates); (iii) rough handling; (iv) inadequate firing drills (for example, failure to set electronic time fuses properly); (v) incorrect launch profiles (for example, air-delivered weapons dropped too low may not have time to arm themselves properly); (vi) poor strike angles (a munition impacting at too shallow an angle may lead to fuse failure); (vii) terrain types (for example, soft ground increases the risk of fuse failure); (viii) heavy precipitation (some fuses may initiate early due to the

are devastating; over 90% of those killed or injured when explosive weapons are used in populated areas are civilians. Many weapons are ill-suited for use in populated areas due to their inherently indiscriminate impact in such settings, where military targets are intertwined with civilian lives and civilians pay the toll of the attacks. These weapons often cause widespread destruction and indiscriminate effects on the lives of civilians. Their remnants have disastrous consequences for communities long after the conflict is over.

ERW victims are predominantly male; this is mostly related to the division of labour. It has resulted in economic implications for the family and community as a whole, as the principal breadwinner is killed or disabled. Although women are not at high risk from ERW, they bear the burden of the long-term consequences, looking after a disabled husband or child, while continuing household work without effective social support. Many have to assume the responsibilities of head of household and earn an income, breaking cultural constructions. Death or injury has serious economic implications for households. The internal armed conflict has affected the country, and the government's support has been minimal. Continuing death and injury from ERW has impeded resettlement, rehabilitation and delayed people from rebuilding their lives and livelihoods.[20]

ERW also affects schools, community centres, places of worship and cemeteries, preventing people from returning to normal lives. This may create frustration and anger that could result in violence, endangering the peace process. Though most ERW may not be harmful to the environment as such, detonated explosives are toxic. Once detonated, ERW can be toxic and contaminate soil and water through secondary exposure.[21]

ERW and Children

Many innocent children have lost their lives and limbs due to disturbing or inadvertently coming into contact with ERW. It poses a greater risk to children when they are involved in economic activities such as

---

resistance caused by rain, leading to sub-munition deployment at the wrong time); and (ix) interaction with other items of ordnance.

20 Large-scale destruction of homes, cultivations, roads, schools, and hospitals in in the Vanni region of Sri Lanka in 2009 was caused by explosive weapons. Report of the Secretary-General's Panel of Experts on Accountability in Sri Lanka, 31 March 2011, available at: www.un.org/News/dh/infocus/Sri_Lanka/POE_Report_Full.pdf, visited 22 July 2011.

21 Explosive Remnants of War: ERW in Sri Lanka, Landmine Action, May 2003

collecting firewood or playing in an area infested with ERW. Children also deliberately tamper with ERW out of curiosity when they do not recognise it as a dangerous munition or to demonstrate bravery. In Poland, an explosion from war remnants killed nearly 4,000 people, including 3,000 children, and injured over 8,000, of which nearly 7,000 were children. The devastating effects of explosive weapons on children are wide-ranging and can reverberate long after conflict. Child survivors of explosive weapons in populated areas (EWIPA) have recorded devastating physical injuries. Some lose their sight, hearing or limbs, while others lose the ability to speak. Children who have been injured, especially those left with disabilities, have different physical rehabilitation needs from adults and, in situations where resources are limited, they are less likely to receive age-appropriate assistance.[22]

The lives of children who survive a bombardment, even those who are not physically injured, are significantly altered. They endure distress or post-traumatic disorders such as persistent fear, severe anxiety, difficulty sleeping or concentrating, nightmares, withdrawal or a loss of appetite, which can interfere with their physical and cognitive development.

Children are also particularly vulnerable to the reverberating effects of explosive weapons. Damage to schools and hospitals can cause children to bear the consequences of conflict for the rest of their lives. Destruction of play areas prevents access to spaces that are essential for children's development. Damage to a power plant, bridge, or water pipe can disrupt access to water and sanitation, increasing the risk of disease outbreaks. In protracted conflicts, children under 5 are more than 20 times more likely to die from diarrheal disease linked to unsafe water and sanitation than from

22 In 2009, a total of 3,956 new casualties from ERW and victim-activated improvised explosive devices (IEDs) were recorded in 64 countries. It was discovered that children made up more than half of all casualties in 14 countries: Afghanistan, Chad, Eritrea, Georgia, Guinea-Bissau, India, Jordan, Kuwait, Mali, Mozambique, Nepal, Philippines, Somalia, Somaliland, and Sudan. In some countries, child casualties, particularly due to ERW, were on the rise again after several years of decreases, for example In Afghanistan. In Chad, children made up 95% of all casualties. In the Philippines, child casualties, accounting for more than 50% of all casualties, were identified for the first time since 2005. In Bosnia and Herzegovina, the number of child casualties was the highest since 2004. In Eritrea, overall casualty figures decreased significantly in 2009, but the number of child casualties remained consistent and increased to 76% from 50% of civilian casualties in 2008. The vast majority of child casualties were boys (80%). In many countries, child survivors have to end their education prematurely due to the long period of recovery and the accompanying financial burden of rehabilitation. Impact of Mines/ERW on Children, Landmine and Cluster Munition Monitor: Fact Sheet, November 2010.

the actual violence. Even after conflict subsides, the effects of explosive weapons can be felt for years to come. Landmines and remnants of war still claim many lives across the world. Children are particularly vulnerable, often attracted to them for their colourful appearance and unaware of how dangerous they are.[23] ERW in Sri Lanka posed a greater risk to children than landmines. In the Jaffna peninsula, during the year 2000, 78% of ERW victims were children.

Socio-economic Impact

The presence of explosive remnants of war in post-conflict communities has undeniable socio-economic impacts. The most obvious socio-economic impacts of ERW are the deaths and injuries they cause.[24] The survivors of ERW are often economically and socially marginalised. Their ability to support their families and contribute productively to local community life is reduced, adversely affecting agriculture and other economic activities. Continuing incidents from ERW may also sustain and reawaken feelings that create tension and possible violence, again affecting the ceasefire.

There is strong evidence that, like APM, the threat from ERW compounds the existing developmental problems of affected communities by modifying their social and economic patterns. The presence of ERW prevents the use and rehabilitation of community infrastructure and resources, including housing, water and irrigation, schools and villages, clinics and markets and the roads. Clearance activities are often needed before they can be used or repaired. ERW presence dissuades the inhabitants of affected communities from certain types of land use, or makes exploitation of local resources less efficient. Ultimately, land denial not only affects economic productivity; it can also produce wholesale change in traditional social and economic practices.

23 Explosive weapons in populated areas: Why children are particularly vulnerable to explosive weapons, available at: https://www.unicef.org/children-under-attack/explosive-weapons-populated-areas.

24 It is usually difficult for the local population to coexist with ERW contamination without either accidental exposure to risks or some form of deliberate engagement with the ordnance in an effort to manage the risks they are facing. ERW contamination also contributes to a general atmosphere of insecurity and fear in many post-conflict communities. ERW accidents do occur from people accidentally striking items while farming or building fires above buried ordnance. A significant proportion of accidents occur because people deliberately interact with ordnance that they find. *Explosive remnants of war and mines other than anti-personnel mines: Global Survey 2003-2004*, Landmine Action, March 2005, London, UK, pp. 8-9.

ERW and other military debris have value as an economic resource in many poor communities. It can provide access to cash within communities where this is otherwise rare. For those on the margins of society, ERW can be the mainstay of their economic survival. This leads people to undertake high-risk activities to locate and scrap ERW, a major cause of accidents in Laos, Eritrea, Guinea-Bissau and Chad.

Besides having the highly visible impacts on mortality and morbidity, the presence of ERW alienates a population's access to critical agricultural, forestry and pastoral resources, which are necessary for restoring livelihoods. ERW also delays the return of the IDPs and the refugees. The land rights situation becomes critical in the conflict-torn States affected by ERW, where land access can be denied or disrupted for years or even decades. ERW contamination not only leaves a profound social, economic and political footprint on the locations where they are located, but their presence also has significant repercussions on larger, adjacent areas.[25]

ERW is not only a post-conflict threat in war-torn societies, but it can also affect adjacent countries or territories not directly involved in conflict. Laos and Cambodia are the two examples of the 'spill-over' of the ERW threat. Although not directly involved in the conflict between North Vietnam and the US, huge quantities of ordnance were dropped on both countries during the 1960s and 1970s by the US to interdict the Ho Chi Minh Trail. As a result, very large numbers of ERW of almost every type of air-delivered ordnance, including large high-explosive bombs, continue to pose a severe threat to communities within Laos and Cambodia, as well as Vietnam.[26] To a lesser extent, similar phenomena have occurred in the vicinity of Central Africa. While most fighting in recent years has been centred on the Democratic Republic of Congo, troop movements and fighting have sometimes strayed into adjoining countries. While this has not resulted in high casualties, but has created impediments to land use,

25 Once violence ends, displaced persons often seek to re-establish their homes and livelihoods, creating a surge of land and property problems, which can be exacerbated by the enduring presence of ERW. Depending on the size of the displaced population and the duration of displacement and conflict, land and property issues can quickly become one of the primary features of a post-war phase. The re-establishment of ownership, use and access rights to land after a war ends is often very difficult as people try to reclaim what they lost. Failure to effectively address these problems can serve as the basis for renewed conflict and armed confrontation. Unruh, Jon, and Alexandre Corriveau-Bourque, Volatile Landscapes: the Impact of Explosive Remnants of War on Land Rights in Conflict Affected Countries, Issue 18, *Journal of Peace, Conflict & Development*, December 2011, p. 8-11.

26 Explosive Remnants of War: A Global Survey: Landmine Action 2003.

infrastructure development and activities such as livestock grazing and hunting.[27]

The Dangers from ERW and Mines

The dangers posed by ERW and APMs are as follows. [28]

- Injuries or deaths can take place at a distance from the explosion, depending on the ordnance involved; the danger area can vary from a few meters to several hundred meters.
- Items of UXO could be more powerful and lethal than anti-personnel mines; depending on the kind of ordnance, UXO incidents may result in a greater proportion of deaths than incidents involving mines.
- When UXO accidents do not involve deaths, they typically result in severe wounds, such as fragmentation injuries to the abdomen and chest, which often include damage to vital organs, amputation of limbs, and loss of vision or hearing.
- ERW are generally found on the surface and are more visible, resulting in a higher interaction of people. However, ERW can also be found sub-surface, where clearance can be difficult; for example, aircraft bombs can be found buried up to several meters.
- ERW are unpredictable and can be detonated at any time under a variety of stimuli: by pressure, by hit or kick or by simple touch. ERW often respond differently to the same action: an item of UXO can explode after being kicked once, or it may explode after ten kicks.
- Unlike mines, it is difficult to identify the reason for the failure of ERW.

Environmental Impact

ERW contamination denies the safe use of agricultural land. It renders large tracts of agricultural land unusable, wreaking environmental and economic devastation. Refugees returning to their conflict-ravaged

27 *Explosive Remnants of War and Mines other than Anti-personnel Mines: Global Survey 2003 -2004*, Landmine Action, London, 2005.

28 *Explosive Remnants of War (ERW): Warnings and Risk Education*, Geneva International Centre for Humanitarian Demining, Geneva, Switzerland, May 2003, pp. 9-10.

countries face this life-threatening obstacle to rebuilding their lives. Many people leave the land and drift to the towns, while the poorest elements of society in ERW affected countries take risks to survive. ERW can even prevent tourism by denying access to cultural heritage sites.

Wild elephant populations are also affected by ERW and landmines as they roam in search of food. In several cases, elephants working for humans are injured in remote areas and are unable to be helped for many days. The emotional and physical distress that the elephants experience is often accompanied by the emotional distress of the handler who is dependent on the elephant's well-being for sustenance. In many cases, the injured elephants need to be put down as a result of the inherent difficulty in finding veterinary help and keeping the wounds and amputations of an elephant clean. In Sri Lanka, according to wildlife veterinarians, as many as 10 elephants were killed or injured each year by ERW or landmines.[29]

As the principal chemical component of ERWs, explosives present a significant risk to the environment, primarily from toxicity towards environmental receptors. The most commonly used secondary explosive is the nitro-aromatic 2,4,6 trinitrotoluene (TNT), which dissolves quickly when exposed to water (200 mg/L) or rainfall. TNT and similar compounds are toxic to humans, animals and plants. Even at very low concentrations, long-term health effects can occur. However, this is dependent on TNT contaminating drinking water sources, which is often prevented by rapid degradation of TNT in soils containing high organic content . 10 11 The risk of TNT contamination is higher if there is a higher groundwater risk. There is also a risk in sandy soil, which does not contain significant organic material, as TNT will not be as rapidly degraded and may travel to groundwater or run off into surface water. TNT will typically biodegrade to a DNT isomer. DNT is highly toxic for humans, since it can convert

29 On April 4, 2011--International Mine Awareness Day-- while many advocates for mine removal were celebrating the inclusion of 10 more states to the Mine Ban Treaty, two elephants were killed in Sri Lanka by landmines. This comes after a decision made by the Sri Lankan government to relocate the Sri Lankan Nature Conservatory to a former war zone containing as many as 1.5 million active landmines, proving even more that elephant safety depends on the actions taken and decisions made by humans in affected regions. Windy Borman, *Sri Lanka Moves Elephants Into Former War Zone, Landmines Remain,* January 10, 2011, The Eyes of Thailand, available at: http://www.eyesofthailand.com/2011/01/10/sri-lanka-elephants-landmines/; Windy Borman, *2 Elephants Step on Landmines in Sri Lanka on International Mine Awareness Day,* 4 April 2011, The Eyes of Thailand, available at: http://www.eyesofthailand.com/2011/04/04/2-elephants-step-onlandmines-in-sri-lanka-on-intl-landmine-awareness-day/.

haemoglobin to methaemoglobin at a relatively low threshold limit of 0.13 mg/L.

RDX (Nitramine cyclotrimethylenetrinitramine) is another common secondary explosive, frequently used in combination with TNT, which has significantly different environmental properties. For example, RDX is significantly less soluble (30 mg/L) than TNT, but also much less susceptible to degradation in soil and therefore more likely to leach through soil. It therefore may travel rapidly through all soil types to groundwater. RDX presents a degree of toxicity for humans, animals and plants, and particularly in humans has been linked to increased risk of cancer. Since RDX is less susceptible to degradation, it may remain in the environment for long periods of time and the effect on a receptor (e.g. humans through potable water sources) may not materialise until tens of years after contamination has been released. Often, TNT and RDX are used as a mixture in an explosive weapon. When combined in this way, it may affect how long it takes for the TNT and RDX to leach from an explosive device into the soil. Once in the soil, it will behave as described above, since by that point the two explosives are unlikely to interact.

Polymer-bonded explosives (PBX) are frequently used in aircraft munitions. These behave somewhat differently in the environment. For example, due to the plastic matrix, leaching of the energetic component from the fill tends to take significantly longer, reducing the quantity of explosive exposed to the environment, particularly in bulk fills. However, after detonation, particularly when not in the intended design mode, such as a second-order demolition in situ, or a low-order mechanical break-up or deflagration, significant pieces of PBX can be deposited in the area. These can present a toxicity risk to any foraging fauna. In addition, these PBXs can be carried by surface water to other environments where the explosive content may leach over long periods of time. As expected, the plastic component may take many years to degrade, although degradation and subsequent explosive leachate is more rapid in climates with significant temperature cycling and light. In addition to its explosive constituents, PBX may also contain aluminium or oxidisers such as ammonium perchlorate, which may also have an impact on the environment.

Many of the bombs that land on soft and highly fertile land fail to detonate. They continue to render the land hazardous. Due to the danger of unexploded bombs, many farmers avoid using tractors and other agricultural techniques that could increase agricultural production. ERWs also adversely affect soil quality. Unexploded bombs and landmines can leak heavy metals and toxic waste into the soil, polluting land and water. In rare cases, contaminants from a landmine have been detected up to 6km away from the initial explosion site. The methods for clearing unexploded ordnance also contribute to land degradation. Heavy demining equipment can damage fertile topsoil and contribute to erosion. Some methods of disposal of ERWs and landmines, such as controlled detonations, can also release contaminants into the soil. For instance, the Halgurd-Sakran National Park in north-eastern Iraq, a region that has seen decades of armed conflict, shows evidence of the release of hazardous metals such as lead, cadmium and arsenic into the soil following demining activities. These contaminants pose significant risks both to local ecosystems and human health through direct contact and the contamination of water sources and food chains. There are also risks of contamination through inhaling or ingesting dust.

According to Berhe (2000), land degradation caused by ERWs and landmines can be classified into three groups: access denial, loss of biodiversity, and chemical contamination, resulting in the loss of productivity. The effects of an explosion depend on the concentration of ERWs and mines in a unit area; chemical composition and toxicity of the ERW/mines; previous uses of the land, and alternatives that are available for the affected populations.

Access denial: The most prominent ecological issue associated with ERWs and landmines (or fear of them) is denial of access to vital resources (where "access" refers to the ability to use resources, in contrast to "property", the right to use them). The presence and fear of the presence of even a single UXO or mine can discourage access for agriculture, water supplies and possibly conservation measures. Access denial can also have positive effects on the environment. When a mined area becomes a "no-man's land", plants and vegetation have a chance to grow and recover.

Loss of biodiversity: Unexploded ordnances and mines can threaten biodiversity by wiping out vegetation and wildlife during explosions or demining. This extra burden can push threatened and endangered species to extinction. Shrapnel, or abrasions of bark or roots caused by detonated mines, can cause the slow death of trees. When land mines make land unavailable for farming, residents resort to the forests to meet all of their survival needs. This exploitation furthers the loss of biodiversity. Many of the biodiversity loss hotspots of the world are severely affected by ERWs and landmines. According to Nachon (2000), a large number of species are threatened or endangered due to many factors, including the presence of

ERWs or landmines in their habitat or migratory paths and are shown in the Table below:[30]

S. No.	Country	Species Diversity	
		Number of Species Found	Number of Species at Risk
1.	Vietnam	9494+	434
2.	Angola	766+	125
3.	Afghanistan	5076+	53
4.	Somalia	4568+	80
5.	Cambodia	n/a	62
6.	Mozambique	6835+	28

Table: Species of living things at risk in REW/mine-affected countries

Chemical contamination: A Place where a mine or military ordnance has exploded tends to be contaminated, particularly with heavy metals. Products produced from the explosives, both organic and inorganic substances, are most likely to be long-lasting, water-soluble and toxic even in small amounts. They are absorbed directly or indirectly into soil, water bodies, microorganisms and plants with drinking water, food products or during respiration. Toxic compounds can also find their way into bodies of water and accumulate in land animals, fish and plants. They can act as a nerve poison to hamper growth with deadly effects in human beings.

The low availability of land (access denial), degradation of the soil, combined with chemical contamination of land and loss of flora and fauna diversity, all contribute to decreased productivity of previously productive land. Land degradation from the ERWs and mines results in a downward spiral of both soil and vegetation, thus loss of productivity. Toxic remnants of war are poisonous or hazardous substances resulting from military activities. They include: radioactive material, white phosphorus, mustard agents, halogens, heavy metals, dioxins and other human carcinogens. Some toxic

30 Nachon CT. 2000. Environmental Aspects of the International Crisis of Antipersonnel Landmines and the Implementation of the 1997 Mine Ban Treaty: Thematic Report. Landmine Monitor Report 2000. International Campaign to Ban Landmines, NY.

remnants are a direct result of armed conflict. Agent Orange used in the Vietnam War contained dangerous dioxins that continue to damage people and the environment today. Toxic remnants of war can result in many adverse health effects in humans and widespread environmental damage. Toxic remnants of war also interact with the effects of climate change.

Environmental Impact of Explosives in Marine Environment: There are significant quantities of abandoned ordnance in oceans worldwide, and of increasing relevance as they are being rediscovered during infrastructure developments such as the installation of windfarms. In general, the environmental impact of ordnance at sea tends to be limited to the local area, e.g. chemical compounds (organic and inorganic), reducing oxygen availability and subsequently driving marine organisms to other areas, or causing degrees of toxicity. Underwater noise from unintended detonations of unstable ordnance may also have an environmental impact, and recent research suggests that the impact from underwater noise is more significant than has previously been suspected. Metal corrosion is also more rapid in saline waters, and it is common to see elevated concentrations of metal near underwater ordnance. At sea, contamination tends to dilute rapidly once beyond the immediate vicinity; however, this does not necessarily diminish the significance of marine contamination from explosive ordnance.

Removal of ERW

Once a conflict is over, the stockpiles of unexpended ammunition pose a serious hazard as abandoned ordnance deteriorates over time, and it becomes difficult to relocate them. This is particularly true with poor-quality or old ammunition, which further deteriorates in high temperatures. There is an additional problem where stocks of abandoned ordnance include small arms and their ammunition, which can be plundered by armed gangs at the end of an armed conflict.[31]

ERW and their clearance have a serious impact on land rights in countries recovering from armed conflict. Apart from the highly visible impacts on mortality and morbidity, the presence of ERW alienates a population's access to critical agricultural, forestry and pastoral resources, necessary for restoring livelihoods. ERW also delay the return of displaced populations,

31 Keeley Robert, Understanding Landmines and Mine Action, September 2003, p.6.

thwarts the reconstruction of infrastructure, and disrupts land and property restitution and security.[32]

In order to ensure that removal or the destruction of ERW causes minimum impact on the local environment, the following is recommended.[33]

1. ERW should be disposed of in a manner that minimises environmental impact, avoids contamination of the land and water and has minimal effect on flora and fauna. In cases where ERW are to be destroyed in situ, and there is a risk to property or infrastructure, protective works must be used.

2. Debris, rubble, wire and other remains of obstacles removed from a demining worksite must be disposed of in accordance with local waste management regulations.

3. Demining organisations must not obstruct or divert the natural flow of watercourses unless absolutely necessary for the operation. They must consult the local community before undertaking diversions.

4. Demining organisations must ensure that the impact of demining on air quality (smoke, dust and toxic fumes) is minimised and the local communities and authorities are informed about the scope and duration of degradation.

5. Burning of vegetation should be avoided; however, when it is inescapable, proper procedures and control measures should be

32 Jon Unruh Jon and Alexandre Corriveau-Bourque, Volatile Landscapes: the Impact of Explosive Remnants of War on Land Rights in Conflict Affected Countries, *Journal of Peace, Conflict & Development,* Issue 18, December 2011, p. 7-25.

33 Explosive ordnance disposal (EOD) is the term used to describe the specific technical procedure for the detection and disposal of items of unexploded ordnance. The EOD procedure depends upon the type of terrain and variety of munitions that are likely to be in the affected area. Where items are buried underground, metal detectors have to be used to locate the ordnance. The actual disposal procedure usually involves the destruction of unexploded ordnance using an explosive charge. Sometimes UXO has to be destroyed where it is, since moving the item may be dangerous and could result in its premature detonation; at other times, UXO is gathered in a central location to be destroyed in a 'bulk demolition' (many items simultaneously). Large items such as aircraft bombs, particularly if they are close to vital infrastructure, are disposed of by a dismantling process sometimes involving the removal of the explosives for disposal elsewhere. *Explosive Remnants of War: ERW in Sri Lanka*, Landmine Action, May 2003, p, 24.

applied. Burning should not be undertaken during night hours, and it should not be started unless there are sufficient fire-fighting arrangements.

6. Stockpile destruction must be planned and conducted in a manner that minimises the impact on the environment. If required by the national authorities, an 'environmental impact assessment', be undertaken.

7. Rubbish from the site must be disposed of at approved dumping sites. Rubbish pits must be located away from watercourses and wells, so as not to contaminate groundwater. Human waste should not be discharged into water courses or onto the soil surface.

8. Demining organisations must ensure that planning is undertaken to prevent any spills of fuel, oil and lubricant (FOL). FOL storage facilities should not contaminate the soil or groundwater.

9. Toxic or hazardous waste products of demining operations must be disposed of under the directions of national authorities.

10. International standards must be observed while transporting hazardous, toxic or flammable materials.

11. While demining is undertaken in areas of cultural or historical importance, demining organisations must take all possible steps to prevent damage to these sites. Where human remains are encountered, action in accordance with IHL should be undertaken.

12. Environmental incidents must be reported to the national authority as soon as practicable after the incident occurred.

13. On completion of demining operations, equipment, surplus materials, and waste must be removed.

14. As far as possible, the local community should be involved in demining operations.

Removal of ERW: The CCW Protocol V

The Protocol V to CCW on ERW is a major achievement of IHL. It strengthens the law in areas where no specific rules previously existed. The Protocol was adopted in 2003 to address one of the deadliest threats faced by civilians in post-conflict situations.[34] It establishes new rules that require the parties to a conflict to clear ERW, to take measures to protect civilians from the effects of these weapons and to assist the efforts of international and non-governmental organisations working in these areas.

The Preamble to Protocol manifests the willingness of the States Parties to observe generic preventive measures, through voluntary best practices specified in a Technical Annexe of the Protocol. The Protocol is applicable on the land territory including internal waters of High Contracting Parties.[35] It deal only with the ERW from conventional weapons and does not address the post-conflict problems arising from the use of biological, chemical or nuclear weapons.

The Protocol is applicable in both international and non-international armed conflicts.[36] Article 1(3) states that the Protocol will apply to the situations arising from the conflicts referred to in paragraphs 1 to 6 of Article 1 of the CCW as amended on 21 December 2001. This is a reference to the amendment adopted by the Second CCW Review Conference that extends the scope of application of CCW Protocols I-IV to non-international armed conflict. The amendment stipulated that the scope of application for other CCW protocols would be determined on a case-by-case basis. Article 1(4) clarified that the Protocol's main operative provisions apply to ERW produced after the Protocol's entry into force for the relevant State.

34 The CCW Protocol V on Explosive Remnants of War was adopted in November 2003 and entered into force on 12 November 2006. It has been ratified by 99 States as on September 30, 2025.

35 Article 1 (2) Protocol V on Explosive Remnants of War, 2003.

36 As a result of its application to non-international armed conflicts, the Protocol refers to "High Contracting Parties" and "parties to an armed conflict". The former is the equivalent of "States Parties", i.e. States that have formally ratified or acceded to the Convention and the Protocol. The phrase "parties to an armed conflict" is a reference to non-State actors (i.e. organized armed groups) and is the formula used in Amended Protocol II to the CCW, which also applies to non-international armed conflicts. As used in Protocol V, "parties to an armed conflict" does not encompass States involved in a conflict that have not ratified or otherwise expressed their consent to be bound by the Protocol. Such States are not bound by it. Maresca Louis, A New Protocol on Explosive Remnant of War: The History and Negotiation of Protocol V to the 1980 Convention on Certain Conventional Weapons, Vol. 86, No. 856, *International Review of the Red Cross*, December 2004, p. 824.

The Clearance of ERW

Article 3 of the Protocol establishes rules on clearance of ERW. It provides that explosive munitions, other than landmines, must be cleared once the fighting has ended. Each State Party and party to armed conflict is responsible for the clearance of these remnants in the affected territory under its control [Article 3 (1)]. In cases where a user of explosive ordnance which has become ERW, does not exercise control of the territory, the users is to provide assistance, to facilitate the marking and clearance of the ERW in territory outside their control that have been produced during military operations. Such assistance may be technical, material, financial or in the form of personnel. It may be provided directly to the party in control of the territory where the explosives are found, or through a third party such as the United Nations, international agencies or NGOs. Under Article 3(3), after the cessation of active hostilities, the State Parties and party to an armed conflict shall take the following measures in affected territories under their control, to reduce the risks posed by ERW: (i) survey and assess the threat posed by ERW; (ii) assess and prioritise needs and practicability in terms of marking and clearance, removal or destruction; (iii) mark and clear, remove or destroy ERW; and (iv) take steps to mobilise resources to carry out these activities. This responsibility relates to the clearance of ERW immediately after the end of active hostilities and does not mean after the conclusion of a formal peace agreement. Clearance is to begin as soon as feasible in affected areas and must not wait for a formal declaration of peace between the parties.

EO typically comprises a series of explosive components known as an explosive train, usually encompassing a detonator, a booster and a main charge. These components all have the potential to cause environmental contamination when either, (i) initiated in their intended mode, (ii) abandoned in the environment, or (iii) disposed of by Open Burning Open Detonation (OBOD) techniques. EO abandoned for long periods of time will corrode and potentially leach significant quantities of explosive into the environment. The following table summarises the most likely ways that EO and associated disposal activities can contaminate the environment.[37]

37 Guide to Explosive Ordnance Pollution of the Environment, The Geneva International Centre for Humanitarian Demining (GICHD, December 2021, pp. 87.

Table: Summary of the most likely ways explosive ordnance and associated scenarios could contaminate the environment

Explosive-Ordnance	**Impact on Land**	**Impact on Water**	**Impact on Air**
Buried in Ground	Explosive ordnance or energetic materials, metals and casing breakdown into soil-Erosion of metals and plastics, solubilisation of energetic materials by weathering.	There may be secondary impacts on water e.g., surface and ground water from soil contamination,	Likely to cause impact on air quality or atmosphere in this form.
Open Burning	Residues from open burning and from particulate falling to the ground, may comprise metals, explosives residues and ash that are solubilised or carried into soil by weathering.	There may be secondary impacts on water, e.g., surface and ground water from soil contamination.	Emissions of greenhouse and toxic gases to atmosphere causing temporary local air quality issues and contribution to climate change.
Open Detonation	Physical land damage, and distribution of explosive and metal residue in the environment solubilised or carried into soil by weathering.	There may be secondary impacts on water e.g., surface and ground water from soil contamination.	Emissions of low levels of greenhouse and toxic gases to atmosphere causing contribution to climate change.
Sea dumping	Metals will corrode enabling energetic materials to leach into environment. Metals and energetic materials may accumulate in sediments.	Localised high concentration of metals and energetic materials potentially causing deoxygenation of water. Rapidly dilutes with distance from ERW.	No impact of air.

Recording and Sharing of Information

The lack of information on the used or abandoned ordnance in an armed conflict is an important detriment to effective removal or destruction of ERW. The immediate transmission of such information by the parties to an armed conflict can significantly improve an organisation's ability to respond swiftly to ERW. Article 4 of the Protocol accordingly stipulates that State Parties and parties to an armed conflict must record and retain information on the use or abandonment of explosive ordnance "to the maximum extent possible and as far as practicable." Parties are subsequently required to share this information without delay after the cessation of active hostilities with other parties, the UN or other organisations involved in risk education or the marking and clearance of contaminated areas.

The information that the parties to an armed conflict are expected to record are listed in the Protocol's Technical Annex. These include the types and amounts (number) of explosive ordnance used; the areas targeted with these weapons; the types, amount and location of abandoned explosive ordnance; and the general location where unexploded ordnance is known to exist or is likely to be found. The Annex also provides details the information that should be transmitted to the other parties and relevant organisations. The Technical Annex sets out voluntary best practices and its contents are not legally binding. However, as parties to the armed conflict are bound by Article 4 to record, retain and transmit information to facilitate the rapid removal of explosive remnants of war as well as risk education, the article's effective implementation will require that the information recorded matches the specifications in the Technical Annex.[38]

Precautions to Protect Civilians and Humanitarian Organisations

Article 5 of the Protocol stipulates that the parties to an armed conflict must take all feasible precautions in territory under their control to protect civilians and civilian objects from the effects of ERW. Article 5 specifically provides:

> High Contracting Parties and parties to an armed conflict shall take all feasible precautions in the territory under their control affected by explosive remnants of war to protect the civilian population, individual civilians and civilian objects from the risks and effects of

38 Maresca Louis, A New Protocol on Explosive Remnant of War: The History and Negotiation of Protocol V to the 1980 Convention on Certain Conventional Weapons, Vol. 86, No. 856, *International Review of the Red Cross*, December 2004, p. 824.

> explosive remnants of war. Feasible precautions are those precautions which are practicable or practicably possible, taking into account all circumstances ruling at the time, including humanitarian and military considerations. These precautions may include warnings, risk education to the civilian population, marking, fencing and monitoring of territory affected by explosive remnants of war, as set out in Part 2 of the Technical Annex.

As regards minimising the effects of ERW on the operations of humanitarian organisations, Article 6 states that the High Contracting Parties and parties to a conflict must protect such organisations from the effects of ERW. It also states that each party must provide information on the location of ERW to humanitarian organisations involved in demining operations.

Assistance and Cooperation

Under Article 7, State Parties facing problems posed by existing ERW have the right to seek and receive assistance from other States and relevant organisations in dealing with them. At the same time, each High Contracting Party, having expertise in ERW is required to provide assistance, where necessary and feasible. The qualifications in this article; 'where appropriate', and 'as necessary and feasible', show that this provision was intended to be a flexible one and was not meant to be absolutely binding for the parties.[39] Article 10 establishes that High Contracting Parties will consult and cooperate with each other on all issues related to the Protocol's operation.

Article 9 mandates State Parties to implement generic preventive measures aimed at minimising the occurrence of ERW. It includes a range of activities taken before the use of EXO to ensure that weapons will explode as intended. A number of general best practices are listed in Part 3 of the Protocol's Technical Annex. They include standards for munitions manufacturing, storage, transport and handling, and the training of personnel. Article 11 promotes compliance with the Protocol and stipulates that a State Party must issue appropriate instructions and procedures and make sure that its personnel receive training consistent with the Protocol's provisions. It also requires State Parties to work bilaterally, through the UN or through other international procedures, to resolve any problems that may arise in the Protocol's interpretation or application.

39 Maresca Louis, A New Protocol on Explosive Remnant of War: The History and Negotiation of Protocol V to the 1980 Convention on Certain Conventional Weapons, Vol. 86, No. 856, *International Review of the Red Cross*, December 2004, p. 830.

There are certain shortcomings in the Protocol. It contains many qualifying phrases in its key provisions. These include phrases such as "where feasible" and "as soon as feasible". These phrases, if abused, could undermine the effectiveness of the Protocol. It is felt that it would be difficult to implement the Protocol's operational provisions in situations where there was not sufficient good will between the parties to conflict. However, there are opposing views [40] that such clauses were intended to provide a degree of flexibility to deal with the practical difficulties and complexities that the governments and armed forces often face in post-conflict situations.

Explosive weapons play an important role in the military doctrines of states. While using weapons during an armed conflict is a military decision, modern combat operations have introduced a dilemma: what to do with ERW that remain after a conflict ends. Such weapons not only threaten the post-conflict safety of civilians and military personnel but can also be a major impediment to economic development. The CCW Protocol V, imposes obligations on States to remediate the 'serious post-conflict humanitarian problems' caused by the ERW. In order to ensure post-use clearance, specific technical requirements, such as increased reliability, self-destruct capabilities and delectability, must be considered by the manufacturers to reduce civilian casualties from ERW in post-conflict situations. The States involved in armed conflict as well as the UN must provide technical, material and financial assistance to facilitate removal of ERW in affected areas.

Action Taken by States

A number of States have adopted measures to remove ERWs and landmines and several of them have established specific mine action plans and put in place specific administrations or institutions dealing with demining. Bosnia and Herzegovina took significant measures and issued a Law on Demining accompanied by the 2018-2025 Strategy on action against mines, succeeding in clearing more than 2/3 of its suspected hazardous areas. Croatia has established a specific framework for demining, which includes the Act on mine action and the National mine action strategy. Croatia, moreover, developed domestic standards based on a set of standards and guidelines established by the International Mine Action Standards (IMAS), and established a Croatian Mine Action Centre. In Cyprus, the National

40 Maresca Louis, A New Protocol on Explosive Remnant of War: The History and Negotiation of Protocol V to the 1980 Convention on Certain Conventional Weapons, Vol. 86, No. 856, *International Review of the Red Cross*, December 2004, p.834.

Guard is the responsible authority for demining operations. In Germany, explosive ordnance disposal is predominantly assigned to the local authorities. Hungary has set up the Mine Action Programme and the task of demining belongs to the Bomb Disposal and Mine-searcher Battalion of the Hungarian Armed Forces. In North Macedonia, the Direction for Safety and Rescue is the responsible national institution for protecting from unexploded ordnance, including area search, detection of explosive devices and their destruction. Romania has a specific Ministry of Defence Explosive Ordnance Disposal structure responsible for the intervention and cleaning of unexploded ordnance.

Canada has developed public education as a means to reduce unexploded ordnance risk and thanks to the Unexploded Explosive Ordnance Program, which identifies and catalogues legacy sites, assesses risks, and works to reduce unexploded ordnance risk. In some countries affected by contaminated land, international agencies, including the UN, civilian companies, and civil society organisations take part in demining activities together with national authorities. In Slovenia, the National Civil Protection Unit is responsible for unexploded ordnance protection, functioning under the Administration of the Republic of Slovenia for Civil Protection and Disaster Relief. In North Macedonia, national institutions have been assisted by international agencies, including the UN, to conduct several demining actions at targeted areas.[41]

At the international level, several states have developed international co-operation in order to locate and clear mines.[42] The US Department of Defence, and the US Agency for International Development (USAID) work together with foreign governments and international organisations undertakes humanitarian mine action programmes. The UK armed forces provide an explosive ordnance disposal capability in the UK and worldwide. India's approach to Mine Action is multi-faceted and comprises contributions through UN Peacekeeping, bilateral assistance and training, domestic R&D & deployment of solutions, collaboration with international organisations and civil society. It spans demining operations, public awareness outreach,

41 For more details see: Mine Action Review (2021) Mitigating the environmental impacts of explosive ordnance and land release. Available at: https://blogs.icrc.org/law-and-policy/2021/12/16/environmental-impacts-explosive-ordnance/; Mine Action Review (2023) Clearing the Mines 2023- Angola. Mine Action Review; NPA. Available at: https://www.mineactionreview.org/assets/downloads/Angola_Clearing_the_Mines_2023.pdf.

42 Domagoj Hajdukovic, Post-conflict time: defusing ticking time bombs for a safe return of displaced populations, Parliamentary Assembly, Council of Europe, June 06, 2024.

victim assistance, victim rehabilitation through financial, employment and health assistance and legislative protection to disabled victims. This reflects our commitment to disarmament and humanitarian objectives. India has trained mine clearance teams working in Cambodia, Lao PDR, Angola, Benin and Afghanistan. India has provided support for mine clearance tasks in Sri Lanka and has organised workshops for several foreign delegations including from Bhutan, Bangladesh, Australia and Vietnam.[43]

Complications of Climate Change

Climate change is one of the most pressing issues of our time. Climate change not only complicates mine action activities, it also impacts local communities, places pressure on local resources and land, and may force people to move and resettle. Climate hazards visible today, like as droughts, floods and wildfires, also intensify the impact of ERWs and landmines. Floods and heavy rainfall can unearth landmines and other unexploded ordnance, sometimes displacing them into areas previously considered safe. High temperatures from heatwaves can also cause abandoned munitions to explode. Reportedly, six different munition sites exploded across Iraq during scorching hot summers in 2018 and 2019, when temperatures regularly topped 45°C. apparently, heatwaves were responsible for a similar arms dump explosion in Jordan in 2020.[44]

The presence of ERWs in the environment can hamper responses to climate events. In easter part of Ukraine, the heavy contamination of forests with landmines and tripwires prevented fire crews from responding effectively to wildfires in 2020. Recently, unexploded bombs from the second world war were detonated by wildfires in the North York Moors, UK. In 2023, Storm Daniel in Libya destroyed two dams and subsequently caused flooding in large parts of the eastern city of Derna. The displacement of unexploded ordnance and ammunition stores caused by the flooding complicated recovery efforts. Climate disasters and environmental change can also prevent communities from benefiting from land that has been cleared of ERW after the end of war. Landmines and ERWs have a lasting

43 Remarks by Ms. Nutan Kapoor Mahawar, Additional Secretary, Indian Council of World Affairs, at the Symposium on Mine Action: Pathway to a Safer World, New Delhi, November 14, 2024, available at: https://www.icwa.in/show_content.php?lang=1&level=2&ls_id=12014&lid=7303.

44 For more details se: IPCC (2019) Climate Change and Land: IPCC Special Report on Climate Change, Desertification, Land Degradation, Sustainable Land Management, Food Security, and Greenhouse Gas Fluxes in Terrestrial Ecosystems. Cambridge University Press.

impact, not only on human life but also the environment. Climate change is only making the threat more unpredictable and challenging to address.[45] Without firm action, toxic remnants of war will continue to pose long term threats to communities and ecosystems. The effects of climate change are wide-ranging and can lead to more intense rainfall, increased risk of floods and landslides, more frequent and intense dry spells, higher average temperatures, increased risk of wildfires, warming oceans, and rising sea-level.[46] Women and girls face higher risks and heavier burdens from the consequences of climate change, since they depend more on natural resources, spend disproportionately more time securing food, water and fuel, and struggle more under climate change pressures.[47] The impacts of armed conflicts and climate-related disasters increase societal vulnerability to subsequent climate hazards.[48]

Conclusion

There are a number of armed conflicts raging around the world. Conflicts and climate-related events are becoming more frequent, intense, complex, and longer lasting. Together, they accelerate land degradation, a process that can take centuries to recover from, with even more time needed to restore land fertility. Similarly, climate-related events add an additional layer of complexity to the already challenging task of mitigating the risks posed by ERWs. In addition to their devastating human toll, these conflicts are all wreaking on the natural environment. One of the key ways war leads to environmental harm is by leaving behind unexploded weaponry and APMs. Explosive ordnance is a potential source of environmental pollution. APM and other EO kill or injure thousands of people each year. Globally, an estimated 60 million people live in areas affected by, and facing, the dangers and indirect consequences caused by landmines and other explosive ordnance. Climate change will present additional challenges for

45 Daria Yehorova, How unexploded bombs cause environmental damage – and why climate change exacerbates the problem, The Conversation, September 3, 2025, available at: https://theconversation.com/how-unexploded-bombs-cause-environmental-damage-and-why-climate-change-exacerbates-the-problem-242535.

46 Cottrell, Linsey and Stowe, Carlie. Climate Change and Extreme Weather: How Can Mine Action Programs Adapt to Our Changing Environment? *The Journal of Conventional Weapons Destruction*, Vol. 25, Issue 2, Article 6, 2021.

47 UN Women. Explainer: How gender inequality and climate change are interconnected. UN Women 28, 2022.

48 Mariagrazia D'Angelia and Paola Vesco, Assessing the impacts of armed conflict and climate related disasters on vulnerability: a Machine Learning approach, Department of Peace and Conflict Research, Uppsala University, June 10, 2024, pp. 14.

all countries affected by EO in terms of both how mine action operations are carried out and the way that EO-contaminated areas and communities will be affected. Climate change will affect regions differently, depending on shifting weather patterns, extreme weather conditions, climate resilience and any coping or national adaptation strategies in place. This will impact areas that are prone to flooding, landslides, or landscape fires more severely, and people living in these areas may also be less able to adapt to or withstand climate trends or shocks. climate change is also predicted to increase the risks for the marine environment caused by the large-scale dumping of munitions after World War II.

Post-War Waste and Environmental Degradation

Vasudha Bali

Abstract

Wars and armed conflicts have a devastating impact not only on the lives but also leave long-term scars on the environment as well. Besides dead and injured bodies, post-war countries are left with remnants of war, toxic chemical residues, depleted uranium munitions, radioactive debris, and hazardous industrial waste. These war wastes are not inert; they continue to impact the environment. This paper examines the environmental impact of post-war waste, explores shortcomings in current international law and International Humanitarian Law, and proposes legal and institutional reforms to enhance accountability.

Despite witnessing such devastating ecological consequences of war waste, international laws lack a coherent framework to address it. The principles of International Humanitarian Law (IHL), as embodied in the Geneva Conventions of 1949 and their Additional Protocols of 1977, provide some protection for the natural environment. Yet, these provisions are notoriously difficult to enforce, owing to the high conjunctive threshold ("widespread, long-term and severe") and the broad discretion accorded to military necessity. The absence of a unified international legal framework for military waste management is striking. Existing treaties cover fragments of the problem.

This article seeks to fill that analytical gap. It examines the nature and impact of post-war military waste, traces the historical evolution of the legal framework, evaluates existing international instruments and customary law, and analyses case studies from Vietnam, Iraq, the Balkans, Ukraine, Antarctica, and outer space. It argues that the current regime is fragmented and inadequate, leaving accountability gaps that perpetuate environmental injustice. The article concludes by proposing a global governance framework, including the negotiation of an International Convention on Military Waste Management, codification of clearance and remediation duties into IHL, and the application of the polluter-pays principle to aggressor states.

Introduction

Wars and armed conflicts have a devastating impact not only on the lives but also leave long-term scars on the environment as well. Besides dead and injured bodies, post-war countries are left with remnants of war, toxic chemical residues, depleted uranium munitions, radioactive debris, and hazardous industrial waste. These war wastes are not inert; they continue to impact the environment by contaminating soil, water, and air long after the cessation of conflict and war.[1] Use of Agent Orange by the United States of America (U.S.), large-scale air pollution during the Gulf Wars, and the ongoing conflict in Ukraine are strong reminders of war waste whose consequences endure across generations.[2]

Despite witnessing such devastating ecological consequences of war waste, international laws lack a coherent framework to address it. The principles of International Humanitarian Law (IHL), as embodied in the Geneva Conventions of 1949 and their Additional Protocols of 1977, provide some protection for the natural environment. Article 35(3) of Additional Protocol I prohibits warfare methods "intended, or may be expected, to cause widespread, long-term and severe damage to the natural environment."[3] Article 55 supplements this by affirming that the natural environment must be protected against such damage, as it is essential to civilian survival.[4] Yet these provisions are notoriously difficult to enforce, owing to the high conjunctive threshold ("widespread, long-term and severe") and the broad discretion accorded to military necessity.

1 See generally, Hailemariam Meaza et al., "Managing the Environmental Impacts of War: What Can Be Learned from Conflict-Vulnerable Communities?" *Science of the Total Environment*, vol. 927 (2024).

2 Olena Hanoshenko, Mykola Halaktionov & Marion Huber-Humer, "Exploratory Study on the Impact of Military Actions on the Environment and Infrastructure in the Current Ukraine War with a Specific Focus on Waste Management," *Waste Management & Research* (2024), pp. 1–15 at p. 4

3 Protocol Additional to the Geneva Conventions of 12 August 1949, and Relating to the Protection of Victims of International Armed Conflicts (Protocol I), 1125 UNTS 3, art. 35(3).

4 *Id.* at art. 55

Parallel developments in International Environmental Law (IEL) — such as the 1976 Convention on the Prohibition of Military or Any Other Hostile Use of Environmental Modification Techniques (ENMOD Convention), the 1989 Basel Convention on the Control of Transboundary Movements of Hazardous Wastes and Their Disposal, and the 2001 Stockholm Convention on Persistent Organic Pollutants — provide useful normative tools but were not drafted with armed conflict in mind.[5] States frequently argue that environmental treaties are suspended during hostilities, creating a governance vacuum precisely when environmental protection is most needed.

Concern about military waste grows deeper in the "global commons," where it transcends territorial boundaries. The Antarctic Treaty, 1959, and its 1991 Madrid protocol were able to forestall the idea of dumping the Cold War-era nuclear waste in Antarctica.[5] However, it highlights the fragile image of safeguards in times of geopolitical rivalry. In outer space, anti-satellite (ASAT) missile tests were conducted by China in 2007, the U.S. in 2008, India in 2019, and Russia in 2021, which raised the militarisation of space along with clouds of orbital debris that remain hazardous for decades.[6] The Outer Space Treaty, 1967, and the Space Liability Convention, 1972, though they call for peaceful use of outer space, do not contain provisions for explicit duties to remediate space debris, highlighting the regulatory gap in this new form of warfare.

The humanitarian implications of post-war waste are equally severe. The United Nations Mine Action Service estimates that landmines and unexploded ordnance (UXOs) continue to claim thousands of civilian lives annually, with children disproportionately affected.[7] Toxic remnants from chemical and radiological warfare produce chronic illnesses, birth defects, and displacement. Economically, the costs of clearance and remediation often exceed the capacity of affected states, diverting resources away from reconstruction and development. As Al-Muqdadi and Al-Ansari observe in the case of Iraq, "radioactive debris still contaminates farm fields,

---

5 Antarctic Treaty, 402 UNTS 71 (1959), art. V; Protocol on Environmental Protection to the Antarctic Treaty, 30 ILM 1455 (1991).

6 Daryl G. Kimball, Arms Control Today, *available at:* https://www.armscontrol.org/act/2022-05/news/us-commits-asat-ban#:~:text=In%202007%2C%20China%20used%20a%20ground%2Dbased%20SC%2D19,to%20destroy%20a%20failed%20U.S.%20intelligence%20satellite accessed on 26 September, 2025.

7 United Nations Mine Action Service, Annual Report 2022, available at: https://www.unmas.org accessed on 15 September 2025.

residential areas, and roadsides decades after the first Gulf War," a problem exacerbated by lack of funds and weak governance.[8]

Against this backdrop, the absence of a unified international legal framework for military waste management is striking. Existing treaties cover fragments of the problem: the Chemical Weapons Convention mandates destruction of chemical stockpiles, the Biological Weapons Convention prohibits biological warfare agents, the Convention on Certain Conventional Weapons (CCW) Protocol V addresses ERWs, and the Treaty on the Prohibition of Nuclear Weapons (TPNW) prohibits nuclear weapons while requiring environmental remediation and victim assistance.[10] However, none of these instruments integrates humanitarian protection with environmental justice into a comprehensive governance regime.

This article seeks to fill that analytical gap. It examines the nature and impact of post-war military waste, traces the historical evolution of the legal framework, evaluates existing international instruments and customary law, and analyses case studies from Vietnam, Iraq, the Balkans, Ukraine, Antarctica, and outer space. It argues that the current regime is fragmented and inadequate, leaving accountability gaps that perpetuate environmental injustice. The article concludes by proposing a global governance framework, including the negotiation of an International Convention on Military Waste Management, codification of clearance and remediation duties into IHL, and the application of the polluter-pays principle to aggressor states.

Nature and Impact of Post-War Military Waste

Military waste, an umbrella term used for the vast array of hazardous remnants generated during and after armed conflict, includes, in itself, "explosive remnants of war (ERWs), toxic residues from chemical weapons, biological weapons, depleted uranium, other radioactive materials, and conventional hazardous waste such as plastics, asbestos, and heavy metals."[9] It extends not only to terrestrial battlefields but also into global

8 K. Al-Muqdadi & N. Al-Ansari, "Nature, Size and Contaminated Areas of the Waste of War in Iraq," *Journal of Earth Sciences and Geotechnical Engineering*, vol. 3, no. 3 (2013), pp. 93–107 at p. 95.

9 Joshua O. Reno, *Military Waste: The Unexpected Consequences of Permanent War Readiness* (University of California Press, Oakland, 2019), p. 22.

commons like the oceans, Antarctica, and outer space, creating pollution that transcends borders and generations.[10]

Explosive Remnants of War

After wars and armed conflicts, the most visible form of military waste is ERWs, including UXOs, landmines, and cluster munitions, creating a staggering amount of humanitarian damage. According to the United Nations Mine Action Service, "more than 60 countries remain contaminated by landmines and UXOs, causing thousands of civilian casualties annually."[11] According to the United Nations Mines Action Service (UNMAS), since "1983, 45,900 Afghan citizens have been killed or injured, with children being disproportionately affected, often mistaking ordnance for toys."[12] They also contaminate soil, making farmlands unusable, obstructing development projects, and displacing communities, affecting the economy as well. "The clearance of ERWs is technically demanding and financially prohibitive; despite decades of demining initiatives, full remediation remains elusive in countries such as Cambodia, Afghanistan, and Angola."[13]

In Humanitarian Law, Protocol V of the Convention on Certain Conventional Weapons (CCW), 2003, obliges parties to conflict to "clear, remove or destroy explosive remnants of war after hostilities".[14] Theoretically, it is a significant step towards the codification of state duty. However, the implementation and compliance mechanisms are not strong. The Protocol relies on voluntary cooperation, leaving affected states dependent on international assistance.

Chemical and Biological Residues

.Toxins such as chlorine, sarin, mustard gas, anthrax, etc., have a devastating and long-term impact on the environment. Agent Orange, a defoliant herbicide used by the U.S. in the Vietnam War, caused widespread loss

10 Jacob Darwin Hamblin, "Environmental Diplomacy in the Cold War: The Disposal of Radioactive Waste at Sea During the 1960s," *International History Review*, vol. 24 (2002), pp. 348–375 at p. 351.

11 UNMAS, *note* 7

12 UNMAS, Afghanistan, available at: https://www.unmas.org/en/programmes/afghanistan accessed on 29 September 2025.

13 UNMAS, *note* 7

14 Convention on Certain Conventional Weapons, Protocol V on Explosive Remnants of War, 2399 UNTS 100 (2003), art. 3

of farmland, forests, water contamination, and soil contamination, leaving toxin residues in food chains for generations.[15] It impacted generations with cancer and congenital disabilities.[16] It is believed that in 2018, the Syrian government used chlorine gas on residents of Doma City.[17] Such attacks continue to pose a danger to society and the environment.

Similarly, biological weapons can have a devastating effect on society.[18] "During World War I (WWI), also referred to as 'The Great War,' Germany implemented a pioneering biowarfare program as part of a broader military strategy to undermine Allied forces by targeting their logistical and supply capabilities".[19] According to the authors, "Several tens of thousands of these deaths were due to the deliberate release of pathogens or toxins, mostly by the Japanese during their attacks on China during the Second World War."[20]

The Chemical Weapons Convention, 1993 (CWC) prohibits "the development, production, and stockpiling of chemical weapons and mandates the destruction of existing arsenals."[21] Similarly, though the CWS is effective in many respects, it does not explicitly address the long-term impact of contamination from such chemicals. It also lacks accountability for states and corporations responsible for such environmental devastation. Similarly, the Biological Weapons Convention, 1972 (BWC) "prohibits

15 Arnold Schecter et al., "Agent Orange and Its Associated Dioxin: Assessment of Environmental and Human Health Effects in Vietnam," *Environmental Science and Pollution Research*, vol. 13, no. 1 (2006), pp. 5–10 at p. 7.

16 *Ibid*

17 UN Security Council, 'Reasonable Grounds to Believe' Syrian Government Used Chlorine Gas on Douma Residents in 2018, Head of Chemical Weapons Monitoring Organization Tells Security Council, available at: https://press.un.org/en/2023/sc15194.doc.htm, assessed on 29 September 2025.

18 *See generally,* David Pimentel and Marcia Pimentel, "Bioweapon Impacts On Public Health And The Environment" *Wm. & Mary Envtl L. & Pol'y Rev.*, vol. 30 (2006), p. 625

19 Nikolakakis I, Michaleas S N, Panayiotakopoulos G, *et al.*, "Instances of Biowarfare in World War I (1914–1918)", *Cureus*, vol. 16, no. 4 (2024), DOI: 10.7759/cureus.59329

20 Friedrich Frischknecht, The history of biological warfare, *Science & Society*, vol. 4, (2003), p. S47

21 Convention on the Prohibition of Chemical Weapons, 1974 UNTS 45 (1993), arts. I–IV

the development and stockpiling of biological agents but provides no framework for remediating areas affected by their past use or testing."[22]

Radioactive and Nuclear Waste

Nuclear detonations and testing, the use of depleted uranium (DU) munitions, have remained one of the most persistent forms of military waste. DU, employed in armour-piercing projectiles, was first used in Iraq in 1991 and subsequently in Kosovo, Bosnia, and Afghanistan.[23] Al-Muqdadi and Al-Ansari report that Iraq remains dotted with radioactive contamination from DU shells, with hundreds of polluted sites identified by national and international agencies.[24] Radioactive dust disperses through wind and water, spreading contamination far beyond impact zones.

At a broader scale, Cold War practices of ocean dumping illustrate the transboundary risks of nuclear waste. According to Jacob Hamblin, "the Soviet Union and Western powers secretly disposed of nuclear reactors and radioactive debris at sea in the 1960s, often in violation of emerging environmental norms."[25] Such activities foreshadowed modern concerns about accountability for environmental harms in the global commons.

While treaties such as the Treaty on the Non-Proliferation of Nuclear Weapons (NPT, 1968) and the Treaty on the Prohibition of Nuclear Weapons (TPNW, 2017) regulate nuclear arsenals, they provide limited guidance on the remediation of nuclear-contaminated environments.[26] This highlights a lacuna between disarmament obligations and environmental responsibilities.

22 Convention on the Prohibition of the Development, Production and Stockpiling of Bacteriological (Biological) and Toxin Weapons (BTWC), available at: https://www.nti.org/education-center/treaties-and-regimes/convention-prohibition-development-production-and-stockpiling-bacteriological-biological-and-toxin-weapons-btwc/, assessed on 15 September 2025

23 Wayne E. Briner, The Evolution of Depleted Uranium as an Environmental Risk Factor: Lessons from Other Metals, *Int. J. Environ. Res. Public Health*, vol. 3, no.2 (2006) p.129

24 K. Al-Muqdadi & N. Al-Ansari, *note 8*

25 Jacob Darwin Hamblin, "Environmental Diplomacy in the Cold War: The Disposal of Radioactive Waste at Sea During the 1960s," *International History Review*, vol. 24 (2002), pp. 348–375 at p. 359

26 Treaty on the Non-Proliferation of Nuclear Weapons, 729 UNTS 161 (1968); Treaty on the Prohibition of Nuclear Weapons, 72 UNTS 122 (2017).

Conventional Hazardous Waste

Wars also generate massive quantities of conventional hazardous waste. Demolition of infrastructure produces asbestos, heavy metals, and plastics, which contaminate air and water when improperly disposed of. Hanoshenko et al. note that in Ukraine, the destruction of cities has created waste volumes comparable to World War II, overwhelming waste management systems.[27] Toxic debris is often dumped in uncontrolled landfills or waterways, exacerbating environmental and public health crises.

Similarly, post-war contexts see abandoned military vehicles, fuel depots, and industrial facilities releasing pollutants into soil and groundwater. These "silent remnants" rarely receive the same legal or political attention as ERWs or chemical weapons, yet their long-term impact on sustainable reconstruction is profound.

Proxy and Irregular Warfare

Non-state actors used in wars and armed conflicts by the nation-states further creates a problem of responsibility. In the Syrian war, the militia ISIS used "Scorching Earth Tactics"[28] by burning the oil fields.[29] Rogue non-state actors may use indiscriminate weapons that pollute the environment. However, the "Ambiguity of responsibility" complicates the remedy, like if non-state actors commit environmental crime, is the sponsoring state liable?

Military Waste in the Global Commons

Military waste extends beyond national borders into areas of shared international concern. The Antarctic Treaty, 1959, and its Madrid

27 Olena Hanoshenko, Mykola Halaktionov & Marion Huber-Humer, "Exploratory Study on the Impact of Military Actions on the Environment and Infrastructure in the Current Ukraine War with a Specific Focus on Waste Management," *Waste Management & Research* (2024), pp. 1–15 at p. 6.

28 The Scorched-Earth Tactics means "the military tactic of destroying everything that enables the enemy to wage war, including crops, livestock, buildings, and infrastructure. A scorched-earth policy may be implemented by an army advancing through enemy territory to punish resistance and reduce enemy capability or by a retreating army to leave nothing of military value to the opposing force." available at https://www.britannica.com/topic/scorched-earth-policy, assessed on 28 September 2025.

29 UNEP, The Fog of War, available at: https://www.unep.org/news-and-stories/story/fog-war#:~:text=Battle%20for%20Mosul%20triggers%20environmental,town's%20sheep%20have%20turned%20black., assessed on 17 September, 2025.

Protocol, 1991, prohibit nuclear explosions and radioactive waste disposal in Antarctica, preventing Cold War-era proposals for nuclear dumping.[30] However, enforcement depends on state cooperation, and climate change raises new concerns about historic waste buried in ice re-emerging.

In outer space, military tests such as China's 2007, the U.S.'s 2008, India's 2019, and Russia's 2021 anti-satellite (ASAT) missile strikes generated thousands of pieces of orbital debris, many of which will remain aloft for decades, posing collision risks to satellites and spacecraft.[31] The Outer Space Treaty, 1967, and Liability Convention, 1972, impose state responsibility for damage caused by space objects but do not create binding duties for debris removal. This regulatory gap exemplifies the inadequacy of current frameworks to govern military waste in emerging theatres.

Humanitarian, Environmental, and Economic Consequences

The humanitarian cost of military waste is measured in casualties, chronic illnesses, and displacement. The environmental cost includes biodiversity loss, soil infertility, and water contamination. Economically, waste clearance diverts billions of dollars from reconstruction and development, locking post-conflict societies into cycles of poverty and instability. As Joshua Reno observes, "military waste is not merely a by-product of war but an enduring condition of permanent war-readiness."[15] Its ubiquity underscores the urgency of integrating waste management into the law of armed conflict and international environmental governance.

Historical Evolution of the International Legal Framework

The legal recognition of environmental damage in warfare has evolved gradually, often in response to catastrophic conflicts that revealed the inadequacy of existing norms. From early humanitarian principles in the Hague Conventions to the integration of environmental clauses in modern treaties such as the ENMOD Convention and Additional Protocol I to the Geneva Conventions, international law has developed piecemeal. Yet, war incidents show a consistent conflict between military necessity and environmental protection.

30 Protocol on Environmental Protection to the Antarctic Treaty, 30 ILM 1455 (1991), art. 7.

31 Space Debris from Anti-Satellite Weapons, available at: https://www.ucs.org/sites/default/files/2019-09/debris-in-brief-factsheet.pdf#:~:text=The%20bottom%20row%20gives%20estimates%20of%20the,the%20Chinese%20ASAT%20test%20in%20January%202007., assessed on 20 September 2025.

Early Humanitarian Restraints

Restrictions on methods of warfare started with the Hague Convention, 1899 and 1907. "Article 23(g) of the 1907 Hague Regulations prohibits the destruction or seizure of enemy property unless imperatively demanded by the necessities of war."[32] Although it had no focus on the environment, it was a landmark step as it gave early recognition to the fact that war cannot be unrestrained. Similarly, the "Martens Clause,"[33] included in the preamble to the Hague Conventions and later reiterated in the Geneva Conventions, affirms that "in cases not covered by existing treaties, civilians and combatants remain under the protection of the principles of humanity and the dictates of public conscience."[34] Even though the clause explicitly does not mention environmental protection, due to its open-ended nature, it has been invoked to extend humanitarian protection to the natural environment.[35]

The Geneva Conventions and Post-World War II Developments

Conventional IHL in the form of the Geneva Convention, 1949, offered limited protection for the environment.[36] Despite many instances of environmental devastation in the two world wars through strategic bombing, scorched earth tactics, and chemical warfare, the focus of the Geneva Convention remained on human casualties.

However, post World Wars, the U.S. use of napalm and Agent Orange in Korea and Vietnam, respectively, raised concerns for recognition of environmental problems, and legal restrictions on ecological destruction. These also prompted debates in the United Nations (UN) about the legality of ecological warfare.

---

32 Hague Regulations Respecting the Laws and Customs of War on Land, annexed to the onvention (IV) Respecting the Laws and Customs of War on Land, 1907, art. 23(g).

33 "It is named after Fyodor Fyodorovich Martens, who introduced the clause for the first time in the Preamble of the 1899 Hague Convention." ICRC, Martens Clause, available at: https://casebook.icrc.org/a_to_z/glossary/martens-clause, assessed on 30 September 2025

34 Hague Convention (II) on the Laws and Customs of War on Land, 1899, preamble (Martens Clause).

35 Dieter Fleck, "The Martens Clause and Environmental Protection in Relation to Armed Conflicts", *Goettingen Journal of International Law*. Vol. 10, no. 1, (2020), pp. 243-266, at p. 264

36 Geneva Conventions of 12 August 1949, 75 UNTS 31, 85, 135, 287

Emergence of Environmental Consciousness

In 1970, in response to environmental manipulation as a weapon of war, like cloud seeding to cause a flood, the Convention on the Prohibition of Military or Any Other Hostile Use of Environmental Modification Techniques, 1976 (ENMOD) was negotiated. "Article I prohibits the hostile use of environmental modification techniques with widespread, long-lasting, or severe effects."[37]

In addition to ENMOD, the Additional Protocol to the Geneva Convention, 1977, has also played a significant role in environmental protection during wartime. Article 35 (3) prohibits "warfare methods expected to cause widespread, long-term, and severe damage to the natural environment. Article 55 mandates environmental protection as essential to civilian survival.[38]

Governing the Global Commons

Parallel to developments in IHL, a series of treaties emerged to regulate military activity in the global commons, particularly Antarctica and outer space—domains where environmental harm could have profound and lasting transboundary effects. The Antarctic Treaty of 1959 demilitarised the continent by prohibiting military bases, weapons testing, nuclear explosions, and the disposal of radioactive waste. Its environmental framework was significantly reinforced by the 1991 Madrid Protocol, which banned all activities related to mineral resource extraction and instituted comprehensive environmental impact assessment requirements. Although these instruments deterred Cold War proposals to dump nuclear waste in Antarctica, legacy pollution from earlier research and military activities persists, and climate change now threatens to expose buried contaminants.

In outer space, the 1967 Outer Space Treaty similarly restricts military activities by prohibiting the placement of nuclear weapons in orbit and obligating states to prevent harmful contamination of the space environment. The 1972 Liability Convention further establishes state responsibility for damage caused by space objects. Yet neither treaty directly addresses the rapidly growing problem of space debris, including that generated by anti-satellite (ASAT) testing. As military operations

37 Convention on the Prohibition of Military or Any Other Hostile Use of Environmental Modification Techniques, 1108 UNTS 151 (1976), art.

38 Protocol Additional to the Geneva Conventions of 12 August 1949 (Protocol I), 1125 UNTS 3 (1977), arts. 35(3), 55

expand into the space domain, the absence of binding obligations for debris mitigation or removal highlights significant regulatory gaps.

Together, these instruments demonstrate an evolving understanding that environmental protection in warfare must extend beyond terrestrial battlefields to shared global domains. They reflect the recognition that military activities in remote or extraterrestrial environments can produce global or long-term consequences, necessitating legal regimes tailored to the unique vulnerabilities of these commons.

Customary Law and Judicial Developments

Customary international law also evolved to encompass environmental protection in conflict. The International Court of Justice (ICJ), in its 1996 Advisory Opinion on the Legality of the Threat or Use of Nuclear Weapons, affirmed that the environment "is not an abstraction but represents the living space, the quality of life and the very health of human beings, including generations unborn."[39] Though the Court stopped short of declaring nuclear weapons illegal, it laid that environmental considerations form part of humanitarian law.

The ICRC's Customary IHL Study codifies rules prohibiting methods of warfare that cause widespread, long-term, and severe damage to the environment (Rule 45) and requiring precautions to protect civilian populations and the natural environment (Rule 83).[40] These rules, while not binding treaty provisions, reflect a growing consensus that environmental protection is integral to humanitarian norms.

Despite these advances, the historical evolution of international law reveals persistent tensions. States remain reluctant to limit their military freedom of action, invoking sovereignty and necessity. Enforcement and accountability of states are minimal.

Humanitarian and Customary Norms

The Geneva Conventions and Additional Protocol I (1977) include Articles 35(3) and 55, which prohibit warfare methods causing "widespread, long-

39 Legality of the Threat or Use of Nuclear Weapons, Advisory Opinion, ICJ Reports 1996, p. 226 at p. 241

40 Jean-Marie Henckaerts & Louise Doswald-Beck, *Customary International Humanitarian Law: Volume I – Rules* (ICRC, Cambridge University Press, 2005), Rules 45, 83

term and severe" environmental damage.[41] However, their conjunctive threshold has been criticised for rendering them ineffective in practice.

Customary IHL, as codified by the ICRC, prohibits warfare that causes disproportionate environmental harm (Rule 45) and requires precautions to protect civilians and the environment (Rule 83).[42] These rules, while influential, lack enforcement mechanisms and depend on voluntary compliance.

Soft Law and Institutional Frameworks

Soft law instruments and institutional practices supplement treaty law. UNEP's *Post-Conflict Environmental Assessments* provide scientific documentation of war's environmental toll, as in Kosovo, Afghanistan, and Lebanon.[43] UN General Assembly resolutions, such as Resolution 47/37 (1992) on the protection of the environment in armed conflict, affirm state responsibility to safeguard the environment.[44] The ICRC's *Guidelines on the Protection of the Natural Environment in Armed Conflict* consolidate applicable rules and best practices, serving as a practical reference.[45] Although not binding, these initiatives shape state behaviour and contribute to the progressive development of law.

International Legal Instruments Governing Military Waste

If environmental protection during war is weak, governance of post-war military waste is minimal. There is no comprehensive framework. Some provisions provided in different international agreements create weak obligations, gaps in enforcement, and uncertainty regarding state responsibility.

41 *note* 38

42 Jean-Marie Henckaerts & Louise Doswald-Beck, *Customary International Humanitarian Law: Volume I – Rules* (ICRC, Cambridge University Press, 2005), Rules 45, 83

43 United Nations Environment Programme, *Kosovo: Post-Conflict Environmental Assessment* (UNEP, Geneva, 1999), p. 11

44 UNGA Res. 47/37, "Protection of the Environment in Armed Conflict," UN Doc. A/RES/47/37 (25 November 1992), para. 3.

45 ICRC, *Guidelines on the Protection of the Natural Environment in Armed Conflict* (Geneva, 2020), p. 5.

Weapons-Specific Treaties

- **Convention on Certain Conventional Weapons (CCW) & the United Nations Mine Action Service (UNMAS)**

Protocol V of CCW on "Remnants of War", 2003, is the first instrument to impose post-war waste management obligations. Article 3 requires "parties to clear, remove, or destroy ERWs as soon as feasible after active hostilities."[46] Article 4 "obliges states to record and transmit information about ERWs, facilitating clearance operations." However, prospective application, lack of strong enforcement, and voluntary cooperation limit its applicability.

On the other hand, the UN body, UNMAS, "works to eliminate the threat posed by mines, explosive remnants of war and improvised explosive devices by coordinating United Nations mine action, leading operational responses at the country level, and in support of peace operations, as well as through the development of standards, policies and norms."[47] It is implementing the UN Mine Action Strategy Plan 2019-23 which aims at world free from threat of mines, ERWs & IEDs.[48]

- **Chemical Weapons Convention (CWC)**

CWC prohibits "development, stockpiling, and use of chemical weapons, mandating destruction of existing arsenals under international supervision."[49] Article IV requires "each state party to destroy chemical weapons in accordance with agreed verification measures," while Article V "obliges the destruction of chemical weapons production facilities." The Organisation for the Prohibition of Chemical Weapons (OPCW) oversees compliance and its successes.[50] However, it is not a post-war waste management body and does not address long-term contamination from chemical residues used in warfare and left as waste.

46 CCW Protocol V on Explosive Remnants of War, 2399 UNTS 100 (2003), art. 3

47 UNMAS, "Who are We", available at: https://www.unmas.org/en/who-we-are, assessed on 30 September, 2025

48 UNMAS STRATEGIC PLAN 2019-2023, available at: https://unmas.org/sites/default/files/documents/unmas_strategic_plan_2019-2023.pdf, assessed on 30 September, 2025

49 Convention on the Prohibition of Chemical Weapons, 1974 UNTS 45 (1993), art. I.

50 OPCW, available at: https://www.opcw.org/, assessed on 20 September 2025

- **Biological Weapons Convention (BWC)**

The 1972 Biological Weapons Convention prohibits the development, production, and stockpiling of biological agents, requiring their destruction or diversion to peaceful purposes.[51] However, the BWC is criticised for lacking verification mechanisms and compliance bodies. While effective in stigmatising biological warfare, it is silent on post-conflict waste issues, such as the disposal of contaminated materials or the remediation of affected environments.

- **Nuclear Weapons Treaties: NPT and TPNW**

The Treaty on the Non-Proliferation of Nuclear Weapons, 1968 (NPT) establishes "obligations to prevent proliferation and advance disarmament, while recognising the right to peaceful nuclear energy."[52] It does not address the environmental obligations. However, Article 6 of the Treaty on the Prohibition of Nuclear Weapons, 2017 (TPNW), "obliges states parties to assist victims and remediate the environment contaminated by nuclear weapon activities."[53] Although not widely ratified, it does recognise environmental remediation as part of disarmament.

Environmental and Hazardous Waste Conventions

- **Basel Convention (1989)**

The Basel Convention on the Control of Transboundary Movements of Hazardous Wastes and Their Disposal, 1989, regulates "international transfers of hazardous waste, including potentially military waste."[54] Although it is not meant for post-conflict waste disposal, it requires that "when states attempt to export military waste for disposal abroad."[55] However, like other instrument challenges of enforcement, illicit transfers, and "toxic dumping" persist.

51 Biological Weapons Convention, 1015 UNTS 163 (1972), art. I

52 Treaty on the Non-Proliferation of Nuclear Weapons, 729 UNTS 161 (1968), arts. I–III

53 Treaty on the Prohibition of Nuclear Weapons, 72 UNTS 122 (2017), art. 6

54 Basel Convention on the Control of Transboundary Movements of Hazardous Wastes and Their Disposal, 1673 UNTS 57 (1989), arts. 4–6

55 Overview of Basal Convention, available at: https://www.basel.int/theconvention/overview/tabid/1271/default.aspx, assessed on 26 September, 2025

- **Stockholm and Rotterdam Conventions**

Many Toxic chemicals, like flame retardants and pesticides, are found in military applications. The Stockholm Convention on Persistent Organic Pollutants, 2002, seeks to eliminate or restrict the production of such toxic chemicals.[56] Similarly, the Rotterdam Convention, 1998, "establishes a prior informed consent procedure for hazardous chemicals and pesticides." None of these treaties explicitly addresses armed conflict, but recognises a "polluter-pays" approach and duty of care that can be invoked for wartime pollution.

- **UNCLOS and marine dumping prohibitions**

The London Convention, 1972, and its 1996 Protocol ban the dumping of hazardous waste at sea, which includes military sources. The 1982 United Nations Convention on the Law of the Sea (UNCLOS) prohibits the dumping of toxic or hazardous waste at sea.[57]Yet during the Cold War, both the United States and the Soviet Union disposed of radioactive waste in oceans, highlighting weak enforcement and secrecy in military operations. Hamblin documents how nuclear submarines and reactors were deliberately sunk, often with little regard for international obligations.[58] Today, UNCLOS obligations are clear, but accountability for historic dumping remains elusive.

Critical Appraisal

This survey of instruments reveals a fragmented legal landscape. Weapons treaties address specific categories of military waste but rarely impose remediation obligations. Environmental treaties provide broad prohibitions but are often sidelined in wartime. Commons regimes such as Antarctica and outer space demonstrate successful prevention but weak remediation frameworks. Customary law and soft law expand normative expectations but lack binding force. The cumulative effect is a governance regime that recognises the problem of military waste yet fails to integrate humanitarian protection with environmental justice in a comprehensive way.

56 Stockholm Convention on Persistent Organic Pollutants, 2256 UNTS 119 (2001), arts. 3–4

57 United Nations Convention on the Law of the Sea, 1833 UNTS 3 (1982), arts. 192–196

58 Jacob Darwin Hamblin, "Environmental Diplomacy in the Cold War: The Disposal of Radioactive Waste at Sea During the 1960s," *International History Review*, vol. 24 (2002), pp. 348–375 at p. 362

Case Studies & State Practices

This part covers a detailed case study to reveal how military waste appears in diverse contexts and the failure of the legal framework to respond.

Vietnam and the Legacy of Agent Orange

The U.S. attack on Vietnam is one of the classic examples of environmental devastation through chemical warfare. Between 1961 and 1971, the U.S. sprayed millions of litres of Agent Orange, an herbicide, thereby causing vast areas of deforestation and destroying agricultural land.[59] The dioxin component of Agent Orange, TCDD, proved highly toxic, causing deforestation, water contamination, cancers, and congenital disabilities in exposed populations.[60]

Despite extensive scientific evidence, accountability under international law has been limited. The Geneva Conventions in force at the time contained no explicit environmental protections, and the ENMOD Convention and Additional Protocol I were negotiated only after the war. Vietnamese victims pursued civil claims in U.S. courts against chemical companies, but these were dismissed on grounds of sovereign immunity and the political question doctrine.[61] The case highlights the absence of legal mechanisms for redress in historic conflicts and highlights the inadequacy of existing treaties in addressing long-term contamination.

The Balkans and Depleted Uranium

The NATO interventions in the Balkans during the 1990s introduced international attention to depleted uranium (DU) munitions. Used in Kosovo and Bosnia, DU shells left radioactive contamination on battlefields. The UN Environment Programme (UNEP) conducted post-conflict assessments, finding elevated uranium levels in soil and water near impact sites.[62] Local populations reported increased cancer rates, though causality remains contested.[63]

---

59 Arnold Schecter et al., "Agent Orange and Its Associated Dioxin: Assessment of Environmental and Human Health Effects in Vietnam," *Environmental Science and Pollution Research*, vol. 13, no. 1 (2006), pp. 5–10 at p. 7

60 Ibid

61 *Vietnam Association for Victims of Agent Orange v. Dow Chemical Co.*, 373 F. Supp. 2d 7 (E.D.N.Y. 2005)

62 UNEP, *Depleted Uranium in Kosovo: Post-Conflict Environmental Assessment* (UNEP, Geneva, 2001), p. 18

63 Id. at p. 22

From a legal perspective, DU munitions are not explicitly prohibited by existing treaties. Protocol V of the CCW addresses explosive remnants but not toxic residues like DU. Attempts to regulate DU under customary law have failed, as major military powers resist restrictions. The Balkans thus illustrate how scientific uncertainty and political resistance undermine accountability for toxic remnants of war.

The Gulf Wars and Iraq's Contaminated Landscape

Iraq exemplifies the cumulative burden of military waste. The 1991 Gulf War saw widespread destruction of infrastructure and the ignition of Kuwaiti oil wells, producing massive air pollution and oil spills.[64] The 2003 invasion left an additional legacy of depleted uranium contamination, asbestos-laden demolition debris, and abandoned military equipment. Al-Muqdadi and Al-Ansari document over 300 contaminated sites, many near civilian populations.[65]

Despite obligations under Protocol I to protect the environment and under human rights law to safeguard health, occupying powers failed to implement comprehensive remediation. Iraq lacks the technical and financial capacity to address the problem, and no international mechanism has compelled accountability. The UN Compensation Commission addressed some environmental claims arising from Iraq's invasion of Kuwait, but no equivalent mechanism exists for Iraq as a victim state.[66]

Ukraine and the Collapse of Waste Management

Russia's invasion of Ukraine since 2022 has produced unprecedented volumes of military and civilian waste. Hanoshenko et al. report that demolition debris, hazardous industrial residues, and asbestos from destroyed buildings overwhelm Ukraine's waste management systems.[67] Nuclear power plants, including Zaporizhzhia, face risks of accidental release, raising the specter of radiological contamination on a continental

64 United Nations Compensation Commission, *Report and Recommendations Made by the Panel of Commissioners Concerning the First Instalment of Claims for Environmental Damage*, UN Doc. S/AC.26/1999/22 (1999), para. 9

65 K. Al-Muqdadi & N. Al-Ansari, *note 8*, p. 96

66 *Ibid*

67 Olena Hanoshenko, Mykola Halaktionov & Marion Huber-Humer, "Exploratory Study on the Impact of Military Actions on the Environment and Infrastructure in the Current Ukraine War with a Specific Focus on Waste Management," *Waste Management & Research* (2024), pp. 1–15 at p. 6

scale. The destruction of the Kakhovka Dam in 2023 released vast quantities of pollutants into the Dnipro River, affecting ecosystems and communities downstream.[68]

Legal frameworks have proven inadequate. As an occupying power, Russia is obliged under Article 56 of Geneva Convention IV to ensure public health and hygiene.[69] Yet in practice, environmental protections remain unenforced. International assistance, while vital, cannot substitute for binding obligations on aggressor states. Ukraine thus demonstrates the scale of modern military waste and the impotence of current legal regimes.

Antarctica and Prevented Dumping

During the Cold War, both the United States and the Soviet Union considered Antarctica a potential nuclear waste dump. Proposals were thwarted by the 1959 Antarctic Treaty and its 1991 Madrid Protocol, which prohibit radioactive waste disposal and require environmental protection.[70] These instruments prevented catastrophic contamination of a fragile ecosystem. However, historic military and research activities left localised pollution, including abandoned fuel depots and waste sites. Climate change may re-expose buried waste, raising questions about long-term accountability.[71] Antarctica illustrates both the preventive potential of strong treaties and the challenges of remediation.

Outer Space and Orbital Debris

Outer space represents a new frontier of military waste. Collisions with satellites or spacecraft could cause cascading debris events, threatening global communications, navigation, and climate monitoring.

The Outer Space Treaty (1967) prohibits harmful contamination, and the Liability Convention (1972) establishes responsibility for damage caused

68 UNEP, "Rapid Environmental Assessment of the Kakhovka Dam Destruction," UNEP Report, June 2023, p. 4

69 Geneva Convention (IV) Relative to the Protection of Civilian Persons in Time of War, 75 UNTS 287 (1949), art. 56

70 Antarctic Treaty, 402 UNTS 71 (1959), art. V; Protocol on Environmental Protection to the Antarctic Treaty, 30 ILM 1455 (1991), art. 7

71 Alan Hemmings, "Waste and Environmental Management in the Antarctic," *Polar Record*, vol. 43, no. 224 (2007), pp. 271–288 at p. 277

by space objects.[72] However, neither instrument creates binding obligations for debris removal. As military competition in space intensifies, the absence of a comprehensive regime for orbital waste mirrors the gaps in terrestrial military waste governance.

State Practices

Military manuals and policy statements of some countries reveal growing concern for the environment post-conflict. For example, defence manuals of Canada,[73] Australia,[74] and the UK[75] emphasise environmental security in operations, and Norwegian[76] and Dutch[77] forces require environmental impact assessments in conflict planning. The compensation in the Gulf War by the United Nations Compensation Commission (UNCC) is a leading example of where political will exists, showing that states have used existing mechanisms to hold aggressors responsible for environmental damage.[78] It

72 David Wright, "Space Debris from Anti-Satellite Tests," *Scientific American*, vol. 296 (2007), pp. 36–43 at p. 40

73 National Defence Canada, Defence Energy and Environment Strategy (2020-2023), available at: https://eda.europa.eu/docs/default-source/ifceed2/national-strategies/canada---the-defence-energy-and-environmental-strategy-2020---23.pdf#:~:text=The%202020%2D2023%20DEES%20provides%20a%20framework%20for,efficiency%20are%20factored%20into%20our%20decision%20making., assessed on 26 September, 2025

74 Adjusting Military Forces to the New Security Environment, the Case of Three 'Middle Powers': Australia, The Netherlands and Norway, available at: https://www.realinstitutoelcano.org/en/analyses/adjusting-military-forces-to-the-new-security-environment-the-case-of-three-middle-powers-australia-the-netherlands-and-norway/#:~:text=Adjusting%20Military%20Forces%20to%20the,Australia%2C%20The%20Netherlands%20and%20Norway, assessed on 26 September, 2025

75 The UK Comments On Requests For Information From The International Law Commission Contained In Chapter III Of Its Report Of Its 67™ Session (A/70/10), available at: https://legal.un.org/ilc/sessions/68/pdfs/english/poe_uk.pdf#:~:text=United%20Kingdom%20response.%20Multilateral%20environmental%20agreements%20are,also%20examples%20in%20the%20context%20of%20the, assessed on 26 September, 2025

76 Timothy J. Grout, Thesis on Norwegian Security Policy and New Environmental Challenges, Naval Postgraduate School, Monterey CA, available at: https://apps.dtic.mil/sti/tr/pdf/ADA307707.pdf, assessed on 26 September 2025

77 *note* 79

78 UN Commission Awards Compensation for Environmental and Public Health Damage from 1990-91 Gulf War, available at: https://www.asil.org/insights/volume/9/issue/25/un-commission-awards-compensation-environmental-and-public-health-damage, assessed on 27 September 2025

not only awarded compensation for measurable resource losses, but under the Security Council mandate expanded the concept of injury to include pollution and health damage.[79]. Kuwait's national court in 1990 accepted UNCC damage assessments to size Iraqi assets.[80]

These case studies highlight recurring patterns: devastating environmental and humanitarian consequences, weak or absent accountability mechanisms, and reliance on voluntary cooperation. Scientific uncertainty, political resistance, and fragmented legal regimes allow for such devastating acts. The international community has been reactive but has failed to take proactive actions against waste prevention, remediation, and liability

Challenges in Post-War Military Waste Governance

From the above discussion, it can be concluded that post-war military waste governance is affected by structural, technical, and political deficiencies. Such challenges limit the effectiveness of existing regimes and continue cycles of environmental injustice.

Technical and Scientific Challenges

Post-war military waste clearance poses many technical and scientific challenges. The major problem of ERWs is that they spread over vast areas, requiring years for detection and clearance.[81] Modern conflicts generate toxic debris like asbestos, heavy metals, and radioactive dust that require specialised scientific and technical expertise. Such toxic debris and DU remain contested, allowing culprits to downplay risks and evade responsibility.[82] Similarly, the health and ecological consequences of Agent Orange and nuclear radiation were seen over the years, which complicates efforts to quantify damage and establish liability. On the other hand, the removal of debris from outer space poses technical challenges and is not cost-effective.[83]

79 *Ibid*

80 UN, Iraq makes final reparation payment to Kuwait for 1990 invasion, available at: https://news.un.org/en/story/2022/02/1111632, assessed on 27 September 2025

81 United Nations Mine Action Service, "Annual Report 2022," available at: https://www.unmas.org accessed on 15 September 2023

82 *See generally*, Nada Al-Duaij, "Environmental Law of Armed Conflict", (2002) (S.J.D. dissertation, Pace University School of Law), available at http://digitalcommons.pace.edu/lawdissertations/1/, assessed on 1 September, 2025

83 David Wright, "Space Debris from Anti-Satellite Tests," *Scientific American*, vol. 296 (2007), pp. 36–43 at p. 41

Fragmentation of Legal Frameworks

A major challenge lies in the fragmentation of international law. Military waste is governed by a patchwork of regimes — IHL, IEL, arms control treaties, and commons governance treaties — none of which provide comprehensive coverage.

Weapons treaties such as the Chemical Weapons Convention (CWC) and Biological Weapons Convention (BWC) prohibit the use and stockpiling of specific categories but do not impose duties of environmental remediation. The CCW Protocol V addresses ERWs but excludes toxic residues such as depleted uranium. Environmental treaties such as the Basel and Stockholm Conventions regulate hazardous substances in peacetime but are often sidelined during armed conflict.[84]

This fragmentation leads to overlaps, lacunae, and selective compliance. States exploit legal ambiguity to avoid liability, arguing that specific instruments do not apply in wartime or that obligations are suspended. In the absence of a uniform framework, the enforceability of environmental protection is challenging.

Financial Constraints and Unequal Burdens

The financial burden of remedying military waste is high and difficult to determine. Remediation also requires continuous investment, and post-conflict states are already weakened economically and lack the funds to take such efforts. Aggressor states often evade responsibility, and the absence of the polluter pays principle in the framework makes it more difficult to ascertain responsibility.

Weak Enforcement and Accountability Mechanisms

Even if obligations exist, enforcement mechanisms and intentions are weak. Besides, the Organisation for the Prohibition of Chemical Weapons under CWC, most instruments lack comparable mechanisms. The CCW lacks compliance bodies; the BWC has no verification regime. The International Criminal Court (ICC) theoretically has jurisdiction over environmental crimes in war under Article 8(2)(b)(iv) of the Rome

84 Basel Convention on the Control of Transboundary Movements of Hazardous Wastes and Their Disposal, 1673 UNTS 57 (1989); Stockholm Convention on Persistent Organic Pollutants, 2256 UNTS 119 (2001)

Statute, but prosecutions have been nonexistent due to the high threshold of proof.[85]

Similarly, UN General Assembly resolutions and UNEP assessments carry moral and political weight but lack binding force. In practice, enforcement depends on voluntary cooperation, international pressure, or ad hoc mechanisms such as the UN Compensation Commission. Without institutionalised accountability, violations persist with impunity.

Political Resistance and Sovereignty Concerns

The politicisation of military waste governance is another obstacle. States are reluctant to accept binding obligations that may constrain their military freedom of action or expose them to liability. Major military powers resist restrictions on depleted uranium munitions, oppose negotiations on space debris treaties, and reject stronger accountability for environmental harms.[86] Sovereignty concerns exacerbate the problem.

Towards a Global Governance Framework

Thus, the challenges discussed above require an urgent need for a coherent framework. The current reactive regime needs to be more proactive by integrating humanitarian, environmental, and accountability principles in a unified system. For that, the following suggestions could be looked into.

Proposal for an International Convention on Military Waste Management

The most important step could be a negotiation of a "Convention on Military Waste Management". Such a step could consolidate scattered obligations, codify duties of prevention, clearance, remediation, and accountability. The convention could provide for a procedure to identify, record, and disclose all forms of military waste. This can address the major gap of "absence of systematic reporting requirements" in the existing law. The occupying country must be required to perform remedying and clearance obligations similar to Protocol V of the CCW. Obligations should include the safe destruction of ordnance, decontamination of polluted sites, and restoration of ecosystems.

85 Rome Statute of the International Criminal Court, 2187 UNTS 3 (1998), art. 8(2)(b)(iv)

86 International Coalition to Ban Uranium Weapons, "Uranium Weapons: Current Status," Policy Brief (2021), p. 4

Most importantly, the convention should establish a polluter-pays principle, mandating that aggressor states bear financial responsibility for remediation. This would operationalise equity and prevent the disproportionate burden from falling on post-conflict societies.

Finally, the CMWM should include monitoring and enforcement mechanisms, such as an independent supervisory body (similar to the OPCW for the CWC), with powers to conduct inspections, verify compliance, and adjudicate disputes. Without enforcement, obligations risk remaining rhetorical.

Integration into International Humanitarian Law

While a new convention would be ideal, integration into existing frameworks remains essential. The Geneva Conventions' Additional Protocols could be amended or reinterpreted to lower the threshold of environmental damage from the conjunctive "widespread, long-term and severe" to a disjunctive test ("widespread, long-term or severe"), enabling broader accountability.

Moreover, the law of occupation (Geneva Convention IV, art. 56) should be read to impose an explicit duty to maintain environmental hygiene, obliging occupying powers to remediate hazardous waste and restore waste management systems. This would align environmental protection with humanitarian concerns for civilian health.

Expansion of Environmental Regimes

Environmental treaties such as the Basel, Stockholm, and Rotterdam Conventions should explicitly apply during armed conflict. States often claim suspension of treaty obligations during hostilities, creating governance vacuums. Clarifying that prohibitions on hazardous waste dumping, transboundary movements, and toxic chemicals remain binding in wartime would close significant gaps.

Similarly, UNCLOS provisions on marine pollution should be expanded to explicitly prohibit naval practices involving the dumping of hazardous military waste. The Antarctic Treaty and Madrid Protocol provide preventive models that could inspire binding regimes for outer space debris management, where military competition poses escalating risks.

Accountability Mechanisms

Accountability remains the weakest link. A model can be drawn from the United Nations Compensation Commission (UNCC), established after

Iraq's invasion of Kuwait, which adjudicated environmental claims and awarded compensation for environmental damage.[87] A similar mechanism could be created to address military waste, funded by responsible states and contributions from the international community.

The International Criminal Court (ICC) could also play a role by interpreting Article 8(2)(b)(iv) of the Rome Statute — prohibiting methods of warfare causing widespread, long-term, and severe environmental damage — to encompass negligent or reckless management of military waste. While prosecutions may remain rare, even symbolic cases could strengthen deterrence.

Linking to Sustainable Development Goals

Military waste governance must also be linked to the Sustainable Development Goals (SDGs). Waste remediation directly supports SDG 3 (health), SDG 6 (clean water), SDG 12 (responsible consumption), and SDG 16 (peace, justice, and strong institutions). By framing military waste as a sustainable development issue, international institutions can mobilise broader political will and funding, integrating remediation into reconstruction programs.[88]

Role of International Institutions and Soft Law

Institutional actors should be empowered to play stronger roles. The International Committee of the Red Cross (ICRC) should expand its Guidelines on the Protection of the Natural Environment in Armed Conflict to include detailed rules on waste management.[89] The United Nations Environment Programme (UNEP) should be given a permanent mandate to monitor and assess military waste globally, with reporting obligations to the UN Security Council.

In outer space, the UN Committee on the Peaceful Uses of Outer Space (COPUOS) should adopt binding debris mitigation standards, moving beyond voluntary guidelines. Similarly, the UN Environment Assembly

87 United Nations Compensation Commission, *Report and Recommendations Made by the Panel of Commissioners Concerning the First Instalment of Claims for Environmental Damage*, UN Doc. S/AC.26/1999/22 (1999), para. 9.

88 United Nations, *Transforming Our World: The 2030 Agenda for Sustainable Development*, UN Doc. A/RES/70/1 (2015), Goals 3, 6, 12, 16

89 ICRC, *Guidelines on the Protection of the Natural Environment in Armed Conflict* (Geneva, 2020), p. 5

(UNEA) could adopt resolutions affirming state responsibility for remediation, reinforcing normative expectations.

Feasibility and Political Obstacles

Admittedly, political resistance from major military powers remains a formidable obstacle. States may oppose binding obligations that constrain military flexibility or expose them to liability. Yet history shows that progress is possible: the stigmatisation of chemical and biological weapons, the adoption of the CWC and BWC, and the preventive success of the Antarctic Treaty illustrate how normative evolution can overcome resistance. Momentum for reforms needs to be created through civil society, scientific evidence, and humanitarian requirements.

Conclusion and Recommendations

The damage caused by war does not end when the fighting stops. Besides immediate loss of life and property, the toxic waste of war causes long-term damage to the environment and life. This waste can poison land, water, and people for generations. From chemical sprays like Agent Orange to radioactive debris, oil spills, and even missile junk orbiting Earth, the war impacts far beyond the battlefield. Yet the current international rules are weak and patchy. Some treaties are weapon-specific, while others deal with hazardous substances in peacetime, but none provide a comprehensive framework of accountability for post-war waste. A recent example of Ukraine's waste is added to many such earlier incidents. And as discussed, the global commons are also not completely immune from such wastes.

To address this problem of military waste, several steps are necessary. Firstly, a new global treaty should be created that clearly sets rules for identifying, reporting, cleaning up, and holding polluters accountable. Secondly, the IHL should be updated to include environmental protection as a duty, rather than an afterthought. Thirdly, existing environmental treaties must be explicitly applied during wartime to prevent hazardous dumping. Fourthly, strict accountability is key. The possibility of creating a compensation commission to handle the claims and the inclusion of ecocide as a war crime should be explored. Fifthly, efforts should be made to link the UN Sustainable Development Goals, showing that cleaning up war waste is not just about security, but also about health, clean water, responsible consumption, and peace. Finally, international institutions must be strengthened. The Red Cross could expand its guidance, UNEP could monitor waste more systematically, the space committee should adopt strict debris standards, and the UN Environment Assembly should back these obligations.

These reforms, though bold and difficult, are necessary. Without these, the cost of toxic war will continue to fall on communities that can least afford it. At the centre of this whole issue is "justice". Peace is not only about stopping violence, it also means repairing the damage that war leaves behind. If we continue to ignore military waste, the environment will remain an invisible casualty, and future generations will inherit poisoned lands and waters. True peace, therefore, requires a clear, enforceable, and fair system to manage and clean up the waste of war.

Chemical Weapons: Sea Dumping

U C Jha

Oceanic Sanctuary?

Oceans accommodate.[1] Oceans have become our default dumping grounds, reflecting a reckless assumption that their vastness can endure any abuse.[2] With no single owner, these global commons are exploited for hazardous waste—nuclear, chemical, and explosive. Instead of a sanctuary, the ocean floor is now a perilous depository, justified by dangerously naïve thinking. Believing the sea's immensity would diffuse risk, policymakers downplayed the hazards, trusting that toxicity would dissipate or decompose naturally.[3] This faith in dilution has proven misguided—and the consequences are mounting.

A classic case of this policy was the US Department of Defence Operation CHASE (Cut Holes and Sink 'Em) to dispose of unwanted munitions at sea. The operation lasted till August 18, 1970. That day, the *SS LeBaron Russell Briggs* sailed for the last time, and as the ship reached 400 km east of Cape Kennedy, Florida, the US soldiers bored into its hull, allowing the incoming seawater to force it downwards. The vessel came to rest at the ocean bed over 5,000m below the surface of the Atlantic Ocean. Its cargo bay held, among other materiel, more than 12,000 M55 rockets, each of which was loaded with about five kg of sarin.[4]

1 Srimad Bhagwad Gita in *shalok* 2.70 gives a simile of ocean to build capacity without perturbation and remain steady irrespective of what flows in.

2 David M. Bearden, 2006, *US Disposal of Chemical Weapons in the Ocean: Background and Issues for Congress,* Congressional Research Service.

3 Geoff Plunkett, 2003, *Chemical Warfare Agent Sea Dumping off Australia,* Department of Defence, Australia, pp. 18–19.

4 Newman, Joshua and Dawn Verdugo, Building Awareness of Sea-dumped Chemical Weapons, Disarmament Forum: Maritime Security, pp. 45-54, available at: https://

Contrary to misplaced optimism, chemical weapon materials have not remained sealed at dumping sites. An estimated 1.6 million tons now threaten oceans—especially vital coastal regions[5]—yet this is likely an undercount, as poor records conceal the true scale. We lack critical knowledge of dump site locations and conditions. The horrifying reality: munitions have surfaced or washed ashore, turning hidden hazards into immediate dangers for ecosystems and human populations.

Chemical Weapons Usage

Toxic chemicals had been used as tools of war for thousands of years, using techniques such as poisoned arrows, arsenic smoke, or noxious fumes. A massive use of chlorine gas[6] occurred in Ypres, Belgium, on April 22, 1915.[7] A gas arms race began with the Allies building up their own gas supplies and capturing German cylinders. The gas was initially delivered by cylinders and pipes, which had to be installed in the darkness of no-

---

unidir.org/wp-content/uploads/2023/09/maritime-security-en-319.pdf, accessed October 06, 2025.

5 A highly conservative estimate made in 2017, estimated the total amount of chemical munitions on our ocean and sea floors to reach 1.6 million tons. Kathryn Millett, Accountability for Old, Abandoned, and Sea Dumped Chemical Weapons, 2021, available at: Twenty-Sixth Session of the Conference of the States Parties (CSP-26) to the Chemical Weapons Convention The Hague, The Netherlands, November 29 – December 3, 2021.

6 Chlorine is two and a half times denser than air so it stays close to the ground when released and it also sinks into trenches, shell holes and bunkers. Chlorine gas also disperses over a reasonably short time to safe levels, enabling assaulting troops to safely occupy the gassed area. Germany already manufactured vast quantities of chlorine for the dye industry, pharmaceutical production, bleaches and water purification. Chlorine gas is fatal in a few minutes at a concentration of 1,000 parts per million (ppm) and 400 ppm is fatal if exposure is for more than 30 minutes. Chlorine is highly corrosive and kills by destroying lung tissue probably by forming hydrochloric acid when dissolved in lung fluid.

7 In April 1915, at Langemark-Poelkapelle near the ruins of Ypres, Belgium, the German army amassed 5,700 cylinders of liquid chlorine under pressure and waited for a favourable breeze to blow towards the enemy. The liquid would become a gas on its release from the cylinders. At around 5pm on April 22, about 160 tons of chlorine gas was released over ten minutes and wafted slowly towards French and French Algerian positions. The French watched in complete astonishment as a ghostly 1-2 m high green fog slowly drifted ever closer to them. The allied soldiers noted a strong irritating odour like a mixture of pepper and pineapple, and then began to wheeze, cough, choke and suffocate. Many men would literally 'drown' in the gas. Over a few minutes about 800–1,400 soldiers were killed and another 4,000 injured. Many thousands ran away in panic.

man's land. Defence against Chlorine gas was also discovered very soon.[8] This led to the development of a new, more lethal gas: phosgene. This gas is easy to manufacture by mixing carbon monoxide and chlorine, then exposing the mixture to sunlight. Soldiers exposed to phosgene gas were treated similarly to chlorine poisoning, including bed rest and oxygen therapy. Phosgene was often mixed with chlorine gas to help spread the denser phosgene. The Allies referred to this mixture as 'white star' after the markings on their gas shells. The Germans painted their chlorine/phosgene shells with a green cross. Chlorine and phosgene mixture gas attacks were used extensively during the Battle of the Somme from July to November 1916.

Development of a more lethal gas weapon: mustard gas, also referred to as sulphur mustard, soon followed. Gas masks and clothing offered no protection against this new weapon. The effectiveness of sulphur mustard was not in its lethality but in its ability to injure large numbers of soldiers for prolonged periods. It also contaminated land and equipment, meaning that assets such as heavy field guns exposed to mustard had to be abandoned, at least temporarily, and were therefore 'silenced'. Sulphur mustard could lie on the ground for weeks or months and be spread by later shelling. Soldiers were often exposed just by sitting or lying on the ground.[9] Sulphur mustard also contains chlorine and is very soluble in fat, penetrates clothing and leather and is absorbed easily through the skin. It is a vesicant, meaning a blister agent. Mustard gas can also form reactive intermediate compounds that attack cellular DNA, causing cancer. It was first used by the Germans in July 1917 at Ypres.

Mustard gas is almost odourless, and contact with the skin initially produces no ill effects. After an hour or so, the skin starts to itch, becomes erythematous, the eyes become inflamed, and vomiting is common. The

8 Covering the mouth and nose with a damp cloth was partially effective in reducing the effects of the gas. Simple gauze pads filled with cotton waste worn over the mouth and nose and motor-cycle goggles were rapidly issued to troops on both sides. These pads worked more effectively when dipped in bicarbonate of soda which was kept in buckets in the front-line trenches. The next stage was the development of the Hypo helmet in May 1915. A P Padley, Gas: the greatest terror of the Great War, Anaesth Intensive Care, 2016, available at: https://journals.sagepub.com/doi/pdf/10.1177/0310057X1604401S05.

9 A technique for large scale production of mustard gas was developed by two German scientists, Wilhelm Lommel and Wilhelm Steinkopf, in 1916. They originally called it Lost after their surnames. A P Padley, Gas: the greatest terror of the Great War, Anaesth Intensive Care, 2016, available at: https://journals.sagepub.com/doi/pdf/10.1177/0310057X1604401S05.

skin would then blister severely, and by the time the men reached a casualty clearing station, they were often blind. The blisters would get larger and larger, slough, become infected, and cause unbearable pain. Inhalation of mustard gas caused little in the way of symptoms initially. Over hours, the mucous membranes of the lung would be burnt and stripped away, resulting in immense pain and bleeding. The Germans called mustard gas 'yellow cross' as this was painted on the mustard gas shells. The British called it HS ('hot stuff' or 'Hun stuff') and the French called it Yperite (after Ypres). Gas was very effective at creating panic and terror in the soldiers of the First World War and greatly added to the misery and discomfort of life in the trenches. Mustard gas was particularly dreaded. Poisonous gas changed the history of warfare forever and is still being used as a weapon. Even today, an unknown number of countries have or are suspected of having stockpiles of poisonous gas.[10]

Sea Dumping of Chemical Weapons

Obsolete, damaged or malfunctioning conventional weaponry and/or canisters were dumped in the Atlantic, Arctic, Indian, Pacific and Southern Oceans.[11] Sea dumping of chemical weapons as a means for their disposal remained a common practice in the post-World War era, which continued even up to the 1980s. There is an uncertainty about the amounts and locations of dumped chemical warfare materials. Munitions dumped in these sites range from conventional munitions, phosphorous devices, to mustard gases. Dumping operations included dumping overboard from

10 A P Padley, Gas: the greatest terror of the Great War, Anaesth Intensive Care, 2016, https://journals.sagepub.com/doi/pdf/10.1177/0310057X1604401S05.

11 One of the most heavily used areas for dumping of conventional and chemical warfare munitions is the Beaufort's Dyke, a 200 to 300 meters deep trench, located between Scotland and Northern Ireland. It has been estimated that over 1 million tons of munitions have been dumped in the Beaufort's Dyke since the early 1920s. Very large quantities of munitions were also dumped in the Skagerrak. It is reported that some 168,000 tonnes of ammunition were dumped in water depths of 600 to 700 meters. These munitions were dumped by sinking vessels loaded with the munitions and some 26 such vessels were dumped in the Skagerrak, south east of Arendal. One of the concerns relating to phosphorous devices is that the containers they were dumped in may now be in an advanced state of decay. Hart, John, 'A Review of Sea-Dumped Chemical Weapons', presented at The Environment and the Common Fisheries Policy, Threats to and Constraints on Sustainability (Greenwich Forum) January 27, 2000, The Royal Society, 6 Carlton House Terrace, London, Great Britain; Surikov and Duursma. 1999. Dumped CW Agents in European Seas, in Duursma Egbert K. (ed.), *Dumped Chemical Weapons in the Sea – Options*, Netherlands: Dr. A. H. Heineken Foundations for the Environment.

vessels and by sinking ships containing chemical weapons and munitions. According to Beldowski (2018), Chemical Weapons were sea-dumped at over 300 places, out of which only 127 sites are documented in the following locations:[12]

- The Arctic, Indian and Pacific Oceans.
- The East and West Coasts of Canada and the United States.
- The Gulf of Mexico.
- The Australian, New Zealand, Indian, Philippines, Japanese, UK and Irish Coasts.
- The Barrents Kara, White Caribbean, Black, Red, Baltic, Mediterranean and North Seas.

As the seas worldwide are impacted by underwater munitions, either dumped in the seas or deployed during combat, these pose an environmental health risk and impair the sustainable economic development of all coastal waters. In general, related risks from chemical sea-dumping include acute toxicity in case of direct contact, chronic toxicity based on enrichment in the food chain, potential access to chemical weapons and contaminated agents by terrorists and progressive corrosion resulting in a decrease in the manageability of the ammunition as well as increasing rates of toxic emissions. According to Beddington and Kinloch (2005), there are three basic types of danger that munitions dumped at sea can cause:

(i) Direct physical contact with either chemical or conventional munitions resulting in threats to human health;

(ii) Contamination of marine organisms and the environment in the vicinity of dumped munitions and the consequent potential for some concentration of toxic contaminants entering wildlife and human food chains; and

(iii) Spontaneous explosions, which can be directly life-threatening, besides having the potential to spread material away from the

12 Jacek Beldowski, Terrence Long and Martin Soderstrom, "Introduction" in Jacek Beldowski, Robert Benn and Eyup Turmus (Eds.), *Towards the Monitoring of Dumped Munitions Threat (MODUM) A study of Chemical Munitions Dumpsites in the Baltic Sea*, Springer, 2018, pp. 2-3.

dump sites, thereby increasing the potential for more of it to come into direct physical contact with individuals.[13]

The threats include:

(i) Acute toxicity to marine organisms of agents and breakdown products released into the water.[14]

(ii) Chronic toxicity on marine organisms of long-lived contaminants in the sediments.

(iii) Bioaccumulation or biomagnification of released contaminants in the food web.

(iv) Threat to human safety if munitions are caught in commercial fishing nets or encountered during oil and gas resource development activities.

(v) Regional economic effects if commercial fish stocks are reduced in size, if sales of commercially important species are affected by contamination with released agents or breakdown products, or if additional large areas are closed to fishing and oil and gas resource development activities.[15]

(vi) Explosive chemicals like TNT and its derivatives are known for their toxicity and carcinogenicity and pose a great threat to the marine environment. In addition to the acute risk of detonation and chronic threat to the marine environment, leaking explosive

---

13 Beddington, J. and Kinloch, A.J., 2005. Munitions dumped at sea: A literature review, IC Consultants Ltd., Imperial College London, 2005. Available at: http://www.mod.uk/NR/rdonlyres/77CEDBCA-813A-4A6C-8E59-16B9E260E27A/0/ic_munitions_seabed_rep.pdf, accessed February 29, 2012.

14 Marine organisms can be exposed to arsenic in sediments in several ways. These include absorption of dissolved arsenic from the water or sediments through the skin and gills, eating other organism containing arsenic in their tissues or guts, ingesting contaminated sediments as a food source while feeding on benthic organisms. Ocean Dumping of Chemical Munitions: Environmental Effects in Arctic Seas, May 1997, MEDEA, Para 8.4.3.

15 Commercial fishing activities could be affected if areas were to be closed to fishing because either fish stocks are contaminated with hazardous materials or chemical munitions could be capture by fishing nets. Loss of fishing areas could substantially reduce the quantities of catch and increase fishing pressure on the remaining areas. Ocean Dumping of Chemical Munitions: Environmental Effects in Arctic Seas, May 1997, MEDEA, Para 8.6.5.

chemicals may enter the marine food chain and directly affect human health upon consuming contaminated seafood.[16]

(vii) Chemical weapons can also impact the genetic code of life forms exposed to them. Exposure to Mustard gas can cause cross-links in DNA, which corresponds with an increase in gene mutation and cancer cell development.

Major Culprits

Most sea-dumping of chemical and conventional munitions started after World War I and continued throughout World War II and the Cold War, and up to the 1970s, when the world began to understand the impact of these dumps on marine ecosystems and the environment in general. Like with other wastes, burial of chemical weapons was the accepted disposal method up until the 1970s and at least four major powers disposed of massive quantities of captured, damaged, and obsolete chemical warfare (CW) material by dumping them into the oceans.[17]

USA

For over 50 years, from 1918 to 1970, the United States (US) dumped more than 350,000 tons of surplus, damaged and captured chemical warfare material.[18] The US, during 'Operation Davey Jones Locker,' from 1946 to 1948, scuttled eleven ships containing chemical munitions in the North Sea and in the Skagerrak Strait (between the North and Baltic Seas).[19] Under

16 Edmund Maser and Jennifer S. Strehse, "Don't Blast": blast-in-place (BiP) operations of dumped World War munitions in the oceans significantly increase hazards to the environment and the human seafood consumer, Archives of Toxicology, 2022, https://doi.org/10.1007/s00204-020-02743-0.

17 Millions of pounds of Mustard Gas (a chemical weapon developed during World War I), other chemical weapons, bombs, torpedoes, artillery shells, and munitions were routinely disposed by the United States. Although many munition dump areas are marked on navigation charts, numerous areas where munitions were discarded remain unmarked. There is also evidence suggesting that munitions were frequently "short dumped," meaning dumped outside of the designated areas by contractors hired to take them to the intended locations. United States Coast Guard, Safety Alert 02-24, Dangerous Bycatch from Discarded Munitions Remains a Present Day Hazard, February 20, 2024, available at: https://www.dco.uscg.mil/Portals/9/DCO%20Documents/5p/CG-5PC/INV/Alerts/USCGSA_0224.pdf.

18 Bearden, David M., The US Disposal of Chemical Weapons in the Ocean: Background and Issues for Congress, CSR report for Congress, January 3, 2007.

19 Mark Frondorf, "Special Study on the Sea Disposal of Chemical Munitions by the United States," in Alexander Kafka (ed.), Sea-Dumped Chemical Weapons: Aspects,

orders of the US occupation authority, Japan[20] also dumped CW material off its coast. As of 2000, poison gas shells abandoned by the Imperial army are still being found near the seabed off the coastal town of Kanda.[21] Mitchell (2020) describes in detail the US practice of dumping chemical weapons in the Pacific, which were captured in Japan's Okunoshima Island:

> Between August 15, 1945, when Emperor Hirohito announced his nation's surrender, and the arrival of Allied troops in Japan two weeks later, Japan's skies turned black as officials burned documents that could be used as evidence against them in war crimes trials. On Okunoshima Island, the army incinerated reports, dismantled some production facilities, and dumped munitions at sea, fearing American reprisal. Wartime intelligence had alerted the Allies to the existence of Japan's chemical weapons program, so American officers arriving in Tokyo conducted interrogations to discover its location. In October, Allied troops landed on Okunoshima, where they found the factories largely intact and vast stockpiles of chemical weapons. At the time, Australian troops administered the region, but with little experience in handling chemical weapons, they asked the US for assistance. Experts from the US Army's Chemical Warfare Service arrived on Okunoshima and drew up plans to remove the poisons. With memories of dangerous conditions fresh in their minds, the island's previous workers refused to return, so the Allies ordered the Teikoku Rayon Company to send a crew. In the following weeks, 300 of these workers gathered approximately 15,000 tons of weapons and 3,000 tons of base chemicals from Okunoshima and neighbouring islands.
>
> The US military devised a two-stage plan: first, destroy the weapons, then destroy the facilities. Starting in May 1946, workers loaded the poisons onto two American ships and ran a pipe from the island's Yellow Agent storage tanks to pump the poisons onto the vessels. One man died when he was exposed to blister agent on one of the ships, and another ninety were injured when the hose from shore to ship was severed in a storm. Following the accident, an American

---

Problems and Solutions, Springer, 1996, pp. 35-40.

20 At the end of World War II, the Imperial Japanese Army left a number of unexploded shells filled with poison gas used as munitions.

21 Critics assail secrecy over unexploded chemical weapons left by Imperial Japanese Army, The Japan Times, December 27, 2019, available at: https://www.japantimes.co.jp/news/2019/12/27/national/unexploded-chemical-weapons-used-by-imperial-japanese-army/

officer ordered workers at gunpoint to retrieve the broken pipe from the seabed; one man developed blisters from head to toe, hospitalising him for three months. After the loading work had been completed, the two ships sailed south, where, overlooked by an Allied submarine, they were sunk in the Pacific. Back on Okunoshima, the Allies faced the problem of how to dispose of the remaining stocks of Red Agent, which, due to its buoyancy, could not be dumped at sea. Workers packed some of the weapons into air-raid shelters and burned them; one worker lost his arm when the propellant exploded. Tens of thousands of vomit agent canisters were stacked in caves and doused with seawater and bleach, a mixture the Allies believed would render safe the arsenic-based munitions. The caves' entrances were then plugged with concrete blocks. Nine out of ten workers involved in Okunoshima's wartime production and postwar cleanup suffered serious health damage, especially respiratory tract cancers and chronic bronchitis; others committed suicide.[22]

Europe

According to Maria (2021), there are about 50,000 tons of chemical munitions buried in the Baltic[23] alone, and 190,000 tons more to the north in the Skagerrak Strait.[24] One of the locations with the highest confirmed amount of sea-dumped CW, which is relatively proximate to human settlements and at relatively low depth (<100 m), is the Bornholm Deep in the Baltic Sea. This is where the main part of the dumping of mostly

22 John Mitchell, *Poisoning the Pacific: The US Military's Secret Dumping of Plutonium, Chemical Weapons and Agent Orange*, London: Rowman & Littlefield, 2020, pp. 15-17.

23 The Baltic Sea Marine Ecosystem is a semi-enclosed sea situated in northern Europe and encompasses a surface area of approximately 394,000 sq km Nine coastal countries (Denmark, Estonia, Finland, Germany, Latvia, Lithuania, Poland, Russia and Sweden) surround the Baltic Sea and are involved in national, regional and international agencies to manage the sea and its resources. The Baltic Sea countries benefit considerably from their utilization of the Baltic Sea, both economically and socially. Benefits derived include jobs, income, natural resources, and various other contributions to economic growth and personal well-being. Baltic Marine Environment Protection Commission, Annual Report 2023, HELCOM activities report for the year 2023, p. 28. Available at: https://helcom.fi/wp-content/uploads/2024/06/Annual-report-2023.pdf.

24 Maria Paula Rubiano, The ocean is a giant dump for chemical weapons. Can we clean it up before it's too late? April 12, 2021, https://www.popsci.com/story/environment/chemical-weapons-dumped-in-ocean/.

German chemical warfare agents and conventional munitions occurred in the Baltic Sea. [25]

By an estimate, 302,857 tons of CW munitions were left over in Germany and the UK after World War II, most of which were eventually dumped in the oceans. However, because of sparse records, the total quantity of CW material discarded at sea will never be known. [26] Whilst both conventional and chemical munitions have been dumped into the Baltic Sea, chemical munitions are considered to be more harmful and more difficult to recover. In the Skagerrak, there have been at least about 250,000 tonnes of chemical and conventional munitions dumped, along with probably more than 74 ships. East of Bornholm, a minimum of about 32,000 tonnes of chemical munitions have been dumped, and about 2,000 tonnes near the island of Gotland. Russia has dumped at least 160,000 tons of chemical weapons in the seas.[27] Other countries also participated in sea-dumping, especially after World War II. The lack of information on the location of dumped chemical weapons poses a great danger. Additionally, some states are reluctant to fully share their information and knowledge on dumped munitions.[28]

Australia

During World War II, chemical munition stocks were held at many sites around Australia.[29] At the end of World War II, at least 21,000 tons

25 Ilias Mohammed Abdullah Christensen, et.al., Acute toxicity of sea-dumped chemical munitions: luminating the environmental toxicity of legacy compounds, Global Security: Health, Science and Policy, 2016, Vol. 1:1, pp. 39-50, DOI: 10.1080/23779497.2016.1219962.

26 David M. Bearden, US Disposal of Chemical Weapons in the Ocean: Background and Issues for Congress (Washington, DC: Congressional Research Service, May 24, 2006; Fredrick Laurin, "Scandinavia's underwater time bomb," *Bulletin of the Atomic Scientists*, Vol. 47 (2), p. 11.

27 Interfax, "Ministry: 'Tonnes' of chemical weapons 'buried' at sea," Moscow, December 7, 1995.

28 Overview of Past Dumping at Sea of Chemical Weapons and Munitions in the OSPAR Maritime Area, 2010 update, OSPAR Commission, 2020, pp. 17, available at: https://www.ospar.org/documents?v=7258.

29 For its part, Australia had reserved the right to use chemical weapons in order to retaliate. The stocks of chemical munitions in Australia were held under General MacArthur's Chemical Warfare Plan for the South West Pacific Area (SWPA). Although their use was dependent on the joint agreement of General MacArthur and the Australian Prime Minister, the stocks were stored in Australia under US Army, Royal Australian Air Force (RAAF), Australian Army or Navy supervision. None of the chemical warfare materials stockpiled in Australia were used during combat and at

of chemical weapons were dumped in Australian seas by the US Army and the Australian defence forces.[30] In Australia, the sea dumping of large amounts of chemical warfare materials had largely ceased by 1948; however, there have been a few more dumping episodes since then, in 1956/1957, 1965 and 1970. Confirmed cases of dumping occurred in the seas off three states: Queensland (east of Cape Morton and Townsville), New South Wales (south-east of Sydney) and Victoria (west of King Island). Some of the chemical weapons were loaded onto decommissioned ships, which were scuttled under supervision. The remainder were dumped in containers or as loose shells or bombs. Mustard gas (sulphur mustard) was the most common type of chemical warfare agent dumped at sea. There were several incidents of contact during the disposal operation involving workers handling the chemical weapons and the members of the public encountering munitions that had floated to the shore. One of the most heavily used areas for dumping of conventional and chemical warfare munitions is the Beaufort's Dyke, a 200 to 300-meter-deep trench located between Scotland and Northern Ireland. It has been estimated that over one million tons of munitions have been dumped in the Beaufort's Dyke since the early 1920s. Since World War II, there have been few incidents of accidental recoveries of chemical warfare materials from the marine environment. As the dump sites in Australian waters are located in areas rarely fished or known to be foul, the risk of accidental recovery by a trawler is low. In 1999 and 2000, on two separate occasions, a mustard gas-filled shell was located at the same quarry as sand dredged from Moreton Bay.

Reasons for Sea Dumping

Storage of a large amount of chemical weapons was considered impractical as the cost of proper management and/or in-land disposal would far

---

the end of the war the material required disposal. Chemical Munitions Sea Dumping off Australia, Australian Government: Department of Defence, 2018, p. 6.

30 The weapons which were dumped included: aircraft bombs of various weights charged with phosgene and mustard gas; aircraft spray installations charged with mustard gas; and steel drums of various capacities (31/3 gallons15 to 90-gallon drums) charged with mustard gas. The areas in which a depth of 500 fathoms could be easily accessed and thus could be designated as suitable for disposal. Before chemical munitions were dumped at sea, tests were often conducted on the individual types to assess their buoyancy in the marine environment.19 It was later recognized that not all the dumped chemical weapons settled to the seabed as some material was recovered from the shore. Chemical Munitions Sea Dumping off Australia, Australian Government: Department of Defence, 2018, p. 8-9.

exceed its monetary value.[31] The short-sighted dumping of chemical warfare materials exemplifies the dark legacy of a few developed states and their cynical attitude towards the environment. Some of the reasons for the disposal of CW material at sea are as follows:

- The oceans were considered to have an unlimited absorptive capacity and unlimited space for disposal.
- It was considered a safer alternative compared to land-based incineration.
- Dumping was regarded as the best method of disposal, as the quantities were too great to burn.
- It was a cheap, quick and easy option.
- It was thought that the vastness of the sea would mitigate any environmental or health risks posed by CW agents.
- CW would lose their toxicity over time through natural chemical decomposition
- Old ships were available for disposal operations.
- There were relatively very few people to complain about dumping, because no one was there to see what was being done.
- There was little understanding of the possible danger to human safety and the ecology of the sea during that time.

Environmental Impact

The CW munitions and agents at disposal sites in seas pose a threat to the marine ecosystem, to the regional economy based on exploitation of these ecosystems and to human health and safety. After decades of lying on the seafloor, the metal shells of the dumped munition items are corroded, and their toxic compounds leak out and get distributed in the marine environment. Marine dumped chemical munitions react differently in water depending on the agent they contain. The munition shell may break open during the dumping operation or may corrode over time, allowing the agent to leak out. Nerve agents and many other agents hydrolyse, or

31 Geir Petter Novik, Morten Sommer and E. B. Abrahamsen, A Risk-Increasing Safety Strategy? Evaluating the Traditional Risk-mitigating Strategy in Dealing with Dumped Ammunition and Explosive Remnants of War, *Journal of Military and Strategic Studies*, Vol. 22, No.1, 2022, pp. 1-37.

break down and dissolve once they come into contact with water, and are therefore rendered harmless in a relatively short amount of time. Mustard gas, however, is insoluble in water, and most injuries that have occurred when fishermen come into contact with marine-dumped chemical munitions have resulted from mustard gas. Phosphorous devices also present long-term problems. Advice to date has been that if left undisturbed on the seabed, they pose no risk. If disturbed, as was the case in the Irish Sea's Beaufort's Dyke dumpsite during pipe laying, these positively buoyant devices may float to the surface and represent a real risk to the seafarers and to the general public should they be washed ashore.[32]

Activities like deep-sea trawling could further aggravate the situation, as a corrosive marine environment for over five decades has been gradually eroding the cases of hazardous chemicals dumped. In the future, more of these munitions may begin to wash up on the shores and beaches of the coastal countries.[33] As marine activities increase, encounters with munitions may become the norm and complete fish stocks and their habitats may be threatened from munitions constituents such as lead azide, lead styphnate, picric acid and mercury fulminate.[34] Dumped munitions have been found floating or washed ashore.[35] Health and environmental risks from these munitions are inevitable, but the extent is still uncertain.

32 Charlotte Koutras, War Remnants and the Pollution of the Sea, Workshop Report, 2009, https://www.europarl.europa.eu/RegData/etudes/divers/join/2009/410194/EXPO-SEDE_DV(2009)410194_EN.pdf.

33 In addition to contamination of seawater, there have been concerns among the public that chemical weapons could wash ashore, or that they could be retrieved accidentally during dredging operations or trawl fishing along the seabed. The likelihood of such events is difficult to predict. Generally, the greater the depth of disposal, the less likely that accidental retrieval or washing ashore would occur. Although ocean currents could move weapons into shallower waters and present a greater safety risk, the accumulation of sediment and marine growth could help anchor weapons to the seabed, making them less susceptible to movement. Bearden, David M., The US Disposal of Chemical Weapons in the Ocean: Background and Issues for Congress, CSR report for Congress, 3 January 2007, available at: http://www.fas.org/sgp/crs/natsec/RL33432.pdf, accessed October 21, 2012.

34 Long, T., 2005. Introduction to sea dumped munitions and hazardous wrecks, 2005. Available at: http://www.cnsopb.ns.ca/environment/pdf/sea/terry_longs_presentation.pdf, accessed 28 February 2012.

35 The corrosion of the chemical weapon shells and rounds which were dumped five to six decades ago is progressing fast now. It is feared that major quantities of chemical agents will leak into the sea in the near future. Beyond the immediate impact of a further depletion of the world's endangered fish stocks, poisonous agents will enter the food chain via plankton. Seismic pluses have potential to damage thin skin chemical

Degrading Marine Environment

The hazards posed by the CW materials to the marine environment have many facets. Heavy metals, arsenical compounds, explosives, persistent chlorinated compounds and other artificial compounds (xenobiotics) are of special concern and can adversely impact fishermen, offshore construction and maintenance workers, sub-surface entrepreneurs, harbour staff and workers, recreational divers, and seafood consumers.

The information on bioaccumulation, distribution, metabolism, and toxicity of CW agents in marine species is limited. However, in recent years, there have been some achievements regarding the knowledge on bioaccumulation and the biological effects of phenyl-arsenic CW agents. These dumped CW agents pose a risk to marine biota living in the vicinity of dumping sites.

Fishery is one of the important employment sources. Fishermen have been the main group affected by CW agents in the immediate post-WWII period.[36] The risk of coming into contact with the dangerous materials was seen to be highest when fishing inside or near the former dumping areas. For this reason, these sites are marked on the official sea charts together with additional information, where fishing activities, anchoring and extracting seabed materials are not advisable. However, due to the former practice of en-route dumping and the ensuing relocation of sea-dumped materials, there is also a risk when fishing is carried out outside the marked dumpsites.

The rapid growth of the offshore industry is accompanied by changes in human behaviour, thereby raising many new issues related to the dumping of conventional and chemical waste at sea. The use of the seabed for offshore activities such as resource extraction and construction is rapidly

munitions, which could dramatically increase the numbers of chemical releases in an area at one time. If a dump site is disturbed enough to cause some sort of release, it could decrease the fish stock by approximately 70%.

36 During the period from 1985 to 1995, Dutch fishermen reported 350 cases of chemical weapons being recovered in fishing nets from the Baltic, with some instances of injury to these fishermen resulting from contact with recovered chemical agents. During the period from 1995 to 2000 (the last year available for complete records), each year Danish fishermen recovered, on average, approximately eight chemical munitions a year with 236 kilograms of active agent from the Baltic. In 2000 alone, there were 11 incidents involving the recovery of 512 kilograms of active chemical agents, some of these chemical weapons disposed of in ocean waters continue to pose a threat to the environment after their chemical agents have decomposed into arsenic, phosphorus, and acids able to change pH of water.

developing and increases the likelihood of encounters with dumped munitions. Offshore construction sites are a good example: where piles are rammed into the seabed, there is a possibility of encountering munitions buried deep in the sediment. Available technologies to detect objects in terrestrial soil are insufficient, as are most of the present solutions for underwater detection. The increased drilling of boreholes for geological surveys also increases the threat of coming into contact with toxic substances, which might occur if a chemical warfare object is punctured in the process or if examined sediment core samples include sediment that has been contaminated with chemical warfare agent mixtures. The increasing amount of activity on the seafloor also increases the risk of coming into contact with chemical warfare agents.

The emergency response sub-surface personnel related to underwater operations could be exposed to an elevated probability of coming into contact with chemical warfare agents in the vicinity of dumpsites or scattered munitions, be it directly and indirectly, intentionally or unintentionally. Poor underwater visibility, the large variety in shapes of chemical warfare material containers and the degree of their corrosion and colonisation by biota pose a challenge to even recognising the potential danger.

Wrecks are of special interest to recreational divers. Most chemical munitions were dumped in the Baltic Sea at depths exceeding 80 m. Availability of highly sophisticated and affordable equipment enables even non-professional divers to conduct ever deeper dives, which increases the likelihood of divers or their equipment coming into contact with chemical warfare materials. Earlier, more than 100 children from a holiday camp were injured while playing with a barrel they found on a beach in Poland. The partly corroded barrel was leaking its brown-black contents of liquid sulphur mustard, and at least four children suffered severe injuries, especially irreversible eye damage.

The highest likelihood of getting into direct contact with chemical warfare materials in the Baltic Sea is through commercial fishing. Sea-dumped chemical warfare agents may potentially have adverse impacts on humans via the food chain. The magnitude of harm that the sea dumped hazardous waste may cause to the local food chain and marine environment is illustrated by the sudden death of more than two million starfish washed ashore and thousands of other marine species that inhabited the polluted marine areas of the Arctic Ocean in 1990. Fish, marine mammals and seabirds may also come into direct contact with the chemical warfare materials themselves (e.g., leaking munitions or lumps of chemical warfare agent) or via contaminated food.

Legal Control on Chemical Weapons

Use of Chemical Weapons was long stigmatised by an association with both unnecessary cruelty and unfair play. Because of this, international efforts to ban chemical weapons took a prominent position in many early disarmament agreements. In 1675, the first international agreement limited the use of chemical weapons when France and Germany signed an agreement prohibiting the use of poison bullets. In 1874, the Brussels Convention on the Law and Customs of War prohibited the employment of poison or poisoned weapons, and the use of arms, projectiles or material to cause unnecessary suffering, although the agreement never entered into force.

The use of poison and poisoned arms was prohibited by the 1899 Hague Convention (II) with Respect to the Laws and Customs of War on Land and its annexe: Regulations concerning the Laws and Customs of War on Land.[37] In the same conference, Declaration (IV, 2) concerning Asphyxiating Gases was also adopted. It declared, "The Contracting Powers agree to abstain from the use of projectiles, the sole object of which is the diffusion of asphyxiating or deleterious gases. The Declaration is only binding on the Contracting Powers in the case of a war between two or more of them. It shall cease to be binding from the time when, in a war between the Contracting Powers, one of the belligerents shall be joined by a non-Contracting Power."[38] The 1907 Hague Convention (IV) respecting the Laws and Customs of War on Land and its annexe: Regulations concerning the Laws and Customs of War on Land, restated the prohibition on the use of poison and poisoned weapons. [39]

37 The rules embodied in the Regulations were partly reaffirmed and developed by the two Protocols Additional to the Geneva Conventions of 1949 adopted in 1977.

38 The Declaration also stated, "The non-Signatory Powers can adhere to the present Declaration. For this purpose, they must make their adhesion known to the Contracting Powers by means of a written notification addressed to the Netherlands Government, and by it communicated to all the other Contracting Powers. In the event of one of the High Contracting Parties denouncing the present Declaration, such denunciation shall not take effect until a year after the notification made in writing to the Government of the Netherlands, and forthwith communicated by it to all the other Contracting Powers.

39 Article 23 (a) of the Annexed Regulation.

The 1925 Protocol for the Prohibition of the Use of Asphyxiating, Poisonous or Other Gases, and of Bacteriological Methods of Warfare (the 1925 Geneva Protocol), though it did not prohibit the development, production or possession of chemical weapons, it only bans the use of chemical and bacteriological (biological) weapons in war. Several countries signed the Protocol with reservations permitting them to use chemical weapons against countries that had not joined the Protocol or to respond in kind if attacked with chemical weapons. In the years since the Geneva Protocol entered into force, some of these States Parties withdrew their reservations and accepted an absolute ban on the use of chemical and biological weapons.

Even after the 1925 Gas Protocol became effective, many developed countries spent considerable resources on the development of chemical weapons. Chemical weapons were used by a number of countries in the 1920s and 1930s, and the discovery of powerful nerve gases in the late 1930s renewed interest in the field. During World War II, all the major powers involved in the war anticipated that chemical weapons would be used on a large scale; however, the war saw limited use of these weapons. During the Cold War, the US and the Soviet Union maintained enormous stockpiles of tens of thousands of tonnes of chemical weapons.

In 1972, the international community adopted the London Convention to ensure a global ban on dumping hazardous materials into the Ocean, including chemical weapons.[40] However, the ocean dumping of chemical weapons continued.[41] The 1993 Chemical Weapons Convention (CWC)[42]

40 The Convention on the Prevention of Marine Pollution by Dumping of Wastes and Other Matter, known as the 1975 London Convention, has been ratified by 84 states. The Convention prohibited the dumping of "materials in whatever form (e.g., solids, liquids, semi-liquids, gases or in a living state) produced for biological and chemical warfare". This regime had also been fully incorporated into the London Protocol 1996, which had entered into force in 2006 and would eventually replace the London Convention. However, the Convention (and Protocol) did not cover materials dumped before the entry into force of the Convention. The parties to the London Convention (and subsequently the parties to the London Protocol) were, however, aware that, in the 1980s to 1990s, parties to the Helsinki Convention had considered the issue of chemical warfare munitions that had been dumped in the Baltic Sea in the wake of the First and Second World Wars in some detail and had agreed to leave those munitions where they had been dumped.

41 Grant Dawson, International Law and Sea-dumped Chemical Weapons, Oxford University Press, 2023, p. 16.

42 The 1993 Convention on the Prohibition of the Development, Production, Stockpiling and Use of Chemical Weapons and on their Destruction (the Chemical Weapons

entered into force in 1996. The Convention aims to eliminate an entire category of weapons of mass destruction by prohibiting the development, production, acquisition, stockpiling, retention, transfer or use of chemical weapons by States Parties. States Parties, in turn, must take the steps necessary to enforce that prohibition in respect of persons (natural or legal) within their jurisdiction. All States Parties have agreed to chemically disarm by destroying any stockpiles of chemical weapons they may hold and any facilities which produced them, as well as any chemical weapons they abandoned on the territory of other States Parties in the past. But the treaty did not address what countries should do with the weapons created and dumped in the seas before 1985. In accordance with Article III (2) and Article IV (17) of the CWC, a State Party to the CWC is not required to declare or destroy chemical weapons dumped at sea before January 1, 1985 or buried on its territory before January 1, 1977 and which remain buried. According to Dawson (2023), the drafters of the CWC clearly intended to exempt sea-dumped chemical weapons from the provision mandating the declaration, storage, and destruction of chemical weapons.[43]

There is a significant loophole in the responsibility of the states to destroy stockpiles and mitigate long-term environmental damage caused by sea-dumped chemicals. As of date, no official notifications of sea-dumping operations have been submitted to the Organisation for the Prohibition of Chemical Weapons (OPCW) ever since the CWC came into effect. This lack of oversight and accountability constitutes a key lacuna in global regulation.[44]

The recovery of sea-dumped chemical munitions has been characterised as a "high cost – high risk operation" that may cause the release of a great amount of chemical agents in the marine environment or even casualties.[45]

Convention or CWC), is comprised of a Preamble, 24 Articles, and 3 Annexes — the Annex on Chemicals, the Verification Annex, and the Confidentiality Annex.

43 Grant Dwson, *International Law and Sea-Dumped Chemical Weapons*, Oxford: Oxford University Press, p. 73.

44 Critics assail secrecy over unexploded chemical weapons left by Imperial Japanese Army, The Japan Times, December 27, 2019, available at: https://www.japantimes.co.jp/news/2019/12/27/national/unexploded-chemical-weapons-used-by-imperial-japanese-army/.

45 N. H. A. Van Ham, "Investigations of risks connected to sea-dumped munitions," in T. Missiaen and J. P. Henriet (eds), Chemical munition dump sites in coastal environments, Brussels: Federal Office for Scientific, Technical and Cultural Affairs (OSTC), Federal Ministry of Social Affairs, Public Health and the Environment 2002, p. 92.

According to Zanders (2002), the coastal State may destroy such chemical weapons which have been dumped at sea before 1985 underwater by following only the rules applicable to the protection of the marine environment and the safety of divers.[46]

Risk Mitigation

There could be three possible scenarios for the disposal of sea-dumped chemical munitions: (i) Careful monitoring, but no action to disturb them;[47] (ii) Recovery of dumped munitions followed by disposal;[48] and (iii) Isolation of the dumping sites. Any positive action on sea-disposed ammunition must, of course, be balanced against the potential harm to marine life, as well as the increased explosives safety risk to workers and the surrounding communities.[49] There are serious safety risks associated with the clean-up of dumpsites, as well as an increased risk of dispersing hazardous substances. The most common management practice is to leave munitions on the seabed and allow them to disintegrate naturally. If munitions must be removed from the seabed, the potential of new techniques that allow neutralisation without explosion should be considered.

46 J. P. Zanders, "Dealing with chemical weapons dumped in bodies of water," in T. Missiaen and J. P. Henriet (eds), Chemical munition dump sites in coastal environments, Brussels: Federal Office for Scientific, Technical and Cultural Affairs (OSTC), Federal Ministry of Social Affairs, Public Health and the Environment 2002, p. 150.

47 Our current risk management strategy is still based on the erroneous assumption that if the ammunition is left alone, it will slowly become harmless over time. Geir Petter Novik, Morten Sommer and E. B. Abrahamsen, A Risk-Increasing Safety Strategy? Evaluating the Traditional Risk-mitigating Strategy in Dealing with Dumped Ammunition and Explosive Remnants of War, *Journal of Military and Strategic Studies*, Vol. 22, No.1, 2022, pp. 1-37.

48 The recovery of munitions from dump sites is a high cost - high risk operation. Mechanical forces may induce a reaction of the munitions, leading to damage or even casualties. The handling of corroded munitions may cause the release of large quantities of toxic compounds. In principle, however, recovery will be the only action that can actually solve the problem and reduce the risks. It is absolutely necessary that the recovered munition must be handled in a special disposal facility according to the present environmental standards. Nico H. H. Van Ham, "Investigations of risks connected to sea-dumped munitions," in T. Missiaen and J.P. Henriet (ed.), Chemical munition dump sites in coastal environments, Federal Office for Scientific, Technical and Cultural Affairs (OSTC), Federal Ministry of Social Affairs, Public Health and the Environment, Brussels 2002, p. 92.

49 US Department of Defense, *Research Related to Effect of Ocean Disposal of Munitions in U.S. Coastal Waters* (Washington: US Department of Defense, 2016).

The growing pressure for offshore constructions, like wind power stations and underwater cables, as well as the concern about the possible adverse impacts on the marine environment, has raised the discussion about prospective monitoring campaigns in areas where CWs have been submerged.[50] Dumped munitions, and in particular the disturbance of dumped munitions by seabed activities, e.g. fishing, sand and gravel extraction, dredging and dumping operations and the placement of cables and pipelines, is an important issue and should be addressed. Details of the locations of all dumpsites and areas where munitions are detected on the seabed must be maintained. Any seabed activities to be undertaken within or close to these locations should be subject to a full assessment of the potential risk before the approval of these activities by national authorities.

In the last two decades, several European Union-funded international projects (MERCW, CHEMSEA, DAIMON and DAIMON 2) and NATO (MODUM) have targeted dumped munitions in the Baltic Sea, focusing on their detection, distribution, environmental fate of the toxic substances and their ecological effects, risk assessment and mitigation strategies, including decision support for end-users. However, the major question remains unresolved: should they be removed or left untouched?

The possibility of having an international convention on the "disclosure of chemical weapons disposed of at sea and pollution preparedness, response and cooperation," as suggested by Morris (2005),[51] could be ruled out because major states like the US, UK and Russia, who were responsible for dumping, are unlikely to take responsibility for their irresponsible acts. To mitigate any future environmental harm from these sea dumped chemical weapons, the UN should take four actions: (i) supplement the CWC with an agreement that requires disclosure all at-sea chemical weapons dumpsites and their contents, even those currently exempt from disclosure, (ii) adopt the best practices for decontamination of the chemical weapons dumped at sea and respond to the governments that are now dealing with this threat, (iii) adopt a research, monitoring, and emergency response system monitored by a UN designated body, and (iv) create a Fund to award

50 Hanna Niemikoski et.al., Evidence of environmental threat caused by sea-dumped chemical warfare agents: Exposure status of hagfish in the skagerrak strait, Environmental Pollution, No. 366, 2025, p. 6.

51 George Michael Morris, 'Truth in Chemical Weapons Disposal: A Call for an International Convention on the Full Disclosure of Chemical Weapons Disposed of at Sea and Pollution Preparedness, Response and Co-Operation, University of Baltimore Journal of Environmental Law, vol. 12 (2005), pp. 165-190.

damages and restoration compensation to individuals and territories affected by chemical weapons dumped at sea.

Conclusion

The year 2025 marked the 110th year of the first large-scale use of chemical weapons in the First World War, killing over one million people with chemical warfare agents.[52] Today, carelessly sea-dumped chemical warfare agents severely endanger the marine ecology, exacerbating the devastating changes to marine life and habitats already struggling under threat from climate change and other human activities. As human oceanic activity continues to expand, all aspects of the blue economy are at risk from the threat of chemical weapons abandoned within almost all of our oceans and seas. Once unreachable chemical weapons dump sites are becoming increasingly accessible and in danger of being disturbed, posing dangers to human and marine life, and the number of human encounters by fishermen and others with abandoned munitions continues to rise. By an estimate, the total amount of chemical munitions lying on the ocean floor would be more than three million tons.[53]

There were two different methods of dumping: throwing overboard, which was done in the Baltic and sinking old ships. There is sufficient evidence that almost all oceans and seas were used for dumping chemical and/or conventional ammunition. Some of the dumping sites are well-known and documented. However, some of them are still hidden in archives of marine military operations. Establishing the legal framework applicable to sea-dumped chemical weapons is necessary to effectively tackle the pollution of the marine ecosystems.

The applicable legal framework has to be a combination of the UNCLOS, environmental law, as well as disarmament law. In addition, there is also a human rights dimension.[54] In the last few decades, advances in technology

52 Ilias Mohammed Abdullah Christensen, et.al., Acute toxicity of sea-dumped chemical munitions: luminating the environmental toxicity of legacy compounds, *Global Security: Health, Science and Policy*, 2016, Vol. 1:1, pp. 39-50, DOI: 10.1080/23779497.2016.1219962.

53 Maria Paula Rubiano, The ocean is a giant dump for chemical weapons. Can we clean it up before it's too late? April 12, 2021, https://www.popsci.com/story/environment/chemical-weapons-dumped-in-ocean/.

54 Alexander Lott, Pollution of the Marine Environment by Dumping: Legal Framework Applicable to Dumped Chemical Weapons and Nuclear Waste in the Arctic Ocean, Nordic Environmental Law Journal, 2015, pp. 57-69.

have also expanded deep-sea exploration and industrial activity, heightening the risk of accidental encounters with chemical dump sites. International chemical disarmament has also made considerable progress. However, no international law or treaty mandates the removal of chemical weapons or their breakdown products from the oceans directly. The time to act is now to protect our future generations.

Part IV

Legal Norms and Accountability

Legal Framework -Environment and Explosive Warfare

Bharathi M

Abstract

The use of explosive weapons in armed conflict has long been associated with immediate human casualties and infrastructure destruction. However, their enduring environmental consequences remain underexplored in both legal and policy discourse. This paper investigates the ecological footprint of explosive weapons, drawing on interdisciplinary research from environmental science, international humanitarian law (IHL), and conflict studies. Explosive remnants of war (ERW), including unexploded ordnance and toxic residues, contribute to soil degradation, water contamination, and biodiversity loss, as documented in U.C. Jha's Weapons of War: Environmental Impact and the AOAV report "The Broken Land". Case studies from Iraq, Syria, and Ukraine reveal how explosive weapons devastate ecosystems and hinder post-conflict recovery. The UNEP and Project Ploughshares reports further highlight the disproportionate impact of such weapons in urban and populated areas, where environmental damage compounds civilian suffering.

This paper critically examines the adequacy of existing legal frameworks, particularly the ENMOD Convention, Additional Protocol I to the Geneva Conventions, and customary IHL in addressing environmental harm during armed conflict. Drawing on recent scholarship from the International Review of the Red Cross and the Journal of Peace Research, it identifies normative gaps and enforcement challenges in current legal regimes. The paper argues for the integration of environmental protection into the conduct of hostilities through clearer legal norms, enhanced accountability mechanisms, and the operationalisation of the 2022 Political Declaration on Explosive Weapons in Populated Areas (EWIPA). It concludes by advocating for a more ecologically conscious interpretation of IHL, aligning the laws of war with global sustainability goals and the evolving concept of environmental security.

Introduction

Explosive weapons have long been central to the conduct of modern armed conflicts, profoundly shaping the trajectory of warfare and its impact on societies. These weapons—including bombs, artillery shells, landmines, and improvised explosive devices—cause catastrophic human suffering and infrastructure destruction. However, their extensive and lasting environmental consequences are only beginning to receive the focused attention they deserve within academic, legal, and policy discourses.

The environmental footprint of explosive warfare is multifaceted, with immediate and long-term repercussions for land, water, air, and ecosystems. When detonated, explosive weapons can devastate landscapes, release toxic substances, and generate vast amounts of rubble and military debris. Soil contamination from heavy metals and explosive residues, along with water pollution caused by hazardous chemicals and damaged infrastructure, poses serious risks to human health, agriculture, and natural habitats. In regions such as Iraq, Syria, and Ukraine, persistent pollution, ecosystem collapse, and threats to biodiversity are well documented, compounding the suffering and challenges faced by war-affected communities.

Beyond the initial destruction, explosive remnants of war—unexploded ordnance and landmines—continue to endanger civilians and impede recovery for years after conflicts end. These remnants restrict access to farmland, contaminate vital water resources, and threaten wildlife. The destruction of industrial, water, and energy facilities further contributes to cross-sector environmental risks, sometimes resulting in large-scale pollution incidents that extend beyond national borders.

Despite the severity of these impacts, international law struggles to provide adequate protection for the environment during armed conflict. While the ENMOD Convention and Additional Protocol I to the Geneva Conventions contain provisions addressing environmental harm, they are limited by ambiguous language, narrow definitions, and enforcement challenges. Customary international humanitarian law recognises the importance of minimising environmental damage, but practical mechanisms for accountability and prevention remain elusive.

There is a growing acknowledgement among scholars, international organisations, and humanitarian agencies of the need to strengthen legal norms and integrate environmental protection into the laws of war. Recent policy initiatives, such as the 2022 Political Declaration on Explosive Weapons in Populated Areas (EWIPA), aim to focus attention on the disproportionate harm caused in urban settings and advocate for preventive measures, monitoring, and remediation efforts.

This paper explores the profound environmental impacts of explosive weapons used in armed conflict, focusing on the multifaceted damage they inflict on ecosystems, soil, water, and air quality. Drawing on case studies and interdisciplinary research, it documents how explosive weapons generate toxic remnants of war that persist long after hostilities cease, hindering recovery and posing significant risks to human health and biodiversity. The paper critically examines the limits of existing legal frameworks—such as the ENMOD Convention, Additional Protocol I to the Geneva Conventions, and customary international humanitarian law—in addressing these harms. It identifies key normative gaps and enforcement challenges that undermine effective environmental protection during conflict.

Building on recent scholarship and international policy developments, including the 2022 Political Declaration on Explosive Weapons in Populated Areas (EWIPA), the research argues for stronger integration of environmental safeguards into the laws of war. It advocates clearer legal norms, enhanced accountability mechanisms, and the operationalisation of political commitments to protect civilians and ecosystems in conflict zones alike. Through this holistic and ecologically conscious approach, the paper aims to align the governance of armed conflict with broader global sustainability goals and the evolving concept of environmental security, offering recommendations for improved legal and policy responses to limit the environmental footprint of explosive warfare.

The Ecological Footprint of Explosive Arms

Armed conflicts are notorious for causing immense destruction and human suffering, which has led to the development of international treaties such as the Geneva Conventions, global norms, and military guidelines to mitigate humanitarian consequences[1]. While the direct human toll of warfare is well established, growing concern now focuses on how conflicts

1 ICRC, *Guidelines for Military Manuals and Instructions on the Protection of the Environment in Times of Armed Conflict,* 311 International Review of the Red Cross (1996), available at https://www.icrc.org/en/doc/resources /documents/article/other/57jn38.htm (accessed on 8 September 2025).

and military activities generate widespread pollution, inflict severe damage on ecosystems, and pose long-term threats to civilian health. Wars directly harm the environment through toxic hazards caused by shelling industrial facilities, remnants from weapons and munitions, mass displacement of populations, environmental destruction linked to extractive industries that fund conflicts, damage to sanitation infrastructure, and deliberate targeting of natural resources. Additionally, war-driven economies indirectly cause ecological degradation, for instance, through artisanal oil refining or large-scale charcoal production[2]. A further driver of environmental harm is the collapse of governance systems, including the weakening of environmental institutions and laws that normally prevent exploitation and mismanagement.

Throughout history, armies have deliberately destroyed ecosystems through tactics such as burning crops or poisoning wells, often as retribution against civilian populations[3]. With the emergence of modern weapons technologies after the invention of gunpowder and later the Industrial Revolution, militaries gained the capacity to cause large-scale ecological destruction. World War I, through prolonged shelling, polluted the battlefields with heavy metals[4], while in World War II, oil fields in Romania became deliberate targets. The 20th century saw the environmental devastation of nuclear weapons testing and the widespread spraying of toxic defoliants such as Agent Orange in Vietnam. Even after the Cold War, conflicts continued to scar the natural environment. For example, retreating Iraqi forces set hundreds of Kuwaiti oil wells ablaze in 1991, creating massive fires and pollution. The Balkan Wars destroyed critical industrial sites[5], while in Iraq and Syria, ISIS exacerbated environmental and humanitarian disasters by setting alight oil wells and burning the Al Mishraq Sulphur factory in 2016—an attack that released sulfur dioxide, killing dozens,

2 David Jensen & Steve Lonergan, "Natural Resources and Post-Conflict Assessment, Remediation, Restoration and Reconstructions: Lessons and Emerging Issues," in David Jensen & Steve Lonergan (eds), Assessing and Restoring Natural Resources in Post-Conflict Peacebuilding (Routledge, 2012)

3 Bronwyn Leebaw, "Scorched Earth: Environmental War Crimes and International Justice," 12(4) Perspectives on Politics 770 (2014).

4 Eline Meerschman, Lieven Cockx, Mohammad M. Islam et al., "Geostatistical Assessment of the Impact of World War I on the Spatial Occurrence of Soil Heavy Metals," 40(4) Ambio 417 (2010).

5 United Nations Environment Programme, Assessment of Environmental Hot Spots: Serbia and Montenegro (2004), available at https://postconflict.unep.ch/publications/assessment.pdf (last visited 10 September 2025).

hospitalising over 1,500, and displacing countless civilians. Similarly, the ongoing war in Ukraine has seen the bombardment of chemical facilities, releasing toxic materials into the air and water[6].

The dangers created by military munitions persist long after wars end. Munitions, explosives, and rocket propellants contaminate soil, air, and water both during battle and over extended post-conflict periods. These materials introduce heavy metals, toxins, and even radioactive contaminants into ecosystems. Beyond the battlefield, scrapped tanks, vehicles, and poorly stored or abandoned ammunition pose additional hazards. Unplanned explosions at storage sites and contamination from firing ranges highlight the risks linked to munitions. In particular, depleted uranium munitions employed in the Balkans, the Gulf Wars, and later in Syria have been a major cause of concern for human health and environmental sustainability[7]. The precautionary principle, central to UNEP's risk assessment strategies and endorsed by UN General Assembly resolutions, calls for a cautious approach when dealing with such ordnance, given their long-lasting risks.

Environmental destruction during war undermines humanitarian well-being and obstructs post-conflict economic reconstruction. The collapse of vital infrastructure often fuels health crises. In Yemen, for instance, damage to water supplies and sewage systems triggered a massive cholera outbreak that infected over a million people. In Iraq and Syria, water shortages combined with weakened governance and halted waste collection systems led to multiple disease outbreaks, disproportionately affecting vulnerable groups such as children, pregnant women, and the elderly[8]. Similarly, in Ukraine, repeated shelling of water filtration facilities put hundreds of thousands at risk, not only by interrupting safe water access but also by

6 OSCE, Environment Assessment and Recovery Priorities for Eastern Ukraine (2017), available at https://www.osce.org/project-coordinator-in-ukraine/362566 (last visited 10 September 2025).

7 S. Oakford, "The United States Used Depleted Uranium in Syria" (2017) *Foreign Policy* https://foreignpolicy.com/2017/02/14/the-united-states-used-depleted-uranium-in-syria/ accessed 10 September 2025 S. Oakford, "The United States Used Depleted Uranium in Syria," Foreign Policy (2017), available at https://foreignpolicy.com/2017/02/14/the-united-states-used-depleted-uranium-in-syria/ (last visited 10 September 2025).

8 W. Zwijnenburg, Scorched Earth and Charred Lives: Human Health and Environmental Risks of Civilian-operated Makeshift Oil Refineries in Syria (PAX, 2016), available at https://www.paxforpeace.nl/publications/allpublications/scorched-earth-and-charred-lives (last visited 10 September 2025).

threatening to release hazardous substances like chlorine. Conflicts can also encourage unsafe livelihoods. In Syria, the destruction of oil infrastructure contributed to the spread of artisanal oil refining, where entire families, including children, laboured under highly toxic and unsafe conditions.

The physical destruction of urban environments brings additional ecological risks. In Iraq and Syria, devastated cities generated millions of tons of rubble, often mixed with industrial, medical, or household waste. Building materials pulverised by bombings may themselves contain asbestos or heavy metals, causing chronic health risks. Gaza offers a particularly dire scenario, where years of conflict, combined with blockades and poor infrastructure, have gradually poisoned the environment. According to UN assessments, the region may soon become uninhabitable due to worsening waste management failures, over-pollution, and insufficient resources to sustain the population.

Beyond infrastructure and urban impacts, armed conflicts often devastate entire ecosystems. Warfare contributes to desertification, deforestation, and widespread land degradation. Shelling in southern Turkey and northern Iraq during dry summers sparked large wildfires that decimated woodlands. Meanwhile, refugee and internally displaced communities in Bangladesh, Lebanon, and Syria rely heavily on firewood, accelerating deforestation. Similarly, armed groups have exploited forests for charcoal production, as in the case of Al-Shabaab in Somalia[9]. Post-conflict rebuilding also strains natural resources: quarrying and riverbed excavations for cement production following wars in Lebanon (2006) and Iraq (2016) disrupted water levels and natural river flows, further destabilising ecosystems.

Ultimately, the environmental toll of armed conflict becomes inseparable from its humanitarian impact. Pollution, ecological destruction, and the collapse of environmental governance combine to create acute crises during wars and undermine long-term recovery prospects. From scorched earth tactics in ancient conflicts to modern high-tech weaponry, warfare continues to poison ecosystems, cripple public health, and erode the foundations of sustainable reconstruction.

9 A. Bolognesi, F. Vrieling & H. G. Rembold, "Rapid Mapping and Impact Estimation of Illegal Charcoal Production in Southern Somalia Based on WorldView-1 Imagery," 25 Energy for Sustainable Development 40 (2015), available at https://www.sciencedirect.com/science/article/pii/S0973082614001318 (last visited 10 September 2025).

Direct Environmental Consequences

War and militarism have far-reaching environmental impacts that begin before active conflict and extend well beyond its conclusion. Prior to fighting, the resources required for military forces—such as minerals, oil, and land—lead to high energy consumption, significant greenhouse gas emissions, and widespread disruption of ecosystems. Military bases and training grounds cover vast areas, sometimes restricting public activity and affecting biodiversity. The disposal of military equipment, especially hazardous weapons and emerging pollutants, leaves long-term pollution, while high expenditures often divert attention and resources away from sustainable development and environmental protection[10].

During and after conflicts, the direct destructive activities—from large-scale vehicle movements to explosive ordnance—inflict physical harm on landscapes, cities, and habitats. Warfare in urban areas generates massive debris, pollutes the air and soil, and damages critical infrastructure like water treatment plants. Attacks on industrial, oil, or nuclear sites can trigger severe spills and long-term contamination. Legacies such as landmines, chemical remnants, and unregulated military scrap create continuing risks for ecosystems and public health. Displacement of people intensifies pressure on resources and weakens governance, causing further environmental degradation. Even in the post-conflict phase, weak oversight and slow recovery can hinder restoration, amplifying pollution, soil damage, and biodiversity loss. While opportunities exist to support sustainable recovery and build peace around shared natural resources, the overwhelming disruption to environmental systems and regulatory frameworks has proved far more damaging in the aftermath of war.

Related Case Study

When a rocket landed in her apartment block in Eastern Ukraine, Lyudmilla (58) described the experience as if "there was flour everywhere in the air, it was white, I couldn't see anything. It was like very thick fog." This vivid depiction illustrates the environmental and health impacts of explosive weapons in populated areas. Explosive weapons generate intense blast waves and fragmentation, which cause buildings to collapse

10 University of Queensland, "Conflict Pollution, Washed-up Landmines and Military Emissions – Here's How War Trashes the Environment" (21 November 2023), available at https://public-health.uq.edu.au/article/2023/11/conflict-pollution-washed-landmines-and-military-emissions-%E2%80%93-here%E2%80%99s-how-war-trashes-environment (last visited 10 September 2025).

and send debris flying[11]. The blast pressure propels fine particles such as pulverised building materials into the air. These particles often contain toxic substances like asbestos and heavy metals, which pose respiratory hazards to civilians and clean-up workers exposed to the conflict rubble. Beyond immediate injuries, these toxins have been linked to longer-term health risks, including antimicrobial resistance, evidenced by wound contaminations in veterans and civilians in conflict zones such as Mosul, northern Iraq. The inhalation of debris contributes to respiratory illness and complicates recovery efforts in affected communities.

The environmental impact extends beyond the immediate blast area, particularly when essential infrastructure is targeted or collateral damage occurs. Conflicts in Syria, Yemen, and Iraq saw repeated attacks on water and sanitation facilities, severely compromising access to clean water and hygienic sewage disposal. This destruction has fuelled widespread outbreaks of communicable diseases such as cholera, affecting millions of civilians in densely populated urban centres. Industrial and chemical facilities in conflict zones present additional environmental threats. When facilities like the Mishraq Sulphur Factory in northern Iraq were set ablaze, releasing plumes of toxic sulfur dioxide, or chemical plants in eastern Ukraine's Donbas region are at risk, pollutants spread through air, soil, and water, rendering entire regions potentially uninhabitable. These industrial complexes often house hazardous chemicals that, if leaked, contaminate groundwater and surrounding ecosystems, with long-lasting effects on agricultural productivity and food security. Furthermore, the environmental degradation wrought by explosive weapon use compounds through soil contamination, destruction of ecosystems, and pollution of water sources, necessitating urgent environmental remediation and health protection measures. These patterns highlight how the environmental consequences of explosive weapons are multifaceted, affecting human health directly and indirectly by compromising the essential systems that support life in conflict-affected regions.

Indirect and Long-Term Environmental Effects

Armed conflicts inflict indirect and long-term environmental damage that persists well beyond the cessation of hostilities, compounding humanitarian crises and hindering sustainable development. One major

11 NEW, Roos Boer & Wim Zwijnenburg, "Exploring the Links Between Environmental Harm and the Use of Explosive Weapons," INEW Blog, available at https://www.inew.org/exploring-the-links-between-environmental-harm-and-the-use-of-explosive-weapons/ (last visited 8 September 2025).

indirect effect is the degradation of soil quality caused by the physical disruption from vehicles, explosions, and heavy machinery that compact and erode soil, reducing its fertility and agricultural potential. Moreover, military ordnance introduces toxic heavy metals such as lead and cadmium into soils, contaminating vast areas and posing chronic health risks as pollutants accumulate in food chains. The destruction of infrastructure during wars also results in water contamination, as damaged pipelines, treatment plants, and industrial facilities release chemicals and pathogens into rivers and aquifers, exacerbating disease outbreaks and compromising drinking water availability. These events often lead to sedimentation and the disruption of aquatic ecosystems, affecting biodiversity and community livelihoods dependent on fisheries[12]. This contamination can render water sources unsafe for decades, severely impacting human health and economic recovery.

Air pollution is another significant long-term consequence of armed conflict. Explosions and industrial fires emit large quantities of toxic gases and particulate matter, including nitrogen oxides, sulfur dioxide, and fine particulate pollutants (PM2.5 and PM10)[13], which contribute to respiratory illnesses, cardiovascular diseases, and acid rain. The conflict in Ukraine exemplifies such impacts, generating vast emissions equivalent to several European nations and releasing large amounts of pollutants from ongoing shelling of industrial sites and fossil fuel infrastructure. Additionally, war-related deforestation and the use of chemical defoliants degrade carbon sinks, further intensifying climate change risks. Beyond environmental degradation, armed conflicts weaken governance structures and environmental oversight, disrupting conservation efforts, increasing illegal resource exploitation such as logging and mining, and hampering post-conflict environmental recovery[14]. The continued use of hazardous military practices, including burn pits and landmine clearance, perpetuates pollution and environmental health hazards for displaced civilian

12 Geneva International Centre for Humanitarian Demining (GICHD), *Guide to Explosive Ordnance Pollution of the Environment* (Dec. 2021).

13 California Air Resources Board, Inhalable Particulate Matter and Health (PM2.5 and PM10), available at https://ww2.arb.ca.gov/resources/inhalable-particulate-matter-and-health (last visited 4 September 2025).

14 Carl Renan Estrellan & Fukuya Iino, "Toxic Emissions from Open Burning," 80(3) Chemosphere 193 (2010), doi:10.1016/j.chemosphere.2010.03.057, available at https://www.gichd.org/fileadmin/uploads/gichd/Publications/EO_Pollution_of_the_Environment_v17_web_01.pdf (last visited 12 September 2025).

populations and veterans alike[15]. Addressing these long-term challenges requires coordinated international efforts to integrate environmental protection into peacebuilding and post-conflict reconstruction strategies, ensuring sustainable recovery and reducing the risk of renewed resource conflicts.

Environmental Damage During Occupations

Occupations, whether short-lived or prolonged for decades, present unique challenges to environmental protection. While occupying states have clear obligations to protect the civilian populations under their control, their duties regarding environmental protection are often less explicitly defined, creating legal and practical gaps. Occupations frequently obstruct sustainable development by limiting access to critical materials and technologies or deterring investment in environmental infrastructure. Pre-existing environmental programs may be suspended or replaced by new administrations with different priorities[16]. In an era of intensifying climate change, such disruption severely hampers the ability of occupied communities to adapt effectively to environmental shifts, increasing their vulnerability to climate-induced hazards.

Infrastructure damage during conflicts typically extends into the occupation phase, with many key environmental facilities left destroyed or unrepaired due to lack of funding or political will. For example, water and sanitation systems in occupied territories often deteriorate progressively, leading to critical public health challenges. Resistance efforts by occupied populations, including protests or sabotage, may inadvertently exacerbate environmental damage. Moreover, the increased military presence—through vehicle movement, training exercises, or construction of barriers like walls and fences—disturbs ecosystems, disrupts wildlife corridors, and restricts communities' access to essential natural resources. Military bases and facilities, particularly those managed with poor waste controls,

15 Down To Earth, "Invisible Damage: From Stratosphere to Marine Life, Impact of Ongoing Wars Pervasive & Long-term" (25 June 2025), available at https://www.downtoearth.org.in/climate-change/invisible-damage-from-stratosphere-to-marine-life-impact-of-ongoing-wars-pervasive-long-term-2 (last visited 10 September 2025).

16 Michael W. Meier, "Protection of the Environment During an Occupation," *Lieber Institute, West Point* (12 May 2023), available at https://lieber.westpoint.edu/protection-environment-during-occupation/ (last visited 25 September 2025).

contribute pollutants that degrade land and water quality, adversely affecting local populations[17].

Environmental degradation during occupations is further compounded by inequitable resource management. Occupying powers often engage in resource extraction and control that disproportionately benefit them while neglecting the rights and needs of the occupied population. Over-extraction of water, minerals, or other natural assets can lead to long-term depletion and pollution[18]. In many cases, environmental oversight under occupation is inadequate or biased, enabling unchecked degradation. The occupied communities frequently face poorer environmental services, limited access to clean resources, and elevated pollution levels compared to the occupying populations[19]. Politically motivated development projects initiated by occupiers may overlook environmental protection, leading to major infrastructure works executed with minimal environmental supervision. This exploitation and neglect intensify disparities and ecological harm within occupied territories.

Environmental Damage After Conflicts

The end of armed conflicts rarely marks a clear endpoint for environmental damage. Post-conflict environments are often marked by persistent low-level violence, insecurity, and institutional fragility, impeding effective environmental governance and restoration. Weak state control during fragile peace transitions limits the capacity to enforce environmental laws, monitor pollution, or manage natural resources sustainably. Competing social and economic priorities regularly side line environmental concerns, leaving ecosystems and public health vulnerable. In some cases, peace agreements create fragmented and unstable political systems, further complicating governance over environmental resources.

One of the immediate environmental legacies after conflicts is the accumulation of vast quantities of rubble and debris in urban areas, such

17 Michael W. Meier, "Protection of the Environment During an Occupation," *Lieber Institute, West Point* (12 May 2023), available at https://lieber.westpoint.edu/protection-environment-during-occupation/ (last visited 25 September 2025).

18 Waad Abualrob, *Protection of the Environment under International Law During Occupation: International Humanitarian, Human Rights and Environmental Law* (Routledge, 2025) ISBN 9781032850825.

19 Waad Abualrob, *Protection of the Environment under International Law During Occupation: International Humanitarian, Human Rights and Environmental Law* (Routledge, 2025) ISBN 9781032850825.

as the eight million tonnes of rubble left in Mosul following the conflict. If rubble is not properly managed, it becomes a source of pollution, releasing dust, asbestos, and toxic materials into the environment. Additionally, the looting of industrial sites exposes toxic substances to the surrounding communities. Many environmentally damaging coping mechanisms adopted during conflict—such as artisanal resource extraction or unsafe waste disposal—persist into the post-conflict period, prolonging ecological stress[20].

Land rights and ownership disputes often arise in post-conflict areas with high displacement, complicating land use and contributing to environmental pressures. Returnees may expand agriculture into previously undisturbed ecosystems, accelerating deforestation and habitat loss. Studies document that deforestation rates commonly increase in post-conflict countries, frequently outpacing governmental capacity for regulation and oversight[21]. The extended presence of military forces beyond active hostilities also carries environmental risks. Military base operation, closure, or transfer often leaves behind pollution, contaminated sites, and hazardous waste. Practices such as the use of burn pits have exposed both military personnel and civilian populations to toxic substances, resulting in long-term health problems[22].

The clearance of landmines and unexploded ordnance, while necessary for safety, can cause soil degradation and localised pollution. Released lands may experience altered use patterns, sometimes leading to further environmental exploitation. Climate change compounds these risks by exacerbating contamination and affecting land and water management in vulnerable post-conflict settings. Finally, the damage inflicted by conflicts extends deeply into environmental governance. Environmental protection

20 Daniëlla Dam-de Jong, "Protection of Natural Resources and the Environment under International Humanitarian Law," in *International Law and Governance of Natural Resources in Conflict and Post-Conflict Situations*, ed. Daniëlla Dam-de Jong (Cambridge University Press, 2015) 200–260, available at https://doi.org/10.1017/CBO9781316145425.009

21 Lingjie Kong and Yuqing Zhao, "Remedying the environmental impacts of war: challenges and perspectives for full reparation," **International Review of the Red Cross** No. 924 (2023), available at: https://international-review.icrc.org/articles/remedying-the-environmental-impacts-of-war-924 (last accessed 20 September 2025).

22 H. Meaza, "Managing the environmental impacts of war: what can be done?" **876 Science of the Total Environment** (2024) 162868, available at: https://doi.org/10.1016/j.scitotenv.2023.162868 (last accessed 20 September 2025).

programs, pollution control efforts, biodiversity conservation, and climate adaptation strategies usually suffer setbacks lasting years after hostilities end. The environmental costs of reconstruction can be substantial, as the rebuilding of cities and infrastructure demands large quantities of natural resources, potentially generating secondary environmental impacts if sustainability is not prioritised[23]. To address these multifaceted challenges, comprehensive long-term planning and international support are essential to promote ecological recovery, reinforce governance frameworks, and sustainably manage natural resources in post-conflict environments.

Legal Frameworks

Environmental protection during armed conflict is governed by a complex and evolving legal framework designed to minimise harm to natural ecosystems and human populations. While the laws of war primarily seek to protect civilians, the environment is intrinsically linked to human survival, making its protection an essential component of international humanitarian law (IHL). Various treaties and customary laws attempt to regulate the conduct of hostilities to prevent widespread, long-term, and severe environmental damage. However, challenges such as vague definitions, high thresholds for violations, limited enforcement mechanisms, and the balancing of military necessity with environmental protection hinder the full realisation of these protections. The key legal instruments are the ENMOD Convention, Additional Protocol I to the Geneva Conventions, and evolving customary international humanitarian law.

The ENMOD Convention (1976)

The Environmental Modification Convention (ENMOD) is a specialised treaty that prohibits the military or any hostile use of environmental modification techniques that have "widespread, long-lasting, or severe effects[24]." It addresses actions that deliberately manipulate natural processes—like weather modification or geological interventions—to cause environmental harm. Despite its pioneering status, the convention's impact is limited: it is rarely invoked, and its narrow scope restricts its

23 International Law Commission, ***Draft Principles on Protection of the Environment in Relation to Armed Conflicts*** (2022), available at: https://legal.un.org/ilc/texts/instruments/english/draft_articles/8_7_2022.pdf.

24 International Committee of the Red Cross, "The environment and warfare," available at: https://www.icrc.org/en/law-and-policy/environment-and-warfare (last accessed 8 September 2025).

application mostly to large-scale, state-level environmental manipulation rather than localised or indirect damage caused in armed conflict[25]. Terms such as "widespread" and "long-lasting" remain subject to different interpretations, providing leeway for belligerents to skirt prohibitions.

Additional Protocol I (1977) to the Geneva Conventions

Additional Protocol I supplements the Geneva Conventions with explicit provisions concerning environmental protection during armed conflict. Article 35(3) prohibits the use of methods or means of warfare that are expected to cause "widespread, long-term and severe damage" to the natural environment[26]. Article 55 further mandates parties to take care to protect the environment from such damage and forbids using the environment as a target for reprisals. These articles incorporate the principle of proportionality, which requires balancing anticipated military advantage against potential environmental damage. However, the enforcement of these provisions is complicated by the stringent thresholds set for prohibited damage and ambiguous terms, making legal action rare. The protocol lacks detailed mechanisms for monitoring or sanctioning violations, limiting its effectiveness in preventing environmental harm during hostilities[27].

Customary International Humanitarian Law (IHL)

Customary IHL reflects evolving state practices and opinions that increasingly recognise environmental protection as part of the laws regulating armed conflict[28]. It encompasses general rules prohibiting attacks that cause extensive environmental damage disproportionate to the military gain, reinforcing the principles enshrined in treaties. However, the customary framework remains underdeveloped concerning

---

25 JP Hupy, "The environmental footprint of war," (2008), available at: https://www.jstor.org/stable/20723680 (last accessed 6 September 2025).

26 International Committee of the Red Cross, ***Protocol I Additional to the Geneva Conventions*** (1977), available at: https://ihl-databases.icrc.org/en/ihl-treaties/api-1977

27 Maya Brehm, ***Protecting Civilians from the Effects of Explosive Weapons in International Humanitarian Law*** (2014), available at: https://www.academia.edu/29736309/Protecting_civilians_from_the_effects_of_explosive_weapons_in_International_Humanitarian_Law.

28 ***Practical Guide to Humanitarian Law***, "Customary international law," available at: https://guide-humanitarian-law.org/content/article/3/customary-international-law/ (last accessed 18 September 2025).

the environment, with considerable ambiguity around what constitutes prohibited damage, how responsibility is assigned, and the scope of protections. This vagueness restricts judicial and enforcement actions and complicates the response to modern environmental threats posed by new military technologies and tactics[29]. Additionally, customary IHL is traditionally anthropocentric, focusing on civilian protection and often failing to recognise the environment as a rights-bearing entity deserving independent protection.

Emerging Developments and Challenges

In recent years, there has been growing momentum to strengthen environmental protection in warfare. The International Committee of the Red Cross (ICRC) has issued guidelines for military manuals to better integrate environmental obligations into armed forces' conduct. Furthermore, there are calls to recognise "ecocide" as a distinct international crime under the Rome Statute of the International Criminal Court (ICC), targeting severe and wanton environmental destruction during conflicts. These initiatives aim to clarify legal standards and promote accountability. However, despite these advances, enforcement remains hampered by political interests, limited mechanisms for investigation and prosecution, and the complexity of proving environmental harm in conflict settings. Ensuring effective protection will require enhancing legal clarity, reinforcing monitoring and accountability, and integrating environmental considerations into military planning and peacebuilding frameworks.

Gaps and Limitations in Current Legal Regimes

Despite progress, international legal frameworks regulating environmental harm during armed conflict face significant shortcomings. One of the core challenges revolves around vague definitions and ambiguous terminology embedded in crucial treaties like the ENMOD Convention and Additional Protocol I to the Geneva Conventions[30]. Terms such as "widespread," "long-term," and "severe" damage are left without concrete, universally agreed-upon thresholds or metrics, which results in wide interpretive latitude for

29 Hithcliff N. Oyas, *International Humanitarian Law: The Use of Explosive Weapons on Populated Areas* (2015), available at: https://www.academia.edu/13744177/International_Humanitarian_Law_The_use_of_explosive_weapons_on_Populated_areas (last accessed 8 September 2025).

30 Geneva Environment Network, "Protecting the environment in armed conflict" (30 May 2025), available at: https://www.genevaenvironmentnetwork.org/resources/updates/protecting-the-environment-in-armed-conflict/

states and combatants. This vagueness allows parties engaged in hostilities to circumvent obligations by arguing that their destructive acts fall short of these criteria, limiting the practical reach of existing protections.

Another fundamental limitation is the persistent tension between environmental protection and the principle of military necessity. The law acknowledges military operations often entail collateral damage; however, enforcement and compliance regularly grant expansive deference to military objectives. This deference can justify significant environmental destruction if deemed essential or advantageous to military goals. Moreover, the escalating complexity and technological sophistication of modern warfare—including asymmetric conflicts and novel weapons systems—pose challenges for existing legal frameworks originally designed with conventional warfare in mind[31]. These novel contexts strain the enforceability and relevance of traditional environmental safeguards.

Accountability and enforcement mechanisms remain particularly weak under the current system. While international humanitarian law formalises duties to minimise environmental damage, actual investigative, prosecutorial, and penal processes for violations are rudimentary. Reporting by states on environmental impacts during conflict is largely voluntary and often insufficient, leading to gaps in transparency and oversight. The absence of binding obligations or international enforcement bodies specifically dedicated to war-related environmental harm means that many violations go unpunished. Additionally, the anthropocentric focus of IHL prioritises civilian protection and tends to sideline environmental rights as independent protections[32]. This limits legal recognition for ecosystems, biodiversity, and collective ecological interests that extend beyond direct human well-being.

31 International Committee of the Red Cross, *Guidelines on the Protection of the Natural Environment in Armed Conflict: Rules and Recommendations under International Humanitarian Law, with Commentary* (ICRC 2020), available at: https://www.icrc.org/sites/default/files/document_new/file_list/guidelines_on_the_protection_of_the_natural_environment_in_armed_conflict_advance-copy.pdfhttps://www.icrc.org/sites/default/files/document_new/file_list/guidelines_on_the_protection_of_the_natural_environment_in_armed_conflict_advance-copy.pdf

32 *International Society of International Law Yearbook on International Humanitarian and Human Rights Law (2001), available at: http://www.worldlii.org/int/journals/ISILYBIHRL/2001/13.html*

Policy Perspectives and Recent Innovations to Strengthen Protection

The growing international recognition of the environmental devastation wrought by armed conflict has prompted a wave of policy innovation and normative reinforcement. United Nations Environment Programme (UNEP) reports and studies by civil society groups such as Action on Armed Violence (AOAV) and Project Ploughshares emphasise the critical need to address environmental harm caused by explosive weapons, particularly in densely populated urban environments. These sectors are especially vulnerable because environmental degradation in cities amplifies humanitarian suffering, hampers recovery, disrupts public health, and leads to prolonged displacement[33].

Significant policy momentum was achieved through the 2022 Political Declaration on Explosive Weapons in Populated Areas (EWIPA), a multilateral commitment where states recognised the grave risks explosive weapons pose to civilians and the environment. This declaration calls on parties to armed conflict to adopt measures that prevent or reduce the use of explosive weapons in densely populated areas, integrate environmental considerations into military doctrines, and endorse clearer standards that govern the conduct of hostilities vis-à-vis environmental protection.

Alongside international political agreements, influential organisations such as the International Committee of the Red Cross (ICRC) and the International Law Commission (ILC) have produced guidance aimed at translating legal principles into operational military protocols[34]. ICRC's Guidelines for Military Manuals and Instructions encourage armed forces to embed precautionary measures, minimise environmental harm during hostilities, and prepare for post-conflict environmental restoration. These efforts recognise that environmental protection is not merely a legal obligation but a strategic imperative linking humanitarian security to ecological sustainability[35].

33 *"Laws of armed conflict and environmental protection," [2001] ISILYBIHRL 5, available at: http://www.worldlii.org/int/journals/ISILYBIHRL/2001/5.html.*

34 International Law Commission, *Draft Principles on Protection of the Environment in Relation to Armed Conflicts* (2022), available at: https://legal.un.org/ilc/texts/instruments/english/draft_articles/8_7_2022.pdf

35 International Committee of the Red Cross, "Protecting the environment in armed conflict," International Review of the Red Cross No. 924 (2023), available at: https://international-review.icrc.org/reviews/irrc-no-924-environment

In addition, there is an emerging normative trend advocating for the criminalisation of severe environmental destruction during conflict, commonly described as "ecocide." Proposals to include ecocide within the Rome Statute of the International Criminal Court reflect a growing international consensus that major environmental damage caused by warfare should be treated as an international crime. While this concept remains under debate, it represents a significant evolution toward more robust accountability frameworks capable of deterring and addressing egregious ecological harm.

Toward a More Comprehensive and Enforceable Framework

The environmental protection regime in armed conflict has laid important normative foundations, but significant improvements are required to meet the challenges of contemporary warfare. Current treaties and customary norms set essential prohibitions but fall short due to vague terms, high thresholds for application, and insufficient enforcement. Military necessity continues to overshadow environmental concerns, allowing potentially avoidable ecological damage to occur with limited accountability[36].

However, policy innovations like the EWIPA declaration and military doctrinal reforms provide promising avenues for progress. Strengthening state commitments, clarifying legal standards, and expanding institutional capacities for monitoring and enforcement are integral to elevating environmental protection in armed conflict. The development of ecocide as a prosecutable crime could represent a pivotal step toward greater deterrence and justice for environmental damages in war[37].

Ultimately, safeguarding the environment during armed conflict is inseparable from protecting civilian populations and ensuring post-conflict sustainability. The future of international humanitarian law must embrace clearer, more precise legal norms complemented by operational guidelines and binding accountability mechanisms. Only through such comprehensive evolution can the international community effectively balance military

36 Yoram Dinstein, "Protection of the environment in international armed conflict," 5 Max Planck Yearbook of United Nations Law (2001) 523–549, available at: https:// www.mpil.de/files/pdf1/mpunyb_dinstein_5.pdf

37 John Borrie and Maya Brehm, "Enhancing civilian protection from use of explosive weapons in populated areas: building a policy and research agenda," **International Review of the Red Cross** No. 883 (2011), available at: https://international-review. icrc.org/sites/default/files/irrc-883-borrie-brehm.pdf.

necessity with the urgent imperative to preserve ecosystems, biodiversity, and human well-being in times of war and peace.

Suggestion and Conclusion

Suggestion: Strengthening Legal, Policy, and Operational Frameworks

- **Environmental Impact of Explosive Weapons**

The environmental devastation caused by explosive weapons in armed conflicts is immediate and long-lasting, demanding a thorough reevaluation of legal frameworks, policy measures, and operational practices. Explosive weapons not only destroy infrastructure but also severely damage ecosystems, soil, water, and air quality, leaving toxic remnants that persist long after hostilities end. These impacts threaten human health, biodiversity, and post-conflict recovery, creating complex humanitarian and ecological challenges. While international instruments such as the ENMOD Convention, Additional Protocol I to the Geneva Conventions, and customary international humanitarian law offer guidance for environmental protection, their effectiveness is limited by ambiguous terms, high thresholds for violations, and enforcement gaps. Addressing these challenges requires a multi-dimensional approach integrating clearer legal norms, robust enforcement, operational safeguards, and sustainable post-conflict recovery.

- **Clarifying Legal Norms**

Legal norms must evolve to include precise definitions of terms such as "widespread," "long-term," and "severe" damage, reducing interpretative ambiguities that allow harmful acts to escape accountability. Thresholds for violations should cover not only large-scale damage but also cumulative and indirect effects, ensuring broader protection of ecosystems and civilians. Another critical gap concerns toxic remnants of war, including unexploded ordnance, explosive residues, and heavy metals, which contaminate soil and water, impede agriculture, and cause chronic illnesses. Legal instruments should mandate clearance, remediation, and risk communication, while military manuals and operational guidelines should embed environmental protection throughout planning, targeting, and post-conflict operations.

- **Strengthening Accountability and Enforcement**

Strengthening accountability and enforcement mechanisms is equally vital. Current institutional structures for monitoring environmental compliance are insufficient. Dedicated international bodies or enhanced mandates for existing institutions such as the International Criminal Court (ICC) and the United Nations Environment Programme (UNEP) are needed to investigate, document, and hold perpetrators accountable for violations of environmental law and international humanitarian law. Systematic state reporting, independent assessments, and reliable data collection—particularly in inaccessible regions—should be prioritised. Collaboration with humanitarian demining organisations, environmental NGOs, and international scientific communities can improve monitoring accuracy. Technological innovations, including remote sensing and environmental forensics, provide essential tools for documenting damage and supporting legal interventions.

- **Integrating Environmental Safeguards into Military Operations**

Operationalising environmental safeguards in military doctrine is essential to prevent harm. Armed forces must integrate environmental considerations into planning, targeting, training, and operations. Guidelines developed by the International Committee of the Red Cross (ICRC) and similar bodies can translate legal obligations into actionable procedures. Measures should include restrictions on explosive weapons in populated areas and ecologically sensitive zones, promotion of less destructive alternatives, and training on risk identification and mitigation. Expanding international agreements like the 2022 Political Declaration on Explosive Weapons in Populated Areas (EWIPA) can build political consensus, while states should align national legislation and military doctrine with these standards, supporting environmental education and risk management within armed forces.

- **Post-Conflict Environmental Recovery**

Post-conflict environmental recovery is essential for sustainable peacebuilding. Clearance of explosive remnants must be coupled with environmental assessments to guide remediation and prevent secondary contamination. Reconstruction should employ green technologies, conserve biodiversity, support water management, and promote sustainable agriculture to reduce future resource conflicts.

International cooperation and technical support are critical for restoring ecological infrastructure and governance capacity, enabling both ecological and social resilience.

Conclusion

The intersection between armed conflict and environmental harm underscores the growing importance of environmental security as a fundamental dimension of global peace and stability. The use of explosive weapons inflicts immediate human suffering while simultaneously degrading ecosystems, undermining public health, and compromising sustainable development. These impacts perpetuate cycles of poverty, displacement, and instability, highlighting the inseparability of civilian protection and environmental stewardship. Strengthening legal frameworks, enhancing enforcement mechanisms, operationalising environmental safeguards in military practice, and promoting sustainable post-conflict recovery are essential measures to mitigate the environmental footprint of warfare.

Protecting the environment in armed conflict is not a peripheral concern; it is central to upholding human dignity, ecosystem integrity, and intergenerational equity. By embedding these principles into international humanitarian law, military practice, and policy-making, the global community can minimise the catastrophic legacy of explosive weapons, ensuring that environmental protection becomes an integral part of conflict governance. This holistic approach reinforces the principle that safeguarding the environment is inseparable from protecting civilians and building lasting peace—a critical responsibility for this generation and the ones to come.

The Rome Statute and Environmental Destruction

Yash Sinha

War Crime of Environmental Destruction

The international community has long recognised the imperative to prosecute the most egregious breaches of international law. The establishment of the International Criminal Court (ICC) through the Rome Statute in 1998 was a landmark achievement, providing a permanent judicial body with jurisdiction over the most serious crimes of concern to the global community: genocide, crimes against humanity, war crimes, and the crime of aggression.[1] These serious violations of the laws and customs are applicable in international and non-international armed conflicts, typically involving actions that target protected persons or objects, or that breach fundamental values of humanity and proportionality in warfare.

Throughout history, acts committed during war have caused substantial harm to the environment. The natural environment is increasingly recognised as a silent casualty of modern armed conflicts. The main impacts of armed conflict on the environment are habitat destruction and loss of wildlife, over-exploitation and degradation of natural resources and pollution.[2] Although wartime environmental damage is as old as war itself, the technological advancement in weapon systems and modern tactics have raised the scale of destruction of ecosystems.[3] This raises the issue of commitment to accountability and justice to ecological harm.

1 Article 5 of Rome Statute deals with Crimes within the jurisdiction of the Court states, "1. The jurisdiction of the Court shall be limited to the most serious crimes of concern to the international community as a whole. The Court has jurisdiction in accordance with this Statute with respect to the following crimes: (a) The crime of genocide; (b) Crimes against humanity; (c) War crimes; (d) The crime of aggression".

2 U C Jha, *Weapons of War: Environmental Impact* (KW Publishers 2017) 1.

3 ibid.

Therefore, the research examines the existing provisions within the international legal architecture, particularly through the Rome Statute of the ICC, to determine their inherent effectiveness in establishing definitive accountability and generating an appropriate level of deterrence in the prosecution of intentional environmental destruction as a codified war crime.

Intentional Destruction of the Environment During Warfare

During armed conflicts, environmental damage is virtually unavoidable, especially given the use of modern weaponry that often contains a significant amount of toxic materials.[4] Even without deliberate destruction, warfare leads to fires, air pollution, soil contamination, threats to human health, and risks to wildlife.[5] These conflict and war-related environmental damages can persist for centuries, as common sources of contamination include the release of components from explosive devices, ammunition and weapons of mass destruction, oils and lubricants used in military vehicles.[6] However, the environmental devastation is not only a byproduct of war and militarism, but has also been implemented as a military strategy since ancient times.[7] These potential military strategies were designed to demoralise the enemy population, denying them sustenance and permanently crippling their ability to recover.

Over the centuries, parties engaged in conflict have *deliberately and intentionally* inflicted ecological damage as a means of harming their adversaries. History has witnessed many deliberate acts aimed at destroying the natural environment in order to achieve strategic goals and safeguard State sovereignty during the course of a military conflict.[8] The ancient world provides numerous examples of intentional weaponisation of the environment; these tactics involved destroying resources, infrastructure

4 Iryna Rekrut, 'Environmental Damage is a War Crime: Analysing the Legal Implications of the Russian Armed Invasion's Environmental Impact on Ukraine' (2024) 114 J Crim L & Criminology 93, 99.

5 ibid.

6 Naomi L J Rintoul-Hynes, 'Environmental considerations for post-war reconstruction of Gaza' (2025) 54 Ambio 1980

7 Bronwyn Leebaw, 'Scorched Earth: Environmental War Crimes and International Justice' (2014) 12(4) Perspectives on Politics 770.

8 Steven Freeland, *Addressing the Intentional Destruction of the Environment During Warfare Under the Rome Statute of the International Criminal Court* (Intersentia 2015) 5.

and food supplies. A famous, though possibly apocryphal, example is the Roman practice of salting the city of Carthage and poisoning the surrounding soil with salt to prevent future fertilisation, rendering their soil infertile and preventing the city's resurgence.[9]

In the modern era, contemporary industrial and chemical capabilities have amplified the potential for destruction to unprecedented levels. During the Vietnam War between 1961 and 1971, the United States military implemented *'Operation Ranch Hand'* and sprayed 12 million gallons of herbicides, including the infamous Agent Orange, over more than 6 million acres in Vietnam, destroying vast tracts of mangrove forests and upland jungles.[10] These defoliants were used to clear vegetation that provided cover for 'enemy soldiers' and destroy crops. It destroyed 8% of Viet Nam's cropland with long-term effects including massive soil erosion, collapse of biodiversity and widespread dioxin contamination of the ecosystem.[11] Also, during the Gulf War of 1991, retreating Iraqi forces systematically detonated 700 Kuwaiti oil wells and dumped up to four million barrels of crude oil into the Persian Gulf.[12] This strategic sabotage released a massive amount of toxic smoke and simultaneously caused vast quantities of oil to be pumped into the Red Sea.[13] Further, it has been estimated by Human Rights Watch that, during the course of the 2003 invasion of Iraq, United States and British forces used almost 13,000 cluster bombs - containing almost two million munitions - 1.9 tonnes of depleted Uranium, causing very significant environmental damage, the extent of which may still not be known for a considerable period of time.[14]

More recently, the Russian armed invasion of Ukraine has impacted the natural environment in multiple ways, leaving in its wake a trail of burnt forests, thousands of dead animals, nature reserves littered with land mines, and contaminated water, air and soil.[15] There has been substantial evidence indicating that the Russian forces have *'deliberately targeted gas pipelines,*

9 Leebaw, 'Scorched Earth' (n 7) 770.

10 ibid.

11 Freeland (n 8) 5.

12 Freeland (n 8) 21.

13 Leebaw, 'Scorched Earth' (n 7) 770.

14 Freeland (n 8) 7.

15 Rekrut (n 4) 97.

water infrastructure, and local crops and wildlife.'[16] Ukraine's Ministry of Environmental Protection and Natural Resources has calculated that around 30% of the country's protected areas, covering more than 1.2 million hectares, are affected by the hostilities.[17]

Further, the Israel-Gaza conflict has caused a public health crisis and threatened long-term food and water security. Since the 7th October 2023 attack by Hamas and the retaliation by the Israeli military, approximately 70% of Gaza's buildings, sewage pumps/wastewater treatment plant and agricultural land have been destroyed or damaged.[18] Hence, the conflict has been described as an 'environmental catastrophe'.[19] The impact has been significant and multifaceted, affecting both the immediate and long-term health of the ecosystem and human population.[20] In addition, the conflict has also contributed in carbon emissions and climate change.[21] This intentional environmental destruction causes additional, unnecessary suffering in times of war and afterwards.

It is clear that the above military actions are not incidental but strategic calculations aimed at exploiting the enemy's dependence on the land to force surrender or permanent subjugation. It has to be acknowledged that the intentional destruction of the natural environment during armed conflict – often referred to as environmental warfare or ecocide – is the grim reality of modern combat. The nuclear, biological and chemical weapons undoubtedly have a disastrous effect of potentially killing many thousands of people; alternatively, they also have effects that may persist for the environment, in some cases indefinitely.[22] Some of such acts may also represent a breach of the fundamental human rights of the targeted individuals.[23] The relationship between human security and a safe habitable

16 Sarah Keisler, 'Environmental Warfare in Ukraine: Should We Prosecute Eco-Crimes Like War Crimes?', GEORGETOWN SEC. STUD. REV. (May 16, 2022).

17 United Nations Development Programme (UNDP), 'Environmental Damage Assessment', *UNDP Ukraine* <https://www.undp.org/ukraine/projects/environmental-damage-assessment> accessed 15 November 2025.

18 Rintoul-Hynes (n 6) 1979.

19 ibid.

20 Yulius Gunawan, Gratia Adonia Wibowo and Muhamad Hikam Arumbinang, 'Foreign Fighters in the Ukrainian Armed Conflict: An International Humanitarian Law Perspective' (2023) 6 Volksgeist J Ilmu Huk dan Konstitusi 145.

21 ibid.

22 Freeland (n 8) 8.

23 ibid.

environment is vital, particularly in relation to access to natural resources. However, these actions may weaken the chances of lasting peace. Thus, irrespective of the initial cause of a conflict, environmental degradation and resource depletion can trap the affected States into a vicious cycle of escalating poverty, compounded with political instability, further leading to recurrent armed conflict, and greater environmental damages with even greater poverty.[24]

Therefore, to deal with these critical ecological harms, international and domestic law have developed legal frameworks prohibiting such acts, which enable the categorisation of environmental damage as a war crime.[25]

International Legal Framework For Environmental Protection

The laws have traditionally been used to regulate acts that may affect the environment. International law increasingly recognises links between environmental and ecological rights and human rights.[26] It is broadly accepted that customary international law requires that one's actions do not cause significant destruction to the environment so as to threaten fundamental human rights.[27] The argument logically follows that international legal regulation intended to protect the environment should lead to accountability in appropriate circumstances for those individuals who intentionally set out to significantly damage the environment.[28]

Hence, the legal regulations in response to acts of intentional environmental destruction during armed conflict fundamentally relate to the binding character and its associated enforcement mechanism.[29] In addition, the protection mechanism is not only governed by existing *jus in bello* treaties but is also potentially dependent on hundreds of multilateral treaties and bilateral instruments.[30] While primarily designed for peacetime regulation, certain principles codified within these instruments may retain applicability during hostilities, extending the scope of ecological safeguards in armed

24 Jha (n 2) 2.

25 Rekrut (n 4) 99.

26 Freeland (n 8) 22.

27 ibid.

28 ibid.

29 Freeland (n 8) 23.

30 ibid.

conflict.[31] Moreover, the protection mechanism, even in armed conflict, is supported by a number of other mechanisms beyond formal law, notably through the use of *'soft law'* guidelines on international environmental law.[32]

Inherently, the inter-relationship between intentional environmental destruction, human security and armed conflict requires that effective enforcement measures exist at the international level.[33] Both national law and regional law only play a very limited role in addressing such *'green crimes'*. Generally, the national laws suffer from a lack of jurisdictional consistency, their punitive character, and are not appropriate in dealing with the transboundary ecological consequences.[34] Simultaneously, regional instruments risk exacerbating inter-regional disparities.[35] Therefore, the following are the most relevant existing international legal mechanisms provided for the protection of the environment during armed conflicts:

- **Protection under International Humanitarian Law (IHL)**

The evolution of multilateral treaties or bilateral instruments regulating the intentional destruction of the environment during warfare have developed alongside the advent of military technology and the rise of environmental consciousness.[36] These treaties are binding on State Parties, who are under an obligation to perform the terms of the relevant treaty in good faith - in accordance with the principle of *pacta sunt servanda*.[37] The laws and customs of war had their origin in the customary practices of armies on the battlefield and have existed in various forms almost since antiquity.[38] However, the first significant attempt to codify the law of war came in 1863, when American President Lincoln issued General Order authorising the so-called *'Lieber Instruction'* or the *'Lieber Code'*,[39] which introduced

31 ibid.

32 ibid 24.

33 ibid 29.

34 ibid 26.

35 ibid 28.

36 ibid 47.

37 Vienna Convention on the Law of Treaties, opened for signature 23 May 1969, 1155 UNTS 331: 8 ILM 679 (entered into force 27 January 1980) (VCLT), article 26.

38 Freeland (n 8) 50.

39 Instructions for the Government of Armies of the United States in the Field, promulgated as General Order No. 100, 24 April 1863.

a set of legal guidelines to be applied at the time of the American Civil War. Following on from the Lieber Code, a number of other States drafted military manuals during the second half of the 19th Century.[40]

Further, the carnage of the Second World War led the International Committee of the Red Cross (ICRC) to convince the international community to adopt the four Geneva Conventions in 1949, laying down the normative framework for the protection of victims of armed conflict.[41] This marked the development of first international treaty to define specific rules of warfare,[42] partly inspired by Henri Dunant's account of the Battle of Solferino.[43] The agreement established principles, including relief for the wounded, neutrality of medical staff, and the use of the red cross symbol, now serve as a foundational platform for the future multilateral treaties on the laws of war. Therefore, currently, the corpus of *jus in bello* encompasses over a hundred instruments.[44]

In particular, the Fourth Convention on the Protection of Civilian Persons in Time of War relates to the protection of the environment, albeit indirectly.[45] Such as the Article 53 of the Convention provides that:

> *'Any destruction by the Occupying Power of real or personal property belonging individually or collectively to private persons, or to the State, or to other public authorities, or to social or cooperative organisations, is prohibited, except where such destruction is rendered absolutely necessary by military operations.'*[46]

Similarly, with the passage of time, substantial and significant conventional norms have gradually developed to regulate a broader spectrum of military activities conducted during armed conflict. Concurrently, with respect to

40 These included Prussia (1870), The Netherlands (1871), France (1877), Russia (1877 and 1904), Serbia (1878). Argentina (1881), Great Britain (1883 and 1904) and Spain (1893).

41 Jha (n 2) 370.

42 Geneva Convention for the Amelioration of the Condition of the Wounded and Sick in Armed Forces in the Field (adopted 12 August 1949) 75 UNTS 31 (entered into force 21 October 1950).

43 Henry Dunant, A Memory of Solferino (International Committee of the Red Cross 1986)

44 Freeland (n 8) 51.

45 Jha (n 2) 370.

46 Geneva Convention Relative to the Protection of Civilian Persons in Time of War (adopted 12 August 1949) 75 UNTS 287 (entered into force 21 October 1950) art 53.

the issue of intentional environmental destruction during the course of warfare, the most important of the *jus in bello* treaties that developed were the Hague Conventions of 1899 and 1907, the four Geneva Conventions of 1949, the Convention on the Prohibition of Military or Any Other Hostile Use of Environmental Modification Techniques of 1976 (ENMOD)[47], and the Additional Protocols I and II (AP I & II) to the Geneva Conventions of 1977, out of which the obligations arising under Hague and Geneva instruments were reaffirmed by United Nation Security Council in a number of Resolutions relating to the protection of civilians in armed conflict.[48]

Beyond the key treaties and instruments mentioned, there are several other treaties prohibiting specific weapons that could cause severe environmental harm. This includes various treaties relevant to the issue of intentional destruction to the environment such as the St. Petersburg Declaration,[49] the Geneva Protocol for the Prohibition of the Use in War of Asphyxiating, Poisonous and Other Gases, and of Bacteriological Methods of Warfare,[50] the Hague Convention for the Protection of Cultural Property in the Event of Armed Conflict,[51] the Biological Weapons Convention,[52] the Chemical Weapon Convention,[53] the Ottawa Convention on the Prohibition of the

47 Convention on the Prohibition of Military or Any Other Hostile Use of Environmental Modification Techniques (adopted 10 December 1976, opened for signature 18 May 1977, entered into force 5 October 1978) 1108 UNTS 151.

48 Freeland (n 8) 58.

49 Declaration Renouncing the Use, in Time of War, of Explosive Projectiles Under 400 Grammes Weight (St Petersburg Declaration) 11 December 1868, 138 CTS 297.

50 Protocol for the Prohibition of the Use in War of Asphyxiating, Poisonous or Other Gases, and of Bacteriological Methods of Warfare (Geneva Protocol) 17 June 1925, 94 LNTS 65 (entered into force 8 February 1928).

51 Convention for the Protection of Cultural Property in the Event of Armed Conflict (Hague Convention 1954) opened for signature 14 May 1954, 249 UNTS 240 (entered into force 7 August 1956).

52 Convention on the Prohibition of the Development, Production and Stockpiling of Bacteriological (Biological) and Toxin Weapons and on their Destruction (Biological Weapons Convention) 10 April 1972, 1015 UNTS 163 (entered into force 26 March 1975).

53 Convention on the Prohibition of the Development, Production, Stockpiling and Use of Chemical Weapons and on their Destruction (Chemical Weapons Convention) 13 January 1993, 1974 UNTS 45 (entered into force 29 April 1997).

Use, Stockpiling, Production and Transfer of Anti-Personnel Mines and on their Destruction.[54]

However, in light of modern development and the history associated with the *jus in bello* regime, it reveals that while general rules regarding the conduct of hostilities may be decisive in determining the lawfulness of adopting specific means and methods in warfare.[55] It is argued that the effective imposition of present provisions is still lacking, provided that these legal obligations only provide some indirect protection to the natural environment in armed conflict. Particularly, because these IHL provisions tend to focus on aspects of the environment that impact upon humans rather than envisage the environment as an object itself in need of protection.[56] For example, the prohibition on pillage, the prohibition on the destruction of dams and dykes that may cause the release of dangerous forces and thus cause severe losses among the civilian population, and the prohibition on the destruction of 'foodstuffs, crops, livestock, drinking water installations and supplies and irrigation works',[57] all serve primarily to protect persons rather than the environment.[58]

- **Protection under Customary International Law (CIL)**

There are a number of important principles of customary international law that underpin the conduct of armed conflict. These principles apply to all States, operating independently of, as well as coincidentally with the provisions of all relevant *jus in bello* treaties to which combatants may be bound.[59] The classic description of what constitutes a rule of customary international law could be understood through the judgement of International Court of Justice (ICJ) in the *North Sea Continental Shelf*

54 Convention on the Prohibition of the Use, Stockpiling, Production and Transfer of Anti-Personnel Mines and on their Destruction (Ottawa Convention) 18 September 1997, 2056 UNTS 211 (entered into force 1 March 1999).

55 Hilaire McCoubrey and Nigel D White, *International Law and Armed Conflict* (Dartmouth 1992) 236.

56 Sandesh Sivakumaran, *The Law of Non-International Armed Conflict* (Oxford University Press 2012) 526.

57 Protocol Additional to the Geneva Conventions of 12 August 1949, and Relating to the Protection of Victims of Non-International Armed Conflicts (Protocol II) 8 June 1977, 1125 UNTS 609 art 4(2)(g), 14, 15.

58 Shivkumaran (n 56) 526.

59 Freeland (n 8) 175.

Cases.[60] The Court confirmed that customary international law evolves over time, and is derived from sufficient evidence of both the 'settled practice' of States, as well as *opinio juris* (recognition as law), which it described as 'a belief that this practice is rendered obligatory by the existence of a rule of law requiring it'.[61]

Similarly, in the traditional view, customary international law is defined by two essential components: an objective element (State practice) and a subjective or psychological element (*opinio juris*). It establishes a universal nature, unlike the conventional principles, compelling adherence virtually from all the States with subject to the exception of the so-called persistent objective rule. This obligation includes preventing the breach of the customary rules and punishing the perpetrators of international crime i.e., environmental degradation, particularly during armed conflict – binding each State regardless of any specific treaty obligation it may, or may not, have accepted.

In addition, it is also evident that these *jus in bello* rules are found in customary laws.[62] The observations of the Nuremberg Military Tribunal in 1946[63] - admittedly, when there were considerably fewer *jus in bello* treaties in force-that:[64]

> *[t]he law of war is to be found not only in treaties, but in the customs and practices of states which gradually obtained universal recognition, and from the general principles of justice applied by jurists and practiced by military courts. This law is not static, but by continual adaptation follows the needs of a changing world. Indeed, in many cases treaties do no more than express and define for more accurate reference the principles of law already existing*

60 North Sea Continental Shelf Cases (Federal Republic of Germany v. Denmark and Federal Republic of Germany v. The Netherlands) (Judgment) [1969] ICJ Rep 3. para 77.

61 Freeland (n 8) 120.

62 Oonagh E Fitzgerald, 'Implementation of International Humanitarian and Related International Law in Canada', in Oonagh E Fitzgerald (ed), *The Globalized Rule of Law: Relationships between International and Domestic Law* (2006) 625, 627.

63 International Military Tribunal for the Trial of the German Major War Criminals at Nuremberg (Nuremberg Military Tribunal)

64 France and others v Göring and others (Judgment and Sentence) (1947) 41 AJIL 172, 219.

This interpretation of *jus in bello* treaties necessitates considering relevant customary international law principles, as indicated by Article 31(3)(c) of the Vienna Convention.[65] Further, it is affirmed by the International Court of Justice (ICJ) in *the Legality of Threat or Use of Nuclear Weapons Advisory Opinion* that:

> *a great many rules of humanitarian law applicable in armed conflict are so fundamental to the respect of the human person and 'elementary considerations of humanity'... [and] are to be observed by all States whether or not they have ratified the conventions that contain them, because they constitute intransgressible principles of international customary law*

Also, these customary international principles are sometimes identical in their terms to conventional provisions related to the intentional environmental destruction during armed conflict.[66] However, despite potential textual similarities, these two sources of law – customs and conventions – may be ultimately applied in varying ways in relation to a specific factual circumstance.[67] Drawing from the jurisprudence of, in particular, the International Court of Justice, there are several fundamental *jus in bello* principles that clearly represent rules of customary international law and have concrete application in relation to situations where acts are done with the intent to cause significant damage to the environment during armed conflict. It includes the principle of humanity, the principle of military necessity, the principle of distinction and the principle of proportionality.

Further, the Rules 43 to 45 of the International Committee of the Red Cross (ICRC) study on customary IHL expressly deal with the protection of the environment during the conflict.[68] The general principles on the conduct of hostilities, contained in Rule 43, particularly apply to the natural environment. It states:[69]

> *(a) no part of the natural environment may be attacked, unless it is a military objective,*

65 VCLT art 31(3)(c).

66 Freeland (n 8) 127.

67 ibid.

68 Jean-Marie Henckaerts and Louise Doswald-Beck, *Customary International Humanitarian Law*, vol I (Cambridge University Press 2005) rules 43–45.

69 ibid rule 43.

> *(b) destruction of any part of the natural environment is prohibited, unless required by imperative military necessity, and*
>
> *(c) launching an attack against a military objective, which may be expected to cause incidental damage to the environment, which would be excessive in relation to the concrete and direct military advantage anticipated, is prohibited.*

Whereas Rule 44 requires armed forces to employ methods of warfare with due regard for the natural environment, taking all feasible precautions to avoid or minimise incidental damage so as to incorporate the precautionary principle.[70] Finally, Rule 45 absolutely prohibits the use of methods or means of warfare intended or expected to cause widespread, long-term, and severe damage to the natural environment, and it also forbids using environmental destruction as a weapon.[71] Furthermore, from the existing international legal obligations and from State practice concerning the protection of the environment against the effects of armed conflict, the ICRC has drafted *Guidelines for Military Manuals and Instructions on the Protection of the Environment in Times of Armed Conflict*[72], which offers a model for national military manuals. They prohibit military or any other hostile use of environmental modification techniques having widespread, long-lasting or severe effects as the means of destruction, damage or injury to any other State party.[73] They also prohibit attacks against the natural environment by way of reprisals.[74] Under these guidelines, the States are urged to enter into further agreements providing additional protection to the natural environment in times of armed conflict.[75]

Subsequently, the ICRC has also released the *2020 Guidelines*,[76] which aim to protect the natural environment in armed conflict, contributing a

70 ibid rule 44.

71 ibid rule 45.

72 International Committee of the Red Cross (ICRC), *Guidelines for military manual and instructions on the protection of the environment in the time of armed conflict* (Geneva 1994).

73 U C Jha, *International Humanitarian Law: The Laws of War* (Vij Books India Pvt Ltd 2011) 221.

74 Ibid.

75 Ibid.

76 International Committee of the Red Cross (ICRC), *Guidelines on the Protection of the Natural Environment in Armed Conflict: Responsibilities and Recommendations relating to the environment in armed conflict* (Geneva 2020).

practical way to promote respect for and protection of the legal obligations, such as in the prohibition of indiscriminate attacks, the proportionality in attack or the duty to take precautions in attack, predominantly during armed conflict. These guidelines are tools to facilitate the adoption of concrete implementation measures so as to strengthen the protection of the environment.

However, while these customs and principles apply in the circumstance of protection to intentional destruction of the environment during hostilities, there are significant shortcomings in relation to these customary rules, as they are largely characterised by vagueness and uncertainty.[77] This stems from several factors, including the difficulties associated with specifying the precise scope of the rules, the traditional and overarching importance accorded to considerations of military advantage, the imprecise status and value rendered to the environment, the inherently destructive nature of warfare, or the overall complexity of the issues involved.[78]

- **Protection under International Environmental Law (IEL)**

The IEL has rapidly developed since the 1972 Stockholm Declaration,[79] which was the first significant statement of international principles relating to environmental protection. As the environmental consequences of nuclear weapons became a subject of discussion following their use during the Second World War.[80] It led to specific reference within the declaration, addressing them directly under its principle 26,[81] which states:

> *[m]an and his environment must be spared the effects of nuclear weapons and all other means of mass destruction. States must strive to reach prompt agreement, in the relevant international organs, on the elimination and complete destruction of such weapons*

Further, the development of the 1982 World Charter for Nature contained a number of general principles relating to the environment and armed conflict, including that '[n]ature shall be secured against degradation caused by warfare or other hostile activities' and '[m]ilitary activities damaging to

77 Freeland (n 8) 159.

78 ibid.

79 Declaration of the United Nations Conference on the Human Environment (16 June 1972) UN Doc A/CONF.48/14/Rev1 (1972 Stockholm Declaration).

80 Freeland (n 8) 103.

81 1972 Stockholm Declaration Principle 26.

nature shall be avoided.'[82] In addition, the 1992 Rio Declaration provided that:[83]

> *[t]he environment and natural resources of people under oppression, domination and occupation shall be protected*

> and:[84]

> *[w]arfare is inherently destructive of sustainable development. States shall therefore respect international law providing protection for the environment in times of armed conflict and* cooperate in its further development, if necessary

Although these instruments, considered non-binding soft law, provide crucial guidelines and standards for environmental conduct that often influence State actions. While not legally enforceable treaties, their concepts frequently evolve into binding treaties or customary international laws, thereby generating international legal obligations. Furthermore, in terms of its applicability (or otherwise) to environmental damage, Philippe Sand suggests classification of different IEL treaties in times of armed conflict in the following ways:[85]

> *(a) treaties that expressly exclude their applicability in relation to damage that occurs as a result of war or armed conflict;*
>
> *(b) treaties that allow for total or partial suspension at the instigation of one of the Parties;*
>
> *(c) treaties that require the consequences of hostilities to influence subsequent decisions under the relevant treaty;*
>
> *(d) treaties that expressly exclude their applicability to any military activities, even during times of peace;*
>
> *(e) treaties that expressly apply to specific activities associated with the conduct of hostilities;*
>
> *(f) treaties that expressly or impliedly apply at all times.*

---

82 United Nations General Assembly Resolution 37/7 (28 October 1982) UN Doc A/RES/37/7 on the World Charter for Nature, Annex, principles 5, 20.

83 Declaration on Environment and Development (adopted 14 June 1992) UN Doc A/CONF.151/26/Rev.1 (vol I) (1992) annex I (Rio Declaration) Principles 23.

84 Rio Declaration, Principles 25.

85 Philippe Sands, *Principles of International Environmental Law* (2nd ed, 2003), 309-10.

In more general terms, Edith Brown Weiss, while acknowledging that most IEL treaties do not indicate whether they are applicable during an armed conflict, asserts that some treaties can only effectively fulfil their purposes if they do continue to apply during times of hostilities.[86]

Also, drawing from the *Trail Smelter Arbitration* principles, many of these IEL agreements give rise to obligations on States to exercise *'due diligence'* to prevent environmental damage to other States - or, in some cases, to areas beyond the territorial jurisdiction of any State – arising from activities under their jurisdiction or control.[87] It asserts that accountability arises from the failure to exercise the requisite standard of care, which are typically not punitive in nature. This reflects the lack of development of international law concerning environmental protection during wartime. Also, subsequently, there are very few multilateral IEL treaties that specifically address environmental protection during war, whereas most existing agreements are typically silent regarding its applicability once hostilities begin, leading to 'insufficient uniformity of opinion' among States on this matter.[88]

It demonstrates that the broad IEL framework has no established and comprehensive treaty regime, particularly to provide for accountability in respect to the intentional destruction of the environment during armed conflict.[89] Rather than creating a punitive and deterrence-focused regime, the framework adopts the traditional principle of State responsibility.[90] It incorporates notions of liability and obligating the State to provide reparation or compensation for violations, without addressing the specific issue of individual criminal responsibility.[91] Moreover, where the conventional environmental limitations do exist, the compliance is non-uniform and often relies heavily upon the requisite political will within the international community.[92]

Therefore, this calls for a further specific legal instrument to fill the existing gaps in accountability, that is possibly through the prevailing framework

86 Freeland (n 8) 108.

87 ibid 105.

88 ibid 106.

89 ibid 113.

90 ibid 116.

91 ibid.

92 ibid 115.

under the Rome Statute or otherwise through an amendment to the Statute of the ICC, which could establish ecocide as a distinct crime against peace, aligning environmental destruction with the most serious crimes under international law and thereby introducing the element of individual criminal responsibility that the current International legal regime lacks.

Deconstruction of The Rome Statute of ICC

One of the most recent works in the field of environmental protection has been the adoption of the Rome Statute of the ICC, granting the court jurisdiction over certain acts causing environmental damage.[93] The Court has been given the mandate to play a role when certain international crimes, particularly in circumstances where *'the most serious crime of concern to the international community as a whole'* has been committed.[94] It has the power to exercise jurisdiction with respect to circumstances that may occur *in the future* - that is, any time after the Rome Statute came into force on 1st July 2000.[95] However, even when the ICC operate within the current jurisdictional limits of the Rome Statute, the Statute is not static. There is nothing that restricts the future inclusion of further crimes within the statute, provided that all necessary procedural requirements are complied with.[96]

In the context of international crimes, to support the argument that certain acts which constitute crimes against humanity relate to circumstances where the environment has been intentionally targeted are particularly specified in article 7(1)(h) and 7(1)(k) of the Rome Statute. These include:[97]

> *[p]ersecution against any identifiable group or collectivity on political, racial, national, ethnic, cultural, religious, gender or other grounds that are universally recognised as impermissible under international law, in connection with any act referred to in this paragraph or any crime within the jurisdiction of the Court*
>
> and:[98]

93 Jha (n 74) 218.

94 Freeland (n 8) 183

95 ibid.

96 Ibid 185.

97 Rome Statute of the International Criminal Court (adopted 17 July 1998, entered into force 1 July 2002) 2187 UNTS 90, art 7(1)(h).

98 Rome Statute, art 7(1)(k).

> *[o]ther inhumane acts of a similar character intentionally causing great suffering, or serious injury to body or to mental or physical health*

Hereby, the deliberate destruction of a habitat or of access to clean and safe water or food on a significant scale could, in certain circumstances, represent a breach of the fundamental human rights of the individuals within a targeted group, as perhaps might some other acts of environmental destruction.[99] Hence, theoretically, the scope of Article 7(1)(h) of the Rome Statute may extend to certain acts that intentionally target the environment during armed conflict, provided that the acts also fulfil the overarching elements of crimes against humanity set out in the chapeau of Article 7.[100] This includes a 'widespread or systematic attack directed against any civilian population'.[101] In essence, for a crime against humanity to be committed, it is necessary to demonstrate that the civilian population is the 'victim' or 'primary object' of such an attack.[102]

Yet, this existing framework fails to address the unique nature of the intentional destruction of the environment during armed conflict as an international crime.[103] Since the environment is deliberately targeted as the victim or primary object—and not the civilian population—this specific victim prospect distinguishes it from other core international crimes, meaning the consequences of this act generally will not fall within crimes against humanity.[104]

However, the provision within the Rome Statute that specifically criminalises environmental damage during international armed conflict is Article 8(2)(b)(iv). It specifies that 'in particular when committed as part of a plan or policy or as part of a large-scale commission of such crimes',[105] a war crime within the jurisdiction of the Court includes:[106]

> *Intentionally launching an attack in the knowledge that such an attack will cause incidental loss of life or injury to civilians or damage to*

99 Freeland (n 8) 201.

100 ibid 202.

101 ibid.

102 Judgement, *Prosecutor v. Dragoljub Kunarac, Radomir Kovac and Zoran Vukovic*, Case No. IT-96-23 and IT-96-23/1-A, Appeals Chamber, 12 June 2002, para 91.

103 Freeland (n 8) 204.

104 ibid.

105 Rome Statute, art 8(1).

106 Rome Statute, art 8(2)(b)(iv).

civilian objects or widespread, long-term and severe damage to the natural environment, which would be clearly excessive in relation to the concrete and direct overall military advantage anticipated

This inclusion represents an attempt to translate the humanitarian norms into actionable criminal law, marking a *'greening'* of IHL provisions. It establishes a war crime based on an excessive collateral consequence of an attack. However, the requirement that the damage must be *'widespread, long-term and severe'*, coupled with the necessary integration of the principle of proportionality, sets an exceptionally high bar for the *actus reus* (the physical element). Hence, demanding a very high threshold of injury to the environment before an act would fall within the scope of the crime.[107]

In addition, Article 30 of the Rome Statute applies as the *mens rea* (the mental element) standard for Article 8(2)(b)(iv).[108] It provides that:[109]

[u]nless otherwise provided, a person shall be criminally responsible and liable for punishment for a crime within the jurisdiction of the Court only if the material elements are committed with intent and knowledge

It establishes a default rule, a *lex generalis* that applies 'unless the Rome Statute or the Elements of Crimes require a different standard of fault.'[110] It includes only direct and indirect intent, to the exclusion of lower mental standards.[111] Here, the indirect intent requires that the offender be aware that the prohibited consequence 'will occur in the ordinary course of events.'[112] In this case, the volitional element decreases substantially and is overridden by the cognitive element, i.e., the awareness that his or her act or omission *will* cause the undesirable proscribed consequences.[113] This dual requirement of both intention and, in particular, knowledge further restricts any possible practical application of article 8(2)(b) (iv).[114]

---

107 Freeland (n 8) 207.

108 ibid 210.

109 Rome Statute, art 30.

110 Catherine Savard, 'What mens rea for ecocide in the Rome Statute?' (2025) The International Journal of Human Rights DOI: 10.1080/13642987.2025.2552468, 3.

111 ibid.

112 ibid.

113 ibid.

114 Freeland (n 8) 210.

But in the absence of a specific environmental crime, the issue of Intentional environmental destruction during armed conflict still appears at best to be a narrowly defined '*add-on*',[115] with very considerable - perhaps even insurmountable - legal hurdles that, for all practical purposes, will serve to curtail any effective prosecution.[116] As the concern associated with criminalising acts that damage the environment in the context of armed conflict requires balancing of damage against the military advantage.[117] In practical terms, this means that environmental issues are 'made secondary' to the interest of military importance.[118] Marking, the decision to criminalise widespread, long-term and severe damage to the natural environment as a war crime, under article 8(2)(b)(iv) as 'a cause for limited celebration, considerable disappointment, and some concern.'[119] Consequently, this approach fails to move beyond the traditional and outdated notion of environmental harm as an unfortunate 'byproduct' of warfare, even in the circumstances of deliberate and intentional damage.[120]

Hence, it is clearly observed that the Rome Statute is fundamentally anthropocentric in its design, prioritising the protection of human life and well-being. The natural environment is thus protected primarily because human life depends on its survival. Even when the Statute does not contain a specific crime of 'crimes against the environment' within the crimes in relation to which the Court has jurisdiction, it does set out the circumstances in which a particular level of damage to the 'natural environment' may constitute a war crime. Therefore, on a cursory read, it is asserted that the inclusion of article 8(2)(b)(iv) of the statute in some aspects may be sufficient.[121] But the fluid nature of intentional destruction of the environment during armed conflict may lead this provision to be simplistic and inaccurate.[122]

115 Mark A. Drumbl, Waging War against the World: The Need to Move from War Crimes to Environmental Crimes, in Jay E. Austin and Carl E. Bruch (eds), The Environmental Consequences of War: Legal, Economic, and Scientific Perspectives (2000), 632.

116 Freeland (n 8) 213.

117 ibid 206.

118 ibid.

119 Drumbl (n 115) 630.

120 Freeland (n 8) 206.

121 ibid 215.

122 ibid.

The blatant disregard to the environment and the potential consequences of such acts 'shock the conscience of humanity', prompting calls for appropriate criminal responsibility.[123] This marks the application of article 8(2)(b)(iv) to be inadequate in addressing such calls due to its uncertainties, the inordinately high threshold of damage required, and the fact that its application is conditional on military contingency.[124] Hence, the current legal framework fails to provide sufficient protection against the intentional targeting of the environment during the armed conflict and thus fails humanity on this issues.[125]

Final Reflection – A Work in Progress

The suffering and devastation caused by contemporary armed conflicts are almost beyond words.[126] Over the ages, there have been many types of victims of armed conflict, but where the environment has been specifically targeted, those responsible have largely gone unpunished.[127] These conflicts have not only destroyed ecosystems but also further deepened the rapidly intensifying global environmental and climate crisis.[128] In the past fifty years, natural ecosystems have declined by almost 50% on average relative to their earliest estimates, and around 25% of animal and plant species are close to extinction, with conflict being an indirect driver of the loss.[129] This is dangerous, among other reasons, because ecosystems and biodiversity are crucial for sustaining human life, as ecosystems are damaged, climate adaptation becomes more difficult, causing further distress to conflict-affected communities that are already among the most exposed.[130]

Though some environmental impacts are unavoidable during an armed conflict, technological development raises an additional difficult question of how to regulate new weapons under conditions of uncertainty about

123 ibid.

124 ibid 216.

125 ibid 216.

126 ICRC, *International Humanitarian Law and the Challenges of Contemporary Armed Conflicts: Building a Culture of Compliance for IHL to Protect Humanity in Today's and Future Conflicts* (30 September 2024) 37.

127 Freeland (n 8) 285.

128 ICRC (n 127).

129 ICRC (n 127) 49.

130 ibid.

their effect on human health and the environment.[131] Nevertheless, these could be reduced or even prevented if the right actions are taken in the right places and at the right times in an attempt to uphold the United Nations Charter's aim to *'save succeeding generations from the scourge of war'*.[132] But as demonstrated in this paper, the position under the *jus in bello* treaty instruments and customary principles, the international environmental law instruments and the jurisdictional mandate of the international criminal justice mechanism clearly point to the fact that the current international regulatory framework is not designed to be sufficient, particularly regarding the act of intentional destruction of the environment during warfare.[133]

While the humanitarian consequences of armed conflict have been increasingly addressed in the relevant *jus in bello* instruments, the international community has been far more resistant to the notion of effectively regulating the environmental consequences,[134] with the result that the interaction between the conduct of armed conflict and the natural environment have been largely under-explored.[135]

However, the mechanism of justice under the existing ICC regime and the Rome Statute could play an integral function with respect to the protection of the environment during armed conflict. It is because ICC is arguably the best-equipped international criminal justice mechanism to deal with this crime of intentional environmental destruction during conflicts, and also that the Statute plays 'a powerful trendsetting role' in articulating and shaping State actions.[136] The conclusion is, therefore, that it is necessary to amend the Rome Statute more appropriately to deal with 'crimes against the environment'.[137] The central rationale to establish this approach is to have a direct and appropriate legal instrument to regulate and criminally punish acts that reach a specified threshold of gravity, specifically the significant intentional destruction of the environment committed in the context of armed conflict. Even when this inclusion of a *sui generis* crime of crimes

131 Jha (n 2) 412.

132 Charter of the United Nations (signed 26 June 1945, entered into force 24 October 1945) 1 UNTS XVI, Preamble.

133 Freeland (n 8) 222.

134 Drumbl (n 115) 620.

135 Freeland (n 8) 220.

136 ibid 226.

137 ibid 285.

against the environment in the Statute, and thus within the jurisdiction of the ICC, will not be an easy task.[138]

In the end, what is required is a significant degree of political will and courage, strong assertiveness by civil society, and an understanding by relevant stakeholders that the threats posed by the ever-increasing destructive capability of modern weapons technology should override military considerations in circumstances where the natural environment is intentionally targeted during armed conflict.[139] Therefore, this level of commitment would surely reflect a work in progress towards greater environmental protection and in achieving much greater effectiveness in the regulation of acts that are intended to cause significant environmental damage during armed conflicts.

138 ibid.

139 ibid.

Climate Crimes of War

Niharika & Shobhit Pratap Singh

Abstract

Armed conflicts have long inflicted collateral damage on the environment, but in the age of accelerating climate crises, such harm can no longer be treated as incidental. Despite mounting evidence that warfare — including military logistics, explosive weaponry, and occupation regimes — contributes significantly to greenhouse gas emissions and ecological collapse, international legal frameworks remain ill-equipped to address such impacts. The laws of armed conflict and international humanitarian law (IHL) largely focus on direct human suffering, marginalising slow-onset or long-term environmental degradation.

This paper critically evaluates the environmental toll of modern warfare through an interdisciplinary lens that synthesises international humanitarian law, environmental law, and climate accountability frameworks. It explores the growing academic and policy momentum around recognising ecocide as an international crime and interrogates whether military-induced carbon emissions should be treated as a form of environmental harm in armed conflict. Drawing from recent conflicts in Ukraine, Gaza, and Sudan, it assesses empirical data on carbon footprints of war, investigates the legal lacunae in addressing such emissions, and examines the feasibility of incorporating carbon accountability mechanisms within existing or reformed international legal structures.

The paper further critiques the gaps in the International Criminal Court (ICC)'s jurisdiction over environmental crimes, the underutilisation of the International Law Commission (ILC) guidelines, and the limited binding power of the ICRC's good practices. It proposes a novel legal-ethical framework that positions war-induced environmental harm as both a violation of intergenerational equity and a breach of planetary boundaries — thereby urging a paradigmatic shift from viewing such damage as permissible collateral to prosecutable climate crimes.

Introduction

Armed conflict in the twenty-first century increasingly manifests not only in human suffering and material destruction but also in serious, enduring damage to the planet's ecological systems. While international humanitarian law has long treated environmental harm as an unfortunate side-effect or "collateral" of war, this framing no longer suffices in a world confronting accelerating climate destabilisation. Modern warfare—through fuel-hungry logistics, bombardment, infrastructure destruction, occupation regimes, debris clearing, and ecological disruption—now contributes measurably to greenhouse gas emissions and ecosystem collapse. Yet, despite mounting empirical evidence, international legal doctrine and institutional mechanisms remain ill-equipped to adjudicate such harm.

This paper seeks to reframe environmental damage from armed conflict as not merely collateral but as a potentially prosecutable climate crime—one that demands recognition through the twin lenses of ecocide and carbon accountability. The core research questions that guide this inquiry are:

1. In what ways do armed conflicts and their associated military, logistical, and infrastructural activities cause significant damage to the environment through greenhouse gas emissions and ecological degradation?

2. Why do existing international legal frameworks — under international humanitarian law, international criminal law, ILC principles, and institutional practice — fail to adequately address such harm?

3. How can environmental damage caused by armed conflict be reframed as climate crime—integrating both ecocide and carbon accountability—as a pathway to legal, institutional, and moral redress?

In the subsequent section, 'Issue of 'Collateral' in Environmental Harm due to Armed Conflicts, ' the paper describes how the conventional label of "collateral environmental damage" functions to suppress the distinctiveness and gravity of ecological harms in wartime. It presents empirical evidence from Gaza, Ukraine, and Sudan to show the multiplicity of direct, indirect, and long-term environmental harms that warfare imposes on ecosystems, soil, air, water, and communities. In the next section of the paper, 'Legal Framework for Protection of Environment during Conflict', the paper interrogates the existing legal architecture—the ENMOD Convention, Geneva Protocols (especially Protocol I), ICRC guidelines, customary law principles, and the ILC draft principles—and shows their conceptual, jurisdictional, and enforcement shortcomings in relation to environmental degradation caused by warfare.

Building on those foundations, the following section, 'Emerging Framework of Ecocide and Carbon Accountability' develops the emerging framework of ecocide and carbon accountability. It explains how the movement to criminalise ecocide, particularly via a proposed Article 8ter to the Rome Statute, offers a doctrinal avenue to hold parties accountable for systemic ecosystem destruction. It further explores how conflict-related greenhouse gas emissions can be measured, attributed, and integrated into climate governance, linking post-conflict carbon reparations to ecosystem restoration.

Together, these parts lead to the last section of the paper – 'Legal–Ethical Framework for Ecocide and Environmental Harm due to Armed Conflicts and its Associated Activities', where a normative and institutional architecture is developed that bridges criminal accountability, reparative justice, and environmental governance. The paper argues for a dual-track model: severe environmental crimes adjudicated via ecocide, and measurable climate liabilities addressed through carbon accountability and reparations. It seeks to move the discourse from ecological casualty to prosecutable climate crime, challenging states and non-state actors to internalise environmental costs even in war.

In sum, this paper charts a new legal-ethical paradigm: war must no longer be an excuse for ecological destruction. The law must evolve so that environmental harm in conflict is not invisible but is instead subject to accountability, remediation, and justice.

Environmental Harm due to Armed Conflicts

Brief Overview

The world is currently experiencing unprecedented levels of conflict and violence, deeply affecting millions. In 2023 alone, more than 170 armed conflicts were documented.[1] By the year's end, nearly 120 million people globally had been forcibly displaced as a result of persecution, conflict, violence, human rights violations, and major disruptions to public order. The devastating impact of war on people is unmistakable, but its harm to the environment often goes unnoticed. Beyond immediate destruction, warfare disrupts ecosystems, exhausts natural resources, pollutes air and water, and threatens the planet's health for generations.[2] Military activities can contaminate fertile land and water when forests are cleared or ecosystems are destroyed to displace populations, as seen in Sudan and Iraq.

In Ukraine, landmines and pollution from shelling and floods threaten soil, waterways, and forests. Clearing these hazards will cost about US$34.6 billion and take decades. In Gaza, conflict has led to the complete degradation of agriculture, land, and water systems. Infrastructure destruction has generated millions of tons of debris, some of which is contaminated with hazardous substances. It has also led to a surge in communicable diseases in Gaza, with the World Health Organisation noting 179,000 cases of acute respiratory infection and 136,400 cases of diarrhoea among children under five-reflecting the effects of damaged infrastructure.

A study by Scientists for Global Responsibility and the Conflict and Environment Observatory estimates that militaries contribute about 5.5% of global greenhouse gas emissions.[3] Military activities, including heavy energy use during conflicts, directly and indirectly intensify the climate crisis, yet emissions from these actions were not fully addressed in the 1997 Kyoto Protocol or the 2015 Paris Agreement due to national security considerations. Damage to chemical industrial sites during war can cause fires and widespread pollution, posing immediate and long-term risks to human health and ecosystems. For example, the 1991 Gulf War saw the uncontrolled burning of over 600 oil wells in Kuwait, releasing

1 Facts and figures: Women, peace, and security available at: https://www.unwomen.org/en/articles/facts-and-figures/facts-and-figures-women-peace-and-security accessed on 24 August 2025.

2 Protecting the Environment in Armed Conflict available at: https://www.genevaenvironmentnetwork.org/ resources/updates/protecting-the-environment-in-armed-conflict/ accessed on 27 August 2025.

3 Estimating the Military's Global Greenhouse Gas Emissions available at: https://ceobs.org/wp-content/uploads/2022/11/SGRCEOBS -Estimating_Global_MIlitary_GHG_Emissions_Nov22_rev.pdf accessed on 1 September 2025.

up to 500,000 metric tons of pollutants daily.[4] In 2006, bombing the Jiyeh power plant in Lebanon spilt 30,000 tons of heavy fuel into the eastern Mediterranean Sea, harming marine life along the coastlines of Lebanon and Syria.[5] Moreover, high-intensity conflicts consume large amounts of fuel, resulting in significant CO2 emissions. For instance, the first three years of Russia's invasion of Ukraine produced 230 metric tons of carbon dioxide equivalent (MtCO2e),[6] comparable to the yearly emissions of Austria, Hungary, the Czech Republic, and Slovakia combined. This is also the first recorded assessment of conflict-related emissions. Large-scale vehicle movement and heavy use of explosives damage sensitive landscapes and geodiversity. Urban explosive weapons pose additional environmental risks by generating debris and rubble, contributing to air and soil pollution.

Conflict-related military hardware and weapons have a long-lasting effect on the environment. In addition to obstructing agricultural access, land mines, cluster munitions, and other explosives contaminate soil and water with harmful substances. Handling abandoned military scrap can be hazardous to one's health because it contaminates groundwater and soil. Marine pollution is a result of damaged ships, submarines, and offshore oil installations.

In addition to the hazardous materials found in many conventional weapons, depleted uranium is also radioactive. Chemical defoliants have caused extensive ecological and public harm, particularly in Vietnam, while incendiary weapons like white phosphorous destroy habitats through fire and toxicity.[7] Acknowledging these effects is vital for harm reduction, environmental recovery, and conflict prevention.[8]

4 The Environmental Impacts of the Gulf War 1991 available at: https://pure.iiasa.ac.at/id/eprint/7427/1/IR-04-019.pdf accessed on 2 September 2025.

5 2006 Jiyeh Power Plant Oil Spill available at: https://www.rempec.org/en/our-work/pollution-preparedness-and-response/response/accident-map/2006-jiyeh-power-plant-oil-spill accessed on 24 August 2025.

6 Warfare now largest source of Ukraine's annual carbon emissions, report warns on third anniversary of Russia's invasion available at: https://earth.org/warfare-now-largest-source-of-ukraines-annual-carbon-emissions-report-warns-on-third-anniversary-of-russias-invasion/ accessed on 5 September 2025.

7 How Does War Damage the Environment? available at: https://ceobs.org/how-does-war-damage-the-environment/ accessed on 11 September 2025.

8 How Conflict Impacts Our Environment available at: https://www.un.org/en/peace-and-security/how-conflict-impacts-our-environment accessed on 10 October 2025.

Case Studies

Gaza

The ongoing conflict in Gaza has led to significant environmental challenges, necessitating urgent assessments and interventions. The United Nations Environment Programme (UNEP) conducted a preliminary assessment at the request of the State of Palestine in December 2023. The assessment highlights visible and less visible environmental impacts, including soil and water contamination.[9] More than 39 million tonnes of debris have been produced, some of which are tainted with asbestos, unexploded ordnance (UXOs), and other dangerous materials. In addition, human remains are interred among this enormous amount of trash. The environmental conditions in Gaza can be studied in the following stages to get a clearer picture:

Pre-Conflict Environmental Conditions in Gaza

The severe environmental degradation faced by Gaza before the escalation of conflict can be attributed to high population growth, unplanned urbanisation, and climate change. Moreover, the nitrate levels in the Coastal Aquifer were six times higher than WHO recommendations. Pollution from untreated wastewater significantly affected marine ecosystems and human health. There were significant investments aimed at improving environmental quality in Gaza such as for construction of wastewater treatment plants and plans to recharge the Coastal Aquifer, construction of the Northern Gaza Emergency Sewage Treatment plant, etc.

Environmental Challenges Post-Conflict

The ongoing conflict has raised diverse significant environmental issues such as:

- **Water and Sanitation crisis**

  Water sources in Gaza-including the Coastal Aquifer, desalination plants, piped water from Israel's Mekorot company, and small-scale suppliers-have been severely disrupted, along with wastewater treatment facilities. According to a 2024 Interim Damage Assessment (WB, EU, UN), 57% of water infrastructure has been

9 Environmental Impact of Conflict in Gaza available at: https://wedocs.unep.org/bitstream/handle/20.500.11822/45739/environmental_impact_conflict_Gaza.pdf?sequence=3&isAllowed=y accessed on 15 September 2025.

destroyed or damaged, costing over US$503 million. By March 2024, water production was less than 5% of normal output, and most wastewater treatment and management sites were inoperable. While some pipeline connections from Israel have been restored intermittently, total water flow remains under a quarter of pre-conflict levels.

Mass displacement to southern Gaza has overwhelmed local water and sanitation systems, with Rafah's population swelling from under 280,000 to around 1.3 million. Untreated sewage is largely concentrated in these areas. As of April 2024, daily water supply ranged from 2-8 litres per person, compared to 85 litres before October 2023. Private operators now supply much less water than before, and prices for tankered water have increased from 20 NIS to 150 NIS. Households, shelters, and IDP centres are rationing supplies, using brackish agricultural wells for drinking, often ingesting unsafe water containing high salt and chemical residues.

- **Solid Waste Management Challenges**

  Solid waste management in Gaza has suffered major disruptions since October 2023, leading to significant public health and environmental risks. Waste transfer to landfills stopped in November due to fuel shortages and security issues, causing rubbish to accumulate-up to 1,200 tons daily from IDP camps, shelters, and host communities. The growing presence of medical waste in hospitals increased disease risks. Waste collection was inconsistent, and informal dumpsites spread throughout the region. Attempts to improve waste management between December 2023 and January 2024 were limited by ongoing conflict and infrastructure damage; five out of six facilities were affected. During gas shortages, residents relied on firewood and burning waste, worsening air quality and respiratory illness risks. Humanitarian agencies launched emergency programmes, including cash-for-work and solid waste transfer initiatives, collecting about 10,000 tons of waste from Rafah and Khan Yunis in early 2024.[10]

10 A Silent Threat: Gaza's Struggle with Solid Waste Management available at: https://stories.undp.org/a-silent-threat-gazas-struggle-with-solid-waste-management accessed on 15 September 2025.

- **Destruction of infrastructure and conflict-related debris**

  Military actions in dense urban areas, such as Gaza, have generated unprecedented amounts of debris, primarily from damaged buildings and infrastructure. This debris often contains hazardous materials like UXOs and human remains, distinguishing it from typical construction waste. By May 2024, over 39 million tons of debris-13 times more than all previous Gaza conflicts combined-had accumulated, with over 107 kg per square metre across the region. More than 60% of Gaza's infrastructure and 62% of homes have been damaged or destroyed, while 62% of roads and most primary transport routes are affected, costing about $358 million. The severity, geographic spread, and density of debris, along with high levels of contamination risk, make this situation unique in scale and complexity.[11]

- **Marine and Coastal Ecosystem Damage**

  Marine ecosystems have been adversely affected by increased pollution and physical damage from the conflict.[12] Unprocessed waste and solid waste from combat have probably increased marine contamination. Humans and marine animals are at danger for health problems due to pathogens linked to sewage-contaminated waterways. About 3,700 people rely on fishing as a primary source of food and income, but the fishing fleet is being physically destroyed and marine pollution is a danger.

- **Agricultural Sector Destruction**

  The agricultural sector has suffered extensive damage, impacting food production and security in Gaza.[13] 42.6% of all crop land has been damaged, with the Gaza governorate experiencing the largest area of damage. Estimated destruction in the agricultural sector amounts to $629 million, affecting trees, greenhouses, and

11 Damage in Gaza causing new risks to human health and long-term recovery available at: https://www.unep.org/news-and-stories/press-release/damage-gaza-causing-new-risks-human-health-and-long-term-recovery accessed on 20 September 2025.

12 War pushes Gaza's environment to full-scale collapse: UNEP report available at: https://www.newindianexpress.com/xplore/2025/Oct/04/war-pushes-gazas-environment-to-full-scale-collapse-unep-report accessed on 5 October 2025.

13 Gaza's agricultural infrastructure continues to deteriorate at alarming rate available at: https://www.fao.org/newsroom/detail/gaza-s-agricultural-infrastructure-continues-to-deteriorate-at-alarming-rate/en accessed on 24 September 2025.

irrigation infrastructure. The widening of the exclusion zone surrounding the Armistice Demarcation Line has limited access to agricultural land. Damage to agricultural land and livestock threatens food security and economic stability in Gaza.

- **Air Pollution Concerns**

  The ongoing conflict in Gaza has led to significant air quality concerns due to numerous fires and hazardous emissions. There are no publicly available air quality statistics for Gaza. Since October 2023, 165 fires have been recorded in Gaza, with major fires visible from Sentinel satellite images. Hazardous chemical emissions are a major concern associated with fires, especially near chemical storage sites. Air quality monitoring stations in Israel reported increased PM2.5 concentrations compared to the previous year. Open burning of waste and materials for cooking increases respiratory and cardiovascular risks among the population.

- **Environmental Contamination from Armed Conflict**

  The conflict has resulted in severe environmental contamination, affecting land, water, and air quality. Over 25,000 tonnes of explosives—the equivalent of two nuclear bombs—have been used in intense warfare. The health of plants and animals is directly threatened by heavy metals and hazardous compounds found in weapons. Elevated concentrations of nickel, chromium, copper, manganese, and lead have been found in contaminated soils. The use of white phosphorus munitions raises concerns about severe burns and environmental persistence.

- **Tunnel System and Its Environmental Impact**

  The extensive tunnel system in Gaza poses risks of groundwater contamination and land instability. Hamas has constructed approximately 500 kilometres of tunnels, which may not meet safety standards. The Israeli Defence Forces have pumped large volumes of water into these tunnels, potentially leading to groundwater contamination. Flooding could cause structural instability, risking surface collapses of buildings and infrastructure. Contaminants from the tunnels, including electrical equipment and munitions, may leach into the groundwater.

- **Humanitarian and Environmental Recovery Needs**

  As of January 2024, damages were around US$18.5 billion, of which US$13.29 billion came from the housing industry. To address the situation, the UN Secretary-General has demanded an urgent humanitarian truce. As soon as circumstances permit, early recovery efforts should start, with an emphasis on resuming vital services like the treatment of wastewater. Environmental assessments are critical to identify contaminants and plan for safe reconstruction efforts.

The Ukraine and Russia Conflict

Since February 2014, a prolonged armed conflict between Russia and Ukraine has generated significant environmental consequences. After Russia's annexation of Crimea, located north of the Black Sea, Ukraine cut off the North Crimean Canal, which had supplied 85% of Crimea's water. As a result, the region has faced severe water shortages. To address this, numerous wells were drilled in Crimea, but this led to increased salinity in both groundwater and soil, resulting in agricultural losses. The impact was made worse by unusual weather in 2020-a winter with little snowfall and a dry spring-which further aggravated the situation.[14]

- **Water Shortages and Industrial Pollution**

  One of the significant ramifications of the ongoing water shortage has been the complete drying up of an acid reservoir situated near the "Crimean Titanium" plant, a major chemical facility known for producing titanium dioxide. The absence of water in this reservoir has resulted in an intensified release of sulphurous anhydride into the atmosphere. This particular compound is recognised as a highly dangerous air pollutant, which can cause severe irritation and impairment of respiratory organs. Upon contact with water, sulphurous anhydride transforms into sulphuric acid, a key contributor to acid rain. Acid rain, in turn, accelerates the acidification of surface waters, leading to soil degradation and posing serious threats to both plant and animal life.[15]

---

14 The Environmental Impact of Military Actions in Eastern Ukraine and the Annexation of the Crimea available at: https://ukraine-analytica.org/the-environmental-impact-of-military-actions-in-eastern-ukraine-and-the-annexation-of-the-crimea/ accessed on 26 September October 2025.

15 Ukraine Conflict Environmental Briefing: Water available at: https://ceobs.org/ukraine-conflict-environmental-briefing-water/ accessed on 29 September 2025.

- **Pre-existing Environmental Vulnerabilities**

  Because some 5,300 heavy industrial businesses were operating in Eastern Ukraine, the region's natural situation was already precarious before the conflict. These consist of mines, oil refineries, power plants, coke factories, and facilities for ferrous metallurgy and chemicals. Due to the increased discharge of harmful chemicals, the onset of military combat has significantly worsened air, land, and water pollution. Fighting-related power outages have frequently forced the closure of water pumps and ventilation systems at coal mines and industrial locations, causing leaks, mishaps, and the release of dangerous materials.

- **Accidents and Chemical Releases**

  During shelling near Donetsk airport in March 2015, a methane release and explosion occurred at the Zasyadko mine, tragically killing miners present underground at the time.[16] Similarly, in May 2015, the Andriivskyi plant caught fire following shelling, which resulted in a massive leak of coke gas containing dangerous substances such as benzene, toluene, naphthalene, hydrogen sulphide, ammonium, and methane.[17] Combat has also resulted in mine water leaks, gasoline and lubricant spills, and the release of heavy metals and nitrates from weapon explosions, which have further contaminated agricultural land and streams with chemicals. Between 2014 and 2017, the Conflict and Environment Observatory recorded more than 500 incidents and interruptions to operations at Eastern Ukrainian industrial facilities. Additionally, throughout this time, 60 of the region's 135 protected natural areas have experienced damage.

- **Escalation of Hostilities and Nuclear Safety Concerns**

  The Russian Federation's recent escalation of hostilities, which resulted in a full-scale conflict, has increased the destruction of infrastructure and the environment over a large portion of Ukraine. The scenario is still developing; therefore, it is unknown how much damage will ensue. But there are now urgent worries

16 33 bodies recovered from eastern Ukraine mine disaster available at: https://edition.cnn.com/2015/03/04/europe/ukraine-miners-trapped accessed on 26 September 2025.

17 Ukraine conflict: The factory that has been shelled 165 times available at: https://www.bbc.com/news/world-europe-32336354 accessed on 29 September 2025.

about the security of Ukraine's nuclear power facilities. In addition to the closed but not yet dismantled Chernobyl nuclear plant, the nation is home to 15 nuclear reactors, including eight that are currently in operation. These facilities might sustain unintentional or intentional damage from missile attacks or disruptions in critical maintenance procedures.[18]

- **Risks to Nuclear Facilities**

  Following the Russian forces' takeover of the facility, the International Atomic Energy Agency (IAEA) has stated that a number of power outages at the Chernobyl plant, including those that affected facilities for storing radioactive waste, have been fixed. The IAEA has also said that during the large-scale war of aggression against Ukraine, which started on February 24, 2022, six of the seven essential pillars for nuclear safety were "compromised or challenged" at Chernobyl. Additionally, since March 4, Russia has controlled the largest nuclear power station in Europe, Zaporizhzhia, and continuous warfare has damaged two of its four power lines and administrative buildings.

- **Unprecedented Challenges for Nuclear Safety**

  The IAEA has warned that the current state of affairs in Ukraine might become unsustainable at critical sites like Zaporizhzhia and has described it as unprecedented, complex, and tough. Amid prolonged conflict in the region, the IAEA's most recent visit to the Zaporizhzhia facility was to evaluate the security systems and the level of damage. The agency reported on September 5, 2022, that the plant had experienced many shelling incidents at or around it, causing damage to the facility and raising considerable concern about the possibility of a catastrophic nuclear disaster that might endanger the environment and human health.

- **International Response and Legal Considerations**

  The Parliamentary Assembly of the Council of Europe, adopted Resolution 2463 (2022),[19] entitled "Further escalation in the

18 Ukraine Conflict environmental brief: nuclear and radiation risks available at: https://ceobs.org/ukraine-invasion-environmental-brief-nuclear-and-radiation-risks/ accessed on 29 September 2025.

19 Further escalation in the Russian Federation's aggression against Ukraine available at: https://pace.coe.int/en/files/31390/html accessed on 10 October 2025.

Russian Federation's aggression against Ukraine," has strongly condemned the "illegal occupation and militarisation of the nuclear power plant in Zaporizhzhia." The resolution also takes into account the Russian Federation's leadership's increased nuclear war threats, which are considered to be against international law and inconsistent with the duties of a nuclear-armed state with a permanent seat on the UN Security Council. Russia declared in early October 2022 that it had violated international law by annexing the Zaporizhzhia nuclear reactor.[20]

- **Protection of Dangerous Installations under International Law**

  In this context, it is important to highlight Article 56 of the Additional Protocol to the Geneva Conventions of 12 August 1949 (Protocol I), which concerns the Protection of Victims of International Armed Conflicts. This article provides special reinforced protection for all "works and installations containing dangerous forces," specifically including nuclear power stations and related installations. Such facilities "shall not be made the object of attack, even where these objects are military objectives, if such attack may cause the release of dangerous forces and consequent severe losses among the civilian population." However, this special protection may cease if the nuclear power plant is providing electric power in regular, significant, and direct support of military operations, and if a military attack is the only feasible way to end such support.

Legal Framework

In the latter half of the 20th century, international legal protections for the environment during armed conflict broadened, through instruments like the UN Convention on Environmental Modification Techniques[21] and Protocol I to the Geneva Conventions. Some of these measures have

20 Juan Pablo Hernández Páez, "Zaporizhzhia Nuclear Power Plant: Ownership and Expropriation of State Assets under International Law", *The Treaty Examiner*, vol. 3 (1) (2023), available at: https://treatyexaminer.com/zaporizhzhia-nuclear-power-plant-ownership-and-expropriation-of-state-assets-under-international-law/ accessed on 29 September 2025.

21 Convention on the Prohibition of Military or Any Other Hostile Use of Environmental Modification Techniques available at: https://treaties.un.org/doc/Treaties/1978/10/19781005%2000-39%20AM/Ch_XXVI_01p.pdf accessed on 30 September 2025.

become customary law, as noted by the ICRC. The 1992 Rio Declaration emphasises respecting environmental protection laws in conflict.

The International Court of Justice acknowledged the overlap between humanitarian and human rights law in its 1996 advisory opinion on nuclear weapons, a principle echoed in later cases and confirmed by bodies such as the UN Human Rights Committee and the European Court of Human Rights.[22] As a result, states involved in conflicts have expanded substantive and procedural obligations-including extraterritorial duties-as the right to a healthy environment gains recognition as a human right.

While both direct and indirect protections exist for the environment during armed conflict, current international instruments generally provide limited safeguards. International humanitarian law primarily focuses on protecting the environment to serve human interests, though recent political efforts suggest a possible shift towards an approach that values intrinsic environmental protection.

From 1955 to 1975, the Vietnam War highlighted environmental destruction as a military tactic, with the United States using weather modification to hinder enemy movement. The United States tried weather modification tactics in Indochina, aiming to increase rainfall and cause mudslides and floods in North Vietnam to hamper enemy movement and disrupt supply routes. These actions prompted the creation of a new international agreement on December 10, 1976, under the United Nations: the Convention on the Prohibition of Military or Any Other Hostile Use of Environmental Modification Techniques (known as ENMOD). ENMOD also remains the only treaty expressly prohibiting the use of environmental modification techniques as weapons, specifically banning actions that cause widespread, long-lasting, or severe effects. In 1977, following the ENMOD Convention, the Additional Protocol (to the Geneva Conventions of 12 August 1949) relating to the Protection of Victims of International Armed Conflicts (Protocol I) was adopted. Articles 55 and 35.3 prohibit methods of warfare intended or likely to cause widespread, long-term, and severe environmental damage, especially where it threatens civilian health or survival. Additionally, attacks on the natural environment as reprisals are banned, and there is an explicit obligation to minimise harm to the environment in warfare.

22 LEGALITY OF THE THREAT OR USE OF NUCLEAR WEAPONS available at: https://www.un.org/law/icjsum/9623.htm accessed on 1 October 2025.

The Council of Europe has established several legal instruments addressing environmental protection, including the Convention on Civil Liability for Damage resulting from Activities Dangerous to the Environment (ETS No. 150)[23] and the Convention on the Protection of the Environment through Criminal Law (ETS No. 172)[24], as well as the Convention on the Conservation of European Wildlife and Natural Habitats (ETS No. 104, "Bern Convention")[25] and the Landscape Convention (ETS No.176)[26]. Convention No. 150 focuses on compensation and prevention of transboundary environmental harm but excludes war-related damages. Convention No. 172 standardises criminal law measures against environmental offences and is currently under revision. Additionally, the Committee of Ministers Recommendation CM/Rec (2022)20 highlights environmental harm from armed conflict and urges recognition of the right to a healthy environment as a universal human right.

Customary international law indirectly protects the environment during armed conflicts through principles like limitation, military necessity, proportionality, discrimination, precautions, and avoidance of unnecessary suffering. The ICRC's Red Cross Guidelines for Military Manuals, first issued in 1994 and updated in 2020, aim to raise awareness and guide states in incorporating environmental protection into military regulations. Based on existing humanitarian law and national practices, these guidelines recommend practical steps for parties in conflict to minimise environmental harm. In 2019, the UN International Law Commission (ILC) introduced 28 draft principles to protect the environment during armed conflicts. After revisions, a final set of 27 principles was adopted on 27 May 2022 and was

submitted to the UN General Assembly, along with ILC comments and recommendations. These principles address gaps in current treaty rules by covering pre- and post-conflict phases and referencing both human rights and environmental law. The General Assembly has recommended these principles for broad dissemination among states and relevant organisations.

23 Convention on Civil Liability for Damage Resulting from Activities Dangerous to the Environment available at: https://rm.coe.int/168007c079 accessed on 1 October 2025.

24 Convention on the Protection of the Environment through Criminal Law available at: https://rm.coe.int/168007f3f4 accessed on 1 October 2025.

25 Convention on the Conservation of European Wildlife and Natural Habitats available at: https://rm.coe.int/1680078aff accessed on 2 October 2025.

26 European Landscape Convention available at: https://assets.publishing.service.gov.uk/media/5a7c1711e5274a1f5cc75b99/8413.pdf accessed on 2 October 2025.

Limitations in the current framework

Existing legal instruments for directly protecting the environment during armed conflict face several challenges. Their scope is limited; for example, the ENMOD Convention only applies between State parties, with just 78 ratifications and 16 signatures to date. While many European countries have joined, 11 have not. The convention prohibits only the use and not the research, development, or preparation of environmental modification techniques. Additionally, key terms such as "environmental modification techniques," "widespread, long-lasting, or severe effects," and "deliberate manipulation of natural processes" remain ambiguously defined. Protocol I (to the Geneva Conventions of 12 August 1949), like the ENMOD Convention, applies only to international armed conflicts and Additional Protocol II relating to the Protection of Victims of Non-International Armed Conflicts lacks direct environmental protection provisions. While 174 states have joined Protocol I, some involved in conflicts that harm the environment, such as Israel, are not parties. There is uncertainty over whether certain provisions are customary law, and many countries, including France and the UK, argue that articles 35.3 and 55 do not cover nuclear weapons. Additionally, environmental protections require harm to be "widespread, long-term and severe," a threshold that is both high and ambiguously defined.

The Council of Europe's conventions Nos. 150 and 172 lack universal acceptance: only nine member States have signed the civil liability convention, with none ratified, and the criminal law convention has fourteen signatories but just one ratification (Estonia). With three ratifications required, neither convention is in force. The Assembly Resolution 2398 (2021)[27] urged reinforcing criminal liability for environmental harm, harmonising liability laws for environmental damage, revising Convention ETS No. 172 to meet current needs, adding ecocide as a crime in national laws, and considering universal jurisdiction for severe environmental crimes under the 1998 Rome Statute of the International Criminal Court. The resolution also calls for stronger civil liability for environmental harm by amending national civil laws, easing the burden of proof through factual presumptions, adding rules for ecological damage, and widening strict

27 Addressing issues of criminal and civil liability in the context of climate change: Resolution available at: https://pace.coe.int/en/files/29512/html accessed on 3 October 2025.

liability where relevant. The Assembly's Recommendation 2213 (2021)[28] also urges replacing Convention No. 172 with a new framework and revising or replacing Convention No. 150.

Most international legal measures to protect the environment during armed conflict were created for international conflicts, but the 2005 ICRC customary law study shows they can also apply to internal conflicts, which are now more common. Despite efforts like the ICRC Guidelines and ILC draft principles to address gaps, there is still no unified legal framework or permanent mechanism to monitor violations and address compensation for environmental damage in armed conflicts. Further, international customary law offers only incidental environmental protection, primarily subordinated to wartime needs and humanitarian concerns. The principle of military necessity prohibits harm to the environment unless linked to military advantage, but this principle can also justify significant environmental destruction during armed conflict if it serves war objectives. Similarly, the principle of proportionality allows for collateral environmental damage if a military objective is important enough to justify the risk. As the value of the target increases, so does the acceptable environmental risk. However, applying these principles in practice is challenging, and environmental concerns often become low priority during conflict, making their protection uncertain.

One of the ways to fill these gaps would be to recognise ecocide at the international level. The developments in his direction have already begun with several States incorporating the concept of ecocide into their domestic law, mostly in their criminal codes. International momentum is also building for establishing ecocide in the context of the Rome Statute of the ICC. Political leaders and parliamentary bodies are supporting this initiative, with regional steps announced by the Nordic Council of Ministers in June 2022 and were called for by the European Parliament in its Resolution 2021/2181(INI)[29] of 17 February 2022 on human rights and democracy to recognise ecocide as an international crime.

28 Addressing issues of criminal and civil liability in the context of climate change: Recommendation available at: https://pace.coe.int/en/files/29514/html accessed on 3 October 2025.

29 European Parliament resolution of 17 February 2022 on human rights and democracy in the world and the European Union's policy on the matter available at: https://eur-lex.europa.eu/legal-content/EN/TXT/?uri=oj:JOC_2022_342_R_0016 accessed on 4 October 2025.

There is, however, one challenge to this- as national and regional interpretations of ecocide vary, establishing an international legal definition requires consensus. While there is no globally recognised definition yet, progress has been made-such as the proposal from the international Independent Expert Panel for the Legal Definition of Ecocide. Domestic laws share common elements, with ecocide applying in both peace and wartime. The first legal definition, found in Article 422 of the Vietnamese Criminal Code, has influenced subsequent national legislation and connects environmental protection to human rights.[30]

Emerging Framework of Ecocide and Carbon Accountability

The proposal to criminalise "ecocide" and to establish mechanisms of "carbon accountability" in the context of armed conflict has emerged as a coherent normative response to the documented ecological and greenhouse-gas (GHG) impacts of modern warfare.[31]

"Ecocide" in contemporary legal drafting has been articulated by an Independent Expert Panel convened by the Stop Ecocide Foundation, which proposed a draft Article 8ter (Ecocide) intended as a complementary crime under the Rome Statute; that draft defines ecocide in terms of "unlawful or wanton acts" committed with knowledge of a substantial likelihood of "severe and either widespread or long-term damage" to ecosystems.[32] The Panel's core text intentionally frames ecocide to capture both peacetime environmental destruction by corporations and states and wartime conduct that results in pervasive ecological collapse, thereby addressing a normative lacuna left by the existing Rome Statute formulation of environmental war crimes.[33] Advocacy for ecocide at the international level has gained traction among states, parliaments and civil society actors who argue that ecosystems deserve protection independent of immediate human casualties, and that imposing criminal responsibility strengthens

30 Environmental impact of armed conflicts: Report available at: https://pace.coe.int/en/files/31460/html#_TOC_d25e150 accessed on 5 October 2025.

31 Legal Definition of Ecocide available at: https://www.stopecocide.earth/legal-definition accessed on 16 September 2025; SGRCEOBS, *note 3*.

32 *Independent Expert Panel for the Legal Definition of Ecocide: Commentary and Core Text*, Stop Ecocide Foundation, June 2021, available at: https://static1.squarespace.com/static/5ca2608ab914493c64ef1f6d/t/60d1e6e604fae2201d03407f/1624368879048/SE%2BFoundation%2BCommentary%2Band%2Bcore%2Btext%2Brev%2B6.pdf?utm_source=chatgpt.com accessed on 17 September 2025.

33 *Ibid.*

deterrence and reparative pathways.[34] Parallel to the ecocide movement, research into the carbon footprint of militaries and armed conflicts has produced novel empirical estimates demonstrating that military activities account for a non-trivial share of global emissions.[35]

A joint study by Scientists for Global Responsibility (SGR) and the Conflict & Environment Observatory (CEOBS) estimated that the world's militaries are responsible for roughly 5.5% of global greenhouse-gas emissions, a scale that exceeds many industrial sectors and which remains largely unreported under current international climate reporting regimes.[36] This empirical finding reframes the climate implications of armed conflict: emissions are not simply incidental but constitute measurable contributions to global warming that ought to be accounted for within climate governance frameworks and reparations discourse.[37]

The intersection of ecocide and carbon accountability raises two complementary legal problems: *definition and threshold* for criminal liability on the one hand, and *measurement, attribution, and redress* for climate harms on the other.[38]

On the definitional axis, the existing Rome Statute contains an environmental war-crime provision (Article 8(2)(b)(iv)) which criminalises intentionally launching an attack knowing it will cause "widespread, long-term and severe damage" to the environment, yet this provision has proven practically inert because of its high thresholds and evidentiary burdens.[39] Proponents of an explicit ecocide offence therefore argue for a doctrinal recalibration: the ecocide definition proposed by the Independent Expert Panel lowers the emphasis on strict military intent and foregrounds notions of "wanton" and "substantial likelihood," thereby widening the

34 Damien Gayle, "What is ecocide and could it become a crime under international law?", *The Guardian*, 31 May 2025, available at: https://www.theguardian.com/environment/2025/may/28/what-is-ecocide-and-could-it-become-a-under-international-law? accessed on 17 September 2025.

35 SGRCEOBS, *note* 3.

36 *Ibid.*

37 How big are global military carbon emissions? available at: https://www.sgr.org.uk/resources/how-big-are-global-military-carbon-emissions accessed 17th September 2025.

38 Stop Ecocide Foundation, *note 32*.

39 Article 8 — War crimes (Rome Statute of the ICC, 1998) available at: https://ihl-databases.icrc.org/en/ihl-treaties/icc-statute-1998/article-8 accessed on 20 September 2025.

scope of culpable conduct while preserving due-process safeguards.[40] On the carbon accountability axis, the core legal challenge is methodological: reliable carbon accounting for military operations and conflict-related emissions is hindered by secrecy, data gaps, and the heterogeneous nature of military supply chains.[41]

Despite these obstacles, methodological advances—combining open-source intelligence (OSINT), satellite remote sensing, lifecycle assessment (LCA) approaches to rubble-clearance and reconstruction, and standard GHG accounting protocols—now make it possible to approximate conflict-related emissions with credible error bounds for attribution and reparations.[42] For example, recent remote-sensing studies have quantified the emissions associated with rubble clearance in Gaza and estimated that clearing 39 million tonnes of debris could itself generate tens of thousands of tonnes of CO2e—thus illustrating how conflict damage creates long-term carbon liabilities linked to both the act of destruction and the post-conflict reconstruction trajectory.

Legal institutionalisation of carbon accountability could proceed along three mutually reinforcing pathways[43]: (1) normative integration — mandating inclusion of military emissions in national GHG inventories and NDCs (Nationally Determined Contributions); (2) reparative mechanisms — requiring belligerents to finance verified carbon mitigation and ecosystem restoration as part of reparations and peace agreements; and (3) market and regulatory instruments — adapting instruments such as CBAMs (Carbon Border Adjustment Mechanisms) and carbon pricing to recognise and penalise conflict-related emissions where appropriate.[44]

In practice, integrating military emissions into the UNFCCC reporting architecture will require political compromises (national security exemptions will be politically salient) but is procedurally feasible given

40 Stop Ecocide Foundation, *note 32.*

41 SGR, *note 37.*

42 Nina Lakhani, "Clearing Gaza rubble could yield 90,000 tonnes of planet-heating emissions" *The Guardian*, 22 July 2025, available at: https://www.theguardian.com/world/2025/jul/22/gaza-rubble-environment-emissions-impact accessed on 20 September 2025.

43 SGRCEOBS, *note 3.*

44 Gaza, *note 9.*

precedents for sectoral inclusion (e.g., aviation, shipping) and recent calls from civil society for increased transparency by defence sectors.[45]

Finally, the normative fusion of ecocide and carbon accountability supports a dual-track enforcement model: criminal accountability (ICC/ecocide) for egregious acts causing systemic ecosystem collapse, and civil/administrative accountability (reparations, carbon offsets, international funds) for measurable climate harms and remediation obligations.[46] Such a model recognises the distinct aims of criminal law (retribution, deterrence) and climate reparative law (restoration, compensation), while offering an integrated pathway for holding states and non-state belligerents responsible for the multi-scalar impacts of contemporary warfare.

Legal–Ethical Framework

This section proposes a practicable legal–ethical architecture for addressing war-related ecological destruction by combining doctrinal reform, institutional innovation, and reparative mechanisms.

The ethical premises that ground this framework are threefold: intergenerational justice (the duty to preserve ecological foundations for future generations), the intrinsic value of ecosystems (ecocentrism), and distributive justice (ensuring that victims of ecological harm receive proportionate remediation).[47]

At the normative level, a reformed Rome Statute incorporating an explicit ecocide offence would supply a doctrinal anchor for criminal responsibility where armed conduct foreseeably causes severe, widespread or long-term ecological collapse.[48] Concretely, an ecocide provision should retain mens rea elements (knowledge or wilful blindness as to the substantial likelihood of severe environmental damage) while accommodating wartime contexts through calibrated defences (military necessity and proportionality subject to strict scrutiny).[49] To preserve legal clarity and avoid overcriminalisation, the ecocide definition should specify thresholds of scale and severity and require proof of causal linkage between the actor's conduct and the

45 SGR, *note 37.*

46 Stop Ecocide Foundation, *note 32.*

47 Stop Ecocide Foundation, *note 32.*

48 Rome Statute of the International Criminal Court available at: https://legal.un.org/icc/statute/english/rome_statute%28e%29.pdf accessed on 25 September 2025.

49 *Ibid.*

ecological outcome, drawing on environmental forensic science and chain-of-custody methodologies.[50]

At the institutional level, the ICC should be complemented by a multilayered architecture: an *International Environmental Tribunal* (or chamber within existing tribunals) for complex environmental damage cases, national incorporation of ecocide offences, and specialised investigative capacities within the ICC's Office of the Prosecutor for environmental crime and carbon attribution.[51] The International Law Commission's 2022 Draft Principles provide a readily usable template for states and institutions to operationalise obligations before, during and after conflict, including remediation, removal of remnants of war, and environmental impact assessments; these normative tools can be harnessed to support prosecutorial and reparative processes.[52]

At the procedural level, robust evidence regimes are essential. This requires standardised methodologies for (a) measuring the carbon footprint and ecological impacts of military operations and attacks; (b) attributing emissions and damage to specific actors; and (c) quantifying remediation costs.[53] State and independent forensic capacities—combining remote sensing, environmental sampling, satellite-derived emissions estimates, and supply-chain analysis—must be recognised in court as admissible scientific proof, and international technical bodies (e.g., UNEP, IAEA for nuclear risks) should be empowered to provide neutral assessments.[54]

For reparative justice, the architecture should link criminal adjudication with restorative instruments: mandatory environmental reparations ordered by the ICC or international tribunals; creation of a dedicated international Environmental Recovery and Carbon Remediation Fund (financed by convicted actors, state contributions, and assessed carbon levies); and integration of carbon-offsetting and restoration projects subject to independent verification and benefits-sharing with affected

50 *Ibid.*

51 The Office of the Prosecutor: Draft Policy on Environmental Crimes Under The Rome Statute, December 2024 available at: https://www.icc-cpi.int/sites/default/files/2024-12/2024-12-18-OTP-Policy-Environmental-Crime.pdf accessed on 25 September 2025.

52 Draft principles on protection of the environment in relation to armed conflicts available at: https://legal.un.org/ilc/texts/instruments/english/draft_articles/8_7_2022.pdf accessed on 26 September 2025.

53 SGRCEOBS, *note 3.*

54 Draft Principles, *note 52.*

communities.[55] Additionally, peace agreements and UNSC mandates should routinely incorporate verified environmental assessments and binding remediation obligations (including binding timelines, financing commitments, and international monitoring), with non-compliance triggering targeted sanctions or conditional assistance.[56]

Finally, the ethical governance of these mechanisms requires democratic oversight and victim-centred participation. Affected populations must have standing in reparative processes, and reconstruction strategies must prioritise local livelihoods, ecological restoration, and low-carbon rebuilding to avoid perpetuating harm through carbon-intensive reconstruction methods.[57]

Policy Recommendations

(1) Adopt an internationally agreed ecocide definition (drawing from the Independent Expert Panel);

(2) Mandate transparent reporting of military emissions and include them in national GHG inventories where feasible;

(3) Establish specialised investigative and prosecutorial capacities for environmental/ carbon crimes at the ICC and national levels;

(4) Create an international remediation fund tied to reparations and carbon remediation; and

(5) Integrate environmental obligations into peace processes and UNSC practice.

Conclusion and Suggestions

This paper argues that the conventional treatment of environmental damage as collateral in armed conflict is no longer defensible in the era of the Anthropocene. Warfare no longer merely destroys infrastructure and human life—it also destabilises ecosystems, contributes significantly to climate change, and imposes intergenerational and planetary costs that the existing legal framework fails to redress. The empirical evidence from Gaza, Ukraine, and Sudan demonstrates the multiplicity of environmental harms—soil contamination, debris carbon emissions, water and sanitation breakdown, toxic residue, and degraded biodiversity—that persist long

55 Stop Ecocide Foundation, *note 32.*

56 Draft Principles, *note 52.*

57 Gaza, *note 9.*

after ceasefires. Meanwhile, the normative lacunae in current law reveal that environmental protection remains subordinated to anthropocentric prerogatives of military necessity and proportionality.

The last two sections of this paper have shown that existing instruments—from the ENMOD Convention to Geneva Protocols to ILC draft principles—are conceptually narrow, limited in applicability, and lack enforcement mechanisms. The proposed framework of ecocide offers doctrinal expansion: criminalising large-scale, reckless environmental destruction, with calibrated mens rea and causation thresholds. Simultaneously, carbon accountability offers a measurable pathway: attributing conflict-related emissions to belligerents, integrating them into climate governance regimes, and linking reparative obligations to carbon mitigation and ecological restoration.

Based on this synthesis, the following suggestions are offered, both practical and visionary:

1. Amend the Rome Statute to include an Ecocide crime (Article 8ter)

   States parties should negotiate a supplemental protocol explicitly recognising ecocide—defined in line with the Independent Expert Panel's draft—parallel to genocide and war crimes. This addition provides a criminal anchor for prosecuting extreme ecological destruction in conflict.

2. Mandate military emissions reporting under UNFCCC / Paris Transparency Framework.

   States should be required to include wartime and peacetime military emissions within their national GHG inventories and NDCs, with confidentiality safeguards for genuine national security concerns. Integrating conflict emissions would close a major blind spot in climate accountability.

3. Establish an International Environmental Recovery & Carbon Remediation Fund

   Proceeds from convicted ecocide perpetrators, assessed carbon levies, and voluntary state contributions should be channelled into a global fund that finances ecosystem restoration, low-carbon rebuilding, soil decontamination, and community rehabilitation in conflict zones.

4. Institute specialised prosecutorial and forensic capacities at ICC and national levels.

   The Office of the Prosecutor at the ICC (and domestic counterparts) should develop dedicated divisions for environmental/ carbon crime. They should build partnerships with scientific institutions, remote sensing agencies, and environmental expert bodies (e.g., UNEP, IAEA) for neutral assessments.

5. Embed environmental clauses in peace agreements and UN mandates

   Post-conflict and peace treaties should include binding environmental impact assessments, remediation obligations, carbon offset obligations, and institutional monitoring by independent agencies. UN Security Council mandates addressing conflict should routinely incorporate ecological accountability provisions.

6. Promote domestic incorporation of ecocide and climate liability laws

   Nations should adopt domestic ecocide statutes rooted in the international definition, and amend national environmental and climate laws to recognise liability for war-related emissions. This ensures complementary jurisdiction and state-level enforcement.

7. Ensure victim participation and democratic oversight.

   Affected communities must have procedural standing in reparative processes; reconstruction strategies should prioritise low-carbon and nature-positive methods. Oversight mechanisms—civil society, international panels—should ensure accountability, transparency, and free prior informed consent in environmental rehabilitation.

If these suggestions are incrementally adopted, they can reorient how we legalise and govern environmental harm in wartime. The broader imperative is a paradigmatic shift: from viewing ecological destruction as collateral to treating it as a dimension of climate justice. War must no longer be an alibi for environmental ruin. In the Anthropocene, to fight a war is to strain planetary boundaries; to fail to prosecute its ecological violence is to deny justice to future generations.

The ICJ's Green Jurisprudence and the MOX Plant Legacy

D Bhuvaneswari & Abarajitha R B

Abstract

The principle of environmental protection in armed conflicts remains a critical challenge underexplored in the eyes of the international legal system. This paper examines this crucial protection through the legacy established in the MOX Plant case, brought by Ireland v. United Kingdom in 2001. The ruling, apart from the emancipation of the doctrine of parallelism via the principle of proximity, has set the rule for the protection of the environment as an obligation persisting alongside humanitarian law at times of hostilities. Apart from raising fragmentation issues, this case was striking the ICJ's emerging Green jurisprudence on environmental protection at conflict zones, whereby emphasising due diligence as a State obligation under treaties like the Geneva Conventions and the ENMOD Convention. The world ruling facilitated the doctrine of parallelism, setting a rule for the protection of the environment as an obligation persisting alongside humanitarian law at times of hostilities. The dispute has raised the challenges in contemporary international law of the fragmentation era that result in overlapping judicial decisions, and is cited by the author as a precedent for a meta-conscious approach of the International Court of Justice. The dispute settlement mechanism of the UNCLOS, striking the ICJ's emerging jurisprudence on environmental protection at conflict zones, whereby emphasising stringent due diligence as a State obligation under treaties like the Geneva Conventions and ENMOD Convention.

Aim and Background of The Study

The legacy of the Mox plant has been facilitated as follows:

1. The States are duly abiding by international environmental

obligations of protecting the environment even during hostilities.

2. This '*erga omnes*' obligation under the International Environmental Law is to co-exist with the principles of protection under the international humanitarian law.

Research Methodology

The research is an ex-post facto research. On evaluation, the research article adopts a mixed research approach i.e analytical, descriptive, comparative, formulative and case law analysis. Further, the study is Law in context research, as it adopts a holistic approach that intertwines IEL and IHL, which goes beyond doctrinal, and critically evaluates how International law is progressively getting shaped, as well as in turn silhouettes the futuristic survival of the Globe. It observes the functioning of the law in a wider spectrum, i.e social, political, economic, historical and tech-driven environment. In addition, through the meaning-making method with reference to the standards of the ICJ, including landmark decisions, the author argues that the statutory obligation of environmental protection in the prevention of transboundary environmental harm extends to times of war. The heart of this dispute prompted the author to reckon "Whether there exists ample recognition and obedience to '*erga omnes*' obligation of environmental protection by the international community, under the current legal mandates?". Thus, to address this gap, the author, through critical arguments, proposes creative legal solutions which would thereby stand catalysing strength to the doctrine of parallelism as proposed via the lens of the World Court observed in the Mox plant legacy. Accordingly, the author seeks to affirm the protection of the environment as an erga omnes obligation, employing an expository research method evaluating the MOX Plant legacy through ICJ's evolving green jurisprudence, thereby reinforcing the imperative of environmental safeguards amid conflicts. The research technique of '*Content Analysis*' further strengthens the '*meta conscious approach*' of the international judicial organs as a golden thread tracing the evolutionary jurisprudence by constructive interpretivism.

Introduction

Armed conflicts inflict not only human casualties but also severe ecological damage. Yet International law largely overlooks the environment during war, favouring "military necessity" over ecological concerns. Peacetime environmental treaties (e.g. UNFCCC,[1] UNCLOS Part XII[2]) establish strong protections, but they are often deemed inapplicable once hostilities begin. The Russian invasion of Ukraine vividly illustrates this neglect: chemical pollutants from destroyed industries and the 2023 Kakhovka Dam breach have devastated the Black Sea's ecosystem. [3]Likewise, Iraq's scorched-earth campaign in Kuwait(1991) left flaming oil wells and thousands of oil lakes, releasing millions of barrels of oil and toxic soot with chronic health and environmental consequences.[4] These examples show that the natural environment remains an "unspoken victim" of conflict.

In this context, the *MOX Plant* case (ITLOS 2001 para 50 of the provisional measures and UNCLOS Arbitral Award) provides crucial insight. Though a peacetime dispute, the MOX Plant teaches that state obligations protecting the marine environment as "ongoing, indivisible, and not suspended by political or security imperatives".[5] Ireland challenged the UK's authorisation of a mixed-oxide fuel plant at Sellafield, claiming UNCLOS violations (Arts. 192, 194) due to radioactive discharge into the Irish Sea.[6] While the tribunal did not enjoin the plant, it emphasised that UNCLOS imposes a due diligence duty to prevent transboundary pollution.[7] In doing so, MOX Plant aligned with the ICJ's broader "green jurisprudence" (e.g. *Nuclear Weapons Advisory Opinion* 1996), recognising that environmental law

1 United Nations, *United Nations Framework Convention on Climate Change*, 9 May 1992, 1771 UNTS 107.

2 United Nations, *United Nations Convention on the Law of the Sea*, 10 December 1982, 1833 UNTS 3, Part XII.

3 UN General Assembly, *Report on the Environmental Consequences of Armed Conflicts in Ukraine*, UN Doc A/78/245 (2023); Dimitar Bechev, *Tackling the Russia-Ukraine War's Environmental Damage in the Black Sea*, Carnegie Endowment Europe (24 February 2025) https://carnegieeurope.eu.

4 Richa Syal, "'Gushing oil and roaring fires': 30 years on Kuwait is still scarred by catastrophic pollution," *The Guardian* (11 December 2021) https://www.theguardian.com; United Nations Environment Programme, *Environmental Assessment of the Kuwaiti Oil Fires*, UNEP/GC/12/Inf.14 (1992).

5 *MOX Plant* (Ireland v. United Kingdom), Request for Provisional Measures, ITLOS Case No. 10, 3 December 2001, ITLOS Reports 2001; *MOX Plant* (Ireland v. United Kingdom), UNCLOS Annex VII Arbitral Award, 2003, RIAA Vol. XXI, §§4498–4505.

6 United Nations, *United Nations Convention on the Law of the Sea*, 10 December 1982, 1833 UNTS 3, Arts. 192, 194, Part XII.

7 Ibid, ITLOS Provisional Measures, pp43–47.

co-exists with human rights and humanitarian law, even under conflict conditions.[8]

However, fragmentation blurs the picture: international humanitarian law (IHL) and international environmental law (IEL) operate in parallel silos. AP I (1977) and the ENMOD Convention (1976) ban extreme ecological harm in conflict (the "widespread, long-term and severe" threshold), but enforcement is weak.[9] The ICJ has addressed environmental harm in various contexts, yet it has not fully defined wartime environmental duties.[10] The MOX legacy offers a doctrinal bridge. We ask whether protection enshrined in treaties like AP I and ENMOD can now be seen as an erga omnes obligation – a duty owed to all humanity endured even in armed conflict.[11] This question has profound implications: if environmental preservation is indeed a jus cogens or erga omnes norm, then its violation (e.g. ecocide) could trigger universal accountability, including a war crime.[12] Our postulate is that the ICJ has gradually enshrined environmental protection as an ongoing erga omnes duty (via cases like *Gabcĩkovo*, *Pulp Mills*, *Nuclear Weapons*).[13] The MOX Plant serves as a pivotal case reaffirming that the "parallelism doctrine" allows environmental obligations to endure through hostilities.[14]

8 ICJ, *Legality of the Threat or Use of Nuclear Weapons*, Advisory Opinion, 8 July 1996, I.C.J. Rep. 66, ¶29–30.

9 Protocol Additional to the Geneva Conventions of 12 August 1949, and relating to the Protection of Victims of International Armed Conflicts (AP I), 8 June 1977, 1125 UNTS 3, Art. 55; Convention on the Prohibition of Military or Any Other Hostile Use of Environmental Modification Techniques (ENMOD), 18 May 1976, 1108 UNTS 151, Art. I.

10 ICJ, *Gabčíkovo-Nagymaros Project* (Hungary/Slovakia), Judgment, 25 September 1997, I.C.J. Rep. 7, ¶53–60; ICJ, *Pulp Mills on the River Uruguay* (Argentina v. Uruguay), Judgment, 20 April 2010, I.C.J. Rep. 14, ¶101–110; ICJ, *Legality of the Threat or Use of Nuclear Weapons*, Advisory Opinion, 8 July 1996, I.C.J. Rep. 66, ¶29–30.

11 Philippe Sands, *Principles of International Environmental Law*, 3rd edn (Cambridge University Press, 2018) 412.

12 Rome Statute of the International Criminal Court, 17 July 1998, 2187 UNTS 3, Art. 8(2)(b)(iv).

13 ICJ, *Gabčíkovo-Nagymaros Project* (n 10); ICJ, *Pulp Mills on the River Uruguay* (n 10); ICJ, *Legality of the Threat or Use of Nuclear Weapons* (n 10).

14 *MOX Plant* (Ireland v. United Kingdom), UNCLOS Arbitral Award, 2003, RIAA Vol. XXI, §§4498–4505.

This study uses a comparative approach, analysing primary sources (ICJ/ITLOS judgments, treaties, UNGA resolutions)[15] and secondary literature. We compare the MOX Plant to IHL rules (AP I, ENMOD) and to ICJ decisions on environmental protection.[16] The analysis assesses environmental due diligence and erga omnes obligations through judicial reasoning and state obligations.[17] Further, considers soft-law developments (ILC draft principles 2022) and proposes reforms to address current gaps.[18] By situating the MOX Plant in the broader jurisprudential matrix, we argue that environmental protection is no longer merely an aspirational policy but a binding international duty applicable not only in peace but during war conflicts as well.[19]

The Doctrine of Parallelism and The MOX Plant Legacy

The *MOX Plant* dispute arose when Ireland objected to the UK's operation of a Mixed Oxide Fuel plant at Sellafield. Ireland alleged that radioactive effluents would pollute the Irish Sea, breaching UNCLOS Articles 192 and 194 (marine environmental protection and pollution prevention).[20] Under Article 290(5) UNCLOS, Ireland sought provisional measures from ITLOS.[21] The Tribunal ordered both parties to cooperate, consult,

15 *MOX Plant* (Ireland v. United Kingdom), ITLOS Case No. 10, Request for Provisional Measures, 3 December 2001, ITLOS Reports 2001; *MOX Plant* (Ireland v. United Kingdom), UNCLOS Annex VII Arbitral Award, 2003, RIAA Vol. XXI, §§4498–4505; United Nations General Assembly, *Resolutions on Protection of the Environment in Armed Conflicts*, UN Doc A/RES/72/33 (2017).

16 Protocol Additional to the Geneva Conventions of 12 August 1949, and relating to the Protection of Victims of International Armed Conflicts (AP I), 8 June 1977, 1125 UNTS 3, Art. 55; Convention on the Prohibition of Military or Any Other Hostile Use of Environmental Modification Techniques (ENMOD), 18 May 1976, 1108 UNTS 151, Art. I; ICJ, *Legality of the Threat or Use of Nuclear Weapons*, Advisory Opinion, 8 July 1996, I.C.J. Rep. 66, ¶29–30.

17 ICJ, *Gabčíkovo-Nagymaros Project* (Hungary/Slovakia), Judgment, 25 September 1997, I.C.J. Rep. 7, ¶53–60; ICJ, *Pulp Mills on the River Uruguay* (Argentina v. Uruguay), Judgment, 20 April 2010, I.C.J. Rep. 14, ¶101–110.

18 International Law Commission, *Draft Principles on the Protection of the Environment in Relation to Armed Conflicts*, UN Doc A/CN.4/L.103 (2022).

19 Philippe Sands, *Principles of International Environmental Law*, 3rd edn (Cambridge University Press, 2018) 412–415.

20 *MOX Plant* (Ireland v. United Kingdom), Request for Provisional Measures, ITLOS Case No. 10, 3 December 2001, ITLOS Reports 2001, ¶¶40–45; United Nations, *United Nations Convention on the Law of the Sea*, 10 December 1982, 1833 UNTS 3, Arts. 192, 194, Part XII.

21 Ibid, Art. 290(5).

and exchange information on the MOX plant's emissions pending the constitution of an Annex VII arbitral tribunal.[22]

Notably, MOX Plant spawned parallel proceedings. Alongside ITLOS, Ireland initiated Annex VII arbitration and a complaint under the OSPAR Convention, while the EU's ECJ was asked to review compliance with European law.[23] These concurrent tribunals did not conflict; instead, the UNCLOS framework (Art. 282) explicitly anticipated such overlaps.[24] The OSPAR tribunal candidly observed that "the adverse character of the MOX Plant operation is subject to parallel set of proceedings," acknowledging ITLOS had already considered key issues.[25] In essence, MOX Plant cemented the parallelism doctrine - the idea that a single issue may be litigated under multiple legal regimes without one overriding the other.[26]

The Doctrine of Parallelism Explained

Although "parallelism" originated as a procedural accommodation in UNCLOS, it has substantive meaning. It asserts that overlapping treaty obligations should co-exist.[27] The MOX Plant league made clear that UNCLOS environmental duties run concurrently with any regional or bilateral rules.[28] Crucially, ITLOS (and later commentators) emphasised that environmental obligations are not "put on hold" when another legal regime (e.g. IHL or EU law) is engaged.[29] This mirrors the ICJ's stance in

22 *MOX Plant* (Ireland v. United Kingdom), ITLOS, Provisional Measures Order, ¶¶46–48; see also UNCLOS Annex VII Arbitral Award, 2003, RIAA Vol. XXI, §§4498–4505.

23 *MOX Plant* (Ireland v. United Kingdom), UNCLOS Annex VII Arbitral Award, 2003, RIAA Vol. XXI, §§4498–4505; OSPAR Commission, *Ireland v. United Kingdom - Complaint Concerning MOX Plant*, OSPAR Case No. 2001/1, 2002, ¶15–16; Court of Justice of the European Union, *European Commission v. United Kingdom*, Case C-459/03, Judgment, 14 December 2004.

24 United Nations, *United Nations Convention on the Law of the Sea*, 10 December 1982, 1833 UNTS 3, Art. 282.

25 OSPAR Commission, *Ireland v. United Kingdom - Complaint Concerning MOX Plant* (n 23), ¶17.

26 Philippe Sands, (n 19) 423–425.

27 Philippe Sands, *Principles of International Environmental Law*, 3rd edn (Cambridge University Press, 2018) 423–425.; Jutta Brunnée, *Legitimacy and Legality in International Environmental Law* (Cambridge University Press, 2008) 177–180.

28 *MOX Plant* (Ireland v. United Kingdom), ITLOS Case No. 10, Request for Provisional Measures, 3 December 2001, ITLOS Reports 2001, ¶¶43–47.

29 OSPAR Commission, *Ireland v. United Kingdom - Complaint Concerning MOX Plant*, OSPAR Case No. 2001/1, 2002, ¶17.

the *Nuclear Weapons Advisory Opinion (1996):* while not making the use of nuclear weapons per se illegal, the Court stressed that *States must take environmental considerations into account when assessing what is necessary and proportionate in military objectives.*[30] In other words, environmental law forms a continuous normative bridge between peace and war. The MOX Plant case illustrates this: even though it was not an armed conflict scenario, the Court treated UNCLOS duties as uninterrupted by concurrent legal processes[31]. The parallelism doctrine thus affirms that environmental protection is a permanent commitment; any doctrine of necessity or conflict of laws must yield to the requirement of safeguarding nature[32].

UNCLOS and Environmental Due Diligence

UNCLOS Part XII imposes robust environmental duties on coastal and flag states. Article 192 mandates that "States have the obligation to protect and preserve the marine environment" while Article 194(1) requires them to take "all necessary measures" to prevent, reduce and control marine pollution[33]. The MOX Plant tribunal interpreted these as due diligence obligations[34]. In practical terms, due diligence meant the UK had to proactively monitor the Sellafield discharges and guard against any harm to Ireland, even absent proof of actual damage.[35] This is akin to the precautionary principle (UN Rio Declaration, Principle 15) and echoes classic transboundary norms (Trail Smelter, *Corfu Channel*)[36]. ITLOS noted that once MOX operations began, increased radioactive emissions into the Irish Sea were inevitable, thus triggering the need for joint monitoring and

30 ICJ, *Legality of the Threat or Use of Nuclear Weapons*, Advisory Opinion, 8 July 1996, I.C.J. Rep. 66, ¶29–30.

31 Philippe Sands (n 27) 425

32 MOX Plant (Ireland v. United Kingdom), UNCLOS Annex VII Arbitral Award, 2003, RIAA Vol. XXI, §§4498–4505.; Ibid; Sands (n 27) 426.

33 United Nations, *United Nations Convention on the Law of the Sea*, 10 December 1982, 1833 UNTS 3, Art. 192, Part XII.; Ibid, Art. 194(1).

34 *MOX Plant* (Ireland v. United Kingdom), ITLOS Case No. 10, Request for Provisional Measures, 3 December 2001, ITLOS Reports 2001, ¶44–47.

35 Philippe Sands, *Principles of International Environmental Law*, 3rd edn (Cambridge University Press, 2018) 415–417.

36 United Nations, *Rio Declaration on Environment and Development*, UN Doc A/CONF.151/26 (Vol. I), 1992, Principle 15.; *Trail Smelter Arbitration* (United States v. Canada), 3 RIAA 1905 (1938/1941), ¶196.;ICJ, *Corfu Channel Case* (United Kingdom v. Albania), Judgment, 9 April 1949, I.C.J. Rep. 4, ¶29.

data exchange[37]. Similarly, the recent ITLOS advisory on climate change has held that GHG emissions now qualify as "marine pollution," activating Article 194(1)'s due diligence in reducing and ultimately eliminating ocean-affecting emissions. In sum, *MOX Plant* reinforced that UNCLOS demands a preventive stance: States must plan and cooperate to pre-empt transboundary pollution, rather than merely address harm after the fact.

Significance of the MOX Plant Legacy

MOX Plant's importance transcends its factual context. It sent a clear signal: environmental obligations cannot be suspended for the sake of security or convenience.[38] The case epitomises the fusion of environmental and human security. Ireland's insistence on cross-border cooperation underscored that protecting the marine environment is as vital as any security measure.[39] As one commentator noted, the ICJ's evolving jurisprudence now treats ecosystems as "living space[s] … essential to the health and well-being of human beings".[40] By affirming continuous obligations even in a complex, multi-fora dispute, MOX Plant prefigured the Court's later rulings (e.g. *Nuclear Weapons*, *Pulp Mills*) where ecology is woven into legal duty.[41] In effect, MOX Plant planted the seeds of the parallelism doctrine in environmental law: no matter how wars or treaties unfold, States remain bound to guard our common natural heritage.[42]

37 *MOX Plant* (Ireland v. United Kingdom), ITLOS Provisional Measures, ¶46

38 *MOX Plant* (Ireland v. United Kingdom), UNCLOS Annex VII Arbitral Award, 2003, RIAA Vol. XXI, §§4498–4505.

39 *MOX Plant* (Ireland v. United Kingdom), ITLOS Case No. 10, Request for Provisional Measures, 3 December 2001, ITLOS Reports 2001, ¶46.

40 ICJ, *Certain Activities Carried Out by Nicaragua in the Border Area (Costa Rica v. Nicaragua)*, Judgment, 16 December 2015, I.C.J. Rep. 665, ¶154; Philippe Sands, *Principles of International Environmental Law*, 3rd edn (Cambridge University Press, 2018) 430.

41 ICJ, *Legality of the Threat or Use of Nuclear Weapons*, Advisory Opinion, 8 July 1996, I.C.J. Rep. 66, ¶29–30. ICJ, *Pulp Mills on the River Uruguay* (Argentina v. Uruguay), Judgment, 20 April 2010, I.C.J. Rep. 14, ¶101–110.

42 Philippe Sands (n 3) 431; Jutta Brunnée, *Legitimacy and Legality in International Environmental Law* (Cambridge University Press, 2008) 180.

The ICJ's Green Jurisprudence and War-Torn Environment

Evolution of the ICJ's Environmental Jurisprudence

Over recent decades, the ICJ has steadily expanded its consideration of environmental issues. In *Corfu Channel* (1949) the Court held Albania responsible for mines that polluted its waters.[43] In *Gabcĭkovo-Nagymaros* (1997), the Court openly acknowledged sustainable development, balancing Hungary and Slovakia's economic plans with river ecology.[44] Perhaps most notably, in *Pulp Mills* on the Uruguay River (2010) the ICJ broke new ground by declaring that a full Environmental Impact Assessment (EIA) is required by general international law before transboundary projects.[45] The Court explained that EIA has become such a universally accepted practice that it is now a duty to conduct one when there is risk of significant transboundary harm.[46] These rulings reflect a clear trajectory: environmental stewardship is no longer peripheral but a core concern of international adjudication. Each judgment reinforces that States must negotiate and cooperate to prevent harm to shared environments, rooting these principles in the corpus of law itself.[47]

The Environment as a Victim of War

International humanitarian law (IHL) has long included environmental protections. AP I (1977) Article 55 imposes a general obligation to "protect the natural environment against widespread, long-term and severe damage," and forbids warfare methods intended or expected to cause such damage.[48] The 1976 ENMOD Convention similarly bans the hostile use

43 ICJ, *Corfu Channel Case* (United Kingdom v. Albania), Judgment, 9 April 1949, I.C.J. Rep. 4, ¶29.

44 ICJ, *Gabčíkovo-Nagymaros Project* (Hungary/Slovakia), Judgment, 25 September 1997, I.C.J. Rep. 7, ¶53–60.

45 ICJ, *Pulp Mills on the River Uruguay* (Argentina v. Uruguay), Judgment, 20 April 2010, I.C.J. Rep. 14, ¶101–110.

46 Ibid, ¶102–104.

47 Philippe Sands, *Principles of International Environmental Law*, 3rd edn (Cambridge University Press, 2018) 432–434.

48 Protocol Additional to the Geneva Conventions of 12 August 1949, and relating to the Protection of Victims of International Armed Conflicts (AP I), 8 June 1977, 1125 UNTS 3, Art. 55.

of environmental modification (ecological warfare) techniques.[49] Yet its enforcement is uneven. The ICJ's 1996 *Nuclear Weapons Advisory Opinion* filled some gaps: it emphatically stated that nothing in IHL or treaty law allows a State to *ignore* environmental impact in planning attacks.[50] In plain terms, "environmental considerations" are integral to assessing necessity and proportionality in any conflict.[51] As the Court put it, respect for the environment "is one of the elements" of necessity.[52] Thus, even absent express treaty prohibitions, the ICJ holds that ecocide (indiscriminate or wanton destruction of nature) is incompatible with the law of armed conflict.[53] This mirrors the Martens Clause's spirit "principles of humanity" extend to ecosystems.

Parallelism between Peace and Conflict

Although the MOX Plant case dealt with peacetime activities, its logical legacy applies to hostilities. By asserting that environmental and security obligations run together, the MOX Plant collapses the artificial law-peace/wartime divide.[54] The ICJ's pronouncement that the environment is humanity's "living space" echoes the Martens Clause: even in a crisis, humanity's conscience and nature's integrity bind all parties.[55] Environmental damage in war is increasingly criminalised. The ICC Rome Statute (1998) expressly classifies causing "widespread, long-term and severe damage to the natural environment" as a war crime. This codification turns environmental protection into an erga omnes duty: everyone owes it to all. Indeed, the ICJ's reasoning has fed into this shift. In *Nicaragua* (2015), for example, the Court remarked that environmental harm transcends national borders and generations. Though not yet fully realised in binding

49 Convention on the Prohibition of Military or Any Other Hostile Use of Environmental Modification Techniques (ENMOD), 18 May 1976, 1108 UNTS 151, Art. I.

50 ICJ, *Legality of the Threat or Use of Nuclear Weapons*, Advisory Opinion, 8 July 1996, I.C.J. Rep. 66, ¶29–30

51 Ibid, ¶29.

52 Ibid, ¶30.

53 Philippe Sands, *Principles of International Environmental Law*, 3rd edn (Cambridge University Press, 2018) 438–439.

54 *MOX Plant* (Ireland v. United Kingdom), UNCLOS Annex VII Arbitral Award, 2003, RIAA Vol. XXI, §§4498–4505.

55 *Certain Activities Carried Out by Nicaragua in the Border Area* (Costa Rica v. Nicaragua), Judgment, 16 December 2015, I.C.J. Rep. 665, ¶154.;Martens Clause, *Preamble to the Hague Convention (II) with Respect to the Laws and Customs of War on Land*, 1899; reaffirmed in AP I, 1977, Preamble.

treaty law, these developments show that under modern international law, environmental care does *not* vanish in the fog of war.[56] The "parallelism" insisted on in the MOX Plant suggests that an attack harming civilians and nature alike cannot invoke an exemption. Ecological integrity implies it is not a luxury of peace but a necessity as a principle that must guide even military strategy.

Environmental Damage as a War Crime

Building on IHL, the Rome Statute has cemented environmental protection among the highest international norms.[57] Article 8(2)(b)(iv) makes it a war crime to attack the environment "widespread, long-term and severe". By doing so, the ICC effectively recognises environmental devastation as a crime against humanity (or against the whole world).[58] This reflects the ICJ's influence: in *Nuclear Weapons*, the Court foreshadowed this by noting that wanton destruction of nature "clearly" breaches existing law. Thus, there is converging jurisprudence that ecosystems themselves have legal protection. When soldiers scorch fields or dump toxins, they risk prosecution not only for civilian suffering but for harming our common future. In sum, the post-MOX era shows a jurisprudential evolution: States are held to account for environmental harm, bridging the gap between sovereign rights and global obligations.[59]

Erga Omnes Obligation and Due Diligence

Conceptual Foundations of Erga Omnes

The concept of erga omnes ("towards all") obligations was crystallised by the ICJ in *Barcelona Traction* (1970), distinguishing duties owed to the world community as a whole (e.g. prohibition of genocide) from strictly bilateral rights.[60] Subsequent cases (*East Timor* 1995, *Bosnian Genocide* 2007) reaffirmed that core humanitarian and self-determination norms fall

56 Jutta Brunnée, *Legitimacy and Legality in International Environmental Law* (Cambridge University Press, 2008) 182–183.

57 Rome Statute of the International Criminal Court, 17 July 1998, 2187 UNTS 90, Art. 8(2)(b)(iv).

58 Philippe Sands, *Principles of International Environmental Law*, 3rd edn (Cambridge University Press, 2018) 438–440.

59 *MOX Plant* (Ireland v. United Kingdom), UNCLOS Annex VII Arbitral Award, 2003, RIAA Vol. XXI, §§4498–4505; Philippe Sands (n 2) 440.

60 ICJ, *Barcelona Traction, Light and Power Company, Limited (Belgium v. Spain)*, Judgment, 5 February 1970, I.C.J. Rep. 3, ¶33.

into this category. Only recently has environmental protection been added to this elite list. In *Certain Activities (Nicaragua v. Costa Rica)* (2015), and especially in *Legality of Nuclear Weapons*, the ICJ hinted that safeguarding the environment is fundamental to human welfare.[61] As noted, the Court described the environment as "living space...essential to the health and well-being of human beings". While not explicitly labelling it *erga omnes*, the tone suggests that environmental protection is approaching that status. Many scholars now argue that a stable climate and intact ecosystems are jus cogens norms non-derogable standards akin to prohibitions on torture. The MOX Plant legacy contributes to this: by treating UNCLOS duties as universal and permanent, it implies that pollution of shared waters offends the whole international community, not just the directly affected state.[62]

Due Diligence in Wartime

The bedrock of transboundary environmental law is due diligence which emphasises that States must act with care to avoid harming others.[63] In peacetime contexts, this means notifying neighbours of dangerous activities, conducting EIAs, and engaging in consultations (as in *Pulp Mills*). *MOX Plant, Pulp Mills* and the recent *International court of justice advisory opinion on Climate change*[64] together confirm that due diligence is a *conduct* obligation: a State must establish legal and regulatory frameworks and exercise vigilance, but it need not guarantee a particular outcome.[65] Crucially, ITLOS has extended this principle into armed conflict. In the 2024 Climate Advisory Opinion, the Tribunal emphasised that compliance with Article 194(1) UNCLOS requires "*stringent due diligence*" even for war-related pollution. It held that a State meets its duty by "put[ting] in

61 ICJ, *Certain Activities Carried Out by Nicaragua in the Border Area (Costa Rica v. Nicaragua)*, Judgment, 16 December 2015, I.C.J. Rep. 665, ¶154.; ICJ, *Legality of the Threat or Use of Nuclear Weapons*, Advisory Opinion, 8 July 1996, I.C.J. Rep. 66, ¶29–30.

62 *MOX Plant* (Ireland v. United Kingdom), UNCLOS Annex VII Arbitral Award, 2003, RIAA Vol. XXI, §§4498–4505.

63 ICJ, *Pulp Mills on the River Uruguay* (Argentina v. Uruguay), Judgment, 20 April 2010, I.C.J. Rep. 14, ¶101–110.

64 Obligations of States in respect of Climate Change, Latest developments, 23rd July 2025, Cf, https://www.icj-cij.org/sites/default/files/case-related/187/187-20250723-sum-01-00-en.pdf?__cf_chl_tk=FWzNUA5uOyR8XvMQNJyd122JwrgCfGJQE2_Itdlt08o-1761464167-1.0.1.1-cjebf4Jp.dD2HdIpzJyl0ttRHRa1atLaSciV9FXAYO4

65 *MOX Plant* (Ireland v. United Kingdom), UNCLOS Annex VII Arbitral Award, 2003, RIAA Vol. XXI, §§4498–4505.; Philippe Sands, *Principles of International Environmental Law*, 3rd edn (Cambridge University Press, 2018) 432–434.

place a national system...and exercising adequate vigilance" to regulate emissions. Applied to warfare, this suggests that military planners must minimise ecological harm (e.g. avoid bombing oil refineries if alternative means suffice) just as they minimise civilian suffering. Failure to do so could constitute a violation of international law even absent intent. In this way, due diligence bridges doctrines: it translates the abstract erga omnes duty into concrete state conduct in both war and peace.[66]

The Fragmentation Challenge

Despite these advances, fragmentation remains an obstacle. IHL, IEL, and human rights law – each approach environmental protection differently.[67] During conflict, IHL sets thresholds (Article 55 AP I), ILC draft principles set guidelines[68], and human rights bodies focus on a clean environment as part of health or life rights. But there is no single treaty that harmonises these.[69] The International Law Commission's 2022 *Draft Principles on the Protection of the Environment in Relation to Armed Conflicts* show promise: they codify existing norms into one instrument. For instance, the Drafts articulate a precautionary duty and mandate legal remedies for war-related harm. Adoption of these principles into a binding convention would be an ideal way to institutionalise the MOX-era parallelism doctrine. Likewise, broader acceptance of the right to a healthy environment (as favoured by UN resolutions and many domestic constitutions) would reinforce that protection of nature is a universal legal value, not left to optional diplomacy.[70] The ICJ, in its advisory jurisdiction, has exhibited the '*meta-modern approach*' could help overcome fragmentation by interpreting

66 Philippe Sands (n 3) 433–434; ICJ, *Certain Activities Carried Out by Nicaragua in the Border Area* (Costa Rica v. Nicaragua), Judgment, 16 December 2015, I.C.J. Rep. 665, ¶154.

67 Protocol Additional to the Geneva Conventions of 12 August 1949, and relating to the Protection of Victims of International Armed Conflicts (AP I), 8 June 1977, 1125 UNTS 3, Art. 55.

68 International Law Commission, *Draft Principles on the Protection of the Environment in Relation to Armed Conflicts*, UN Doc A/77/10, 2022, Principles 3–5.

69 UN Human Rights Council, *Resolution on Human Rights and the Environment*, UN Doc A/HRC/RES/48/13, 2021, ¶3; see also Philip Alston, "Human Rights and the Environment" (2018) 3 *OUP Journal of Human Rights* 235, 240.

70 UN General Assembly, *Human Rights and the Environment*, UN Doc A/RES/76/300, 2022, ¶7; see also constitution of Finland (1999), Art. 20; constitution of South Africa (1996), Sec. 24.

the Martens Clause and due diligence principles in an integrated way.[71] The court has emulated in its constructive interpretation, the doctrine of '*lex specialis*' that the gap between IHL and IEL must be bridged by a common standard, reinforcing that the principles of climate change and those governing armed conflicts must be harmoniously interpreted for the obvious reason that the environment is a victim in every war.[72]

Recommendations and Conclusion

Policy and Legal Recommendations

To translate the MOX Plant insights into concrete law, we propose the following:

- **Codify the ILC Draft Principles into a Convention.** The 2022 ILC draft on the environment in armed conflict should be adopted as a binding treaty. This would merge fragmented rules, establishing clear obligations (e.g. avoiding deforestation as reprisal, mandating EIAs in conflict zones) and enforcement mechanisms.[73]
- **Expand ICJ Compulsory Jurisdiction for Environmental Claims.** States should accept ICJ compulsory jurisdiction (Art. 36(2) Statute) for cases involving environmental damage, including those arising from conflicts. A specialised chamber or environmental court could hear such disputes.[74] This would give teeth to the parallelism doctrine by allowing third-party standing and universal jurisdiction for ecological injuries.
- **Create a UN Environmental Peacekeeping Body.** A UN-backed body (possibly under UNEP or the Peacebuilding Commission) should oversee wartime ecosystem protection. It could deploy "green peacekeepers" to monitor compliance (e.g. satellite tracking

71 Martens Clause, *Preamble to the Hague Convention (II) with Respect to the Laws and Customs of War on Land*, 1899; reaffirmed in AP I, 1977, Preamble.

72 Philippe Sands, *Principles of International Environmental Law*, 3rd edn (Cambridge University Press, 2018) 445–446.

73 International Law Commission, *Draft Principles on the Protection of the Environment in Relation to Armed Conflicts*, UN Doc A/77/10, 2022, Preamble, Principles 1–5.

74 Statute of the International Court of Justice, 26 June 1945, 33 UNTS 993, Art. 36(2). ↩

of forest fires, marine oil spills) and coordinate post-conflict rehabilitation of soils and waters.[75]

- **Recognise Environmental Protection as Jus Cogens.** The international community should work toward declaring and abiding to the prohibition of severe environmental harm a peremptory norm.[76] This might be achieved through a UNGA declaration or a UN environmental court interpreting jus cogens. Achieving jus cogens status would make ecological preservation non-derogable, akin to bans on genocide or slavery.
- **Domestic Implementation of Wartime Environmental Laws.** States must integrate due diligence and environmental protection into military manuals and national defence law.[77]For example, armed forces could be required to train soldiers on IHL's environmental provisions, to include environmental impact scenarios in rules of engagement, and to codify national liability for war-related pollution under domestic law.[78]

Conclusion

The meta-conscious approach is evidenced in the Mox plant as it was quite exceptional in accommodating and balancing modernistic rigidity and modernistic flexibility, by adjudicating ITLOS judicial competence in deciding Mox Plant by application of the doctrine of parallelism, acknowledging the importance of environmental protection being an erga omnes obligation. The court was further convinced by the competency of the European Court's jurisdiction, standing for the promotion of core international law principles of existence in harmony. By this sensible novel and positive adjudication as a conflict reducing mechanism, the author of the article exhibits as the '*meta conscious approach* the international tribunals. This has once again proved to be the primary judicial organ of the world, setting a trend for the peaceful settlement of disputes, in

75 United Nations Environment Programme, *UNEP Strategic Plan 2020–2025*, UNEP Doc., 2020, ¶12–15.

76 Edith Brown Weiss, "Environmental Protection as a Norm of Jus Cogens" (2009) 18 *RECIEL* 161, 165.

77 ICJ, *Certain Activities Carried Out by Nicaragua in the Border Area* (Costa Rica v. Nicaragua), Judgment, 16 December 2015, I.C.J. Rep. 665, ¶154.

78 ICRC, *Customary International Humanitarian Law Database*, Rule 43, Environmental Protection in Armed Conflicts, 2021.

spite of the fragmentation threat lingering the veracity of the existence of International law.

The MOX Plant legacy stands as a beacon of environmental protection in international law, demonstrating that ecosystems - oceans, rivers, forests, and biodiversity are not permissible collateral damage in interstate disputes. At its core, the case crystallised a fundamental principle: environmental obligations are continuous and autonomous, operating as a "parallel track" alongside other legal responsibilities. These obligations do not pause in times of crisis, conflict, or economic expediency. Ireland's challenge to the United Kingdom's mixed oxide fuel plant at Sellafield exemplified the necessity of pre-emptive, preventive action under UNCLOS, emphasising that transboundary environmental harm cannot be ignored even when the threat is potential rather than immediate[79].

The legal innovation in the MOX Plant lies in the doctrine of parallelism. While initially a procedural concept within UNCLOS - allowing multiple fora to adjudicate related claims without jurisdictional conflict - it carries profound normative weight. The doctrine signals that environmental duties, whether derived from treaties, customary law, or soft law instruments, are not subordinate to other obligations. Even when states confront security dilemmas, humanitarian crises, or armed conflict, they remain bound to safeguard nature. MOX Plant thus establishes that environmental protection is not merely an ancillary concern of state practice; it is a central, enforceable obligation[80].

Building on MOX Plant, the ICJ has progressively extended the contours of what has been termed "green jurisprudence." Parallelism also bridges the often fragmented domains of international law. Traditionally, environmental law, international humanitarian law (IHL), and human rights law operated in distinct silos. IHL addresses environmental harm in warfare through Article 55 of Additional Protocol I (1977), forbidding methods of warfare expected to cause "widespread, long-term, and severe" environmental damage. Human rights law increasingly recognises the right to a healthy environment as intrinsic to the right to life and health. International environmental law, codified in conventions such as UNCLOS Part XII, the ENMOD Convention (1976), and the Rio Declaration (1992), imposes preventive obligations, including due diligence and precautionary

79 *MOX Plant* (Ireland v. United Kingdom), UNCLOS Annex VII Arbitral Award, 2003, RIAA Vol. XXI, §§4498–4505.

80 Ibid; Philippe Sands, *Principles of International Environmental Law*, 3rd edn (Cambridge University Press, 2018) 438–442.

measures. MOX Plant demonstrates that these obligations do not disappear in wartime; rather, they operate concurrently, forming a legal and ethical bridge across disparate regimes. The ICJ has emphasised this in its advisory pronouncements, asserting that even absent express treaty prohibitions, States cannot disregard environmental considerations in military planning or conduct. The environment is a continuous subject of legal protection, bridging the gap between peace and conflict.

This perspective reinforces the concept of erga omnes obligations. In *Barcelona Traction* (1970), the ICJ distinguished duties owed to the international community as a whole from strictly bilateral rights. Later jurisprudence, including *East Timor* (1995) and *Bosnian Genocide* (2007), extended this principle to core humanitarian norms. Environmental protection is increasingly recognised within this framework: the ICJ's observations in *Certain Activities Carried Out by Nicaragua* (2015) describe ecosystems as "living space essential to the health and well-being of human beings".[81] MOX Plant reinforces the universality of these duties, establishing that pollution or ecological degradation of shared waters constitutes a wrong not just against a single state but against the international community as a whole. This perspective aligns environmental protection with jus cogens principles, elevating it to non-derogable status akin to prohibitions on genocide or torture.

The evolution of green jurisprudence also influences the codification of norms in instruments such as the ILC's Draft Principles on the Protection of the Environment in Relation to Armed Conflicts (2022). These principles, inspired in part by MOX Plant, articulate precautionary duties, legal remedies, and governance mechanisms to prevent wartime environmental harm. By incorporating these norms into a binding treaty, states could institutionalise the doctrine of parallelism and reinforce '*stringent due diligence*' as a core obligation. The principles ensure that environmental protection is not merely aspirational, but a concrete standard of conduct for governments, militaries, and multinational actors. In practical terms, MOX Plant and its jurisprudential successors advocate for proactive state behaviour. Governments must develop legal frameworks, regulatory systems, and monitoring mechanisms to ensure compliance. Military operations should integrate environmental considerations into planning, rules of engagement, and post-conflict rehabilitation. A UN-backed environmental peacekeeping mechanism could provide oversight, monitoring, and remediation, reflecting the idea that ecological security is

81 UNCLOS, 10 December 1982, 1833 UNTS 3, Part XII, Arts. 192, 194.

inseparable from human security. Such measures would operationalise the erga omnes duty of environmental protection, translating abstract norms into concrete, enforceable actions.

The broader significance of the MOX Plant lies in its normative and moral vision. By framing the environment as a shared asset, the ICJ and related tribunals have fostered an eco-centric consciousness in international law. Professor Frans de Waal aptly reminds us that "the Earth is not inherited from our ancestors but borrowed from our children." The legal wisdom of MOX Plant echoes this maxim, reminding states that failure to protect ecosystems is not merely a policy error, but a breach of duties owed to humanity and future generations. In a world increasingly shaped by armed conflicts, industrial disasters, and climate crises, jurisprudence serves as a moral compass, asserting that ecological destruction is a legal as well as ethical violation.

In conclusion, the MOX Plant legacy, reinforced by ICJ green jurisprudence, articulates a transformative vision of international law. Environmental protection is no longer optional; it is an enduring, universal, and enforceable obligation that co-exists with all other legal duties. The doctrine of parallelism affirms that legal obligations persist across regimes, the erga omnes principle guarantees universal responsibility, and the codification of due diligence ensures practical compliance. Collectively, these developments herald an eco-centric era in international law, whereby reaffirming the international community with the principle that "Earth is not a mere inheritance from our ancestors; rather it is borrowed from our future generations."

Weaving Ecocide into ICC's Jurisdictional Framework

Vinay Juneja, T.V. Subba Rao & Tushar Pal

Abstract

The International Criminal Court (ICC) shifts its ethical reverence towards the cold wounding of Earth's living essence with the ecocide gleaming upon the legal emptiness of the ICC Rome Statute, ICC's fabric must be reweaved, in light of both justice for the people, coupled with the justice for the planet, thereby reweaving the normative foundations of the ICC. Moreover, other International legal sentinels such as International Environmental law (IEnL), International Human Rights Law (IHRL) and International Humanitarian Law (IHL) set themselves as vigilant souls eager to deliver its say in contradiction of Ecocide and other International law disciplines are composed but the voyage into the divine hallways of ICC mechanism is largely uncharted, we lack doctrinal stitching of the legislative framework, thereby leading to weathering of this legal rock.

Does ICC, premeditated to prosecute crimes against humanity, also embrace the voice for the silent suffering of the planet? How can the avenues of justice respond to the poisoned rivers? How can justice cradle the wounds of razed forests? How can justice heal the feel of breathless skies? This article navigates these jurisprudential questions by bracing the dark clouds surrounding the legal conception, one that may risk the ICC sailing ultra vires, beyond its chartered waters. Yet it offers a beacon for the ICC and other International institutions mandated to redress atrocity crimes, especially as they confront those offences that do not bring physical harm, but leave the Earth gasping. In this context, the vision of ecocide as a prosecutable crime within the jurisdictional ambit of ICC becomes not merely time-bound but necessity-bound— it's a call to expand the ethical arc of justice into the environmental arc of justice.

Introduction

From the Amazonian[1] to the Ukrainian[2] event, ecological devastation has emerged as a global problem. One essential way to improve protection is through criminal accountability for serious environmental harm. The first, yet designated as an institution of last resort, the International Criminal Court (ICC)[3], has demonstrated an increasing willingness to handle this kind of injury.[4] In late 2024, the Ecocide as a crime was projected for inset in the Rome Statute.[5]

Although the ICC's framework is chiefly anthropocentric, the pursuit for ecocentric reform has prompted the need to employ IHRL, IHL and IEnL in prosecuting environmental crimes. The suggested crime of ecocide is one form of this intersection. The "sources of law" clause requires more than simply enumerating existing law. Article 21[6] instructs the Court to consider treaties and other international norms, promoting a more "inclusive" approach, but is silent on how to include sources from beyond the inner circle, and ICC jurisprudence has yet to help clarify this ambiguity.[7] In the absence of such case, smooth integration is necessary to avoid exacerbating the fragmented current state of international law,[8] which is particularly evident in relation to environmental protection.[9] This article introduces a framework for integrating IEnL and related regimes into ICC jurisdiction.

1 Climate Counsel, Greenpeace Brasil, Observatorio do Clima (2022).

2 Rekrut (2024).

3 Rome Statute, Article 17(1).

4 Andriy Kostin, "Ecocide as a weapon of war" 21 May 2024.

5 Following ICC's Office of the Prosecutor's (OTP) 2013 and 2016 comprehensive Policy Paper on Environmental Crimes, which is currently undergoing public consultation, ecocide was proposed for inset in the Rome Statute in late 2024.

6 Rome Statute; Article 21 (Applicable law).

7 Hochmayr (2014); McLachlan (2024, pp. 311–312) (providing examples where external sources were reviewed in ICC jurisprudence without a detailed examination of Article 21's functioning).

8 McLachlan (2005, p. 284) (citing Brierly – 'the development of specialized fields of international law, if progressed in isolated compartments, could lead to serious conflicts of laws within the international legal system'); ILC (2006). Cryer (2009) (noting that ICC's 'Elements of Crimes' depart from international customary law on the 'manifest pattern' contextual factor for genocide).

9 Bruch et al. (2021) (reviewing 'IHL, IEnL, ICL, IHRL, the United Nations Charter, and so on' and finding that 'a fragmented and unclear legal framework protects the environment in times of armed conflict').

It discusses both opportunities and obstacles of applying this approach to environmental harm in the use of extrinsic law before the ICC. Prior studies (of Rachovitsa,[10] Galand[11], Feria-Tinta[12], Campbell, McLachlan[13] and Anne Peters[14]) have emphasised the applicability of IEnL principles under the Rome Statute as well as the connections between IHRL, IHL, and International Criminal Law (ICL); however, they have not examined how these sources might be harmoniously integrated under the Article 21 of the Rome Statute. Separately, IEnL and ICL have been attacked at the general conceptual level by a "proliferating critical scholarship on ecocide"[15]. Nevertheless, some of these publications[16] fail to provide any practical way to deconstruct normative tensions under the current international criminal law framework.[17] More importantly, the framework integration model presented here offers a convincing approach to breaking down international law to strengthen its structural stability.

Reintegrating External Normative Frameworks into ICL

In order to comprehend how ICL fits into the larger framework of international law, it is necessary to see its development historically.

10 Rachovitsa in her study on systemic integration refers to the ICC in passing, but makes no mention of Article 21 of the Rome Statute (2017).

11 Galand in his study on IHRL and ICL, Galand refers to IHRL having a systemic effect on ICL, but does not refer to environmental harm in any respect (2019).

12 Feria-Tinta in her study on systemic integration and climate change, makes no reference to ICL and does not question the limited interpretive framing of systemic integration (2024).

13 Campbell McLachlan in his study on systemic integration, refers to Article 21 of Rome Statute but does not address environmental harm in this context (2024).

14 Anne Peters reviews systemic integration and mentions the ICC, but does not refer at all to Article 21 and does not examine how extrinsic materials would be applicable under the Rome Statute (2017).

15 Rekrut (2024) (commenting on ICL and IHL, without mentioning Article 21 of Rome Statute or any other theory of integration). Others have talked about integrating IHL and IEnL, but also without addressing integration under the Rome Statute in any detail.

16 For e.g., Rekrut (2024) (commenting on ICL and IHL, without mentioning Article 21 of the Rome Statute). Others have talked about integrating IHL and IEnL, but without addressing integration under the Rome Statute in any detail.

17 Nishimura (2022) (noting that the international community seeks a 'system of international law that should strive for coherence and consistency').

Although it only became a distinct field after the Cold War[18], its intellectual roots go back centuries. Grotius[19], based on Vitoria's ideas of Statehood and Pacta sunt servanda, conceived of a "common law of nations" that was independent of ecclesiastical authority and defied Machiavellian realpolitik, so provocative that De Jure Belli ac Pacis was banned by the Catholic Church for almost three centuries. His recognition of a right to punish serious transgressions of natural and international law inspired Henri Donnedieu de Vabres, who later advanced a universal jurisdiction based on the universality of punishment.

Through the use of documents like the 1899 Hague Convention, the 1949 Geneva Conventions, and the 1863 Lieber Code, the second stage of development saw the codification of IHL standards that form the basis of ICL[20]. With genocide arising during the Holocaust, and not addressing genocide, the Nuremberg and Tokyo Tribunals applied other fundamental offences. Nevertheless, because of their situational nature, they have not yet established ICL as a completely independent.

In the 1990s, ICL emerged as a distinct field post–Cold War via codification of jurisprudence from ad hoc tribunals for Yugoslavia, Rwanda, and other countries, asserting ICL's independence from ICJ norms, advancing concepts like "overall control" and denial of head-of-state immunity, and establishing a complex, subsidiarity-based system linked to domestic law.[21] International criminal justice developed as a complex jurisdictional order, characterised by deference and subsidiarity, although being linked to domestic systems.[22] Nevertheless, deliberations over the conceptual nitty-gritties of ICL have endured. These deliberations frequently echo Judge Pal's critique of its organisational basis, as articulated in his dissent during the Tokyo Trial.[23]

18 Although some refer to the Nuremberg trials as the emergence of ICL, but at that point it was still *ad hoc*.

19 Grotius (1925, pp. 527–529).

20 Scharf (2022, pp. 25–26). Though ICL has since differentiated itself from IHL and IHRL, though maintaining a close inter-connection, Stahn (2019) ('ICLhas gradually distinguished itself from other bodies of law, such as IHL or IHRL').

21 Refer Schabas (2011, pp. 1–16); Bergsmo et al. (2014).

22 Stahn, 2019, p. 20.

23 Tokyo Tribunal: Judgment of The Honorable Justice Pal, Member from India: "*[N] o particular group of nations can claim to be the custodian of the 'common good'. International life is not yet organized into a community under the rule of law. A*

Originally, critiques of ICL, including Milošević's inquiry into the legitimacy of the ICTY, were rather narrow and legalistic. Today, the critiques seem to focus on democratic deficit, fragmentation, and an alleged selective bias against the Global South.[24] These critiques raise a need to ground ICL in strong theoretical underpinnings and within the larger framework of international law—a goal that recent commentary has sought to further.

Recent efforts have sought to reintegrate ICL within the broader corpus of international law. As cross-cutting issues emerge before bodies such as the UN Security Council, ICJ, and ICC[25], and as peremptory norms gain prominence, the risks of fragmentation and inconsistent outcomes become apparent, undermining predictability and legitimacy.[26] Ecocide exemplifies this challenge, intersecting criminal, environmental, human rights, and humanitarian law.

Beyond IHL, however, these tribunals seldom engaged systematically with other sub-branches of international law.[27] ICC jurisprudence[28] has varied in its responsiveness to external sources,[29] where some chambers have resisted such sources and other chambers have adopted certain procedures despite there being no statutory support for them, which reflects the lack

community life has not even been agreed upon yet. Such an agreement is essential before the so-called natural law may be allowed to function in the manner suggested."

24 Simpson (1997, pp. 4–11).

25 Libya and Sudan constitute earlier examples, whereas Russia's invasion of Ukraine in 2022 and the Israel-Hamas conflict have also seen multiple jurisdictions engaged in litigation.

26 Perez-Leon-Acevedo, 2024; Webb, 2013; Cryer, 2009.

27 Refer ICTY: *Prosecutor v. Dusko Tadić*, Decision on the Defence Motion for Interlocutory Appeal on Jurisdiction, IT-94-1-AR72, 2 October 1995, para.204; Gutierrez Posse (2006).

28 ICC: *Prosecutor v. Lubanga* (ICC-01/04- 01/06), Judgment on the appeal of the Prosecutor against the decision of Trial Chamber I entitled 'Decision on the consequences of non-disclosure of exculpatory materials covered by Article 54(3)(e) agreements and the application to stay the prosecution of the accused, together with certain other issues raised at the Status Conference on 10 June 2008', 21 October 2008, para. 51.

29 ICC: *Prosecutor v. Lubanga* (ICC- 01704-01/06), Decision Regarding the Practices Used to Prepare and Familiarise Witnesses for Giving Testimony at Trial, 30 November 2007, para. 44; Schabas (2016, p. 519).

of scholarship around harmonising international criminal law under the Statute[30] with the broader architecture of international law.

Reconciling the Rome Statute with broader International Law

Systemic integration offers a solution where ICL provides limited guidance on using external sources. McLachlan views Article 21 as codifying this concept without addressing its normative basis, making its evaluation for the ICC timely.[31] Developed by the ILC to harmonise international law, it was most authoritatively outlined in the ILC report chaired by Koskenniemi.[32]

Article 31(3)(c) of the Vienna Convention, which calls for consideration of relevant rules of international law, embodies the principle of systemic integration. Koskenniemi and the International Law Commission (ILC)[33] study group hold that treaties ought to be interpreted within the framework of the broader legal system, using extrinsic sources when it achieves coherence across relevant norms. This point of view is further enriched with the lex specialis, lex posterior, and lex superior, supporting a purposive, interconnected international legal order.[34]

Yet, the interpretive orientation of systemic integration renders its practical utility at the ICC inherently constrained.[35] Article 21 of the Rome Statute goes beyond mere interpretation, allowing the Court to use external law to fill substantive or procedural gaps, exceeding the interpretive scope of Article 31 of the Vienna Convention.[36]

30 ICC: *The Prosecutor v. William Samoei Ruto and Joshua Arap Sang*, Public redacted version of Decision on Defence Applications for Judgments of Acquittal, ICC-01/09-01/11-2027-Red-Corr, 05 April 2016.

31 McLachlan, 2024, pp. 310–311

32 International Law Commission (2006, para. 410); McLachlan (2024, p. 4) (noting that the notion underlying systemic integration first found authoritative expression in the ICJ *Oil Platforms* case); ICJ: *Oil Platforms (Iran v. U.S.)*, 2003 I.C.J. 161 (6 November 2003).

33 International Law Commission, 2006, p. 106.

34 McLachlan, 2024, p. 4.

35 Djeffal, on the meaning of 'interpretive methods' (2015).

36 Article 31 General rule of interpretation

From Interpretation to Application

The uniquely written Article 21 serves as the foundation for integrating international law into the framework of Rome Statute.[37] This clause creates a distinct hierarchy of sources[38] in addition to giving the Court the authority to use a variety of sources, such as applicable foreign treaties[39], international legal principles, and norms. The Statute of the International Court of Justice, in contrast to this cascading three-tiered structure, cites its major sources in an unhierarchical manner and adds auxiliary ways of interpretation.[40] Despite being designed to provide legal certainty, Article 21 serves as a "master key"[41], serving as the fundamental entryway connecting the Court's internal system with the architecture of public international law.

Article 21 establishes a hierarchical cascade[42] of applicable laws. At the first tier, judges must apply the Statute, the Elements of Crimes, and the Rules of Procedure and Evidence in that order.[43] Only when these sources leave a genuine lacuna may external treaties or principles of international law be invoked under Article 21(1)(b).[44] Failing that, Article 21(1)(c) permits reliance on general principles derived from national legal systems.

37 Hochmayr (2014, p. 655) (noting that 'Article 21 of the International Criminal Court (ICC) Statute represents the first international law provision specifying the law to be applied by an international criminal court').

38 ICC: *Prosecutor v. Germain Katanga*, ICC-01/04-01/07, Judgment pursuant to article 74 of the Statute, Trial Chamber II, 7 March 2014, ('Katanga Trial Judgment'), Para.39. Flynn (2020) ('As an international treaty, all recognized sources of internat ional law would generally apply to the Rome Statute [...]').

39 The French version of the Statute clarifies that the term 'applicable' relates to treaties (*'les traités applicables et les principes et règles du droit international'*).

40 Schabas, 2016, pp. 515–516).

41 The expression draws inspiration from McLachlan's reference to systemic integration as a 'master key', and adapts it to the context of the ICC.

42 In this respect Article 21(1)(a) has a 'hierarchy within the hierarchy'; Bitti (2015, pp. 416– 417). Although Article 21(1)(a) makes no hierarchy between the sources, Article 51(5) of the Rome Statute states that, 'in the event of a conflict between the Statute and the Rules of Procedure and Evidence, the Statute shall prevail.'

43 ICC: *Situation in the Democratic Republic of Congo*, Case No. ICC-01-04-168, Judgment on the Prosecutor's Application for Extraordinary Review, paras.33–34 (13 July 2006).

44 *Katanga* Trial Judgment, para.39.

This funnel leaves a narrow opening for extrinsic sources, further constrained by strict interpretive safeguards: crimes must be strictly construed. These textual bulwarks raise the question of whether Article 21 meaningfully accommodates external sources, particularly in defining substantive crimes.[45] Closer scrutiny reveals notable gaps in the ICC's framework, particularly concerning environmental harm. Likewise, conventions on marine and ship pollution may inform grounds for excluding criminal responsibility under Articles 31(3) and 32 of the Rome Statute.[46] Broader IEnL principles, including the precautionary principle, could shape assessments of mens rea, while treaties like ENMOD and IHL sources are essential in interpreting terms such as "widespread, long-term and severe"[47] under Article 8(2)(b)(iv) and ecocide formulations[48].

To determine how Article 21(1)(b) applies to external legal instruments, the phrase "where appropriate" is key but ambiguous.[49] Since Article 21(1)(b) is already subordinate to 21(1)(a), interpreting "appropriate" solely as addressing legal gaps is redundant. Instead, it likely serves both to identify when external sources are needed and to ensure those sources are relevant to achieving the Statute's aims. Article 21(1)(b) suggests customary international law is typically applicable and has been applied, as in the case of Jordan's inaction on arresting Al-Bashir.[50] Nonetheless, this mode of identifying and applying customary law has faced some critique[51], in part attributable to a lack of clear instruction on the use of extrinsic materials, leading to inconsistently applied methodology.

45 Democratic Republic of the Congo, Appeals Decision 2006, para. 39 ('No gap is noticeable in the Statute with regard to the power claimed in the sense of an objective not being given effect to by [their] provisions'). ICC: *Prosecutor v. Jean-Pierre Bemba Gombo et al.*, Judgment on the appeals of the Prosecutor, Mr Jean-Pierre Bemba Gombo, Mr Fidèle Babala Wandu and Mr Narcisse Arido against the decision of Trial Chamber III entitled 'Decision on Sentence pursuant to Article 76 of the Statute', 8 March 2018, ICC-01/05-01/13-2276-Red, paras 75–76.

46 Robinson, pp. 342–343 (2022).

47 ICC: *Prosecutor v. Ruto and Sang*, 'Reasons for the Decision on Excusal from Presence at Trial under Rule 134 quater, Ruto and Sang' (ICC-01/09-01/11), Trial Chamber V(A), 18 February 2014, paras.56–60.

48 Formulations of ecocide like that proposed by the Independent Expert Panel (Gillett 2022, pp. 99–104)

49 Hochmayr, 2014, pp. 664–666.

50 ICC: *Prosecutor v Al-Bashir*, Judgment in the Jordan Referral re Al-Bashir Appeal, Appeals Chamber, ICC Case No 02/05-01/09-3 (6 May 2019).

51 Schabas, 2016, p. 522.

Article 21's structure is clear, but it doesn't fully explain how to apply international law within its framework. The Rules of Procedure and Evidence reference Article 21 regarding national laws, human rights, aggravating circumstances, and justice-related offences, but lack broad guidance for other international law areas.[52] To address this gap, Koskenniemi's systemic integration under Article 31(3)(c) of the Vienna Convention could be considered. Although the Court often cites Article 31 of the Vienna Convention to interpret the Rome Statute, its use is inconsistent, unclear, and leaves uncertain whether this interpretive method applies only to the Statute itself or also to external laws under Article 21(1)(b).[53]

This confusion demonstrates the Court's muddling of two different functions: the Article 21 Rome Statute process for identifying and prioritising the applicable law ('identificatory' function), and the Article 31 Vienna Convention process for interpreting relevant international law provisions ('interpretive' function).[54] To apply an external legal source is one thing, and it is another to interpret an internal provision using that external source.[55] However, it is not clear in Katanga Trial Judgment[56] whether the Court accounted for these two processes or conflated them in some manner in reducing them to the single category of, e.g. interpreting the Rome Statute.[57]

52 ICC: *Prosecutor v. Thomas Lubanga Dyilo*, ICC-01/04–01/06 A5, Judgment on the appeal of Mr. Thomas Lubanga Dyilo against his conviction, 1 December 2014, para.277. Also refer ICC: *Prosecutor v. Jean-Pierre Bemba Gombo*, ICC-01/05–01/08–3343, Judgment pursuant to Article 74 of the Statute, 21 March 2016, para.70; ICC: *Democratic Republic of Congo*, Decision 2006, para.33 and; ICC: *Situation in Bangladesh/Myanmar* (Decision, 14 November 2019) ICC-01/19, para. 55.

53 *Katanga* Trial Judgment, para.47 (considering that under article 31(3)(c) of the Vienna Convention on the Law of Treaties, the interpretation of the applicable law can also be informed by external sources providing context).

54 The distinction is mentioned in Hochmayr (2014, pp. 656–657). In addition to the identificatory and interpretative functions, there is also the applicative function. However, the study of Koskenniemi shows that he did not take this approach beyond the confines of interpretation; International Law Commission (2006, para. 423).

55 Pauwelyn (2003, pp. 203–204) referring to the *Lockerbie* case, ICJ Reports 1992, para. 42.

56 ICC: *Katanga* Trial Judgment, para.47.

57 See Bitti (2015, pp. 436–437) citing ICC: *Situation in the Democratic Republic of the Congo,* Decision on the Joinder of the Cases against Germain Katanga and Mathieu Ngudjolo Chui, Katanga, 10 March 2008, ICC-01/04-01/07-257, PTC I, ICC, 10 March 2008. But see ICC: Appeals Chamber in *Prosecutor v. Lubanga,* Judgment on the Appeal of Mr. Thomas Lubanga Dyilo against the Decision on the Defence Challenge

Holding individuals accountable for environmental harm requires substantive external norms, but systemic integration only guides interpretation. This article proposes "framework integration" as better suited under Article 21(1)(b), enabling identification, interpretation[58], and application of external law without violating Rome Statute principles, though its practical operation remains unclear.

Re-situating Article 21(1)(b) within the Constitutional Order

In his report for the ILC, Koskenniemi discusses three methods to resolve conflict: (i) lex specialis, (ii) lex posterior, and (iii) status norms[59], but nothing in the ICC's legal frameworks clearly resolves or prioritises applicable law—a precondition for the process of interpretation. While they can lessen inter-system friction, they cannot accomplish a coherent integration.[60] Also importantly, none of these systems will escape the limitations placed by the Rome Statute—for instance, lex specialis caveats defer to the norms of IHL, while Article 50(1) of Additional Protocol I[61] states placement to a civilian/common effect is to be reserved for dubious cases.

Assuming civilian status can bypass proving victim protection, shifting the burden of proof and conflicting with Article 67(1)(i). Lex specialis is limited in ecocide cases involving overlapping regimes, while lex posterior is constrained by Article 24(2). Rigidly applying it could let States override the Rome Statute through new treaties, undermining Article 121(5)'s amendment process.

---

to the Jurisdiction of the Court pursuant to article 19(2)(a) of the Statute, ICC-01/04-01/06-772, 14 December 2006, para.37.

58 Technically, Article 31 of the VCLT could still be used to conduct the interpretive function, insofar as it does not clash with Article 21 of the Rome Statute. Given that the Rome Statute, including Article 21, does not exhaustively specify how to interpret its terms, this allows for resort to Article 31 of the VCLT in accordance with the terms of Article 21(1)(b) of the Rome Statute. Consequently, interpretive guides, such as the 'ordinary meaning' and 'object and purpose' tests remain valid under the framework integration approach.

59 ILC, 2006, para. 412.

60 Colangelo, 2016, p. 21.

61 Article 50(1) of Additional Protocol I would require that '[i]n case of doubt whether a person is a civilian, that person shall be considered to be a civilian'. Article 52(3) of API for a corresponding presumption for protected objects.

Article 21 provides its own expressed hierarchy of legal sources, and while the International Law Commission asserts that any treaty in conflict with jus cogens[62] or supralegislative human rights norms is invalid from the moment of its conclusion, the Rome Statute incorporates numerous normative jus cogens/non-derogable rules[63]—the prohibition against genocide and the core elements of IHL[64]—in its text itself.

Integrative Criteria for Frameworks

The Court's internal law, as provided for by Article 21(1)(a), is apparent, while Article 21(1)(b) does not specify the manner by which to look to external sources.[65] To synergise the Rome Statute with international law in a wider sense, criteria are put forth for how to: decide which norms to use; the order these norms should be used; and the manner in which norms should be interpreted.[66] Each of these criteria is in line with Article 21(1)(b), which states "where appropriate, applicable treaties and the principles and rules of international law, including established principles of armed conflict."[67]

Adjudicative Consistency in Criminal Courts

Adjudicative coherence can serve as a context-specific analytical lens to assess whether the application of various sources of law before the ICC might lead to an "incoherent judicial process,"[68] potentially undermining

62 ILC 2022 Jus Cogens study, Conclusions 10–11.

63 ILC 2022 Jus Cogens study, Conclusion 23 'non-exhaustive list' referring to the prohibition of aggression, the prohibition of genocide, the prohibition of CAH and the prohibition of torture, for example.

64 Bitti (2015, pp. 438–439). But he also argues that there is no such basis to distinguish between the superior status of the law in question (at 440).

65 ICC: *Lubanga* Appeal Judgment, para.277. But see Maučec (2021, p. 24).

66 Colangelo (2016, Part V) (referring to 'precise and concrete "coherence methods" (as opposed to conflict methods), to use in advancing international law's systemic coherence through decisional cross-fertilization in resolving disputes').

67 Adjudicative coherence emanates from the institution's identity as a Court, which is reflected in the Preamble and Article 1 of the Rome Statute among other provisions. *Effet utile* emanates from the Preamble's requirement 'to put an end to impunity for the perpetrators of [atrocity crimes]' and ensure their 'effective prosecution' as well as the structure of Article 21(1)(a) to (c) which provides a cascading web of normative sources designed to avoid the Court lacking a legal basis to act.

68 Gillett (2022, pp. 49–50). For an example of an interpretive approach approximating adjudicative coherence in the context of an international criminal trial, see STL,

or jeopardising the feasibility of the proceedings. This principle is rooted in the ICC's identity as a criminal court, which prioritises core values such as individual culpability, legality, and accurate legal labelling.[69] These values are reflected, for instance, in the introduction to the *Elements of Crimes* for crimes against humanity.

'Since Article 7 concerns international criminal law, its provisions must, consistent with Article 22, be interpreted strictly. Crimes against humanity, as defined in Article 7, constitute some of the gravest offences of international concern, warrant individual criminal responsibility, and require conduct prohibited under universally recognised international law, as affirmed by the principal legal systems of the world.'[70] Adjudicative coherence[71] helps the Court identify and prioritise external legal sources based on their alignment with its core functions.[72] For instance, provisions like Articles 9, 14, and 15 of the ICCPR (and corresponding customary norms in the UDHR) naturally reinforce the Court's due process framework[73]. Similarly, powers such as staying proceedings for abuse of process protect trial integrity and the Court's legitimacy.[74] In such cases, adjudicative coherence supports the integration of external safeguards, including the principle of non-refoulement.[75]

Judgment, *Ayyash et al.* (STL-11-01/T), Trial Chamber, 18 August 2020. paras. 5917–5918.

69 See *Katanga* Trial Judgment, para.50 referring to Article 22. The principle also encompasses the notion of *lex certa*; ICC: *Prosecutor v. Al Bashir*, Case No. ICC-02/05-01/09-3, Decision on the Prosecution's Application for a Warrant of Arrest Against Omar Hassan Ahmad Al Bashir, paras. 128–131.

70 ICC Elements of Crimes, Article 7 Crimes against humanity.

71 Report of Ad Committee on the Establishment of an ICC (1995), UN Doc A/50/22, paras. 52, 57, and Report of Preparatory Committee on the Establishment of an ICC (Proceedings of the Preparatory Committee during Mar.–Apr. and Aug. 1996), UN Doc A/51/22, paras.52, 180, and 185; Grover (2010, p. 552).

72 Koskenniemi (2005, p. 253) ('one man's coherence is not necessarily that of another's.'). See also 303–320, 488.

73 ICC: *Lubanga* Decision to Stay Proceedings 2008. See also Grover (2010, p. 561) ('a suspect or accused may have other rights protected under customary international law or a treaty ratified by the state of which he or she is a national').

74 ICC: *Prosecutor v. Katanga*, Decision on the Application for the Interim Release of Detained Witnesses DRC-D02- P-0236, DRC-D02-P-0228 and DRC-D02-P-0350, Situation in the Democratic Republic of the Congo, ICC-01/04-01/07-3405-tENG, TC II, ICC, 1 October 2013, para.30; Bitti (2015, pp. 439–440).

75 Conversely, other rights, such as social and cultural rights are not central to the Court's operation, though it is conceivable that such rights may be relevant, such as in the

It is noteworthy that, while the principle of legality is foundational, it does not impose undue constraints on the Court's capacity to interpret and apply the law. Specifically, it does not preclude progressive or dynamic readings of ICC law.[76] Rather, it mandates that the judicial construction of an offence must be reasonably foreseeable to an accused at the relevant time, particularly when legal counsel is available.[77]

Effet utile (*ut res magis valeat quam pereat*)

Crucially, while legality is central to ICC proceedings i.e. effet utile or 'effectiveness' (ut res magis valeat quam pereat),[78] it does not artificially limit the Court's ability to interpret and apply the law at hand. While consequential to a teleological approach to interpretation flagged by Article 31(1) of the Vienna Convention's reference to object and purpose of a treaty, it also stems on principles from Article 26 (pacta sunt servanda) and direction from Article 32(b) to avoid manifestly absurd or unreasonable results (e.g, practically results in the provision having no utility whatsoever). The adjudicative coherence standard thus normalises international law as an interpretation of international criminal law while preserving the autonomous character and normative mission as an institution under an anti-impunity intent rather than at its less core function as a humanitarian institution.[79]

The principle of effectiveness encourages the Court to rely on external sources of law, which enhance the functionality and utility of the internal elements of the Rome Statute.[80] Similarly, ad hoc tribunals, faced with the applicable law question, have embraced the principle of effet utile when

---

context of reparations.

76 Maučec (2021, p. 26). Similarly, see Shahabuddeen (2004, p. 1017).

77 ECHR: *SW and CR v. United Kingdom* App No 47/1994/494/576, ECHR (1995) Series A, Nos 335-B and 335-C, at paras 36 and 34; Grover (2010, p. 554); Van Schaak (2008). See also ICTY: Decision on Dragoljub Ojdanić's Motion Challenging Jurisdiction – Joint Criminal Enterprise, IT-99-37-AR72, Appeals Chamber, 21 May 2003, para.38.

78 ICC: *Situation in Uganda*, Decision on the Prosecutor's Application that the Pre-Trial Chamber Disregard as Irrelevant the Submission Filed by the Registry on 5 December 2005, ICC-02/04-01/05, 9 March 2006 para. 25.

79 *Katanga* Trial Judgment, para.46.

80 ICC: *The Prosecutor v. William Samoei Ruto and Joshua Arap Sang*, Decision on Prosecutor's Application for Witness Summonses and resulting Request for State Party Cooperation, ICC-01/09-01/11-1274-Corr2. 17 April 2014.

determining applicable law, including questions of subpoenas.[81] Thus, when the integration of these criteria and framework progresses, effectiveness must never trump the requirement of adjudicative coherence.

Substantive Proximity and the Pursuit of Rome Statute Objectives

Having substantive closeness to the objectives of the Rome Statute acts like a qualitative filter that guides the integration of external legal sources by privileging those sources that are the closest fit with provisions of the Rome Statute and its Preamble. In contrast to the lex specialis test, that relies on hierarchically specific, this standard relies on substantive closeness that facilitates adjudicative coherence and effective resolution.[82]

The proximity criterion provides a practical baseline for identifying pertinent external sources of law. Indicators of proximity include: (i) linguistic identity or linguistic similarity between the external source and the objective or provision of the Rome Statute in question; (ii) subject-matter relevance; (iii) overlap, whether partial or complete, between the parties to an external treaty; and (iv) temporal applicability at the time of the events. The closer an external source is in terms of terminology, subject, parties, and time, the greater weight it should be given in the integration process.

From Disjunction to Concord

Another important component for framework integration is the de-fragmentation of international law, founded on the role of the Court as an international forum within the larger legal order. This is especially important in the context of harms caused by environmental destruction when various legal regimes intersect.[83] An integrated approach allows the Court to create guiding authority for other tribunals outside the Court—that is, Colombia's Special Jurisdiction for Peace (JEP)[84], which must

81 Schabas (2003, p. 860), referring to e.g. ICTY: *Blaškić* Subpoena decision, para.21; *adić* Jurisdictional Decision, para.204; and *Barayagwiza* Decision of 3 November 1999, para.46.

82 Whereas *lex specialis* holds that the particular or specific law which derogates from the general law will be applicable in the situation. See *DRC vs Uganda*, (para.216) with the *Nuclear Weapons* Advisory Opinion (para.25).

83 Shelton (2003, pp. 148–149); Gillett (2023).

84 See Interim Article 5 of the Colombian Constitution, as amended by Constitutional Act 01 of 2017 (granting the JEP jurisdiction over crimes committed before 1 December 2016 in the context of the conflict with the FARC-EP).

reconcile ICL, IHRL, IHL, and domestic criminal law—or the International Tribunal for the Law of the Sea[85], which must apply its Convention along with other rules of international law that are consistent.

At the jurisprudential level, reliance on extrinsic materials to counter fragmentation in international law is well established. President Verzijl expressed this in the *Georges Pinson* arbitration, noting that every treaty must be understood as implicitly referring to general principles of international law on matters it does not explicitly resolve.[86] Pauwelyn similarly proposes a "fallback" on other norms of international law where treaties are silent. The ICJ has adopted comparable reasoning, including in environmental cases such as *Gabcíkovo-Nagymaros*.[87]

The Case of Ecocide and Environmental Harm

Having introduced framework integration as a method to unify disparate strands of international law and identified four criteria for its application at the ICC, it is now pertinent to consider its use in proceedings concerning environmental harm. Ecocide, in its current formulation[88], embodies an intersection of ICL, IEnL, IHRL, and IHL.[89] The principle of legality assumes particular significance in environmental cases, including ecocide, because much of the conduct in question may be perceived by some as socially beneficial or economically productive.

Determining meaning in provisions within a single branch of law is generally not particularly difficult. For example, with respect to bilateral treaties, '[e]ach State brings to the negotiating table a lexicon of its prior participation in treaties (bilateral or multilateral)'.[90] However, from a system such as the Rome Statute, means of identifying, prioritising, interpreting, and applying provisions from multiple external legal sources would be markedly complex. The differences not only may include terminology

85 United Nations Convention on the Law of the Sea, Articles 288, para.1, and 293, para.1.

86 Per Verzijl P, *Georges Pinson case*, Franco-Mexican Commission, AD 1927-8, No. 292, para.50.

87 ICJ: *Case Concerning the Gabcíkovo--Nagymaros Project* (Hungary v. Slovakia), Judgment, ICJ Reports 1997, para.140.

88 For leading formulations of ecocide, see IEP (2021) and Gillett (2022a) definitions referenced above.

89 Gillett (2023). See also Schabas (2003, p. 887).

90 McLachlan, 2005, pp. 283-284.

differences, but also differences in the normative and conceptual bases which underpin these labels, such as diverging understandings of conduct, obligations, and enforcement.[91]

International Environmental Law (IEnL)

IEnL can support the implementation of international criminal law (ICL) by specifying the types and thresholds of environmental harm considered unlawful or wrongful.[92] Its integration into ICL may be guided by analogies from its application in other legal domains. For instance, in General Comment 36 on right to life, the Human Rights Committee drew on key IEL principles, including the precautionary principle, access to information, sustainable resource use, environmental impact assessments, and the obligation to notify other States of emergencies.[93] In the context of IHL, both the International Law Commission (2022) and the International Committee of the Red Cross (2020) have examined environmental protection, but neither has systematically integrated IEnL and IHL frameworks.

The use of IEnL instruments can aid a tribunal in identifying potentially unlawful acts, such as trafficking hazardous waste[94], or conducting maritime polluting operations[95], therefore clarifying the conduct covered by the scope of ecocide under the principle of legality.[96] IEnL instruments can also provide clarity in defining 'serious' or 'severe',[97] as an essential element of the actus reus of Article 8(2)(b)(iv) in the Rome Statute[98], and contribute to a mens rea analysis utilising the precautionary principle, in a

91 Robinson (2008, pp. 927–928). For example, see the term 'person' as used in an international criminal law context, such as Article 67 in the Rome Statute, as opposed to how the term 'person' is used in international trade law.

92 Robinson, 2022, pp. 332– 334

93 HRC: General comment:36, Article 6: right to life, CCPR/C/GC/36, 3 September 2019, para.62.

94 Basel Convention on the Control of Transboundary Movements of Hazardous Wastes and Their Disposal, 1673 UNTS 57, 22 March 1989, Article 9.

95 Protocol of 1978 Relating to the International Convention for the Prevention of Pollution from Ships, 1340 UNTS 61, 17 February 1978, and annexes.

96 See Gillett (2022) definition of ecocide, which links the enumerated underlying acts to existing IEnL conventions; Gillett (2023).

97 See Hulme (2022, pp. 1165–1166) (in the context of the corresponding IHL provisions - Articles 35(3) and 55 of Additional Protocol I).

98 See IEP and Gillett (2022) definitions referenced above.

manner relevant to cases of indirect intent where the accused was aware of a foreseeable risk, but did not intend the implicated harm.[99]

A principal example of IEnL is the obligation to conduct an environmental impact assessment before undertaking activities with potential environmental consequences, which may be relevant in relation to ICC prosecution of environmental crimes. The duty has been acknowledged by the ICJ in the Pulp Mills case[100], ITLOS[101], and has been noted by other bodies, including before military operations, as a duty for precautions.[102]

Sustainable development is another important principle of IEnL. The IEP places sustainable development at the core of its proposed definition of ecocide, with support for its inclusion. Sustainable development may also inform reparations for environmental crimes (by drawing upon the ICJ's observations in Gabcíkovo-Nagymaros[103]).

IEnL principles addressing species depletion, resource exhaustion, and the protection of future generations can inform the assessment of environmental harm's gravity, both for admissibility and for elements of specific crimes.[104] For example, the WTO *Shrimp Turtles* case drew on UNCLOS, the Convention on Biological Diversity, and CITES to define "exhaustible natural resources".[105] Integrating these principles through framework integration supports the de-fragmentation of international law.

International Humanitarian Law (IHL)

Environmental harm is often most severe during armed conflicts, as regulatory protections may be weakened or dismantled. Since many applicable environmental offences are war crimes, IHL will likely play a

99 Gillett (2022, 348) setting out a proposed definition of Ecocide, with a *mens rea* element focused on 'Wilfulness'.

100 ICJ: *Pulp Mills on the River Uruguay* (Argentina v. Uruguay), Judgment, ICJ Reports 2010, para.204.

101 ITLOS: *Responsibilities and Obligations of States Sponsoring Persons and Entities with Respect to Activities in the Area*, Seabed Disputes Chamber of ITLOS, Advisory Opinion of 1 February 2011, paras 145–150.

102 Report of the ILC of its 66th Session, held between 5 May–6 June and 7 July–8 August 2014, A/69/10, para.209.

103 ICJ: *Gabcíkovo – Nagymaros*, para.140.

104 ICJ: *Legality of the Threat or Use of Nuclear Weapons*, Advisory Opinion, [1996] ICJ Reports 226, para.29.

105 McLachlan, 2005, pp. 302–303; Hafner & Binder, 2006, p. 170

central role in prosecutions arising from conflict. While scholars have explored integrating IEnL principles with IHL, tensions remain, as IHL traditionally treats environmental damage as collateral rather than criminal.[106]

Relevant IHL provisions include those on specially protected and civilian objects, which help classify environmental features as enemy property under Articles 8(2)(e)(xii) and 8(2)(b)(xiii).[107] The ICRC's codification of customary IHL and its environmental protection principles offer guidance on issues not explicitly addressed by the Rome Statute[108], such as protected zones of ecological significance. These sources enhance the effet utile of the Statute. Terrorism law[109] may be relevant when environmental harm is linked to coercive acts. Framework integration, provides a structured and principled means for the ICC to navigate these complexities effectively.

Navigating Complexities: Overarching Challenges and Insights

Framework integration, along with the facilitating criteria discussed, offers a robust method for the Court to incorporate external law. Yet, normative challenges remain, requiring careful attention to prevent doctrinal confusion. By centering adjudicative coherence and the principle of legality, however, it cannot justify stretching statutory language—for instance, interpreting "natural person" in Article 25(1) to include corporations, or reading "organisation or institution" in Rule 85(b) to cover non-anthropocentric entities.[110] Framework integration is intended to supplement and enhance the Court's legal toolkit, not to circumvent it.

106 See, e.g. ICTY: Final Report to the Prosecutor by the Committee established to Review the NATO Bombing Campaign against the Federal Republic of Yugoslavia (2000), paras.14–15, 90–91.

107 ICRC Customary International Humanitarian Law Study, Volume I book3 at Rules 43–45.

108 ICRC (2020). See also International Law Commission, 'Principles on the protection of the environment in relation to armed conflict', now reflected in United Nations General Assembly resolution 77/104.

109 See STL: Interlocutory Decision on the Applicable Law: Terrorism, Conspiracy, Homicide, Perpetration, Cumulative Charging (Case No. STL-11-01/I), Appeals Chamber, 16 February 2011.

110 See, e.g. Special Tribunal for Lebanon: Public Redacted Version of Judgment on Appeal, NewTV S.A.L. and Al Khayat (STL-14-05/I/CJ), Appeals Chamber, 8 March 2016.

A related and more intricate challenge is that framework integration might appear to compel States to uphold external treaties through the Rome System. However, framework integration is designed to serve the objectives of the Rome Statute.[111] Using extrinsic legal sources under Article 21 does not make States party to those treaties, nor obligate the ICC to enforce them.[112] In line with adjudicative coherence, the Court should only apply external obligations when there is a clear textual basis, such as where Article 21(1)(b) permits filling gaps in the Rome Statute that State Parties are bound to uphold.

At a conceptual level, the ICC's anthropocentric orientation poses a risk when shifting toward an ecocentric focus. To counter this, the adoption of ecocide should be supported by increased resources, including scientific experts and judges with relevant experience, and sustained dialogue with environmental treaty bodies.

IEnL is often criticised for favoring development, raising concerns that ecocide could legitimise "business as usual" over environmental justice. Yet, such critiques can help shape definitions that criminalise grave harms—like habitat destruction—irrespective of economic or social utility.[113] A mutually reinforcing integration of IEnL and ICL ensures both fields contribute meaningfully while maintaining accountability at the ICC. By incorporating environmental, humanitarian, and human rights law, it offers a principled basis for charges like ecocide, strengthening the Court's framework and reducing uncertainty in environmental cases.

Conclusion

With environmental degradation now on the agenda of the ICC, it is encountering a critical moment for relying upon the external branches of international law. Just as past war crime prosecutions have engaged IHL, so too will cases addressing environmental crime engage principles and instruments of IEnL. While the Rome Statute does permit the movement

111 See above under the heading of 'Reconceptualizing systemic integration as 'framework integration'.

112 See, by analogy, ECtHR, *Verein KlimaSeniorinnen Schweiz and Others v. Switzerland*, no. 53600/20, judgment (Grand Chamber), 9 April 2024, para.453–455 (referring also to *Fedotova and Others v. Russia* [GC], nos. 40792/10 and 2 others, para.167, 17 January 2023).

113 Author's proposed definition of ecocide, which does not pivot on the concept of sustainable development, which is only an element in relation to final underlying act of ecocide.

toward these sources of law, particularly pursuant to Article 21(1)(b), it does not offer much guidance on how judges would exercise this discretion. Furthermore, traditional systemic integration would not be sufficient as it speaks to the interpretation of law, yet not the preliminary-driven consideration of appropriate sources of law.

Integrating frameworks to adjudicate environmental harm improves the adjudication of environmental harm by reference to IEnL as a means of clarifying conduct, terminology, and mensrea, and IHL to weigh environmental harm against the weight of military necessity. The extension of its normative implications goes beyond environmental cases to include aggression cases, new evidence, and digital evidence. Normatively, it provides a framework to apply Article 21 in order to apply the Rome Statute to international law and ensures legality and due process. Most notably, it facilitates ecocentric adjudication within the ICC's anthropocentric framework by reinforcing both normativity and the Court's capability to address consequential environmental harm.

Bibliography

Meenakshi Harith

Abdulraheem Mahmood Y. 2000. 'War-related Damage to the Marine Environment in the ROPME Sea Area, in Austin, Jay E., and Bruch, Carl E., (ed.), *The Environmental Consequences of War: Legal, Economic and Scientific Perspectives*, Cambridge: Cambridge University Press.

Abijola, B. 'Protection of the Environment in Times of Armed Conflict". In Al-Nauimi, N. and Meese, R. (eds.), International Legal Issues Arising Under the United Nations Decade of International Law, 1995, The Hague: Martinus Nijhoff Publishers.

Abouali Gamal, Natural Resources under Occupation: The Status of Palestinian Water under International Law, Vol. 10 (2), *Pace International Law Review*, 1998, p. 411-574.

Adede, Andronico O., 'Protection of the Environment in Times of Armed Conflict: Reflections on the Existing and Future Treaty Law', Vol. 1 (1), *Annual Survey of International & Comparative Law*, Article 7, (1994), p. 161-179.

Adhikari, Jay Ram and Bhim Adhikari, Political Conflicts and Community Forestry: Understanding the Impact of the Decade-Long Armed Conflicts on Environment and Livelihood Security in Rural Nepal, 2010.

Afghanistan: Post-Conflict Environment Assessment, 2003, United Nations Environment Programme (UNEP).

Afriansyah Arie, International Environmental protection During Armed Conflict; Case Study: Israel-Lebanon Conflict, *Jurnal Hukum dan Pembangunan Tahun*, Vol. 38, No. 1, January-March 2008, pp. 35-57.

Al-Dawoody, Ahmed, and Kelisiana Thynne. "Of Date Palms and Dialogue: Enhancing the Protection of the Natural Environment under International Humanitarian Law and Islamic Law." *International Review of the Red Cross*, vol. 106, no. 925, (2024), pp. 350–365.

Al-Duaij Nada. 2004. *Environmental Law of Armed Conflict*, New York: Transnational Publishers.

Al-Hallaq, Abdulrahman, et al. "Environmental Considerations for Post-War Reconstruction of Gaza." Ambio, (2025). Available online at: https://link.springer.com/article/10.1007/s13280-025-02246-1.

Alexander Nicholas G., Airstrikes and Environmental Damage: Can the United States be Held Liable for Operation Allied Force.? Vol. 11, No. 2, *Colorado Journal of International Environmental Law and Policy*, 2000, p. 471-498.

Alfredson Gudmundur. 2010. Human Rights and the Environment, in Leary David & Balakrishna Pisupati (eds.), *The Future of International Environmental Law*, Tokyo: United Nations University Press, p. 127-146.

Amanda Doty, Reshaping Environmental Criminal Law: How Forfeiture Statutes Can Deter Crime, Vol. 18, Issue 3, *Georgetown International Environmental Law Review*, Spring 2006, p. 521-542.

Angurets, O., et al. "Environmental Consequences of Russian War in Ukraine (Report)." (2022). Available at: https://www.researchgate.net/publication/376981280_Environmental_consequences_of_Russian_war_in_Ukraine_2022

Antoine Philippe, International Humanitarian Law and the Protection of the Environment in Time of Armed Conflict", No. 291, *International Review of the Red Cross*, November-December 1992, p. 517-537.

Argren, Rigmor. "The Obligation to Prevent Environmental Harm in Relation to Armed Conflict." *International Review of the Red Cross*, vol. 105, no. 924, (2023), pp. 1208–1226.

Askary, Pouria, and Katayoun Hosseinnejad. "A Possible Legal Framework for the Exploitation of Natural Resources by Non-State Armed Groups." International Review of the Red Cross, no. 924, (2023), pp. 1522–1542.

Assessment of the Environmental Impact of Military Activities During the Yugoslavia Conflict, Prepared by: The Regional Environmental Center for Central and Eastern Europe, June 1999. Available at: http://www.grip.org/bdg/pdf/g1691.pdf.

Augst Robert M, Environmental Damage Resulting from Operation Enduring Freedom: Violations of International Law? *ELR News & Analysis*, Vol. 33, 2003, p. 10668-10681.

Austin, Jay E., and Bruch, Carl E., (ed.). 2000. *The Environmental Consequences of War: Legal, Economic and Scientific Perspectives*, Cambridge: Cambridge University Press.

Australian Defence Force: Environmental Management, Appendix 4, Defence Annual Report 2009-2010, p. 310-315.

Babcock, Hope M., The Problem with Particularized Injury: The Disjuncture Between Broad-Based Environmental Harm and Standing Jurisprudence, Vol. 25, *Journal of Land Use*, Fall 2009, p. 1-18.

Bagshaw, Simon. "The 2022 Political Declaration on the Use of Explosive Weapons in Populated Areas: A Tool for Protecting the Environment in Armed Conflict?" International Review of the Red Cross, no. 924, (2023), pp. 1293-1312.

Baral, N. and J. T. Heinen, The Maoist People's War and Conservation in Nepal, Vol. 24, Issue 1-2, *Politics and the Life Sciences*, (2006), p. 2-11.

Baskoro, Aji. "Environmental Destruction as a Weapon of War: A Human Rights and Humanitarian Law Perspective." Alauddin Law Development Journal, (2024). Available online at: https://journal3.uin-alauddin.ac.id/index.php/aldev/article/view/54352.

Batal al-Shishani, Murad, Environmental Ramifications of the Russian war on Chechnya, *Central Asia-Caucasus Analyst*, 3 May 2006, p. 10-11.

Baudichau, Eva. "Another Brick in the Wall: Climate Change (In)adaptation under the Law of Belligerent Occupation." International Review of the Red Cross, no. 924, (2023), pp. 1337-1364.

Bayoneto M. Victoria, The Former US Bases in the Philippines: An Argument for the Application of US Environmental Standards to Overseas Military Bases, Vol. VI, *Fordham Environmental Law Journal*, (1994), p. 111-155.

"Battlefields to Wastelands: UN Warns Conflicts Are Destroying Ecosystems Worldwide." *United Nations Geneva*, (2025), Available online at https://www.ungeneva.org/en/news-media/news/2025/11/112606/battlefields-wastelands-un-warns-conflicts-are-destroying-ecosystems-worldwide.

Berhe, A.A., The Contribution of Landmines to Land Degradation, Vol. 18, *Land Degradation & Development*, 2007, p. 1-15.

Berman, Eli, and L. González. "Environmental Litigation and State Responsibility in the Wake of Armed Conflict." European Journal of International Law, 2021–2023.

Bhurtel, Jugal, & Saleem H. Ali. 2009. 'The Green Roots of Red Rebellion: Environmental Degradation and the Rise of the Maoist Movement in Nepal', in Mahendra Lawoti & Anup Pahari (eds.), *The Maoist Insurgency in Nepal: Dynamics and Growth in the 21st Century.* New York: Routledge.

Biggerstaff, W. Casey, and Michael N. Schmitt. "Protecting the Environment in Armed Conflict: Evaluating the US Perspective." International Review of the Red Cross, no. 924, (2023), pp. 1267–1292.

Bílková, Veronika. "Environmental Protection in Armed Conflict: Between War and Peace." *International Review of the Red Cross*, vol. 105, no. 924, (2023), pp. 1115–1133. Available online at: https://international-review.icrc.org/sites/default/files/reviews-pdf/2023-12/environmental-protection-in-armed-conflict-between-war-and-peace-924.pdf

Biller, David. "Environmental Destruction as a Method of Warfare: Revisiting the ENMOD Convention." *Journal of International Humanitarian Legal Studies*, vol. 12, no. 2 (2021), pp.115–142.

Biswas Asit K. 2000. 'Scientific Assessment of the Long-term Environmental Consequences of War', In Austin, Jay E., and Bruch, Carl E., (ed.), *The Environmental Consequences of War: Legal, Economic and Scientific Perspectives*, Cambridge: Cambridge University Press.

Blank Laurie and Amos Guiora, Teaching an Old Dog New Tricks: Operationalizing the Law of Armed Conflict In New Warfare, Vol. 1, *Harvard National Security Journal*, (2010), p. 45-85.

Bleise A, P.R. Danesi, W. Burkart, Properties, use and health effects of depleted uranium (DU): A general overview, Vol. 64, *Journal of Environmental Radioactivity*, (2003), p. 93-112.

Bodansky Daniel. 2003. *Legal Regulation of the Effect of Military Activity on the Environment*, Berlin, Erich Schmidt Verlag, pp. 126.

Boden, Tara. "The Environment as a Civilian Object: Rethinking Distinction and Proportionality." *Leiden Journal of International Law*, vol. 36, no. 4, (2023), pp. 920–950.

Bondarenko BB and Kasyanenko, 'Military Pollution—Chemical Waste' in Taipale Ilkka, P. Helena Makela and Kati Juva (ed.). 2001. *War or Health? A Reader*, London: Zed Books, p. 426-430.

Boothby Bill, 'The Law of Weaponry—Is It Adequate'? in Schmitt Michael and Jelena Pejic. (ed.). 2007. *International Law and Armed Conflict: Exploring the Faultlines*; Essays in Honour of Yoram Dinstein, Martinus Nijhoff Publisher, p. 297-316.

Boothby William H. 2009. *Weapons and the Law of Armed Conflict*, Oxford: Oxford University Press.

Borrie John. 2009. *Unacceptable Harm: A History of How the Treaty to Ban Cluster Munition Was Won*, Geneva: United Nations Institute for Disarmament Research.

Bostian Ida L., The Environmental Consequences of the Kosovo Conflict and the NATO Bombing of Serbia, *Colorado Journal of International Environmental Law and Policy*, 1999, p. 230-240.

Bothe Michael, The Protection of Environment in Times of Armed Conflict, Vol. 34, *German Yearbook of International Law*, 1991, p. 54.

Bothe Michael, Environmental Destruction as a Method of Warfare, *Disarmament*, Vol. XV, (1992), No. 2, p. 101-161.

Bothe Michael, Carl Bruch, Jordan Diamond, and David Jensen., International Law Protecting the Environment during Armed Conflict: Gaps and Opportunities, Vol. 92, No. 879, *International Review of the Red Cross*, September 2010, p. 569-592.

Bothe M., Partsch, K.J. & Solf, W.A. 1982. *New Rules for Victims of Armed Conflicts*, Hague: Martinus Nijhoff, p. 746.

Bouvier Antoine, Protection of the natural environment in time of armed conflict, No. 285, *International Review of the Red Cross*, December 1991, p. 567-578.

Bouvier Antoine, Recent Studies on the Protection of the Environment in Time of Armed Conflict, No. 291, *International Review of the Red Cross*, November-December 1992, p. 554-566.

Brantz Dorothee, 'Environments of death: trench warfare on the western front, 1914-1918', in Closmann Charles E., (ed.). 2009. *War and the Environment: Military Destruction in the Modern Age*, USA: Texas A&M University Press, p. 68-91.

Brauer Jurgen. 2011. *War and Nature: The Environmental Consequences of War in a Globalized World*, London: AltaMira Press.

Bray, Daniel. "Environmental Harm and the Laws of Armed Conflict: Thresholds and Challenges." *International and Comparative Law Quarterly*, vol. 72, no. 4, (2023), pp. 980–1005.

Breau Susan, 'Protection of Environment during Armed Conflict', in Shawkat Alam (ed). 2013. *Routledge Handbook of International Environmental Law*, London: Ruotledge, p. 617-632.

Briggs Chad M., et.al., Environmental health risks and vulnerability in post-conflict regions, Vol. 25, No. 2, *Medicine, Conflict and Survival*, April-June 2009, p. 122-133.

Bring O., 'Arms Control and International Environmental Law', in Wahlgren, Peter (ed.). 2000. *International Aspects*, Stockholm Institute for Scandinavian Law, p. 397-417.

Brisman Avi, Crime-Environment Relationship and Environmental Justice, Vol. 6, Issue 2, *Seattle Journal for Social Justice*, 2008, p.727-817.

Bruch, Carl. "Legal Innovation for Environmental Protection in Armed Conflict." *International Review of the Red Cross*, vol. 105, no. 923, (2023), pp. 102–131.

Bruch, Carl E., et. al. 2009. 'Post-conflict Peace Building and Natural Resources', in Ole Kristian Fauchald, David Hunter, and Wang Xi (eds), *Yearbook of International Environmental Law*, Vol. 19, 2008, Oxford: Oxford University Press.

Bunker Alice Louise, Protection of the Environment During Armed Conflict: One Gulf Two Wars, *RECIEL*, Vol. 13(2), 2004, p. 201-213.

Butts Kent Hughes. 1994. 'Why Military is Good for the Environment', in Kakonen Jyrki (ed.), *Green Security or Militarized Environment*, USA: Dartmouth.

Camacho Rincón, Andrea, and Germán Parra Gallego. "Addressing Environmental Damages in Contexts of Armed Conflict: Transitional Justice in Colombia." *International Review of the Red Cross*, vol. 106, no. 925, (2024), pp. 424–449.

Caron David D. 2000. 'The Place of Environment in International Tribunals', In Austin, Jay E., and Bruch, Carl E., (ed.), *The Environmental Consequences of War: Legal, Economic and Scientific Perspectives*, Cambridge: Cambridge University Press.

Carr Paul, "Shock and Awe" and the Environment, Vol. 19, *Peace Review: A Journal of Social Justice*, 2007, p. 335-342.

Carus, W. Seth, *Defining "Weapons of Mass Destruction"*, Centre for the Study of Weapons of Mass Destruction, Occasional Paper, No. 8, Washington, DC: National Defence University Press, January 2012.

Cave, Rosy. 2003. *Explosive Remnants of War in Sri Lanka*, Landmine Action, 2003.

CEOBS & ZOI Environment Network. "War and the Environment in Ukraine: Evidence of Damage." *Journal of Conflict and Environment Studies*, vol. 2, no. 1, (2023), pp. 1–30.

Chamber, W. Bradnee, Towards an Improved Understanding of Legal Effectiveness of International Environmental Treaties, Vol. 16, *Georgetown International Environmental Law Review*, Spring 2004, p. 501-530.

Chamorro Susana Pimiento and Edward Hammond, *Addressing Environmental Modification in Post-Cold War Conflict*, Occasional Paper, USA: The Edmonds Institute. Available at: http://www.edmonds-institute.org/pimiento.html.

Chartier, Robert J., Environmental Issues Associated with Operation Enduring Freedom, *Engineer*, October-December 2003, p. 24-27.

Chefe, Daniel, and Cordula Droege. "The ICRC's Approach to the Environment in Armed Conflict." *International Review of the Red Cross*, vol. 105, no. 924, (2023), pp. 302–333.

Clark, Janine Natalya. "Environmental Harms and Entangled Lifeworld in the Ukraine War." *Journal of Human Rights Practice*, 2025. Available online at: https://research.birmingham.ac.uk/files/272458028/ClarkJ2025Environmental.pdf

Closmann Charles E., (ed.). 2009. *War and the Environment: Military Destruction in the Modern Age*, USA: Texas A&M University Press.

Cohan John Alan, Modes of Warfare and Evolving Standards of Environmental Protection under International Law of War, Vol. 15, *Fla. J. Int'l L.* (2002-03), p. 481-539.

Coleman Kim. 2005. *A History of Chemical Warfare*, New York: Palgrave Macmillan.

Conca, Ken. "Environmental Peacebuilding in Times of War." *International Review of the Red Cross*, vol. 106, no. 925, (2024), pp. 49–78.

Conca Ken and Jennifer Wallace, Environment and Peacebuilding in War-torn Societies: Lessons from the UN Environment Programme's Experience with Post-conflict Assessment, *Global Governance*, Vol. 15, (2009), p. 485-504.

Creta, Somini. "The Environment Is Not a Target: UN Positions on Protecting Nature during Conflict." *International Review of the Red Cross*, vol. 105, no. 924, 2023, pp. 1310–1330. Available online at https://international-review.icrc.org/sites/default/files/reviews-pdf/2023-12/Protection-of-the-Environment-During-Armed-Conflict-International-Review-of-the-Red-Cross-No-924.pdf.

CSO Report on the Application of Environmental Norms by Military Establishments *For submission to the United Nation Environment Programme,* The Sub-Committee on Military Related Environmental Concerns, Vermont Law School International Law Society, February 2008.

Daehler, Curtis C. and Majumdar SK. 1992. 'Environmental Impacts of the Persian Gulf War' in Majumdar SK, Forbes GS, Miller EW and Schmalz (ed.), *Natural and Technological Disasters: Causes, Effects and Preventive Measures*, The Pennsylvania Academy of Science, p. 329-336.

Dahl Arne Willy, Environmental Destruction in War, Vol. XV, No. 2, *Disarmament*, (1992), p. 113-127.

Daoust, Isabelle. "Health and Environmental Effects of Explosive Weapons." *International Review of the Red Cross*, vol. 106, no. 926, (2024), pp. 269–292.

De Hemptinne, Jérôme. "Increasing the Safeguarding of Protected Areas Threatened by Warfare through International Environmental Law." *International Review of the Red Cross*, vol. 105, no. 924, (2023), pp. 1268–1286. Available online at: https://international-review.icrc.org/sites/default/files/reviews-pdf/2023-12/increasing-the-safeguarding-of-protected-areas-threatened-by-warfare-through-international-environmental-law-924.pdf.

Demeyere, Bruno. "Protection of the Environment During Armed Conflict." *International Review of the Red Cross*, vol. 105, no. 924, 31 Oct. 2023, pp. 1167–1168.

DeSaussure, Major Ariane L. The Role of the Armed Conflict During the Persian Gulf War: An Overview, *The Air Force Law Review*, 1994, p. 41-68.

Desgagne Richard, The Prevention of Environment Damage in Time of Armed Conflict: Proportionality and Precautionary Measures, in Horst Fischer and Avril McDonald (eds.), *Yearbook of International Humanitarian Law*, Vol. 3, 2000, p. 109-129.

Deweerdt Sararh, War and the Environment, *World Watch*, Vol. 21 (1), Jan-Feb 2008.

Dhar Aarti, Manmohan calls for saving Himalayan Eco-system, *The Hindu*, 27 October 2009.

Diederich Michael, Law of War and Ecology: A Proposal for a Workable Approach to Protecting the Environment through the Law of War, Vol. 136, *Military Law Review*, Spring 1992, p.137-160.

Dinstein Yoram. 2001. 'Protection of the Environment in International Armed Conflict', In Frowein J.A. and R Wolfrum (ed.), *Max Planck Yearbook of the United Nations Law*, Vol. 5, p. 523-549.

Dorfman Bridget, Permission to Pollute: The United States Military, Environmental damage, and Citizen's Constitutional Claims, Vol. 6, No. 3, *Journal of Constitutional Law*, March 2004, p. 604-622.

Draft International Covenant on Environment and Development, International Union for Conservation of Nature and Natural Resources, Fourth Edition, 2010.

Draulans Dirk and Ellen Van Krunkelsven, The impact of war on forest areas in the Democratic Republic of Congo, Vol. 36, No. 1, *Oryx*, 2002, p. 35-40.

Drucker Major Merrit P., The Military Commander's Responsibility for the Environment, Vol. 11 (2), *Environmental Ethics, (1989), p.* 135-152.

Drumble Mark A., *Accountability for Property Crimes and Environmental War Crimes: Prosecution, Litigation, and Development*, International Centre for Transitional Justice, November 2009.

Drumbl, Mark A., Waging War Against the World: The Need to Move from War Crimes to Environmental Crimes, Vol. 22, Issue 1, *Fordham International Law Journal*, (1998), p. 122-153.

Dudley Joseph P., et. al., Effects of War and Civil Strife on Wildlife and Wildlife Habitats, Vol. 16, No. 2, *Conservation Biology*, April 2002, p. 319-329.

Dycus Stephen, Nuclear War: Still the Gravest Threat to the Environment, Vol. 25 (3), *Vermont Law Review*, (2000-2001), p. 753-771.

Dycus, Stephen, Osama's Submarine: National Security and Environmental Protection After 9/11, Vol. 30, No. 1, *WM. & MARY ENVTL. L. & POL'Y REV.*, (2005), p. 1- 54.

Eifan, Meshari K., Head of State Criminal Responsibility for Environmental War Crimes: Case Study: The Arabian Gulf Armed Conflict 1990-1991, (2007). *Dissertations & Theses.* Paper 2.

El-Baz Faronk and R M Makharita. 1994. *The Gulf War and Environment*, USA: Gordon & Breach Science Publishers.

El-Sayed, Ahmed, et al. "From Conflict to a Climate Future: Unraveling the Nexus between Warfare and Environmental Degradation." *Sustainable Futures*, vol. 14, (2025). Available online at https://www.sciencedirect.com/science/article/pii/S2666188825000954.

Elliot L. Environment and Security: What's the Connection, Issue No. 174, *Australian Defence Force Journal*, 2007, p. 39-52.

Enemark Chrisitian. 2003. *Biological Weapons: An Overview of Threats and Responses*, Working Paper No. 379, Canberra: Strategic and Defence Studies Centre.

Environmental Assessment of the Gaza Strip following the Escalation of Hostilities in December 2008 – January 2009, United Nations Environment Programme, (2009).

Environmental Contaminants from War Remnants in Iraq, NGO Coordination Committee for Iraq, June 2011, available at: http://reliefweb.int/sites/reliefweb.int/files/resources/images... unitionsHumanHealthinIraq.pdf.

Etten Jacob van, Joost Jongerden, Hugo J. de Vos, Annemarie Klaasse, Esther C.E. van Hoeve, Environmental destruction as a counterinsurgency strategy in the Kurdistan region of Turkey, *Geoforum*, Vol. XXX (2008), p. 1-12.

Evans Gareth, *The Responsibility to Protect in Environmental Emergencies*, American Society of International Law, Proceedings of the 103rd Annual Meeting, March 25-28, 2009, Washington, DC, p. 27-32.

Falk, Richard. 2000. 'The Inadequacy of the Existing Legal Approach to Environmental Protection in Wartime', In Austin, Jay E., and Bruch, Carl E., (ed.), *The Environmental Consequences of War: Legal, Economic and Scientific Perspectives*, Cambridge: Cambridge University Press.

Feinstein Barry A., The Applicability of the Regime of Human Rights in Times of Armed Conflict and Particularly to Occupied Territories: The Case of Israel's Security Barrier, Vol. 4, Issue 2, *Northwestern Journal of International Human Rights*, Fall 2005, p. 238-302.

Fernandez, Maria, and Luca Vacchi. "Weaponizing Water: Hydrological Damage and International Humanitarian Law." *International and Comparative Law Quarterly*, vol. 72, no. 3, (2023), pp. 621–650.

Fidler David P. 2000. 'War and Infectious Diseases: International Law and the Public Health Consequences of Armed Conflict', In Austin, Jay E., and Bruch, Carl E., (ed.), *The Environmental Consequences of War: Legal, Economic and Scientific Perspectives*, Cambridge: Cambridge University Press.

Finger Matthias. 1994. 'Global Environmental Degradation and the Military', in Kakonen Jyrki (ed.), *Green Security or Militarized Environment*, USA: Dartmouth.

Forces for Sustainability: Report of the first Peace and Sustainability Session, Peace Palace, The Hague, 14-15 March 2007, Netherlands, The Hague: Institute for Environmental Security.

Fort Timothy L. and Cindy A. Schipani, Ecology and Violence: The Environmental Dimensions of War, William Davidson Institute Working Paper Number 698, May 2004.

Freeland Steven, Human Rights, the Environment and Conflict: Addressing Crimes Against the Environment, *The International Journal of Human Rights*, Vol. 2, No. 2, (2005), p. 112-139.

Freeland Steven, Human Security and the Environment: Prosecuting Environmental Crimes in the International Criminal Court, Available at: http://law.anu.edu.au/anzsil/conferences/2004/proceedings/freeland.pdf.

Gander T.J. 1987. *Nuclear, Biological and Chemical Warfare*, London: Ian Allan Ltd.

Gangwar Abdhesh, Impact of War and Landmines on Environment, Centre for Environmental Education, Available at: http://archive.mtnforum.org/rs/ol/counter_docdown.cfm?fID=1409.pdf.

Garrett Benjamin C. and John Hart. 2010. *Historical Dictionary of Nuclear, Biological and Chemical Warfare*, USA, Maryland: The Scarecrow Press.

Garnett, Stephen. "Biodiversity and Armed Conflict: How Warfare Impacts Species and Ecosystems." *International Review of the Red Cross*, vol. 105, no. 924, (2023), pp. 1331–1352.

Gasser Hans-Peter, For Better Protection of the Natural Environment in Armed Conflict: A Proposal for Action, Vol. 89 (3), *American Journal of International Law*, (1995), p. 637-645.

Gasser, Hans-Peter, Guidelines for Military Manuals and Instructions on the Protection of the Environment in Times of Armed Conflict, *International Review of the Red Cross*, No. 311, (1993), p. 230-237.

Gattini Andrea, The UN Compensation Commission: Old Rules, New Procedures on War Reparations, Vol. 13, *European Journal of International Law*, (2002), p. 161-181.

Gavrysh, Khrystyna. "Prosecuting Individuals for Environmental Harm in the Armed Conflict between Russia and Ukraine: The Case of Destruction of the Kakhovka Dam." *Polish Yearbook of International Law*, vol. 43, (2023), pp. 261–283.

Geib Robin, Poison, 'Gas and Expanding Bullets: The Extension of the List of Prohibited Weapons at the Review Conference of the International Criminal Court in Kampala', in Schmitt M.N. (eds.), Volume 13, *Yearbook of International Humanitarian Law*, 2010, p. 337-352.

Gibbons Owen Thomas, Uses and Effects of Depleted Uranium Munitions: Towards a Moratorium on Use, *Yearbook of International Humanitarian Law*, Vol. 7 (2004), p. 191-232.

Gibson Sarah, Polluters as Perpetrators of Person Crimes: Charging Homicide, Assault, and Reckless Endangerment in the Face of Environmental Crime Vol. 25, *Journal of Environmental Law and Litigation*, (2010), p. 511-558.

Gilbert, Jérôme. "Atmospheric Pollution from Warfare: A Neglected Domain of IHL." *Yearbook of International Environmental Law*, vol. 33, (2023), pp. 142–171.

Gillet Matthew, Prosecuting Environmental Damage Under International Criminal Law, p. 1-11, available at: http://www.esil-en.law.cam.ac.uk/Media/Draft_Papers/Agora/Gillett.pdf.

Gillett, Matthew. "Criminalizing Reprisals Against the Natural Environment." *International Review of the Red Cross*, vol. 105, no. 924, (2023), pp. 1463-1496.

Gillett, Michael. "Ecocide, Environmental Harm and Framework Integration at the International Criminal Court." *Journal of International Criminal Justice*, vol. 22, no. 1, (2024), pp. 81–104.

Gillett, Edward. "Russia–Ukraine Conflict and Environmental Harm: Breaking Down the Evidence." *Global Environmental Politics*, vol. 24, no. 1, (2024), pp. 44–72.

Gilman Ryan, Expanding Environmental Justice after War: The Need for Universal Jurisdiction over Environmental War Crimes, Vol. 22, No. 3, *Colo. J. Int'l Envtl. L. & Pol'y*, (2011), p. 447-471. S-256.

Gleditsch Nils Petter, Armed Conflict and The Environment: A Critique of the Literature, Vol. 35, No. 3, *Journal of Peace Research*, 1998, p. 381-400.

Godschalk Seakle K.B., Green Soldiering – Integrated Environmental management as a Major Contribution towards Military Mission Achievement, available at: http://www.dfac.mil.za/publications/presentations/papers/Article%20MIEM.pdf.

Goldblat, Jozef, Laws of Armed Conflict: An Overview of the Restrictions and Limitations on the Methods and Means of Warfare, Vol. 13, *Bulletin of Peace Proposals*, Oslo, 1982, p. 127-133.

Goldblat Jozef. 1990. The Mitigation of Environmental Disruption by War: Legal Approaches, in Westing Arthur H. (ed.), *Environmental Hazards of War: Releasing Dangerous Forces in an Industrialized World*, New Delhi: Sage. p. 48-60.

Gopal Sriram and Nicole Deller, *Precision Bombing, Widespread Harm; Two Case Studies of the Bombings of Industrial Facilities at Pancevo and Kragujevac During Operation Allied Force, Yugoslavia 1999*, Institute for Energy and Environmental Research November 2002. Available at: http://www.ieer.org/reports/bombing/pbwh.pdf.

Graubart, Jonathan. "Ecocide, Genocide, and the Politics of Environmental Harm." *International Review of the Red Cross*, vol. 105, no. 924, (2023), pp. 1287–1309. Available online at: https://international-review.icrc.org/sites/default/files/reviews-pdf/2023-12/ecocide-genocide-and-the-politics-of-environmental-harm-924.pdf.

Grayson, Catherine-Lune, et al. "The Climate and Environment Charter for Humanitarian Organizations." *International Review of the Red Cross*, no. 924, (2023) pp.1227-1237.

Grayson, Peter. "Explosive Weapons and Long-Term Environmental Degradation." *International Review of the Red Cross*, vol. 106, no. 925, (2024), pp. 17–48.

Greening the Blue Helmets: Environment, Natural Resources and UN Peacekeeping Operations, United Nations Environment Programme (UNEP), Nairobi, 2012.

Guidelines for Military Manuals and Instructions on the Protection of the Environment in Times of Armed Conflict, No. 311, *International Review of the Red Cross*, March-April 1996, p. 230-237.

Guruswamy Lakshman D. and Grillot Suzette R. 2001. *Arms Control and the Environment*, New York: Transnational Publishers Inc. Ardsley.

Haavisto Pekka, 'Kosovo War: First Environmental Impact Assessment', In Talpale Ilkka, P. Helena Makela and Kati Juva (ed.). 2001. *War or Health? A Reader*, London: Zed Books, p. 447-451.

Halle Silja (ed.). 2009. *From Conflict to Peace-building: The Role of Natural Resources and the Environment*, The United Nations Environment Programme (UNEP), pp. 50.

Hamilton, A, A. Cunningham, et al., Conservation in a region of political instability: Bwindi Impenetrable Forest, Uganda, *Conservation Biology*, 14(6), (2000), p. 1722-1725.

Hancock Jan. 2003. *Environmental Human Rights: Power, Ethics and Law*, USA: Ashgate.

Harland Christopher, Anti-Personnel Landmines: Balancing Military Utility and the Humanitarian Cost, *CLAWS Journal*, Summer 2008, p. 236-248.

Harrell Eben, Regional Nuclear War and the Environment, *Times*, January 22, 2009.

Hart, T. and A. Hart, Conservation and civil strife: two perspectives from central Africa, *Conservation Biology*, 11(2), (1997), p. 308-314.

Hashimi, Qadriya, and Ramesh. "Impact of War on the Environment: A Critical Study of Afghanistan." *International Environmental Legal Research Journal*, vol. 1, no. 1, (2023), pp. 52–61.

Hay Alastair W. 2000. 'Defoliant: The Long-term Health Implications', In Austin, Jay E., and Bruch, Carl E., (ed.), *The Environmental Consequences of War: Legal, Economic and Scientific Perspectives*, Cambridge: Cambridge University Press.

Haye Eve La. 2008. *War Crimes in Internal Armed Conflicts*, Cambridge: Cambridge University Press.

Henckaerts Jean-Marie, Towards Better Protection for the Environment in Armed Conflict: Recent Developments in International Humanitarian Law, *RECIEL*, Vol. 9 (1), 2000, p. 13-19.

Henckaerts, Jean-Marie. 2000. 'International Legal Mechanism for Determining Liability for Environmental Damage under International Humanitarian Law', in Austin, Jay E., and Bruch, Carl E., (ed.). *The Environmental Consequences of War: Legal, Economic and Scientific Perspectives*, Cambridge: Cambridge University Press, p. 602-619.

Henckaerts, Jean-Marie and Louise Doswald-Beck. 2005. *Customary International Humanitarian Law*, Vol. I, International Committee of the Red Cross and Cambridge: Cambridge University Press.

Hinde Susan M., International Environmental Court: Its Broad Jurisdiction as a Possible Fatal Flaw, Vol. 32, *Hofstra Law Review*, (2003), p. 727-757.

Hiskes R. P., The Right to a Green Future: Human Rights, Environmentalism, and Intergenerational Justice, Vol. 27, No. 4, *Human Rights Quarterly*, (2005), p.1346–1364.

Homer-Dixon, Thomas F., On the Threshold: Environmental Changes as Causes of Acute Conflict, Vol. 16 (2), *International Security*, (1991), p. 76-116.

Hourcle Laurent R., Environmental Law of War, Vol. 25 (3), *Vermont Law Review*, (2000-2001), p. 653-693.

Hsiao, Elaine (Lan Yin), et al. "Protected Zones in Context: Armed Conflicts and Biodiversity." *International Review of the Red Cross*, no. 924, (2023), pp 1412-1440.

Hübschle, Anna. "Transnational Maritime Environmental Crime, Blue Crimes and Ecocide." *Frontiers in Conservation Science*, 2024. Available online at: https://www.frontiersin.org/journals/conservation-science/articles/10.3389/fcosc.2024.1448316/pdf.

Human Rights Watch. *Toxic Legacy: Environmental Harm from Explosive Weapons in Syria.* (2021). Available online at https://www.hrw.org/report/2021/10/15/toxic-legacy/environmental-harm-explosive-weapons-syria.

Hulme Karen. 2010. A Darker Shade of Green: Is it time to Ecocentrise the Laws of War, in Quenivet Noelle and Shilan Shah-Davis (ed.), *International Law and Armed Conflict: Challenges in the 21st Century*, TMC Asser Press, p. 142-160.

Hulme Karen, Environmental Security: Implications for International Law, Vol. 19, *Yearbook of International Environmental Law*, 2008, p. 3-36.

Hulme Karen, Taking Care to Protect the Environment against Damage: A Meaningless Obligation, *International Review of the Red Cross*, Vol. 92, No. 879, September 2010, p. 675-69.

Hulme Karen. 2004 *War Torn Environment. Interpreting the Legal Threshold*, Leiden: Martinus Nijhoff Publishers.

Humphreys, M., Natural resources, conflict and conflict resolution: uncovering the mechanisms, Vol. 49, No. 4, *Journal of Conflict Resolution*, August 2005, p. 508-537.

Hupy, Joseph, The Environmental Footprint of War, Vol. 14, No. 3, *Environment and History*, (August 2008), p. 405-21.

Huseynov, Rahim. "Chemical Pollution from Armed Conflict: Long-Term Environmental Consequences." *International Review of the Red Cross*, vol. 105, no. 924, (2023), pp. 1353–1371.

Huston Meredith DuBarry, Wartime Environmental Damage: Financing the Cleanup, Vol. 23, *U. Pa. J. Int'l Econ. L.*, (2000), p. 899-929.

Hryhorczuk, Dmytro, et al. "The Environmental Health Impacts of Russia's War on Ukraine." *International Archives of Occupational and Environmental Health* (or *Occupational Medicine* online), 2024. Available online at: https://occup-med.biomedcentral.com/counter/pdf/10.1186/s12995-023-00398-y.pdf. (SpringerLink)

Ignatavicius Gytautas and Vytautas Oskinis, Some aspects of interaction between military activities and environmental protection on Lithuanian military grounds, Vol. 53, *Ekologija*, Supplement, 2007, p.16–21.

Impact of war on the environment: ecocide. *Frontiers in Environmental Science*, (2025). Available online at: https://www.frontiersin.org/journals/environmental-science/articles/10.3389/fenvs.2025.1539520/full.

nternational Committee of the Red Cross (ICRC). "Legal Review: Environmental Protection under IHL." *ICRC Legal Position Papers*, 2020–2024. Available online at: https://www.icrc.org

International Committee of the Red Cross (ICRC). "From Crisis to Recovery: Managing the Environmental Impacts of Armed Conflict." *ICRC Law & Policy Blog*, 2 Dec. (2025), Available online at: https://blogs.icrc.org/law-and-policy/2025/12/02/from-crisis-to-recovery-managing-the-environmental-impacts-of-armed-conflict/.

International Committee of the Red Cross (ICRC), Guidelines for Military Manuals and Instructions on the Protection of the Environment in Times of Armed Conflict. Available at: http://www.icrc.org/eng/resources/documents/misc/57jn38.htm

International Law Commission. *Draft Principles on the Protection of the Environment in Relation to Armed Conflicts.* 2022. Available online at. https://legal.un.org/ilc/texts/instruments/english/draft_articles/8_7_2022.pdf legal.un.org+1

Jabbari-Gharabagh Mansour, Type of State Responsibility for Environmental Matters in International Law, Vol. 33, *RJT*, (1999), p. 59-121.

Jacobsson, Marie G., *Protection of the environment in relation to armed conflicts*, Annex E, Report of the International Law Commission, Sixty-third session, (26 April–3 June and 4 July–12 August 2011), to General Assembly, Supplement No. 10 (A/66/10), p. 358.

Jensen Eric Talbot, The International Law of Environmental Warfare: Active and Passive Damage During Armed Conflict, Vol. 38 (1), *Vanderbilt Journal of Transnational Law* (2005), p. 145-185.

Jensen Eric Talbot and James J. Teixeira, Prosecuting Members of the US Military for Wartime Environmental Crimes, Vo. 17, *The Georgetown International Environmental Law Review*, (2004-05), p. 651-671.

Jones Carol A. 2000. 'Restoration-based Approach to Compensation for Natural Resource Damage: Moving Towards Convergence in US and International Law', In Austin, Jay E., and Bruch, Carl E., (ed.), *The Environmental Consequences of War: Legal, Economic and Scientific Perspectives*, Cambridge: Cambridge University Press.

Jongerden, Joost, et.al., Forest burning as a counterinsurgency strategy, 2006, available at:

http://www.joostjongerden.info/ForestBurning_website.pdf.

Jorgensen Nikolai, The Protection of Freshwater in Armed Conflict, Vol. 3 (2), *Journal of International Law and International Relations*, 2007, p. 57-96.

Kaczan, D., and R. E. Smith. "War-Related Forest Loss and Carbon Emissions: Evidence from Ukraine." *Environmental Research Letters*, 2025.

Kanyamibwa Samuel, Impact of War on Conservation: Rwandan Environment and Wildlife in Agony, Vol. 7, *Biodiversity and Conservation*, 1998, p. 1399-1406.

Kapoor, Radhika, and Dustin A. Lewis. "UN Security Council Practice on the Environment and Armed Conflict." *International*

Review of the Red Cross, no. 924, (2023), pp. 1646-1667. Kellenberger, Jakob. "The ICRC's Evolving Role in Environmental Protection in Conflict." *International Review of the Red Cross*, vol. 105, no. 924, (2023), pp. 1134–1149.

Keller, Laura. "Toxic Remnants of War: Chemical and Industrial Risks in Contemporary Conflicts." *Environmental Science & Policy*, vol. 128, (2022), pp. 47–66.

Kellman Barry. 2000. 'The Chemical Weapons Convention: A Verification and Enforcement Model for Determining Legal Responsibility for Environmental Harm Caused by War', in Austin, Jay E., and Bruch, Carl E., (ed.), *The Environmental Consequences of War: Legal, Economic and Scientific Perspectives*, Cambridge: Cambridge University Press.

Kelly Katherine M., Declaring War on the Environment: The Failure of International Environmental Treaties During the Persian Gulf War, Vol. 7, *American University Journal of International Law and Policy*, (1992), p. 921-950.

Kemkar Neal A, Environmental Peacemaking: Ending Conflict between India and Pakistan on the Siachin Glacier through the Creation of a Trans-boundary Peace Park, *Stanford Environmental Law Journal*, Vol. 25 (1), (2006), p. 1-56.

Kerbrat Yann and Sandrine Maljean-Dubosos (eds.). 2011. *The Transformation of International Environmental Law*, Oxford UK: Hart Publishing Ltd.

Kerr Glenn and Barry Snushall. 2005. *Future Environmental Policy Trend to 2020: Impact on Ship Design and Operation*, Centre for Maritime Policy, University of Wollongong, Commonwealth of Australia.

Khalil, Samer, et al. "Sustainability amid Conflict: Gaza's Environmental, Social, and Economic Struggles." *Journal of Environmental Management*, vol. 358, (2025). Available online at https://www.sciencedirect.com/science/article/pii/S0301479725004098.

Khan Imtiyaz Gul, Afghanistan: Human Cost of Armed Conflict since Soviet Invasion, Vol. XVII, No. 4, *Perceptions*, Winter 2012, p. 209-224.

Killean, Ruaridh. "A Critical Defence of the Crime of Ecocide." *The International Journal of Human Rights & the Environment*, 2025.

Available online at: https://www.tandfonline.com/doi/full/10.1080/09644016.2025.2492441

Kirby Alex, World 'Needs Green Geneva Convention', 10 February 2003, available at http://news.bbc.co.uk/1/hi/sci/tech/2744359.stm.

Kiss Alexandre, International Humanitarian Law and the Environment, *Environmental policy and Law*, Vol. 31/4-5, (2001), p. 223-231.

Kiss Alexandre, State Responsibility and Liability for Nuclear Damage, Vol. 35 (a), *Denv. J. Int'l L.& Pol'y,* (2006), p. 67-83.

Kirk Talbott & Melissa Brown, Forest Plunder in Southeast Asia: An Environmental Security Nexus in Burma and Cambodia, Environmental Change & Security Project Rep., Spring 1998.

Koda, Shinichi, et al. "Assessing Environmental Damage Caused by Armed Conflict: New Methodologies and Challenges." *International Review of the Red Cross*, vol. 105, no. 924, (2023), pp. 1372–1389.

Kolesnikov Sergei and Aleksander Yemelyanenkov, 'Nuclear Pollution in the Former USSR, in Taipale Ilkka, P. Helena Makela and Kati Juva (ed.). 2001. *War or Health? A Reader*, London: Zed Books, p. 420-425.

Kong, Lingjie, and Yuqing Zhao. "Remedying the Environmental Impacts of War: Challenges for Reparation." *International Review of the Red Cross*, no. 924, (2023), pp. 1441-1462.

Koplow David A. 2001. 'Green Chemistry: Dismantling Chemical Weapons While Protecting the Environment', in Guruswamy Lakshman D (ed.) *Arms Control and the Environment*, New York: Transnational Publishers, Inc, p. 143-157.

Koppe Erik. 2008. *The Use of Nuclear weapons and the Protection of Environment During International Armed Conflict*, USA, Oregon: Oxford and Portland.

Kravchenko, Olga. "Toxic Fallout from Shelling of Industrial Sites in Eastern Ukraine." *Environment International*, vol. 192, (2024), pp. 120–145.

Kritsiotis, Dino, The fate of nuclear weapons after the 1996 advisory opinions of the world court, *Journal of Armed Conflict Law*, 1996, p. 95-119.

Landel Morgane, Are Aerial Fumigations in the Context of the War in Colombia a Violation of the Rules of International Humanitarian

Law? Vol. 19, *Transnational Law & Contemporary Problems*, Spring 2010, p. 491-513.

Lanier-Graham Susan D. 1993. *The Ecology of War: Environmental Impacts of Weaponry and Warfare*, New York: Walker and Company.

Larsson Marie-Louise, Legal Definitions of the Environment and of Environmental Damage, Stockholm Institute for Scandinavian Law, Available at:

http://www.scandinavianlaw.se/pdf/38-7.pdf.

Lawrence C. Jessica and Heller Kevin Jon, The First Eco-Centric Environmental War Crime: The Limits of Article 8(2)(b)(iv) of the Rome Statute, Vol. 20 (1), *Georgetown International Environmental Law Review*, Fall 2007, p. 61-96.

Le Billon Philippe, The Political Ecology of War: Natural Resources and Armed Conflicts, Vol. 20, *Political Geography*, 2001, p. 561–584.

Leal Filho, Walter, et al. "War in Ukraine: Environmental Impacts and Human Health." *Frontiers in Sustainable Resource Management*, vol. 3, (2024).

Leaning Jennifer, Environment and health: Impact of war, *Canadian Medical Association Journal*, October 31, 2000, 163(9): 1157-1161.

Leibler Anthony, Deliberate Wartime Environmental Damage: New Challenges for International Law, *California Western International Law Journal*, Vol. 23, No. 1, 1992-1993, p. 67-137.

Lewis Jeff, Unexploded Ordnance and the Environment – a Legacy of Past Practices, Vol. 10. No. 4, *Canadian Military Journal*, (2009), p. 46-52.

Lind Jeremy and Kathryn Sturman. 2002. *Scarcity and Surfeit: The Ecology of Africa's Conflict*, South Africa: Institute for Security Studies.

Linda Nowlan. 2001. *Arctic Legal Regime for Environmental Protection.* IUCN, Gland, Switzerland and Cambridge, UK and ICEL, Bonn, Germany, p. 70.

Lindsey, P., and H. J. Cooper. "Military Activities and Wildlife Conservation: A Review of Recent Conflicts." *Conservation Biology*, (2022).

Littlewood, Jez. 2005. *The Biological Weapons Convention: A Failed Revolution*, England: Ashgate.

Livingstone Ann and Kristine St-Pierre (eds.). 2009. *Environmental Considerations for Building Peace*, The Pearson Papers, Vol. 12, Canada: Pearson Peacekeeping Centre.

Loets Adrian, An Old Debate Revisited: Applicability of Environmental Treaties in Times of International Armed Conflict Pursuant to the International Law Commission's 'Draft Articles on the Effects of Armed Conflict on Treaties', Vol. 21 (2), *RECIEL*, 2012, p. 127-136.

Lopez Aurelie, The Protection of Environmentally-Displaced Persons in International Law, Vol. 37, *Environmental Law*, (2007), p. 365-409.

Lopez Aurelie, Criminal Liability for Environmental Damage Occurring in Time of Non-International Armed Conflict: Rights and Remedies, Vol. 18, *Fordham Environmental Law Review*, (2006-2007), p. 247-248.

Loretz John, The Animal Victims of the Gulf War, The PSR Quarterly, December 1991, Vol. 1, No. 4, p. 221-225. Available at: http://www.ippnw.org/pdf/mgs/psr-1-4-loretz.pdf.

Low Luan and David Hodgkinson, Compensation for Wartime Environmental Damage: Challenges to International Law After the Gulf War, Vol. 35, No. 2, *Virginia Journal of International Law*, (1995), p. 405-483.

Luck Edward C, *Environmental Emergencies and the Responsibility to Protect: A Bridge Too Far*, American Society of International Law, Proceedings of the 103rd Annual Meeting, March 25-28, 2009, Washington, DC, p. 32-38.

Lujala, Paivi, The Spoils of Nature: Armed civil Conflict and Rebel Access to Natural resources, Vol. 47 (1), *Journal of Peace Research*, (2010), p. 15-28.

Lundberg Michael A. The Plunder of Natural Resources during War: A War Crime, Vol. 39 (3), *Georgetown Journal of International Law*, (2008), p. 495-525.

MacKenzie Catherine P., Barking Up the Wrong Tree: Current Challenges in International Environmental Law, Vol. 58, *Virginia Lawyer*, February 2010, p. 44-49.

Machlis Gary E. and Thor Hanson, Warfare Ecology, Vol. 58, No. 8, *BioScience*, September 2008, pp. 729-736.

Majeed Abeer. 2004. *The Impact of Militarism on the Environment: An Overview of Direct & Indirect Effects*, 2004, Canada: Physicians for Global Survival.

Malone Linda A, *Green Helmets: Eco-Intervention in the Twenty-first Century*, American Society of International Law, Proceedings of the 103rd Annual Meeting, 2009, Washington, DC, p. 19-27.

Malone Linda A, Green Helmets: A Conceptual Framework for Security Council Authority in Environmental Matters, Vol. 17, *Michigan Journal of International Law*, 1996, p. 515-536.

Mannion A.M., 2003, T*he Environmental Impact of War and Terrorism*, Geographical Paper No 169, Department of Geography, University of Reading, Whiteknights, UK.

Manual on International Law Applicable to Air and Missile Warfare. 2009. Harvard University, Program on Humanitarian Policy and Conflict Research (HPCR), Bern.

Marauhn Thilo, Environmental damage in times of armed conflict not really a matter of criminal responsibility? *International Review of the Red Cross*, No. 840, (2000), p. 1029-1036.

Marauhn Thilo, Georg Nolte, and Andreas Paulus, Possible Future Trends in International Humanitarian Law, Vol. 28, No. 3-6, *Human Rights Journal*, August 31, 2007, p. 65-75.

Margitay, L., O. Oshurkevych-Pankivska, and Y. Pankivskyi. "Consequences of the Ongoing War in Ukraine on the Environment." *Grassroots Journal of Natural Resources*, vol. 8, no. 1, 2025, pp. 35–51.

Marsh Jeremy J., *Lex Lata* or *Lex Ferenda?*: Rule 45 of the ICRC Study on Customary International Humanitarian Law, Vol. 198, *Military Law Review*, 2008, p. 116-164.

Martin Jean-Christophe. 2011. 'The United Nations Compensation Commission Practice with Regards to Environmental Claims', in Kerbrat Yann and Sandrine Maljean-Dubosos (ed.), *The Transformation of International Environmental Law*, Oxford UK: Hart Publishing Ltd, p. 253-55.

Mason, Michael, 'The application of warfare ecology to belligerent Occupations', in Machlis, Gary and Hanson, Thorand Spiric, Zdravko and McKendry, J. E., (eds.). 2011. *Warfare Ecology: a new synthesis for peace and security*, Germany: Springer, Dordrecht.

Mason, Simon A., and Adrian Muller. 2008. *Linking Environment and Conflict Prevention: The Role of the United Nations*, Centre for Security Studies (CSS), ETH Zurich.

Massingham, Eve, et al. "War in Cities: Why the Protection of the Natural Environment Matters…" *International Review of the Red Cross*, vol. 105, no. 924, (2023), pp.1313–1336.

Matheson Michael J., The Environmental Effects of Nuclear Weapons and the 1996 World Court Opinion, Vol. 25 (3), *Vermont Law Review*, (2000-2001), p. 773-777.

Mathien Timothy R., Environmental Protection and the Law of Armed Conflict: A Study of Current Provisions and a Recommendation for the Future, Vol. VIII, *The Bowdoin Forum: Journal of International Affairs*, Spring 2005, p. 37-65.

Matousek Jiri. 1990. The Release in War of Dangerous Forces from Chemical Facilities, in Westing Arthur H (ed.), *Environmental Hazards of War: Releasing Dangerous Forces in an Industrialized World*, New Delhi: Sage. p. 30-37.

Mavhunga, Tendai. "Mining, Conflict and the Environment in the Sahel." *Environmental Science & Policy*, vol. 146, (2024), pp. 141–158.

Mavrofides, Maria. "Environmental Damage from Conflict-Induced Displacement." *International Review of the Red Cross*, vol. 105, no. 923, (2023), pp. 132–159.

McCallion K.F., Sharma R.H., Environmental justice without borders: The need for an international court of the environment to protect fundamental environmental rights, Vol. 32, No. 3, *The George Washington Journal of International Law and Economics*, (2000), p. 351-365.

McDonald Avril, Jann K. Kleffner and Brigit Toebes (eds). 2008. *Depleted Uranium Weapons and International Law: A Precautionary Approach*, T.M.C. Asser Press.

McEwan A.C. 1988. 'Environmental Effects of Underground Nuclear Explosions', in Goldblat Jozef and David Cox (ed.), *Nuclear Weapon Tests: Prohibition or Limitation*, SIPRI, Oxford: Oxford University Press.

McLaughlin Kathryn and Kathryn Nixdorff (ed.), *Biological Weapons Reader*, The Bio-Weapons Prevention Project (BWPP), Geneva, 2009.

McManus Keith P., Civil Liability for Wartime Environmental Damage: Adapting the United Nations Compensation Commission for the Iraq War, Vol. 33, No. 2, *Boston College Environmental Affairs Law Review*, (2006), p. 417-448.

McNaught L.W. 1984. *Nuclear Weapons and Their Effects*, London: Brassey's Defence Publishers.

McNeely Jeffery A. 2001. 'Environmental Impacts of Arms and War', in Guruswamy Lakshman D (ed.) *Arms Control and the Environment*, New York: Transnational Publishers, Inc, p. 41-58.

McNeely Jeffrey A., Conserving Forest Biodiversity in times of Violent Conflict, *Oryx*, Vol. 37, No.2, April 2003, p. 142-152.

McNeely Jeffery A. 2000. 'War and Biodiversity: An Assessment of Impacts, In Austin, Jay E., and Bruch, Carl E., (ed.), *The Environmental Consequences of War: Legal, Economic and Scientific Perspectives*, Cambridge: Cambridge University Press.

McNeill J.R., 'The Global Environmental Footprint of the US Military', in Closmann Charles E., (ed.). 2009. *War and the Environment: Military Destruction in the Modern Age*, USA: Texas A&M University Press, p.10-31.

Megret Frederic, The Problem of an International Criminal Law of the Environment, Vol. 36 (2), *Columbia Journal of Environmental Law*, (2011), p. 195-257.

Meisels, Tamar. "Environmental Ethics of War: Jus ad Bellum, Jus in Bello, and the Natural Environment." *Conatus: Journal of Philosophy*, vol. 8, no. 2, (2023).

Mensah Thomas A. 2000. 'Environmental Damage Under the Law of Sea Convention', In Austin, Jay E., and Bruch, Carl E., (ed.), *The Environmental Consequences of War: Legal, Economic and Scientific Perspectives*, Cambridge: Cambridge University Press.

Miguel Edward and Gerard Roland, The Long-run Impact of Bombing Vietnam, Vol. 96, *Journal of Development Economics*, 2011, p. 1-15.

Miller Jeferey G. 2000. 'Civil Liability for War-caused Environmental damage: Model from United States Law', In Austin, Jay E., and Bruch, Carl E., (ed.), *The Environmental Consequences of War: Legal, Economic and Scientific Perspectives*, Cambridge: Cambridge University Press.

Mingashang, Ivon, and Christian Tshiamala Banungana. "The International Responsibility of a Belligerent State in the Event of Transboundary Environmental Damage." *International Review of the Red Cross*, vol. 106, no. 925, (2024), p. 469.

Minkova, Lyubomira G. "Ecocide, Sustainable Development and Critical Environmental Law Perspectives." *Journal of International Criminal Justice*, vol. 22, no. 1, (2024), pp. 105–130.

Mishra Charudutt and Anthony Fitzherbert, War and wildlife: a post-conflict assessment of Afghanistan's Wakhan Corridor, Vol. 38, No. 1, *Oryx*, January 2004, p. 102-105.

Moret Leuren, Depleted Uranium: The Trojan Horse of Nuclear War, Vol. 8, No. 2, *World Affairs*, p. 110-135.

Mosher David E., Beth E. Lachman, Michael D. Greenberg, Tiffany Nichols, Brian Rosen, Henry H. Willis. 2008. *Green Warriors: Army Environmental Considerations for Contingency Operations from Planning Through Post-Conflict*, RAND Corporation.

Mossalanejad A., International Security through Environmental Challenges, *Int. J. Environ. Res.*, Vol. 3 (3), Summer 2009, p. 429-434.

Moxley, Charles J., John Burroughs, and Jonathan Granoff, Nuclear Weapons and Compliance with International Humanitarian Law and the Nuclear Non-Proliferation Treaty, Vol. 34, *Fordham International Law Journal,* (2011), p. 595-697.

Murphy Mark, Krishna Prasad Oli, & Steve Gorzula. 2005. *Conservation in conflict: The impact of the Maoist-government conflict on conservation and biodiversity in Nepal.* Winnipeg: International Institute for Sustainable Development.

Murray Richard R. & Kellye L. Fabian, Compensating the World's Landmine victims: Legal Liability and Anti-Personnel Landmine Producers, Vol. 33, *Seton Hall Law Review*, (2003), pp. 303-369.

Muylaert, Anne. "Climate, Conflict, and the Ecology of War." *International Review of the Red Cross*, vol. 106, no. 926, (2024), pp. 149–176.

Nagle Luz E., Placing Blame Where Blame is Due: The Culpability of Illegal Armed Groups in Narco-traffickers in Colombia's Environmental and Human Rights Catastrophes, Vol. 29, *William & Marry Environmental Law and Policy Review*, (2004), p.1-106.

Nair Pavan, The Siachin War: Twenty-five Years On, *Economic & Political Weekly*, March 14, 2009, Vol XLIV, No. 11, p. 35-40.

Nanda, Ved P., International Environmental Norms Applicable to Nuclear Activities, With Particular Focus on Decisions of International Tribunals and International Settlements, Vol. 35 (1), *Denv. J. Int'l L & Policy*, (2006), p. 47-65.

Nasr, D, et. al., Environmental Impacts of Reconstruction Activities: A Case of Lebanon, Vol. 3, No. 2, *Int. J. Environ. Res.*, Spring 2009, p.301-308.

Nicolson Garth L and Marawn Nasralla, 'Gulf War Illnesses', in Taipale Ilkka, P. Helena Makela and Kati Juva (ed.) 2001. *War or Health? A Reader*, London: Zed Books, p. 431-46.

O'Rourke, Catherine, and Ana Martin. "Gender, Conflict and the Environment." *International Review of the Red Cross*, vol. 105, no. 924, (2023), pp. 1600-1622.

Obregón Gieseken, Helen, and Vanessa Murphy. "The Protection of the Natural Environment under International Humanitarian Law: The ICRC's 2020 Guidelines." *International Review of the Red Cross*, vol. 105, no. 924, (2023), pp. 1180–1207.

Okowa Phoebe. 2009. 'Environmental Justice in Situations of Armed Conflict', in Ebbesson Johan and Phoebe Okawa (eds.), *Environmental Law and Justice in Context,* Cambridge: Cambridge University Press, p. 246-47.

Okowa Phoebe N., Natural Resources in Situations of Armed Conflict: Is There a Coherent Framework for Protection? Vol. 9, No. 3, *International Community Law Review*, 2007, p. 237-262.

Omar, Samira A., E. Briskey, R. Misak, and Adel Asem. 2000. "The Gulf War Impact on the Terrestrial Environment of Kuwait: An Overview." In *The Environmental Consequences of War: Legal, Economic, and Scientific Perspectives.* J. Austin and C. Bruch, (eds.), Cambridge: Cambridge University Press, p. 316–337.

Orellana Marcos A. Criminal Prosecution for Environmental Damage: Individual and State Responsibility at a Crossroad, Vol. 17 (2004-2005), *The Georgetown International Environmental Law Review*, p. 673-696.

Page Edward, Theorizing the Link Between Environmental Change and Security, *RECIEL*, Vol. 9 (1), 2000, p. 33-43.

Pantazopoulos, Stavros-Evdokimos. "Navigating Legal Frontiers: Climate Change, Environmental Protection and Armed Conflict." *International Review of the Red Cross*, vol. 106, no. 925, (2024), pp. 366–392.

Parsons, Rymn James, The fight to save the planet: US Armed Forces, 'Greenkeeping', and Enforcement of the law pertaining to environmental protection during armed conflict, Vol. 10, No. 2, *Georgetown International Environmental Law Review*, 1998, p. 482.

Partow Hassan, Environmental Impact of Wars and Conflicts, available at: http://www.afedonline.org/afedreport/english/book12.pdf.

Percival Robert V., Liability for Environmental Harm and Emerging Global Environmental Law, Vol. 25, *Maryland Journal of International Law*, (2010), p. 37-63.

Peterson Ines, The Natural Environment in Times of Armed Conflict: A Concern for International War Crimes Law? *Leiden Journal of International Law*, Vol. 22, issue 2, (2009), p. 325-343.

Peytrignet Gerard, Protection of the Natural Environment in Time of Conflict: Overview of the State of International Humanitarian Law and the Position of the International Committee of the Red Cross (ICRC), available at: http://www.bibliojuridica.org/libros/4/1985/15.pdf.

Plant Glen. 1993. 'Environmental Damage and the Laws of War: Points Addressed to Military Lawyers', in Fox Hazel & Meyer Michael A. (eds.), *Armed Conflict and the New Law, Volume II – Effecting Compliance*, p. 159-174.

Plant, Glen. 1992. *Environmental Protection and the Law of War: a fifth Geneva convention on the protection of the environment in the time of armed conflict*. London; New York: Belhaven, Press.

Polkinghorne Michael and James Cockayne, Dealing with the Risks and Responsibilities of Landmines and their Clearance, Vol. 25, Issue 5, *Fordham International Law Journal*, (2001), p.1187-1204.

Poll Letetia van der and Ashraf Booley, In Our Common Interest: Liability and Redress for Damage Caused to the Natural Environment During Armed Conflict, Vol. 15, *Law, Democracy & Development*, (2011), p. 1-43.

Popovsky Mark, Nanotechnology and Environmental Insurance, Vol. 36, No. 1, *Columbia Journal of Environmental Law*, 2011, p.125-161.

Price, S. V. (ed.). (2003). *War and Tropical Forests: Conservation in Areas of Armed Conflicts*, New York: Food Products Press.

Protecting the Environment During Armed Conflict: An Inventory and Analysis of International Law, November 2009, UNEP, pp.79.

Puleo Lt. Col. Louis J., Conservation Issues on Military Land: Some Thoughts on a Framework for Successful Mission Integration, Vol. 17 (2), *Journal of Land Use and Environmental Law*, (Spring 2002), p. 413-439.

Qandeel, Mais. "The Protection of the Natural Environment in Armed Conflicts and Agent-Based Modelling." *International Review of the Red Cross*, vol. 106, no. 925, (2024), pp. 450–468.

Quinn John P., Richard T. Evans and Michael J. Boock. 2000. 'United States Navy Dvelopment of Operational Environmental Doctrine', In Austin, Jay E., and Bruch, Carl E., (ed.), *The Environmental Consequences of War: Legal, Economic and Scientific Perspectives*, Cambridge: Cambridge University Press, p.156-170.

Rahman Chris and Robert J. Davitt. 2006. *ADF Training in Australia's Maritime Environment*, Papers in Australian Maritime Affairs, No. 18, Australia: University of Wollongong, p. 72.

Rao, N.H., Environmental management: Relevance and implications for management of defence installations for sustainability, *Current Science*, Vol. 88, No. 11, 10 June 2005, p. 1753-1758.

Rappert Brian. 2006. *Controlling the Weapons of War: Politics, Persuasion and the Prohibition of Inhumanity*, London: Routledge.

Rawcliffe, Maj John (ed.), *Operational Law Handbook-JA 422, International and Operational Law*, The Judge Advocate General's Legal Centre and School, US Army, Virginia, 2007.

Raymond, Catherine. "Urban Warfare and Environmental Collapse." *International Review of the Red Cross*, vol. 106, no. 926, 2024, pp. 293–321. (2024).

Reichberg Gregory & Syse Henrik, Protecting the Natural Environment in Wartime: Ethical Considerations from the Just War Tradition, Vol. 37, No. 4 *Journal of Peace Research*, 2000, p. 449-468.

Renaud, Fabrice, and S. Pomponi. "Maritime Pollution and Warfare: Oil, Ports and Underwater Infrastructure." *Marine Policy*, 2021. (2021).

Rest Alfred, Enhanced Implementation of International Environmental Treaties by Judiciary-Access to Justice in International Environmental Law for Individuals and NGOs: Efficacious Enforcement by the Permanent Court of Arbitration, Vol. 1, *MqJICL*, p. 1028,

Reyhani Roman O., The Protection of the Environment During Armed Conflict, Vol. 14, No. 2, *Missouri Environmental Law and Policy Review*, 2007, p. 323-338.

Richards Peter J. & Schmitt Michael N., Mars Meets Mother Nature: Protecting the Environment During Armed Conflict, Vol. 28, No. 4, *Stetson Law Review*, (1999), p. 1047-1092.

Richter Elihu, et. al., Ecocide: A Crime Against Humanity, available at: http://beta.genocidepreventionnow.org/Portals/0/docs/Ecocide_Collegium%20Ramazzini_Richter.pdf.

Riordan Kevin, Protecting Fundamental Human Rights in Times of War—The Means and Methods of Warfare, Human Rights Research, available at: http://www.victoria.ac.nz/nzcpl/HRRJ/vol3/Riordan.pdf.

Roberts Adam. 2000. 'The Law of War and Environmental Damage', In Austin, Jay E., and Bruch, Carl E., (ed.), *The Environmental Consequences of War: Legal, Economic and Scientific Perspectives*, Cambridge: Cambridge University Press.

Roberts Adam, 'Failure in Protecting the Environment in the 1990-1991 Gulf War, in Rowe Peter (ed.). 1993. *The Gulf War 1990-1991 in International and English Law*, London: Sweet and Maxwell, p.111-154.

Roberts Adam, Environmental Destruction in the Gulf War", No. 291, *International Review of the Red Cross*, November-December 1992, p. 538-553.

Roberts Michael, Oil War II: The Environmental Consequences, available at:

http://www.ecu.edu.au/chs/cem/research/reviews%20&%20articles/articles/M_Roberts_art.pdf.

Robinson J.P. Perry, Difficulties facing the Chemical Weapons Convention, Vol. 84, No. 2, *International Affairs*, (2008), p. 223-239.

Robyn Eckersley, Ecological Intervention: Prospects and Limits, available at:

http://www.redorbit.com/news/science/1101311/ecological_intervention_prospects_and_limits/index.html.

Roka Krishna B., Armed Conflict and its Impact on Community Forestry in Nepal, Vol. 26, *Tropical Resources Bulletin*, Spring 2007, Yale Tropical Resource Institute, Yale School of Forestry and Environmental Studies, p. 55-62.

Roscini Marco. 2009. Protection of the Natural Environment in the Time of Armed Conflict, in Bhuiyan Md. J. H., Louise Doswald-Beck, and A.R. Chowdhury (eds.) *International Humanitarian Law - An Anthology*, Nagpur: LexisNexis Butterworths, p. 155-179.

Ross, Marc A., Environmental warfare and the Persian Gulf War: possible remedies to combat intentional destruction of the environment', Vol. 10, *Dickinson Journal of Environmental Law and Policy*, 1992, p. 534.

Rubenson David, Jerry Aroesty and Charles Thompsen, Two Shades of Green: Environmental Protection and Combat Training, RAND's Army Research Division for United States Army.

Sadik M. and McCain J.C. 1993. *The Gulf War Aftermath: An Environmental Tragedy*, Springer.

Saillan Charles de, Disposal of Spent Nuclear Fuel in the United Sates and Europe: A Persistent Environmental Problem, Vol. 34, *Harvard Environmental Law Review*, (2010), p. 461-519.

Saleem Farrukh, Strategic Dialogue is the only answer, *The Times of India*, 17 January 2010.

Sand Peter H., International Environmental Law After Rio, Vo. 4, *EJIL*, (1993), p. 377-389.

Sandoval, Clara. "Environmental Reparations for War-Related Harm: A Victim-Centered Approach." *International Review of the Red Cross*, vol. 106, no. 926, (2024), pp. 210–236.

Sandoz Yves, Chrisotphe Swinarski and Bruno Zimmermann (eds.). 1987. *Commentary on the Additional Protocols of 8 June 1977 to the Geneva Conventions of 12 August 1949*, International Committee of the Red Cross, Geneva: Martinus Nijhoff Publishers.

Sands Philippe. 2003. *Principles of International Environmental Law*, New York: Cambridge University Press, p. 219-316.

Santiapillai Charles and S. Wijeyamohan, The Impact of Civil War on Wildlife in Sri Lanka, *Current Science*, Vol. 84, No. 9, 10 May 2003.

Sassoli Marco, Antoine A. Bouvier and Anne Quintin, 2011. *How Does Law Protect in War?* Volume II, Part II: Cases and Documents, Geneva: International Committee of the Red Cross, p. 621-622.

Sassoli, Marco, State responsibility for violations of international humanitarian law, *International Review of the Red Cross*, Vol. 84, No. 846, June 2002, p. 401-433.

Scheetz Lori, Infusing Environmental Ethics into the Space Weapons Dialogue, Vol. 19, No. 1, *Georgetown International Environmental Law Review*, Fall 2006, p. 57-82.

Schmitt Michal N., Green War: An Assessment of the Environmental law of International Armed Conflict, Vol. 22, No.1, *Yale Journal of International Law*, Winter 1997, p. 1-109.

Schmitt Michael N., Humanitarian Law and the Environment, Vol. 28 (3), *Denv. J. International Law & Policy*, (2000), p. 265-323.

Schmitt Michael N., Investigating Violations of International Law in Armed Conflict, Vol. 2, *Harvard National Security Journal*, (2011), p. 31-84.

Schmitt Michael N. 2000. 'War and the Environment: Fault Line in the Perspective and Landscape', In Austin, Jay E., and Bruch, Carl E., (ed.), *The Environmental Consequences of War: Legal, Economic and Scientific Perspectives*, Cambridge: Cambridge University Press.

Schmitt Michael N., The Environmental Law of War: An Invitation to Critical Re-examination, Vol. 6, *Journal of Legal Studies*, 1995-96, p. 237-271.

Schofield Timothy, The Environment as an Ideological Weapon: A Proposal to Criminalize Environmental Terrorism, Vol. 26, Issue 3, *Boston College Environmental Affairs Law Review*, (1999), p. 619-647.

Schwabach Aaron, Ecocide and Genocide in Iraq: International Law, the Marsh Arabs and Environmental Damage in Non-international Conflicts, (2004), The Berkeley Electronic Press.

Schwabach Aaron, Environmental Damage Resulting from the NATO Military Action Against Yugoslavia, Vol. 25, No. 1, *Columbia Journal of Environmental Law*, (2000), p. 117-140.

Schwabach Aaron, Humanitarian Intervention and Environmental Protection: The Effect of the Kosovo War on the Law of War, Vol. 6, *Columbia Journal of Eastern European Law*, (2001), p. 405.

Schwabach Aaron, Law Regarding Protection of the Environment During Wartime, International Law and Institutions, p. 1-7. Available at: http://www.eolss.net/Sample-Chapters/C14/E1-36-02-04.pdf.

Schwartz, Daniel M., Environmental Terrorism: Analyzing the Concept, Vol, 35, No. 4, *Journal of Peace Research*, (July 1998), p. 483-496.

Scott Karen N. International Environmental Governance: Managing Fragmentation through Institutional Connection, Vol. 12, Issue 1, *Melbourne Journal of International Law*, June 2011, p. 177-216.

Scovazzi Tullio, State Responsibility for Environmental Harm, Ulfstein Geir and Jacob Werksman (ed.), *Yearbook of International Environmental Law*, Vol. 12 (2001), p. 43-67.

Seacor Jesica E., Environmental Terrorism: Lessons from the Oil Fires of Kuwait, Vol. 10, *AM U. J. INT'L L. & POL'Y*, 1994, p. 481-523.

Shaheen, Ali. "The War on the Gaza Strip and Its Consequences on Global Environmental Systems." *Frontiers in Human Dynamics*, 2024. (2024). Available online at https://www.frontiersin.org/journals/human-dynamics/articles/10.3389/fhumd.2024.1463902/full.

Shakya, M. M. and A. Chitrakar (ed.). 2006. *Cost of Conflict on Nepal's Conservation Efforts*, Nepal, Kathmandu: Wildlife Watch Group.

Shambaugh, J., J. Oglethorpe, and R. Ham with contributions from S. Tognetti. 2001. *The Trampled Grass: Mitigating the Impacts of Armed Conflict on the Environment.* Washington, DC: Biodiversity Support Program.

Shapiro, Judith. 2001. *Mao's War Against Nature.* Cambridge: Cambridge University Press.

Sharp Peter, Prospects for Environmental Liability in the International Criminal Court, Vol. 18, No. 2, *Virginia Environmental Law Journal*, 1999, p. 217-243.

Sharp Walter G., The Effective Deterrence of Environmental Damage During Armed Conflict: A Case Analysis of the Persian Gulf War, Vol. 137, Military Law Review, (1992), p.1-66.

Shelton Dinah and Kiss Alexandre, Martens Clause for Environmental Protection, Vol. 30, No. 6, *Environmental Policy and Law*, (2000), p. 285-86.

Sherman Wesley, The Economics of Enforcing Environmental Laws: A Case for Limiting the Use of Criminal Sanctions, Vol. 23 (1), *Journal of Land Use*, Fall-2007, p-87-110.

Shrestha, R. B. and S. Suvedi. 2006. 'Impact of insurgency on community forestry program in Nepal', in Shakya M.M. and A. Chitrakar, *Cost of Conflict on Nepal's Conservation Efforts*, Kathmandu, Nepal, Wildlife Watch Group, p. 209-221.

Shumilova, Oleksandra, et al. "Kakhovka Dam Destruction: Heavy Metals, Sediments and Long-Term Risks." *Environmental Sciences Research Report*, (2025). Available online at https://www.theguardian.com/world/2025/mar/13/destruction-of-ukraine-kakhovka-dam-caused-toxic-timebomb-in-rivers-study-finds.

Sidel Victor W. 2000. 'The Impact of Military Preparedness and Militarism on Health and Environment', In Austin, Jay E., and Bruch, Carl E., (ed.), *The Environmental Consequences of War: Legal, Economic and Scientific Perspectives*, Cambridge: Cambridge University Press, p. 426-443.

Sidel Victor W., Barry S. Levy, and Jonathan E. Slutzman, Prevention of War and Its Environmental Consequences, *Hdb Env Chem*, 2009, p. 21-39.

Sieg Richard, A Call to Minimize the Use of Nuclear Power in the Twenty-first Century, Vol. 9, *Vermont Journal of Environmental Law*, (2008), p. 305-373.

Sierra Leone: Environment, Conflict and Peace-building Assessment, Technical Report, 2010, United Nations Environment Programme, Nairobi.

Sills Joe, Jerome C. Glenn, Elizabeth Florescu and Theodore J. Gordon, *Environmental Crimes in Military Actions and the International Criminal Court -- United Nations Perspectives*, April 2001, Army Environmental Policy Institute, Atlanta.

Simonds S.N., Conventional warfare and Environmental damage Vol. 29, *Stanford Journal of International Law*, (1992), p. 165.

Sinha Uttam Kumar, Environmental Stresses and their security Implications for South Asia, Vol. 30, No. 3, *Strategic Analysis*, July-Sep 2006, p. 599-618.

Singh Shubha, Step out of dangerous terrain, *Hindustan Times*, New Delhi, 19 May 2003.

Sjöstedt, Britta, and Karen Hulme. "Re-evaluating IHL in a Triple Planetary Crisis." *International Review of the Red Cross*, vol.105, no. 924, (2023) pp, 1238-1266.

Skons, Elisabeth, *The Costs of Armed Conflict*, Stockholm International Peace Research Institute Project on Military Expenditure and Arms Production, p. 169-190.

Smith, D. 2001. *Trends and Causes of Armed Conflicts,* Berlin: Berghof Research Center for Constructive Conflict Management.

Smith Tara, Creating a Framework for the Prosecution of Environmental Crimes in International Criminal Law, available at: http://ssrn.com/abstract=1957644.

Smith Tara. 2010. Criminal Accountability or Civil Liability: Which Approach Most Effectively Redresses the Negative Environmental Consequences or Armed Conflict? in Quenivet Noelle and Shilan Shah-Davis (ed.), *International Law and Armed Conflict: Challenges in the 21st Century*, TMC Asser Press, p. 95-120.

Solf, Waldemar A., 'Article 55: Protection of the Natural Environment', in Bothe Michael, Karl Josef Partsch, and Waldemar A. Solf. 1982. *New Rules for Victims of Armed Conflict: Commentaries on the Two 1977 Protocols Additional to the Geneva Conventions of 1949*, Nijhoff, The Hague, p. 347.

Solf Waldemar A., Protection of Civilians Against the Effects of Hostilities under Customary International Law and under Protocol I, Vo. 1, No. 1, *AM. U.J. INT'L L. & POL'Y*, 1986, p. 117-135.

Sprinz Detlef F, Modeling Environmental Conflict, p. 1-12, available at: http://www.uni-potsdam.de/u/sprinz/doc/model.pdf.

Stasiuk, Nadiia. "International Legal and National Mechanisms for Overcoming the Environmental Consequences of Russia's Aggression Against Ukraine." *Law. Human. Environment*, vol. 15, no. 3, (2024), pp. 68–84. Available online at https://environmentalscience.com.ua.

Stenhouse M.J. and V.I. Kirko.1998. *Defence Nuclear Waste Disposal in Russia: International Perspective*, NATO ASI Series, Disarmament Technologies Vol. 18, London: Kluwer Academic Publishers.

Stephen Dale, Human Rights and Armed Conflict—The Advisory Opinion of the International Court of Justice in the Nuclear Weapons Case, Vol. 4, *Yale Human Rights & Development L.J.*, 2001, p. 1-24.

Stewart James G., Corporate War Crime: Prosecuting the Pillage of Natural Resources, New York: Open Society Institute, available at: http://www.pillageconference.org/wp-content/themes/pillage-2010/pillage-manual-10-16-2010.pdf.

Stone Christopher D. 2000. 'The Environment in Wartime: An Overview', In Austin, Jay E., and Bruch, Carl E., (ed.), *The Environmental Consequences of War: Legal, Economic and Scientific Perspectives*, Cambridge: Cambridge University Press.

Suba Chandran D and J Jeganaathan (Ed.). 2011. *Energy and Environmental Security: A Cooperative Approach in South Asia*, New Delhi: Institute of Peace and Conflict Studies.

Sundaram Vinothine, Fighting a Chemical War: The Environmental Impact of War on Iraq and Its Neighboring Regions, Available at: http://www.cwru.edu/med/epidbio/mphp439/Chemical_War.pdf.

Symposium: The Environmental Law of War, A Note from the Editors, Vol. 25 (3), *Vermont Law Review*, (2000-2001), p. 649-651.

Szasz Paul C. International Law Applicable to the Gulf War, Vol. XV, No. 2, *Disarmament*, (1992), p. 101-161.

Tarasofsky Richard G, Legal Protection of the Environment During International Armed Conflict, Vol. XXIV, *Netherlands Yearbook of International Law*, (1993), p. 17-79.

Tarlock, A. Dan, In There a There There in Environmental Law? Vol. 19 (2), *Journal of Land Use*, (Spring 2004), p. 213-254.

Taylor Linda A. 2009. 'The United Nations Compensation Commission', in Ferstman Carla et. at., (Eds.), *Reparations for Victims of Genocide, War Crimes and Crimes Against Humanity: Systems in Place and Systems in Making*, Leiden: Martinus Nijhoff Publishers, p. 197-216.

Teclaff Ludwik A., Beyond Restitution—The Case of Ecocide, Vol. 34, *Natural Resources Journal*, Fall 1994, p. 933-956.

The Continuing Environmental Threat of Nuclear Weapons: Integrated Policy Responses, Vol. 88, No.21, *EOS*, 22 May 2007, p. 228-231.

The Environmental Effects of the Gulf War, Gulf War Environmental Information Service: Impact on the Land and Atmosphere, The World Conservation Monitoring Centre, UK: Cambridge.

The Manual of the Law of Armed Conflict, 2004, UK Ministry of Defence, Oxford: Oxford University Press.

The Military Impact on the Human Environment, SIPRI Yearbook, 1978, p. 43-68.

The Military's Impact on the Environment: A Neglected Aspect of Sustainable Development Debate, A Briefing Paper for States and Non-Governmental Organizations, International Peace Bureau, Geneva, August 2002.

heisen Ole Magnus, Blood and Soil? Resource Scarcity and Internal Armed Conflict Revisited, Vol. 45, No. 6, *Journal of Peace Research*, 2008, p. 801-818.

Themner Lotta & Peter Wallensteen, Armed Conflicts, 1946-2011, Vol. 49 (4), *Journal of Peace Research*, p. 565-575.

Thompson Robert, Radioactive Warfare: Depleted Uranium Weapons, the Environment, and International Law, Vol. 36, *Environmental Law Reporter*, 2006, p.10474-10486.

Threat of modern warfare to man and his environment: An Annotated Bibliography, UNESCO Publication No. 40, UNESCO, 1979.

"Three Years of War in Ukraine: 'Environmental Damage Knows No Borders' as Emissions Rise to New High." *Euronews Green*, Available online at (2025).https://www.euronews.com/green/2025/02/24/

three-years-of-war-in-ukraine-environmental-damage-knows-no-borders-as-emissions-rise-to-n.

Thurer Daniel. 2011. *International Humanitarian Law: Theory, Practice and Context*, Hague Academy of International Law.

Thuillier, Rebecca. "The Role of Transitional Justice in Addressing Environmental Damage: Case Studies from Colombia and Bosnia." *Transitional Justice Review*, (2022).

Tignino Mara, Reflections on the Legal Regime of Water during Armed Conflicts, available at: http://www.afes-press.de/pdf/Hague/Tignino_LegalRegime_Water.pdf.

Tignino, Mara, and Tadesse Kebebew. "A Galaxy of Norms: UN Peace Operations and Protection of the Environment." *International Review of the Red Cross*, vol. 105, no. 924, (2023), pp. 1543-1567.

Tompkins, H., and M. K. Reddy. "Assessing the Carbon Footprint of Warfare: Methods and Early Results." *Environmental Science & Policy*, (2023).

Tomuschat Christian, Draft Code of Crimes Against the Peace and Security of Mankind, Extract from the Yearbook of the International Law Commission, 1996.

Toon Owen B., Alan Robock, and Richard P. Turco, Environmental Consequences of Nuclear War, *Physics Today*, December 2008, p. 37-42.

Trail Smelter Case (*United States v. Canada*), 16 April 1938 and 11 March 1941, Reports of International Arbitral Awards (R.I.A.A.), Vol. III, p. 1905.

Tranquillo Nicoletta, 2007. *Green Casualties of War: The need for international protection of the environment during armed conflicts and the case of the war between Israel and Lebanon in 2006*, Sweden: Lund University.

Traoré, Sâ Benjamin, and Ezéchiel Amani Cirimwami. "Environmental Obligations of Business Entities during Armed Conflicts." *International Review of the Red Cross*, vol. 106, no. 925, (2024), pp. 393–423.

Tu Chelsea H., From Norm to Practice: Comparative Case Studies on International Mechanisms for Wartime Environmental Restitution,

12 May 2008, available at: http://nature.berkeley.edu/classes/es196/projects/2008final/Tu_2008.pdf.

Tucker Matthew L, Mitigating Collateral Damage to Natural Environment in Naval Warfare: An Examination of the Israeli Naval Blockade of 2006, Vol. 57 *NAVAL L. REV.* (2009), p. 161-201.

UN General Assembly Resolution 47/37, 9 February 1993, Protection of the Environment in Times of Armed Conflict, UN Doc. A/RES/47/37.

United Nations OCHA. *Environmental and Humanitarian Consequences of Armed Conflict: Selected Case Studies.* (2021–2024). Available online at https://www.unocha.org.

UNECE (Informal Inter-Agency Coordination Group). *Comprehensive Report: Ukraine Environmental Damage Assessments.* Dec. 2023. (2023).

UNEP Report of the international meeting on environmental norms and military activities, UNEP/Env.Law/Mil/IG/1/2, 10 December 2009.

UNEP. *Environmental Assessment of the Gaza Strip.* (2024). Available online at https://www.unep.org.

UNEP. *Pollution Hotspots in Post-Conflict Iraq: Assessment Report.* (2021). Available online at https://www.unep.org/resources/report/pollution-hotspots-post-conflict-iraq.

UNEP. *State of the Environment in Conflict-Affected Regions*, (2025). Available online at https://www.unep.org/resources/report/state-environment-conflict-affected-regions-2025.

UNEP. *Ukraine: Environmental Impact Assessment of Conflict-Affected Regions*, (2024). Available online at https://www.unep.org.

United Nations Environment Programme (UNEP). *Environmental Rule of Law: A Toolkit for Post-Conflict Recovery*, (2022). Available online at https://www.unep.org.

United Nations Environment Programme (UNEP), and United Nations Centre for Human Settlements (UNCHS). 1999. *The Kosovo Conflict: Consequences for the Environment and Human Settlements.* Geneva, Switzerland: UNEP and UNCHS.

Upreti B.C. 2011. 'Conflict in Nepal: Impact on Nepal and its Cross-border Consequences', in Raghavan V.R. (ed.) *Internal Conflict in Nepal:*

Transnational Consequences, New Delhi: Vij Books India Pvt. Ltd. p. 100-118.

Upreti Bishnu Raj. 2004. *The Price of Neglect: From Resource Conflict to Maoist Insurgency in the Himalayan Kingdom,* Nepal: Bhrikuti Academic Publications, Kathmandu.

Vanasselt Wendy, Armed Conflict, Refugees, and the Environment, *World Resources Institute 2002-2004*, June 2003, p. 25-27.

van Steenberghe, Raphaël. "International Environmental Law as a Means for Enhancing the Protection of the Environment in Warfare: A Critical Assessment of Scholarly Theoretical Frameworks." *International Review of the Red Cross*, vol. 105, no. 924, (2023), pp. 1568–1599.

Vander Vyver Johan D., The Environment: State Sovereignty, Human Rights, and Armed Conflict, Vol. 23, No.1, *Emory International Law Review*, 2009, p. 85-112.

Varisco Andrea Edoardo, A Study of the Inter-Relation between Armed Conflict and natural resources and its Implications for Conflict resolution and Peace-building, *Journal of Peace, Conflict and Development*, Issue 15, March 2010.

Vermeer Arjen, The Laws of War in Outer Space: Some Legal Implications for the *Jus ad Bellum* and the *Jus in Bello* of the Militarisation and Weaponisation of Outer Space, p. 1-18.

Verwey Wil D., Observations on the Legal Protection of the Environment in Times of International Armed Conflict, *Hague Yearbook of International Law*, Vol. 7 (1994), p. 35-52.

Verwey Wil D., Protection of the Environment in Times of Armed Conflict: In Search of a New Legal Perspective, Vol. 8 (1), *Leiden Journal of International Law*, 1995. p. 7-40.

Vietnam and US in joint venture to clean up Agent Orange damage, 17 June 2011, available at: http://www.guardian.co.uk/world/2011/jun/17/vietnam-us-agent-orange-damage.

Vinuales, Dr Jorge E., The Contribution of the International Court of Justice to the Development of International Environmental Law: A Contemporary Assessment, Vol. 32 (1), *Fordham International Law Journal*, (2008), p. 232-258.

Voneky Silja, A New Shield for the Environment: Peacetime Treaties as Legal Restraints of Wartime Damage, *RECIEL*, Vol. 9 (1), 2000, p. 20-32.

Vonkey Silja. 2000. Peacetime Environmental Law as a Basis of State Responsibility for Environmental Damage Caused by War', In Austin, Jay E., and Bruch, Carl E., (ed.), *The Environmental Consequences of War: Legal, Economic and Scientific Perspectives*, Cambridge: Cambridge University Press.

Vyver Johan D van der, The Environment: State Sovereignty, Human Rights and Armed Conflict, Vol. 23, No. 1, *Emory International Law Review*, (2009), p. 85-112.

Wall Andru E. 2002. *Legal and Ethical Lessons of NATO's Kosovo Campaign*, International Law Studies, Vol. 78, Newport: Naval War College, pp. 602.

Walsh Nicolas E. & Wendy S. Walsh, Rehabilitation of landmine victims — the ultimate challenge, *Bulletin of the World Health Organization*, 2003, 81 (9), p. 665-670.

Wantuck Marnie, Broken Arrows: Movement Towards Complete Prohibition of Nuclear Weapons through International Environmental Law, Editorial, *Vermont Journal of Environmental Law*, 2005.

War and the Environment, *World Watch Magazine*, January/February 2008, Volume 21, No. 1.

War Impact on Forest resources and Olive Groves in South Lebanon, Association for Forests, Development and Conservation and UNDP, Final Report, May 2007.

Wartiainen, Felicia. "Time for Environmentarian Corridors in Armed Conflict." *International Review of the Red Cross*, vol. 105, no. 924, (2023), pp 1365-1391.

Water and War: ICRC Response, Geneva: ICRC, July 2009.

Waters Christopher and Ashley Barnes, The Arctic Environment and the Law of Armed Conflict, Vol. 6, No. 4, *Canadian Naval Review*, Winter 2011, p. 16-21.

Weapons of Mass Destruction and the Environment, Stockholm International Peace Research Institute (SIPRI), (1977), London: Taylor & Francis Ltd.

Weisberg Barry. 1970. *Ecocide in Indochina: The Ecology of War*, San Francisco: Canfield Press.

Weistein Tara, Prosecuting Attacks that Destroy the Environment: Environmental Crimes or Humanitarian Atrocities, Vol. 17 (2004-2005), *The Georgetown International Environmental Law Review*, p. 697-722.

Westing Arthur H. 1997. 'Environmental Protection form Wartime Damage: The Role of International Law', In Gleditsch N.P. et al, (eds.), *Conflict and Environment*, Netherlands: Kluwer Academic Publishers, p. 535-553.

Westing Arthur H. 1984. *Herbicides in War: The Long-term Ecological and Human Consequences,* London: Taylor & Francis.

Westing Arthur H. 2000. 'In Furtherance of Environmental Guidelines for Armed Forces During Peace and War', In Austin, Jay E., and Bruch, Carl E., (ed.), *The Environmental Consequences of War: Legal, Economic and Scientific Perspectives*, Cambridge: Cambridge University Press.

Westing Arthur H (ed.). 1990. *Environmental Hazards of War: Releasing Dangerous Forces in an Industrialized World*, New Delhi: Sage

Westing Arthur H, 'Conventional Warfare and the Human Environment', in Taipale Ilkka, P. Helena Makela and Kati Juva (ed.). 2001. *War or Health? A Reader*, London: Zed Books, p. 407-415.

Westing Arthur H, Environmental and Ecological Consequences of War, Conflict Resolution-Vol. II, available at: http://www.eolss.net/Sample-Chapters/C14/E1-40-05-01.pdf.

Westing, Arthur H., Warwick Fox and Michael Renner, *Environmental Degradation as both Consequence and Cause of Armed Conflict*, Working Paper for Nobel Peace Laureate Forum participants by PREPCOM subcommittee on Environmental Degradation, June 2001.

Westing Arthur H. (ed.). 1984. *Environmental Warfare: A Technical, Legal and Policy Appraisal*, SIPRI, London: Taylor & Francis.

Westra Laura, Ecological Integrity and Biological Integrity: The Right to Life and the Right to Health in Law, Vol. 18, No. 3, *Transnational Law & Contemporary Problems*, p. 3-44.

Wexler Lesley, Limiting the Precautionary Principle: Weapons Regulation in the Face of Scientific Uncertainty, Vol. 39, *University of California, Davis*, (2006), p. 459-529.

What Rights for Mine Victims? Reparation, Compensation: From Legal Analysis to Political Perspectives. France: Handicap International, April 2005.

White, Ronald H., et.al., Premature Mortality in the Kingdom of Saudi Arabia Associated with Particulate Matter Air Pollution from the 1991 Gulf War, Vol. 14, No. 4, *Hum. Ecol. Risk Assess*, 2008, p. 645-664.

Winnefeld James A. and Mary E. Morris, Where Environmental Concerns and Security Strategies Meet: Green Conflict in Asia and the Middle East, RAND, 1994, p. 133.

Wirtu, Yonas Desta, and Umar Abdela. "Impact of War on the Environment: Ecocide." *Frontiers in Environmental Science*, (2025). Available online at https://www.frontiersin.org/articles/10.3389/fenvs.2025.1539520/pdf.

Woods Mark, Some Worries about Ecological-Humanitarian Intervention and Ecological Defence, Vol. 21.3, *Ethics & International Affairs*, Fall 2007.

World Bank. *Damage Assessment of Natural Resources in Ukraine.* (2024).

Worldwide Emerging Environmental Security Issues Affecting the US Military. The Millennium Project for the US Army Research Office Scientific Services Program Administered by Battelle, 30 June 2010.

Wyatt Julian, Law-making at the Intersection of International Environmental, humanitarian and criminal Law: The Issue of Damage to the Environment in International Armed Conflict, *International Review of the Red Cross*, Vol. 92, No. 879, September 2010, p. 593-646.

Yemelyanenkov Aleksander and Andrei, 'Military Pollution—Nuclear Waste', in Taipale Ilkka, P. Helena Makela and Kati Juva (ed.). 2001. *War or Health? A Reader*, London: Zed Books, p. 416-419.

York Christopher, International Law and the Collateral Effects of War on the Environment: The Persian Gulf, Vol. 7, *South Africa Journal of Human Rights*, 1991, p. 269-290.

Zahar, Alexande. "Ecocide and the Law of Armed Conflict: Revisiting Thresholds of Environmental Damage." *International Review of the Red Cross*, vol. 105, no. 924, (2023), pp. 1227–1237.

Zemmali Ameur. 2004. The Right to Water in Times of Armed Conflict, in Lijnazaad Liesbeth, Van Sambeek Johanna & Tahziblie Bahia (eds), *Making the Voice of Humanity Heard*, Leiden/Boston, M. Nijhoff, p. 307-318.

Zemmali Ameur, The Protection of Water in Times of Armed Conflicts, No. 308, International *Review of the Red Cross*, September-October 1995, p. 550-564.

Zirojevic Mina, Markovic Milos and Pocuca Milan, Nuclear and Biological terrorism Implication on Environment, Vol. LXII, No. 1144, *The Review of International Affairs*, 2011, p. 97-108.

ZOI Network. *Assessing Environmental Damage in Ukraine: Methodologies and Early Findings*. (2023). Available online at https://zoinet.org/wp-content/uploads/2018/01/Ukraine-assessing-environmental-damage_EN.pdf.

Zwijnenburg, Wim, and Ollie Ballinger. "Emerging Technologies for Environmental Monitoring in Conflict Zones." *International Review of the Red Cross*, vol. 1055, no. 924, (2023), pp. 1497-1521.

Index

E

F

G

H

I

K

M

N

O

P

R

S

T

U

W

Z

www.ingramcontent.com/pod-product-compliance
Lightning Source LLC
Chambersburg PA
CBHW021216250926
51852CB00006B/36
9789347436000